Industry

Industry

Bang on a Can and New Music in the Marketplace

William Robin

OXFORD
UNIVERSITY PRESS

Oxford University Press is a department of the University of Oxford. It furthers the University's objective of excellence in research, scholarship, and education by publishing worldwide. Oxford is a registered trade mark of Oxford University Press in the UK and certain other countries.

Published in the United States of America by Oxford University Press
198 Madison Avenue, New York, NY 10016, United States of America.

© Oxford University Press 2021

All rights reserved. No part of this publication may be reproduced, stored in a retrieval system, or transmitted, in any form or by any means, without the prior permission in writing of Oxford University Press, or as expressly permitted by law, by license, or under terms agreed with the appropriate reproduction rights organization. Inquiries concerning reproduction outside the scope of the above should be sent to the Rights Department, Oxford University Press, at the address above.

You must not circulate this work in any other form
and you must impose this same condition on any acquirer.

Library of Congress Cataloging-in-Publication Data
Names: Robin, William, author.
Title: Industry : Bang on a Can and new music in the marketplace / William Robin.
Description: New York : Oxford University Press, 2021. | Includes index.
Identifiers: LCCN 2020025843 (print) | LCCN 2020025844 (ebook) |
ISBN 9780190068653 (hardback) | ISBN 9780190068677 (epub) | ISBN 9780190068684
Subjects: LCSH: Bang on a Can (Organization)—History. |
Avant-garde (Music)—History—20th century. | Music—Marketing—History—20th century.|
Sound recording industry—History—20th century. | Bang on a Can (Music festival) |
Bang on a Can All-Stars.
Classification: LCC ML26 .B384 2021 (print) | LCC ML26 (ebook) |
DDC 780.78/7471—dc23
LC record available at https://lccn.loc.gov/2020025843
LC ebook record available at https://lccn.loc.gov/2020025844

DOI: 10.1093/oso/9780190068653.001.0001

1 3 5 7 9 8 6 4 2

Printed by Sheridan Books, Inc., United States of America

for Emily

Contents

List of Illustrations   ix

    Introduction   1

1. **Academics**   18
2. **Horizons**   47
3. **Festivals**   75
4. **Funding**   104
5. **All-Stars**   138
6. **Lincoln Center**   161
7. **Record Labels**   190

    Epilogue   221

Acknowledgments   231
Chronology   233
Notes   237
References   281
Index   289

List of Illustrations

1.1	Michael Gordon and David Lang in New Haven, April 1982	23
1.2	Jacob Druckman and Martin Bresnick, 1980s	28
1.3	Michael Gordon Philharmonic, 1980s	31
1.4	David Lang, Michael Gordon, and Julia Wolfe, late 1980s	33
1.5	Sheep's Clothing ambulatory concert at Yale, October 1982	36
2.1	David Lang and Jacob Druckman, September 1985	48
2.2	Meet the Composer advertisement	56
2.3	Press conference for Orchestra Residencies Program, Lincoln Center, 1983	59
3.1	Poster for the 1987 Bang on a Can festival	84
3.2	John Cage, David Lang, Julia Wolfe, and Michael Gordon, May 1992	92
3.3	Cees van Zeeland, Michael Gordon, Julia Wolfe, and Gerard Bouwhuis outside of RAPP Arts Center in 1989	94
3.4	Advertisement for 1989 festival	95
4.1	Bang on a Can's income in 1991 (total of $216,685)	111
4.2	Total annual funding from the New York State Council on the Arts	126
4.3	Annual income, Bang on a Can	133
4.4	Bang on a Can benefit concert honoring John Duffy, 1998	135
4.5	Poster for People's Commissioning Fund at the Knitting Factory, 1998	136
5.1	Bang on a Can All-Stars, mid-1990s	139
5.2	Michael Gordon Philharmonic in 1986	141
5.3	*Music for Airports* at Lincoln Center, 1998	158
6.1	Bang on a Can All-Stars at Walter Reade Theater at Lincoln Center, April 11, 1994	162
6.2	Still from Michael Blackwood, *New York Composers: Searching for a New Music*, 1996	179
6.3	Survey responses: "I have been coming to your events for . . ."	183
6.4	Survey responses: Education completed	183
6.5	Survey responses: Age	184
7.1	Otto Luening and Joseph Dalton at CRI's fortieth anniversary celebration at the New York Public Library for the Performing Arts, October 7, 1994	197
7.2	Cover to *Bang on a Can Live Volume 1*, 1992	199

7.3 Ad for Sony album in Lincoln Center program book, 1995, featuring *Industry* album cover and Peter Serling's photograph 209

E.1 David Lang, Michael Gordon, and Julia Wolfe 223

Industry

Introduction

On a clear New York afternoon on Mother's Day in 1987, three composers hosted a marathon concert in a downtown art gallery. Titled the "Bang on a Can Festival," the event presented nearly twelve hours of avant-garde music, ranging from participatory meditation to cerebral atonality to hard-rocking postminimalism. A half-day of complex contemporary composition was not an easy sell to audiences. But Michael Gordon, David Lang, and Julia Wolfe had tired of the kind of new-music concerts that seemed to cater exclusively to a small clientele of fellow musicians. They wanted to reach a broader public. "When I was in music school the prevailing discourse was that there was no audience for this music," Gordon later wrote. "Julia, David, and I challenged that assumption."[1]

They heavily promoted the concert, mailing out flyers and hanging posters and pitching newspapers for coverage. They kept ticket prices low, sold beer at the venue, and skipped traditional concert trappings like program notes. And it worked: the gallery reached capacity, with more than 400 attendees dropping by into the early hours of the morning. "Our aim in 1987 was to build an audience," Gordon wrote; by such measures, Bang on a Can had triumphed. And they continued to succeed over the subsequent decade as they grew their organization and audience—expanding their marathons into multi-event extravaganzas, forming an ensemble to tour internationally, partnering with prestigious arts presenters, and signing contracts with major record labels— while maintaining their now well-known irreverent ethos.

Around the same time as the May marathon, the advocacy organization Meet the Composer was working on a handbook about how to make a living in contemporary music. Published in 1989, *Composers in the Marketplace* provided useful tips on the basics of copyright, performance, publishing, recording, income streams, publicity, management, and more.[2] Its purpose was practical, but its existence was ideological, serving a larger vision that had become pervasive in these years. Rather than being reclusive academics or bohemian experimentalists, composers might earn income from their work, connect with general audiences, and participate in the musical marketplace. Earlier in the decade, Meet the Composer's founder, John Duffy, had written that his organization had "one ultimate goal: to reclaim composers by restoring them to their rightful place in contemporary society as active, working, useful, recognized, recorded, respected, paid people." In order to achieve such aims, composers needed to be in direct dialogue with the public. They needed to build an audience for new music.[3]

Both the marathon and the thirty-seven page handbook point to an emerging institutional consensus, during an era of broad historical transformation. Contemporary music had long been considered box office poison: inaccessible, academic, full of alienating and atonal sounds. But beginning in the 1980s, in the wake of the popularity of new styles like minimalism and neo-Romanticism, institutions in the United States saw how contemporary music could freshly reengage with a large audience. Meet the Composer arose to make that contact between composers and the public happen; orchestras including the New York Philharmonic and presenters like Lincoln Center saw contemporary music as a means to attract new ticket buyers; and the record industry looked to new music as an opportunity to amass profits. In the final two decades of the twentieth century, American new music turned toward the marketplace: institutions and musicians came to believe that the survival of contemporary composition depended on reaching a broad, non-specialist audience. Bang on a Can traipsed through these developments, searching for ways to grow the listenership for new music. The organization's impressive rise was a product of the individual ingenuity of its three founding composers, but also of significant shifts in the American musical landscape.

As new music turned to the marketplace, it turned away from the norms of a previous era. In the decades following the Second World War, there were two principal visions for the musical avant-garde in the United States. It could serve as an analogue to scientific research, composed by academics for fellow specialists; or it could serve as an exploratory interrogation of conventional practices, created by experimentalists for like-minded listeners. Neither of these musical camps was overtly opposed to their work being presented to a wider public, but neither was explicitly concerned with building an audience for contemporary music. That began to change in the 1980s, as disciples of and dissenters from the so-called worlds of uptown and downtown re-envisioned the place of new music in American society.

Those who advocated for the marketplace turn—a mixture of Ivy League composition professors, foundation directors, festival curators, government bureaucrats, arts center administrators, and record producers—commanded authority at nascent and powerful institutions alike. Looming in the background were congressional Republicans and the religious right, who had no interest in contemporary music but, in protesting purportedly obscene avant-garde photography, fought to eliminate government support for the arts and declared that American artists should embrace the free market. Bang on a Can's story is intertwined with a large, interlocking institutional infrastructure of composers and performers, orchestras and ensembles, public and private funders, presenters and record labels. Not all of them embraced new music's marketplace turn, but all grappled with it.

No One Has Done Anything About the Audience

In May 1966, Aaron Copland addressed a gala at Manhattan's Plaza Hotel, gathered to celebrate the fiftieth anniversary of the Pulitzer Prize, which the distinguished composer had won back in 1945 for his ballet score *Appalachian Spring*. "I've been asked to sort out trends in my field in 300 seconds flat," the composer, born at the dawn of the twentieth century, told the crowd.[4] He began by noting that music had become wrapped up in what he called the "Edifice Complex," the proliferation of new facilities for the performing arts such as New York's own Lincoln Center. "The buildings are brand new, but unfortunately no one has done anything about the audience," Copland coolly noted. The "music-loving public" had remained "staunchly conservative," drawn to new spaces but not to new music.

"For them I am the bearer of brutal tidings," Copland continued. "We are living in the midst of an unprecedented musical revolution." Young composers, he explained, were writing extraordinarily complex music for specialized ensembles rather than symphony orchestras, and even turning to the electronic medium as a means of expression. Along with this "music of highest control," Copland noted a second, major development: "Music that is wayward and unpredictable, relaxedly exploring the charm of chance operations." These twin trends meant that, for those listening to new music, "don't look for any tunes, any continuity, any graspable form, or any propulsive rhythms." Copland ultimately celebrated this new "sense of adventure" among a younger cohort of composers, recalling his own years as a young radical in the 1920s, and concluded by wishing "Good luck to them!" But elsewhere, Copland expressed hesitance about a creeping disconnect, between a generation of probing revolutionaries reinventing music and an arts public that sought out Ludwig van Beethoven instead of Milton Babbitt.[5]

This disconnect had always been part of American composition, but the gap seemed to widen during the first two decades of the Cold War. The United States emerged from World War II as a cultural titan, but neoclassical Americana in the vein of *Appalachian Spring*, pioneered by Copland and his contemporaries after the Depression, started to give way to the more esoteric deliberations of new avant-gardes. There remained a strong commitment to traditionalist methods among prominent figures such as Leonard Bernstein, Ned Rorem, and Copland himself, who remained at the forefront of the classical music establishment. But prestige began to accrue elsewhere. Young American composers were inspired by modernist émigrés such as Arnold Schoenberg and Igor Stravinsky as well as homegrown mavericks like Charles Ives, eager to embrace the new currents of serial music in vogue in Zero Hour–era Europe, and drawn to the technological innovations of the postwar years. It didn't help that, in the midst of the Red Scare—in which Copland himself testified before a Senate committee chaired by Joseph McCarthy—the tonal and patriotic music of the previous era did not sound terribly distant from the state socialist propaganda composed in Soviet Russia.[6] Driven by the baby boom, massive economic growth, increasing educational opportunities, and new forms of patronage, the American musical public was expanding dramatically. During this "cultural boom," audiences gravitated toward the standard classical repertoire presented at Lincoln Center and contextualized on television by Bernstein.[7] But the two musical scenes that Copland described—the one extraordinarily complex and controlled, the other unpredictable and chance-driven—continued to grow on their own. Within a decade or so of Copland's speech, they would become widely known among musicians as "uptown" and "downtown," mapping the geography of Manhattan outwards onto the entire country and labeling distinctive musical styles, communities, and ideologies.

The uptown world—named for its Upper West Side centers of activity such as Columbia University and Merkin Concert Hall—revolved around the academy. In 1958, the vanguard serial composer Milton Babbitt authored an essay he titled "The Composer as Specialist," but which the magazine *High Fidelity* printed under the incendiary headline "Who Cares if You Listen?"[8] In it, Babbitt argued that the serious composer was by nature isolated from the public, who lacked sufficient education to understand the latest developments in modern music. In an "alien and inapposite world," composers should see this isolation as an opportunity, a chance to create their work unhindered by the judgments of the lay listener. He advocated that the composer "do himself and his music an immediate and eventual service by total, resolute, and voluntary withdrawal from this public world to one of private performance and electronic media."[9] And Babbitt led the way, helping found the first-ever PhD program in composition at Princeton in 1962, which led to a proliferation of doctoral programs across the country. Compatriots such as Charles Wuorinen, Mario Davidovsky, and Elliott Carter wrote similarly intellectualized music, and the label of "academic composer" came to stand for the atonal sound of their work, the mathematical techniques undergirding it, and the uneasy relationship it had with mainstream audiences.

A Cold War network of institutions and musicians supported this project, which reflected an ideology of heroically individualist modernism that, in contrast to Soviet socialist realism, epitomized the freedom afforded to artists by American democracy.[10] In the early 1950s, Carter isolated himself in the Arizona desert to write his first string quartet, an innovative piece that showcased the new technique of metric modulation. "I decided for once to write a work very interesting to myself," he later said, "and so say to hell with the public and with the performers too."[11] When it received its European premiere in 1954 in Rome, the quartet cemented Carter's international reputation—the performance was sponsored by the Congress for Cultural Freedom, an arts festival that promoted Euro-American modernism and, not so incidentally, received secret funding from the CIA.[12]

Uptown composers described their work as a form of specialized research, allowing them to tap into new sources of university and foundation patronage in a post-Sputnik moment.[13] In 1970, Wuorinen became the youngest composer to ever win the Pulitzer Prize, for *Time's Encomium*—the first electronic work to receive the award—which he created with the RCA Mark II Synthesizer. The machine was housed at the Columbia-Princeton Electronic Music Center, which Babbitt helped create, and was paid for with a $175,000 grant from the Rockefeller Foundation as part of more than $2 million of Rockefeller funding awarded during the 1960s to create new-music centers at universities across the country.[14] Specialized ensembles, such as the Group for Contemporary Music and Speculum Musicae, arose to play the intricate music created by this faction of composers.[15] The wealthy patron Paul Fromm started his own foundation for new music, which supported a festival at the Tanglewood Music Center, an analytical journal called *Perspectives of New Music*, and major commissions.[16]

The most militant of these musicians proselytized their avant-garde methods as the only path forward. "While the tonal system, in an atrophied or vestigial form, is still used today in popular and commercial music, and even occasionally in the works of backward-looking serious composers, it is no longer employed by serious composers of the mainstream," Wuorinen wrote in the preface to his book *Simple Composition*. "It has been replaced or succeeded by the 12-tone system."[17] That attitude, and the prestige that Wuorinen and his peers acquired along with their pedagogical influence at select major universities, gave rise to the notion of "serial tyranny," that serial music and its authors dominated the musical establishment.[18] Whether or not serialism was tyrannical, academic composers who wrote atonal music commanded significant authority and resources in the decades following the Second World War.

Meanwhile, a little more than a hundred New York blocks south of Columbia University, but sonically worlds away, the downtown musical scene took shape—one whose ethos was shared by composers in San Francisco, Ann Arbor, and other freethinking enclaves across the country. Their spiritual godfather was John Cage, who pioneered the techniques of indeterminacy and chance operations in the 1950s to create works that circumscribed the composer's authorial voice and afforded new freedoms to performers and listeners. Cage's permissive creative philosophy helped give shape to the wide-ranging sphere of experimentalism, encompassing everything from the performance-art happenings of Fluxus to the hushed, longform ruminations of Morton Feldman to the electronic tinkerers of the Sonic Arts Union.[19] Cage and his colleagues, including Feldman and the pianist David Tudor, found their own sources of Cold War institutional patronage—not so much in the United States, but in visits to the Darmstadt and Donaueschingen summer festivals, funded by the West German government, that shook up the European avant-garde.[20]

"The masterpieces of Western music exemplify monarchies and dictatorships," Cage wrote in 1974. "Composer and conductor: king and prime minister. By making musical situations which are analogies to desirable social circumstances which we do not yet have, we make music suggestive and relevant to the serious questions which face Mankind."[21] Post-Cage graphic scores and improvisational practices provided not only new musical languages but also the dissolution of traditional hierarchies. In San Diego, Pauline Oliveros worked with an all-women ensemble on therapeutic body exercises and contemplative text scores, which would develop into her series of *Sonic Meditations*. In New York, La Monte Young guided a small ensemble in evening-length buzzing drone improvisations. In San Francisco, Morton Subotnick helped create the Buchla box, a modular synthesizer whose lack of a conventional keyboard offered revolutionary musical potential. And in Chicago, Muhal Richard Abrams co-founded the Association for the Advancement of Creative Musicians, a collective of Black musicians whose radical compositions transcended genre boundaries, independent of the mostly-white Cagean avant-garde.[22] These wide-ranging activities offered an implicit sociopolitical critique of the primacy of the musical score, eroding the modernist divisions between composer and performer that pervaded the academic scene.

Such efforts were resolutely countercultural, and occasionally aligned with the utopian political projects of the 1960s. Oliveros's sonic meditations were wrapped up in the women's liberation movement, and when she first published them in *Source Magazine* in 1971, they were accompanied by a preface in which the composer announced that she was "a two-legged human being, a female, lesbian, musician, composer, among other things which contribute to her identity."[23] Whereas Young saw the Theatre of Eternal Music as his own compositional endeavor—and his fellow performers as subservient executors of his vision rather than equal collaborators—participating violinist Tony Conrad saw it as an egalitarian project that would "emblematically deny 'composition' its authoritarian function as a modern activity."[24] The AACM's collectivism drew from the spirit of the Black Power Movement; as Abrams and trumpeter John Shenoy Jackson wrote, "The AACM intends to show how the disadvantaged and the disenfranchised can come together and determine their own strategies for political and economic freedom, thereby determining their own destinies."[25] Swept up in the Marxism of the New Left, the expatriate experimentalists of Musica Elettronica Viva improvised in collective performances for, and with, members of the Italian working class.[26] Cage himself sometimes clashed with interpreters such the cellist Charlotte Moorman and the vocalist Julius Eastman, who staged his scores as explicitly transgressive, theatrical performances that foregrounded their gender and sexuality.[27]

Ultimately, neither the uptown academics nor the downtown experimentalists were terribly concerned with attracting a large listenership. Academic composers did care who listened, but they had developed an infrastructure that could support their work mostly outside of the mainstream. Experimentalists saw their creative activities as fundamentally communal, and met at galleries, lofts, and liberal arts campuses that allowed them the freedom to explore outré languages without outside intrusion or the need to fill concert halls.[28] In "The Composer as Specialist," Babbitt described the serious composer as a creator of "a commodity which has little, no, or negative commodity value," and advocated for university patronage so that "the composer would be free to pursue a private life of professional achievement, as opposed to a public life of unprofessional compromise and exhibitionism."[29] Cage was less concerned with growing the audience than with liberating it from the strictures of the traditional concert experience—"An audience can sit quietly or make noises," he wrote in 1966, "People are people, not plants."[30] Much modernist music was alienating to the public, a perspective epitomized in Henry Pleasants's 1955 polemic *The Agony of Modern Music*, which declared "Serious music is a dead art," and that "What we know as modern music is the noise made by deluded speculators picking through its slag pile."[31] When Cage was given a major platform by Leonard Bernstein for the New York

Philharmonic's 1964 Avant-Garde Festival, he presented *Atlas Eclipticalis*, a stridently confrontational electro-acoustic work that incensed members of the orchestra and caused much of the audience to leave during the performance. Those who stayed provided what one critic called "the loudest chorus of boos I have ever heard."[32]

Less than a decade after Copland wished good luck to his younger colleagues, however, a post-Cage and post-Babbitt generation started to find popular support by abandoning, or heavily revising, aspects of the academic and experimental aesthetics. Steve Reich and Philip Glass, who had hung out at Young's downtown loft and in the Bay Area scene, developed a style of minimalism that flirted with traditional tonality and centered on pulsating rhythms. They created their own groups, the Philip Glass Ensemble and Steve Reich and Musicians, to tour works like *Music in Twelve Parts* and *Drumming* to receptive audiences in both art museums and rock clubs. The composer David Del Tredici mastered serial technique at Babbitt's home base of Princeton but defected from uptown by writing a series of orchestral tone poems, based on the Alice in Wonderland mythos, that harkened back to the sound-world of the late nineteenth century. As music director of the New York Philharmonic, the fearsome Pierre Boulez led a popular but short-lived series of "rug concerts," in which young audiences sat on the floor of Avery Fisher Hall to hear Bach and George Crumb alike. John Adams, who had developed a distaste for serialism while studying at Harvard and gradually soured on the post-Cagean scene while teaching in San Francisco, fused the languages of minimalism and neo-Romanticism in symphonic works for the San Francisco Symphony. The year of the American Bicentennial was a pivotal moment: Glass's massive non-opera *Einstein on the Beach* sold out a two-night run at the Metropolitan Opera; Reich's expansive *Music for Eighteen Musicians* debuted to a packed Town Hall, and its 1978 ECM recording went on to sell more than 100,000 copies; and Del Tredici's *Final Alice* made a sensation at its Chicago Symphony premiere, where audiences welcomed the sixty-five minute piece with a lengthy, standing ovation, and a live recording topped *Billboard*'s classical charts.

Neo-Romanticism seemed to appeal to classical music's traditional public, while minimalism chafed against conventional ears but attracted hipper, artsy listeners drawn in from the counterculture. "Composers now are beginning to realize that if a piece excites an audience, that doesn't mean it's terrible," Del Tredici told the critic John Rockwell. "For my generation, it is considered vulgar to have an audience really, really like a piece on a first hearing. But why are we writing music except to move people and to be expressive?"[33] In the early 1980s, Laurie Anderson's "O Superman," a vocoder-led looping riff on an aria by Jules Massenet, rose to number 2 on the British pop charts; Philip Glass produced albums by the new wave band Polyrock and starred in a magazine ad for Cutty Sark whiskey; and the Kronos Quartet dressed in black spandex and played Terry Riley and Jimi Hendrix to capacity crowds. Postmodernism had arrived.[34]

And, by some reports, modernism was dead. "The issue of vanguardism, the whole avant-garde, has burned itself out," John Adams told the *New York Times* in 1987, the year his controversial hit opera *Nixon in China* premiered. "As we approach the end of the century, there is an exhaustion of this intense need to run to the barricades, to forge ahead to the future."[35] Musicians, critics, and scholars argued endlessly whether the so-called "return to tonality" was progressive, or conservative, or whether such political terms should even be applied to the question of musical style.[36] But it's hard to say that the avant-garde died. The academics and the experimentalists never went away—Babbitt and Cage had long, productive careers, and their colleagues and disciples continued their efforts. Plenty of composers never fit neatly into one or the other loose category of uptown and downtown, which many musicians publicly rebuked, as fictitious classifications invented by unsympathetic newspaper columnists. By the 1980s, musical camps had proliferated and fragmented. There were serialists and post-serialists and ex-serialists, vocal improvisers and computer music whizzes and electric guitar virtuosos, symphonic postminimalists and polystylistic saxophonists and traditionalist art-song authors.

At a heated conference on the state of contemporary music held at Manhattan's 92nd Street Y in January 1981, composer George Rochberg declared that modernism has "failed us," critic Samuel Lipman described an atmosphere of "apathy" and "cultural pessimism," violinist Isaac Stern told composers that, in order to have their music performed, "they have to earn it," and *Village Voice* critic Gregory Sandow denounced the proceedings as a "gathering of the uptown tribe" that excluded experimental, rock, and jazz musicians.[37] Ronald Reagan had been inaugurated the week before, and rumors of his desire to slash the budget of the National Endowment for the Arts hovered over the proceedings. But Steve Reich voiced a note of optimism. "I would like to point out that the myth of there being no audience for new music is simply that: a myth," he said. "There is a very large, often young audience for new music, and a lively concert presented at any one of a number of locations in this country will draw them out in large numbers."[38] He had witnessed this popularity firsthand. Three years later, Sandow wrote that "The big news not just downtown but all over the country is really the audience," in a program book essay for the New York Philharmonic's 1984 Horizons series, the sequel to a contemporary-music festival that had become a surprise box-office hit the season prior. Describing the phenomenon of Glass and Reich, he added that "It's a shock to realize that there is a form of serious new music with a large independent public of its own, and that it found that public outside the usual contemporary or classical music concert halls."[39]

The present book picks up where Reich and Sandow left off, during a period of growing understanding about the potential for new music to reach a broad audience. The institutional infrastructure that supported new music's marketplace turn in the United States was largely domestic, and quite unlike the state-sponsored avant-garde that existed in many European countries at the end of the twentieth century, which facilitated a different relationship between new music and the public and in some ways preserved the modernist project.[40] In the 1970s, specific American composers and select musical works had demonstrated that new music could draw out an audience in large numbers. What would occur in the 1980s and 1990s was a large-scale response to this potential for popularity, galvanized by funding organizations like Meet the Composer, picked up by upstart festivals like Bang on a Can, and eventually responded to by prestigious endeavors like Lincoln Center and Sony Classical. The music-loving public was catching up to the musical revolution.

Industry

Michael Gordon's 1992 *Industry*, for amplified cello, opens simply, almost gently. The soloist outlines triadic arpeggios that trail off into held, brooding double-stops. The pattern continues but the tone becomes hazier, as the cellist gradually crescendos, adds vibrato to the held notes, begins to keenly glissando, and, almost imperceptibly, deploys a distortion pedal called the "tube screamer." The scored rhythmic and harmonic material remains largely the same—on the page, it looks almost meditatively still—but the cello starts to screech and growl. In the final third of the nine-minute piece, the cellist mashes out a series of double-stops, barraged with amplified fuzz, building faster and faster into a snarling, headbanging insurgence. The piece was inspired, Gordon wrote, by a "vision of a 100-foot cello made out of steel suspended from the sky."[41]

Industry manifests the sonic ethos of Bang on a Can—classical music conventions serve as a gateway to gritty distortion, precisely notated gestures spell out a sneering, steely provocation. It served as the title track for Bang on a Can's 1995 major label debut on Sony Classical, where it was performed by its original commissioner, the cellist Maya Beiser, a founding member of the

Bang on a Can All-Stars ensemble. A *New York Times* reviewer described the record as "a bruising, bracing slap in the face."[42] And sound worked in tandem with image. The cover of the Sony album depicted a bleak, grayscale power silo, and an accompanying promotional photograph showed the All-Stars, unsmiling and dressed in black, on a rough New York rooftop.

Such aural and visual signifiers are typically invoked in journalistic and scholarly portrayals of Bang on a Can, and align with how Gordon, David Lang, and Julia Wolfe like to describe themselves. "Refining rebellion with discipline is an important idea for our time," the three founders wrote, in a quasi-manifesto published in the Sony album's liner notes.[43] "It's the kind of idea we like at Bang on a Can." Their music was noisy and combative, and has been characterized as instantiating a "post-minimalism of resistance."[44]

But just how rebellious were Bang on a Can? The founding composers studied at a top graduate program in the Ivy League, and one of them briefly worked for the New York Philharmonic. They wrote fully notated music for classically-trained virtuosos. Their first festival in 1987 was both scrappy and tightly coordinated, and Bang on a Can quickly expanded. They built their organization and audience by carefully crafting marketing materials, relentlessly writing grant applications, and starting a touring ensemble to unlock new sources of income. Eventually, they were programming marathons at Lincoln Center and collaborating with A&R at Sony Classical—institutions they attracted because of their ambition and administrative savvy, and because their unruly output provided a hip repackaging of classical music's conventions.

Industry might signal a raucous resistance, but attending to Bang on a Can's institutional practices—their participation in a larger classical- and new-music *industry*—reveals another side. In one account, Bang on a Can is a group of renegades that stormed the musical establishment. In another, they were trained in the establishment, and it's not surprising that they ended up there again. These narratives must be held close together, in productive tension, to reveal how the organization participated in new music's marketplace turn.

There were other areas in which Bang on a Can manifested less of a resistance than one might initially expect. It is not entirely a coincidence that the marketplace turn unfolded in tandem with the Reagan Revolution. The Bang on a Can composers had little in common politically with supply-side conservatives, nor was new music's marketplace synonymous with the so-called free market extolled by neoliberals—Bang on a Can, Meet the Composer, and similar efforts were subsidized by government funding, as well as foundation backing.[45] But their public support soon became imperiled, as American avant-gardists faced harsh cutbacks to government arts funding through the 1980s and 1990s during the vicious Culture Wars battles over the fate of the National Endowment for the Arts. Bang on a Can witnessed the new neoliberal paradigm; their growth, when other institutions struggled, can be attributed to their willingness to accommodate to the vagaries of late capitalism, to envision conditions that allowed their music and musicians to survive, and even thrive, in a tumultuous moment.

Critics of neoliberalism have argued that unfettered markets threaten democracy, and some small-scale analogue of this phenomenon does play out in this story.[46] While Bang on a Can was often described as a "collective," that nomenclature wasn't quite accurate in this period. Although the three founding composers made decisions as a collective, as Bang on a Can grew, it side-stepped a history of democratic governance that was part of the institutional fabric of the postwar American avant-garde, whether in the socialist communalism of student new-music groups, the granting panels of public arts agencies, the self-management of contemporary-music ensembles, or the administrative committees of experimental festivals. In an age of arts austerity, Bang on a Can keenly navigated the marketplace in part because of how their leaders led.

One cannot account for Bang on a Can's rise without accounting for their sound: zealous management aided the organization in achieving success, but the empathic effect of the avant-garde music they fostered gave them a foothold among audiences, fellow musicians, and administrators. The rock-oriented, postminimalist works issued by the three founding composers, as well as the music of their contemporaries and elders they promoted in concerts and recordings, constituted an aesthetic thread that was so tightly interwoven with the organization's identity that critics and scholars have described the existence of "Bang-on-a-Can-ism."[47] The story of Gordon, Lang, and Wolfe's oeuvre is not one of "selling out," of musicians compromising their art in order to reach a larger listenership. A previous generation of American avant-garde composers, whether minimalists or neo-Romantics, did turn toward a language of more immediate communicability in the 1970s, whether driven by their own personal aesthetic journeys or by a desire to reach out beyond a specialist clientele.[48] The Bang on a Can composers instead always stressed that they sought to cultivate new audiences for difficult music, rather than cultivate easy music that would appeal to new audiences. "I never imagined doing something with Bang on a Can that I didn't believe in strictly because I felt like it was important for us to have X number of people at a concert," Lang once said.[49] At the same time, Bang on a Can did change the kind of music they programmed—and the kind of stories they told about themselves—while they expanded into new markets.

This Story

This story of Bang on a Can proceeds chronologically, from the early 1980s to the late 1990s—sometimes looping further back when necessary—to follow the organization as they moved through different institutional settings that were themselves undergoing transition and transformation. It begins at Yale, where Gordon, Lang, and Wolfe attended graduate school in the 1980s and formed strong personal and musical bonds, and briefly looks backward to see how the three composers got there. Though comfortably ensconced in an elite setting, they attended a master's program that cut an unusual profile. Their professors, Martin Bresnick and Jacob Druckman, cultivated a permissive pluralism that allowed the trio to explore musical minimalism during a time that it was largely shunned in the academy. They dabbled in experimental hijinks through the undergraduate collective Sheep's Clothing, which inspired Bang on a Can's marathon concert-format, but did not take to the college students' utopian politics. Instead, they gravitated toward Druckman's ethos of professionalism, which provided the composers and their student peers with a model for how to navigate the marketplace, in contrast to the typical image of the academic composer as Ivory Tower intellectual.

Next is a crucial but unlikely precursor context for Bang on a Can: the New York Philharmonic in the mid-1980s. Before he co-founded a renegade organization that stood apart from the orchestral establishment, Lang spent an important year working as an assistant for Druckman in curating the Philharmonic's third Horizons festival for contemporary music. The three Horizons festivals were closely observed by the Bang on a Can composers and their peers. The first festival in 1983, which celebrated an aesthetic movement that Druckman called New Romanticism, was a blockbuster that pointed toward the potential for young composers to pursue a career in the orchestral world. And that was the point. Horizons was the flagship project of the Orchestra Residencies Program, one of Meet the Composer's principal endeavors. John Duffy launched the residency program—generously subsidized by Exxon, Rockefeller, and the National Endowment for the Arts—to give American composers access to the concert-hall public and cultivate a marketplace spirit nationwide. And while Bang on a Can did not ultimately link up with the symphonic mainstream, Meet the Composer's philosophy and funding galvanized Bang on a Can to launch their first festival in 1987.

That festival represented Gordon, Lang, and Wolfe's entrepreneurial attempt to reimagine what the new-music world should look like. They were dissatisfied with the uptown academics and the downtown experimentalists. Attending concerts all over New York in the mid-'80s, they found both scenes to be stagnant, and isolated from larger audiences. A marathon concert that brought together what the trio called an "eclectic supermix" of musical styles, in an informal, friendly atmosphere, might address their grievances. Seeking to push past the uptown–downtown divide, they placed the serialism of Milton Babbitt and the minimalism of Steve Reich back-to-back in the hope that overcoming longstanding boundaries and feuds would help them reach new listeners. There were both ideological and practical components to the first Bang on a Can festival, ones that set it apart from institutional peers such as the venue Experimental Intermedia and the ensemble Speculum Musicae. For some observers, Bang on a Can provided a symbolic foil for an older annual gathering, New Music America, and the two festivals offered competing visions for new music—the former represented an emerging generation of composers who wrote notated works for virtuoso performers, the latter celebrated a long-established scene of experimental composer-performers. That Bang on a Can was expanding just as New Music America went defunct in the early 1990s reveals a turning point in American new music.

Despite arising in an era of increasingly precarious public funding for the arts, Bang on a Can's annual budget grew from a little under $11,000 to more than $400,000 in less than a decade.[50] It was a turbulent time, as the Culture Wars raged and the fate of new music hung in the balance. With their careful attention to grant applications and dedicated care to fundraising, Bang on a Can succeeded in a period when other new-music institutions, such as the Group for Contemporary Music, faltered. They also positioned themselves as multicultural and audience-friendly just as some major funders, most notably the New York State Council on the Arts, began to explicitly favor subsidizing organizations that prioritized such aims. In 1995, Congress slashed the NEA's budget by 40 percent and eliminated funding for individual artists, affecting new music across the board. Gordon, Lang, and Wolfe responded by starting their own commissioning fund that doubled as a way to build their donor base. As public austerity measures forced American artists into the marketplace, Bang on a Can found new means to support their world.

And as they developed, the organization sought to move outside New York by creating a compact, touring vehicle for their ethos: the Bang on a Can All-Stars, an instrumental sextet founded in 1992. The All-Stars provided an international platform for Bang on a Can, combining six virtuoso performers into a supergroup that epitomized the festival's extroverted image and sound. It also had the auxiliary purpose of unlocking a new stream of earned income for its parent institution. Amplified and accompanied by a rock-inflected repertoire, the All-Stars allowed Bang on a Can to newly emphasize their relationship to popular music and grow their audience on the road. But tensions soon emerged between composers and performers, as Bang on a Can's top-down style of management set the All-Stars apart from predecessor and peer ensembles.

All of this activity caught notice in the highest echelons of classical music and, in 1994, Bang on a Can was invited to present All-Stars concerts and annual marathons at Lincoln Center. Under the direction of the administrator Jane Moss, Lincoln Center looked to new music as a means to reach new audiences, seeking to compete with the popularity of the Brooklyn Academy of Music's Next Wave Festival. For Lang, Gordon, and Wolfe, the decision to bring the downtown marathons to the Upper West Side was fraught—would they be sacrificing their homespun reputation for the big leagues? Bang on a Can's partnering with the classical music establishment ultimately reflects their goal to expand their audience, yet the festival's new home soon became a point of contention among longtime observers.

In the 1990s, Bang on a Can sought out the resources of the record industry. Nonesuch and ECM had already established the possibility for contemporary music to prosper on mainstream labels, rather than the small-scale, non-commercial recording efforts of the past. In their early years, Bang on a Can put out three live albums on the non-profit label Composers Recordings, Inc.—part of CRI's rebranding as a hip proponent of downtown music. But the big news came in 1995, when they made their debut on Sony Classical. This jump to the majors resulted from a strange phenomenon in contemporary music, when a 1992 Nonesuch recording of the Polish composer Henryk Górecki's lachrymose Symphony No. 3 unexpectedly sold hundreds of thousands of copies. Major labels including Sony, BMG, and Philips quickly responded, launching new-music imprints in the hopes of riding a trend. In this moment of speculation, producers such as Tim Page at BMG and Martyn Harry at Sony attempted to tastefully balance art and commerce, but found themselves defeated by the sales demands of label executives. Bang on a Can soon moved from Sony to Philips' Point, where they released their best-selling album, *Music for Airports*, but the partnership didn't last. The record industry started to fall apart and, at the dawn of the twenty-first century, Bang on a Can started their own independent record label.

***

Unfortunately, I missed all of this. I was born shortly after Bang on a Can's second-ever festival and grew up not far from the city where their annual marathons resounded, yet they did not enter my cultural consciousness until much later. I saw the All-Stars deliver a jolting performance of Louis Andriessen's *Workers Union* in college—it was part of a 2008 tour with the Wilco drummer Glenn Kotche—and the concert made a strong impression at the time. Although Bang on a Can staked their claim on attracting a nonmusical, artsy audience, they have also always had a strong appeal to people like my college self: classical-music nerds who were looking for something a bit cooler and louder than the average chamber music concert. As it turns out—again, I don't recall this, but I looked it up—David Lang won the Pulitzer Prize for his doleful *the little match girl passion* the day after that 2008 concert.

In early 2009, I checked out a fat stack of Bang on a Can CDs, including *Industry*, from the college library and ripped them to my computer. I can easily imagine rocking out in my dorm room to David Lang's acerbically groovy *cheating, lying, stealing* or to the tightly-controlled frenzy of Julia Wolfe's *Lick*. Around this time, having obsessed over Alex Ross's *The Rest Is Noise*, I began to consider studying new music as a musicologist.[51] In graduate school, I started to investigate the history of Bang on a Can and their twenty-first century musical legacy.[52] A few years later, it became clear that the account of Bang on a Can that needed to be told was not one that focused on the present day, but instead one that dwelled in a period that I had not lived through as a new-music fan. I wanted to chronicle Bang on a Can not as a group of composers who had netted Pulitzer Prizes, Guggenheim fellowships, and a MacArthur grant, or held prestigious residencies at Carnegie Hall, or shepherded a young generation of musicians with their summer institute. Instead, I wanted to tell an earlier story, one in which they were gaining influence but had not yet become fully consecrated, midcareer composers. Researching the 1980s and 1990s—investigating archival sources, reading newspapers, talking to people, investigating more archival sources, talking to more people—revealed an institutional infrastructure that seemed, to me, hidden in plain sight. Some of these organizations have vanished, others have transformed beyond recognition, and still others simply have never had their stories told. Yet Yale's pedagogy, Meet the Composer's grantmaking, New Music America's sprawl, the New York State Council on the Arts' multiculturalism, Lincoln Center's programming, and Sony's bottom line are inextricable from Bang on a Can's biography. Bang on a Can's persistence in the twenty-first century was part of a broader historical transformation at the close of the twentieth century, as new music pivoted toward the marketplace—this was the story I wanted to tell.

Back in February of 2016, sitting in the kitchen of the TriBeCa loft that Julia Wolfe and Michael Gordon have shared for decades—they married a few years before Bang on a Can started—I asked Wolfe about what had changed in the world of contemporary music since she first came on the scene. "The audience is much more active and alive," she responded.[53] It hadn't been that way when Bang on a Can first started out. "We really built an audience from the ground up." With significant effort, they did. But they were not alone.

1
Academics

In October 1981, the twenty-five-year-old Michael Gordon walked onto the stage of Yale's Sprague Hall and began playing a portable electric organ. The music that pulsated from the amplified instrument, hooked up to a Roland SRE–555 tape delay machine, consisted of a spare polyrhythmic texture. Using the delay system, the composer began to loop two simultaneous, alternating patterns—an upwards, three-note arpeggio in one hand and a downwards, four-note arpeggio in the other, which would switch hands every measure—back unto one another. The musical effect was simultaneous stasis and movement or, as Gordon later described it, a "block of sound" in which "all kinds of things are happening but nothing is happening."[1] At the time, Gordon was fascinated with the music of Steve Reich and Philip Glass, and was seeking ways to reimagine the processes of their early work. His piece, called *The Tree Watcher*, unmistakably belongs to this tradition of musical minimalism, but it is also more self-consciously abrasive, more relentlessly hostile, than much of the minimalist canon. In the final section of the fourteen-minute performance, David Lang, a fellow graduate student in Yale's composition program, joined his friend on stage and began buzzing incessant eighth notes on an amplified hotel bell, creating further feedback in the tape delay that briefly drowned out the already loud organ.

The response was instantaneous and visceral. In the balcony of Sprague Hall, student peers stood up and cheered, but there were also boos, and one faculty member may have yelled "Shut up!" and walked out.[2] Likening the moment to the riotous reaction that greeted the premiere of *The Rite of Spring*, composer and then-student Jeffrey Brooks described hearing *The Tree Watcher* as a transformative moment in his youth, in which in which the persistence of the work's minimalist drive posed "a threat to the music establishment."[3]

"In the early '80s, Yale was still under the sway of twelve-tone serialism," stated a 2010 profile of Lang by the website *Politico*. "When Gordon would do his strange, repetitive pieces, large swaths of the faculty would walk out."[4] *The Tree Watcher* uproar serves as an appropriate origin story for a group of musical renegades like Bang on a Can, and one whose stakes might be familiar to those who know the story of the American postwar musical avant-garde: the Ivy League academy stood as the bastion of uptown, where atonal composers detested the repetitive, countercultural sound and commercial appeal of minimalism. "About one minute of minimalism is a lot, because it is all the same," Elliott Carter famously told *Time Magazine* in 1982. "One also hears constant repetition in the speeches of Hitler and in advertising."[5] Glass, in turn, described the serialists as "maniacs, these creeps, who were trying to make everyone write this crazy creepy music."[6] The sides of the Yale battle, then, would seem to be clear—the minimalist, student vanguard rebelling against the entrenched, serial academic establishment. Downtown invades uptown.

But when asked specifically about this moment in his graduate studies, the story that Gordon tells today is a bit more complicated. "I was probably surprised," he recalled of the faculty booing. After all, he added, "It wasn't so uptight there."[7] He noted that the head of the composition department, Jacob Druckman, was interested in the music of Reich and the Dutch dissonant minimalist Louis Andriessen; so, too, was Gordon's principal teacher Martin Bresnick. And Gordon had successfully applied to Yale with a Reich-inspired piano work. If anything, his professors seemed to welcome minimalists. Further, Druckman, an orchestral composer who would go on to champion an aesthetic he described as New Romanticism, was largely opposed to what he saw as the overly intellectualized exercises of serialism. The booing, as it turns out, came from a sole clarinet professor who served as associate dean. As Bresnick put it, "Conventional musicians got very grumpy."[8]

A full recounting of the *The Tree Watcher* incident instead reveals what Yale was actually like for Gordon, Lang, and Julia Wolfe, who attended its graduate program between 1980 and 1986, and how its atmosphere may have been more welcoming to their aesthetic agendas than one might initially assume. And it suggests something about preconceptions of academic music-making more broadly. Musicologists have long considered the university one of the principal sites for the development of postwar American modernism, taking after Milton Babbitt's "Who Cares if You Listen?" essay and his argument that the university "should provide a home for the 'complex,' 'difficult,' and 'problematical' in music."[9] The history of American graduate studies in composition after the 1962 founding of Princeton's pioneering PhD has largely been analyzed as a kind of Babbitt aftershock, one in which Cold War ideology and patronage constructed a home for mathematical, atonal, and audience-unfriendly music to flourish outside the marketplace.[10] In a lacerating 1966 essay, experimental composer Morton Feldman criticized the insular culture of university composition studios and their attendant foundation support, scholarly journals, ensembles, and electronic music studios as having "created a climate that has brought the musical activity of an entire nation down to a college level."[11] And even though Joseph Straus has partly debunked what he calls the "myth of 'serial tyranny'"—that composers of twelve-tone music ruled the US musical establishment, and especially college campuses, for decades—the impression that twelve-tone music dominated the academy is still hard to shake.[12] Indeed, that narrative is supported, in part, by the Bang on a Can composers' mixed academic experiences prior to their Yale studies.

But Gordon's clarification about Yale in the early 1980s reveals that we may need to approach the academy with a new lens. Graduate programs in composition were not simply a top-down form of pedagogy, in which students accepted or rebelled against their teachers' serial tyranny, but instead a constellation of forces and agents within a multi-faceted institutional setting. Bang on a Can's three founding composers were deeply shaped by Yale's open-minded pedagogy, its professionalized atmosphere, and the experimentalism of the undergraduate collective Sheep's Clothing. In some ways, Yale was both uptown and downtown, an elite university setting and rigorous curriculum that nevertheless allowed students to explore minimalism; in other ways, it was neither, encouraging a relationship to the marketplace that was typically shunned by academics and experimentalists alike. But what is clear is that underlying ethos of Bang on a Can grew directly out of, rather than against, their Ivy League training.[13]

I Wanted to Be a Composer

Born in the second half of the 1950s, Gordon, Lang, and Wolfe were late Baby Boomers who encountered the reverberations of 1960s student radicalism when they arrived at college in the mid-'70s. ("We are the post-hippie generation," Lang once said.[14]) In their pre-Yale academic years, they grappled with the legacy of uptown, studying with professors who encouraged them to utilize serial techniques and discouraged their love of musical minimalism, at institutions that had been shaped by Cold War-era patronage. They grew frustrated with the notion of the musical academy as a retreat from society, but nevertheless chose to continue their studies at Yale.

Gordon had an unusually itinerant early life for a composer who has spent most of the rest of it based in New York. His parents were Eastern European Jewish émigrés—his father left Poland in 1939—and met in New York shortly after World War II. Gordon's grandfather had emigrated from Poland to Cuba and then on to Nicaragua, and his parents subsequently moved there. Born in Miami in 1956—his mother traveled to the states for medical care—the composer grew up in a tiny, immigrant community in the outskirts of Managua, where he began taking piano lessons. When he was eight, Gordon and his family moved to Miami Beach, where he started dabbling in composition, including writing for rock and jazz bands in which he played keyboards as a teenager. His sister's boyfriend was a contemporary music aficionado and gave the young Gordon a record of chamber music by Elliott Carter. Upon the first hearing, Gordon thought that the music was "the ugliest thing I had ever heard," but he kept listening again and again, hearing something he perceived as more sophisticated than rock and pop.[15] He decided that Carter's path was one he wanted to pursue, and started taking composition lessons with a local Juilliard graduate.

He flitted between colleges, briefly attending Boston University—where he obsessively listened to a tape his brother-in-law had made him that mixed George Crumb's *Black Angels*, Steve Reich's *Four Organs*, and medieval organum—then heading closer to home to the University of Florida, where he studied with a Harvard and Michigan grad named Edward Troupin. But New York, the city of Reich, was calling. Gordon moved to Manhattan in 1977, first studying at the Manhattan School of Music and then at New York University, where he finally completed his undergraduate degree. He attended Glass and Reich concerts downtown, but also programs featuring the music of Carter and Mario Davidovsky at Carnegie Recital Hall. Gordon had started to write minimalist-infused music, of which his teacher at Manhattan, who prized the neoclassicism of Paul Hindemith, was highly discouraging. At one point, she told him, "You really don't need to go to school here to write the kind of music you write. Just go and hang out in bars downtown."[16] And he did—in 1979, Gordon started playing in a new wave band, Peter and the Girlfriends, in the downtown art-rock scene.

Though Gordon had yet to find a mentor who fully supported the kind of music he wanted to compose, it wasn't until NYU that he encountered serial pedagogy. His teacher there, the composer Brian Fennelly, was an emblematic uptown figure. Having earned a PhD in music theory at Yale, where he studied with the atonal composer Mel Powell and the prominent theorist Allen Forte, Fennelly published analytical articles for the journal *Perspectives of New Music* and wrote pointillistic twelve-tone works. He expressed little interest in Gordon's minimalist experiments, but helped his student build a rigorous analytical understanding of the inner workings of modernist music by Carter and Anton Webern. It was there that Gordon wrote what he considers his first major composition, *Earthwork*. An episodic piano piece that takes much from the composer's minimalist lodestars, it begins with quick repetitions of bright, open chords before moving on to a bit of sinewy passagework that spells out a twelve-tone row through an additive process reminiscent of Glass. "I really loved that music," Gordon said of his fascination with Reich and Glass in this period, "but when I tried to write something that sounded like it, I got really bored."[17] *Earthwork* expresses some of this restlessness, constantly trying out and discarding sped-up versions of various minimalist phase and pattern techniques. It premiered on an April 1980 concert at NYU featuring compositions with abstract titles like *Solo Piece with Passacaglia* and *Music for Flute and Tape*; Gordon was clearly the odd one out. (Incidentally, the program was partly funded by a grant from Meet the Composer.)

Gordon visited Yale several times and was impressed by the musicianship at the student concerts in its Sprague Hall auditorium.[18] He applied to the master's program and, despite having composed a relatively small number of works, was accepted. He arrived in New Haven in fall 1980, in a class that included composers Scott Lindroth and Michael Daugherty. Despite finding Yale more hospitable than his previous university settings, Gordon never warmed to the academy. He would commute to campus from the city, frequently missing seminars and occasionally private lessons as his downtown band overshadowed his coursework. "I still hated class," he later recalled. "I can't think of a single class in my two years there I wanted to take, or I enjoyed taking and I did the work for."[19]

In his second year, Gordon found a new compatriot in David Lang, a composer who felt entirely at ease in scholastic environs. Gordon and Lang had first met at the Aspen Music Festival's summer composition program several years earlier—Lang was twenty, Gordon was twenty-one—where they became fast enemies. Lang attended Aspen for four summers, and won several student prizes there. "I show up to Aspen and I'm in a class with no less than young David Lang, who is from LA and has already written a hundred pieces of music," Gordon remembered. "He knows everything and knows everybody. He's a total snot-ass. And I'm like a hick from Florida. I don't know anything and I don't know anyone. In this class together, we just hated each other."[20]

Upon re-encountering each other at Yale, however, they quickly became friends (Figure 1.1). Born in 1957, Lang grew up in Los Angeles, and though his family was not particularly musical, they took him to concerts and the opera. It did not take long for artistic ambitions to emerge. In a story he recounts frequently, when Lang was in elementary school, he saw a video of one of Leonard Bernstein's "Young People's Concerts" in which the conductor apparently described how Shostakovich wrote his First Symphony at age nineteen and "became world famous overnight."[21] "I remember thinking, I'm nine years old," Lang later recalled. "I have ten years. I can do that." His path toward composition began, then, with what he called a "tremendous amount of naivete and a tremendous amount of incredible arrogance." He took up trombone seriously and immersed himself in music. Lang composed trombone

Figure 1.1 Michael Gordon and David Lang in New Haven, April 1982. Courtesy of Michael Gordon.

parts to Beethoven's violin sonatas so he could play along with his father's recordings, wrote juvenilia for string quartet and symphony orchestra, and, at age thirteen, started studying composition with the UCLA professor Henri Lazarof.

His parents wanted him to be a doctor, and so Lang went to Stanford for college at age seventeen with the intent of being a chemistry major. But he subsequently changed focus about a half-dozen times, briefly majoring in drama, English, art history, medieval studies, and, by the time he graduated, music. Lang's family was Jewish, from Germany and Lithuania, and he was a self-proclaimed "Russophile"—in high school, he created "The Greater Los Angeles Shostakovich Society"—who spent a summer studying abroad in Russia.[22] Through these intellectual convulsions, Lang's musical activities at Stanford were constant and wide-ranging: he wrote for student composition concerts, started a contemporary music group, worked in the famed Center for Computer Research in Music and Acoustics, arranged for Broadway shows, composed for the jazz band, reviewed performances for the student newspaper, conducted the wind orchestra, and played in the notoriously countercultural marching band.

Lang's music also developed from a Shostakovich-infused style in his high-school years toward what he described as a "very pretty and very spacey and very slow and delicate and transparent" sound under the influence of Lou Harrison, a visiting professor in Lang's first year at Stanford, and after powerful encounters with the music of Harry Partch, Glass, and Reich.[23] Through college, he explored this "California, hippie, spacey" experimental idiom, writing an eight-hour piano piece in his freshman year. And he studied with the young faculty member Martin Bresnick, who helped his student introduce what Lang called an "intellectual rigor" to his music. He graduated from Stanford in 1978.

"I never wanted to go any place but Yale," Lang once said.[24] Intending to continue working with Bresnick, who had joined the Yale faculty in 1976, Lang applied to the School of Music's master's program. But following an administrative error, Lang was not accepted, and Bresnick told him to reapply the next year; rather than wait, Lang went to the University of Iowa in 1978, where he encountered a very different environment.

Iowa represented a stronghold for the Cold War academic avant-garde. In 1965, the Rockefeller Foundation had selected its music department to receive a $100,000 grant to start a new-music center, as part of a $2 million nationwide initiative to establish universities as a home for cutting-edge composition.[25] Twelve campuses were funded across the country, and these laboratories of musical modernism—steeped in the ethos of uptown—had their own specialized contemporary ensembles and electronic music studios. Milton Babbitt served as a regular consultant for the Rockefeller Foundation, and the very first infusion of Rockefeller funding had gone to the Columbia-Princeton Electronic Music Center. One of Lang's principal teachers at Iowa, William Hibbard, had co-founded Iowa's Center for New Music; he was a doctrinaire figure whose music drew on Babbitt's time point system and serialized pitch and rhythm.

Lang hated the snow but appreciated Iowa's academic rigor, where he took courses focused on William Byrd, Brahms, and the history of tuning, studied with several teachers, and benefitted from the Center's ensemble and symposia. His music took a turn from the spacey to the dissonant, and he found the competitive nature of the Iowa studio—in which every graduate student was vying to win a BMI young composer's award—alienating and hostile compared to his previous liberal arts environment. "The teachers hated each other, and they had their students fight their wars," he recalled.[26] "My job was to do something that would squeeze one of the opposing students out." After finishing his master's at Iowa, he decided he had enough of the academy and moved to Boston to work in arts administration; he soon found, however, that he had no time to compose, and decided to return to graduate studies. After a short stint in Harvard's doctoral program, which he felt was too stuffy and removed from concert life, he reapplied to Yale for a second master's degree.[27] By the time Lang arrived at Yale in fall 1981, he had a large catalog of early works, an understanding of a wide array of idioms in contemporary music, and a certain degree of jadedness about the differences between university life and the real world. But he was also highly conventionally credentialed. Bresnick recognized that, unlike Gordon and Wolfe, Lang "from the outset had a complete and thorough and unequivocal training in the world that I live in," by which he meant the academy.[28]

Last to arrive at Yale—after both Lang and Gordon had completed their master's degrees and were living in Manhattan—was Julia Wolfe. Born in 1958, she grew up in northeastern Pennsylvania in a family of music lovers. Her parents regularly attended the symphony orchestra and played classical records at home on Sundays, which, as a child, she found mostly boring. Wolfe started studying piano at age six and, as a preteen, would buy books of show tunes to learn at home. In high school during the '60s, she developed a love for the Beatles and Janis Joplin, and began playing folk guitar and writing songs in the manner of Joni Mitchell.

Studies at the University of Michigan continued to foster Wolfe's countercultural leanings. Michigan had been a hotbed for leftist politics—the first meetings of the Students for a Democratic Society took place there back in 1960—and Wolfe enrolled in the school's Residential College, a still-new program designed to create a liberal arts atmosphere within the larger university. It served as what the campus newspaper called a "testing ground for then-revolutionary educational concepts" including unstructured seminars, a pass-fail system, and student-led courses, and its East Quad dorm became an epicenter for student activism.[29] Wolfe had no particular intention to pursue music, but found her way into a class called "Creative Musicianship" taught by the choral conductor and Alexander Technique specialist Jane Heirich. The Residential College was separate from Michigan's prestigious School of Music, Theatre & Dance, and the course attracted musicians of all skill levels; Heirich encouraged them all to compose. Soon, Wolfe was spending almost all her time on dorm room pianos writing small pieces as exercises for class. "There was no hierarchy of musics," the composer later wrote of Heirich's wide-ranging philosophy. The professor introduced her students to Bach, Brahms, Dave Brubeck, and even Terry Riley—Wolfe has credited "Creative Musicianship" with instilling her with an omnivorous artistic philosophy.[30]

The developing composer flourished in the bohemian atmosphere of the Residential College's living–learning curriculum; she trotted around the Michigan campus with a mountain dulcimer and played in the streets in an all-women's drumming group.[31]

In her final year of college, Wolfe began studying privately with Laura Clayton, a graduate student in composition at Michigan, who introduced her to the music of George Crumb, György Ligeti, Charles Ives, and others. Around this time, while collaborating with a modern dance company, Wolfe heard Reich's *Music for Eighteen Musicians* for the first time and "felt a world crack open"—though she soon discovered that minimalism was shunned by other Michigan composers.[32] Wolfe graduated, but stayed in Ann Arbor, took the music school's theory sequence and, after Clayton moved away, began working with the composition professor George Balch Wilson. Wilson was the longtime director of Michigan's electronic music studio, which had been modeled after the Columbia-Princeton Electronic Music Center. Like Iowa, Michigan's composition studio had been funded by the Rockefeller Foundation, receiving around $84,000 in the late 1960s to establish a contemporary ensemble.[33]

With Clayton, Wolfe had pursued her eclectic liberal arts interests; under Wilson's tutelage, things soon changed. "In my first lesson he had me put aside my somewhat scrawling but definitely lively work for large chamber ensemble and trapeze artists, and gave me a set of ordered pitches with which to write a new work for piano," she later wrote.[34] After working with two supportive and open-minded female mentors, Wolfe chafed under Wilson's discouraging supervision and serial pedagogy, and spent more than two years on the atonal piano work, titled *Seamarks*. "I barely survived my lessons at Michigan," she said in 2016.[35]

Wolfe found other creative outlets. She started an all-female theater company, Wild Swan, that adapted folk stories, in which she acted, wrote scripts, and directed the music, including singing and playing flute and dulcimer. But she also wanted to pursue more in-depth forms of composition, to write complex works that she herself would not perform. In part because of the reputation of its theater department, she considered graduate studies at Yale. On a trip to New York in 1982, she visited a photographer friend, Peter Serling, and met his roommate, Michael Gordon. Gordon and Wolfe went out for breakfast and discussed Yale—he had recently finished the program—and he recommended that she meet David Lang.

Wolfe drove to New Haven and spent an afternoon with Lang, who cracked open a bag of Chips Ahoy cookies and played for her what she described as "this really odd combination of music" including Witold Lutosławski, Laurie

Anderson, and Reich.[36] Wolfe and Gordon began dating while she was living in Ann Arbor. Despite Wilson's dissuasion, she attended the Aspen summer festival, for which she wrote a work for two cellos and percussion and won the student prize. She returned to Ann Arbor and attempted to switch teachers, studying briefly with William Bolcom and George Cacioppo, but ultimately decided to leave Michigan for the East Coast. Wolfe applied to Yale with three compositions: the atonal piano solo, the prize-winning Aspen work, and a new piece for wind instruments and hand clappers inspired by Reich's *Tehillim*. Gordon and Wolfe married shortly before she began studies at Yale in fall 1984.

A Pluralistic Attitude

"Most schools were heavily entrenched in serial music," Wolfe has said of her Michigan days.[37] But if her previous environs fell under the sway of a serial tyranny, Yale was an outlier. Describing the moment of amazement when Bresnick first introduced her to the score for Louis Andriessen's monumental, postminimalist manifesto *De Staat*, Wolfe said that Yale provided "respect for different kinds of artists and music: it wasn't a closed door at all."[38] Gordon agreed, *The Tree Watcher* incident notwithstanding. "It was the first time I was in a kind of creative atmosphere involving new music where it wasn't this kind of mind-deadening, academic, totally intellectual approach," he once said of his graduate school years.[39] Gordon, Lang, and Wolfe had traced similar academic arcs prior to Yale. They had gravitated toward the minimalism of Reich and Glass, but encountered colleagues and professors who were largely unsympathetic and instead encouraged them to explore serial technique. They could have simply dropped out of the academy after completing their undergraduate degrees, and moved to downtown New York or San Francisco and started making music—but even after withstanding serial pedagogy, they still wanted to pursue a form of composition more rigorous than theatrical folk songs or spacey experimentalism. Yale was the place to do so.

Through the 1980s, Yale's graduate composition program was shepherded by Jacob Druckman and Martin Bresnick. In the years before Druckman's arrival, Yale was not associated with one or two dominant composition professors, as was the case with Princeton and Babbitt. The School of Music, which did not offer tenure, typically hired composers on short-term contracts with the potential for regular renewal. Composer Martin Brody, who studied at Yale in the mid-'70s, described the environment then as very "diffuse," with a mixture of hands-on faculty such as Yehudi Wyner and Robert Morris, and prestigious but less attentive guest composers like Krzysztof Penderecki and Tōru Takemitsu.[40]

Druckman briefly taught at Yale in the early 1970s and joined the faculty in 1976 to succeed Wyner as chairman of the composition department. Bresnick had arrived at Yale's undergraduate Department of Music that same year, and would join the graduate School of Music faculty in 1981. As visiting faculty cycled in and out for short terms in this period, Druckman and Bresnick steered the department's culture and curriculum (Figure 1.2). But Druckman was a prestigious midcareer composer, and his professional commitments—serving as a resident composer at the American Academy in Rome, working as the New York Philharmonic's composer-in-residence, preparing a Metropolitan Opera commission—meant that he frequently took leave from teaching. Almost immediately after he was hired at the School of Music, Bresnick was tasked with coordinating the graduate program, despite being only in his mid-thirties.

The school had implemented a rotational system in which students were encouraged to work with a different professor each semester for individual lessons. Druckman embraced this policy, seeking to foster what he called

Figure 1.2 Jacob Druckman and Martin Bresnick, 1980s. Courtesy of the Yale School of Music.

a "pluralistic attitude" in which students explored a range of compositional styles under a diversity of supervision.[41] A student might work with Druckman for a semester, then Bresnick, then a guest composer like Frederic Rzewski. Regularly changing teachers, Gordon's classmate Scott Lindroth recalled, meant that "You're on your own in a sense." Druckman's mentality, he said, was that "You should be able to test out your ideas with people who have very different opinions, be able hold your own and learn what you can."[42] With this scheme, Bresnick and Druckman hoped to avoid the plight of students who closely mimicked their professors—or what Morton Feldman lambasted as a circular, insular system in which "the music of the teacher will be no different from that of the teacher he's teaching."[43]

The rotational scheme was not strictly enforced. Composers interested in the orchestral world, like Gordon and Lang's classmates Aaron Jay Kernis and Michael Daugherty, tended to gravitate toward Druckman; Bresnick carved out a niche for teaching what he called "the outcast composers" such as Gordon and Jeffrey Brooks.[44] Even the outcasts, though, found Druckman unusual for an academic. When Gordon described Yale as a rare exception to the hyper-intellectualized academy, he identified this approach as "Druckman's legacy"—"He hated serial music. He didn't like any of it."[45] Druckman had dabbled in writing serial works earlier in his career, and spent time at the Columbia-Princeton Electronic Music Center in the 1960s. He once quipped that "not being a serialist on the East Coast of the United States in the sixties was like not being a Catholic in Rome in the thirteenth century. It was the respectable thing to do, at least once."[46] His electronic compositions led him to new realizations about timbre and, in the 1970s, he began writing a series of large-scale orchestral works, including the Pulitzer Prize-winning *Windows*, a piece exploring a gestural, freely intuitive style that mixed tonality and atonality, and which he described as "a reaction of 15 to 20 years of strictly controlled post-Webernian structuring, the kind of thing that has held music in a prison."[47] "It had come to the point where students were writing pieces that would sound terrible in the concert hall and yet were very beautifully analyzable in these professional journals," Druckman told an interviewer in 1974. "The battle was being fought in these journals instead of in the concert hall, and this I think is very unhealthy."[48] This perspective would culminate in Druckman's embrace of the moniker New Romanticism, the banner theme for the Horizons festivals he curated as composer-in-residence with the New York Philharmonic.

Gordon worked briefly with Druckman but, indifferent to the orchestra and attempting to develop a new postminimalist idiom, cycled through teachers until finally landing with Bresnick, whom he described as "very respectful of what I was doing."[49] And if Druckman was sympathetic to minimalism, Bresnick was openly welcoming of and well-versed in the style from his years studying and teaching in the Bay Area. Bresnick guided Gordon to continually hone his voice, culminating in the breakthrough piece *Thou Shalt!/Thou Shalt Not!*, which adapts the rhythmic dissonances of *The Tree Watcher* into an ensemble medium. Composed during Gordon's final semester at Yale in 1982, *Thou Shalt* is infused with the spirit of that tape of organum and *Four Organs* that Gordon obsessed over, staging a conflict between a short, repeating modal gesture ("Thou Shalt!") and a second motif that consistently interrupts it ("Thou Shalt Not!").[50] In Gordon's score, the motivic battle is further dramatized by a timbral skirmish: guitar, bass clarinet, and electric keyboard continually reiterate the sinewy, constantly shifting opening riff, but are thwarted by the interjections of tuned drums and marimba playing insistent quarter notes. "I saw him sit at this really crappy upright in my studio and just desperately try to achieve a certain kind of sonority," Bresnick recalled.[51] To perform the piece, Gordon assembled his own makeshift ensemble—the Michael Gordon Philharmonic, an amplified group in which Gordon played keyboards (Figure 1.3). As he wound down work with his art-rock band, the Philharmonic soon stood at the center of his musical life. Most of his music of the 1980s was composed for the ensemble, which included Yale composer and clarinetist Evan Ziporyn.

Though Wolfe took Druckman's orchestration class, she studied exclusively with Bresnick for her four semesters.[52] She has described how her teacher constantly pushed her to make her work stronger and more persuasive, without dogmatism.[53] As Bresnick put it, "If you have an idea about what you want to learn, I want to help you fulfill your idea of what that is. But I also want to subject to a certain very quiet scrutiny what it is that you want to learn."[54] She focused primarily on two pieces at Yale: the woodwind quintet *On Seven-Star Shoes* and the choral work *Song at Daybreak*. A strong feminist consciousness undergirds both pieces. *On Seven-Star Shoes*, the earliest work still in Wolfe's catalog, drew inspiration from the writer Elsa Lasker-Schuller, whom Wolfe identified in a program note as "one of the few women associated with the Expressionist movement."[55] And Wolfe has described the text of *Song at Daybreak*, a thirteenth-century Hebrew hymn, as appealing because it is written from the female perspective: "Take care of the soul, she's turquoise, agate and jasper." Wolfe, Lang, and Gordon have maintained important connections to the traditions of their Jewish heritage throughout their lives and music, and *Song at Daybreak* represents an early example of Wolfe drawing on those influences.

Figure 1.3 Michael Gordon Philharmonic, 1980s. Photograph by Peter Serling.

On Seven-Star Shoes is marked by piquant harmonies reminiscent of the neoclassical Stravinsky, and hiccupping rhythms that evoke Reich's *Tehillim*. Almost halfway through the five-minute piece, Wolfe indicates that the clarinetist switch to bass clarinet and play a riff "funky," an early sign of her music's burgeoning relationship to the vernacular. Though it started as an outgrowth of her Ann Arbor experimental theater days—originally written for wind players and hand clappers—the piece took a more pragmatic turn under the guidance of Bresnick. In one lesson, he mentioned that woodwind quintets were always seeking out new repertoire, and that if she wrote for the instrumentation she would have a better chance of hearing the work publicly performed. So she re-orchestrated it.[56] Wolfe characterized Bresnick's advice as "very practical." "That's part of the Yale mentality too," she said. "You are a composer in this world and how do you function?"[57]

Lang worked primarily with Druckman, although their methods were somewhat at odds. Druckman was more instinctive than cerebral, whereas Lang had developed, from his years at Iowa, an intensive engagement with the kind of pre-compositional maps and restricted musical materials deployed by the theory-minded serialists. The first major work he wrote at Yale, the Vietnam War-inspired violin sonata *illumination rounds*, uses the concept of tracer bullets as a metaphor for contrapuntal interplay between violin and piano, as the latter shadows the highly virtuosic, chromatic passagework of the former.[58] Following its premiere at Carnegie Recital Hall in April 1982, *illumination rounds* won both ASCAP and BMI's student composer prizes. (Take that, Iowans.) A profile in the *Yale Daily News* written shortly afterwards documented the composer's further ambitions as an impresario: "Lang's ultimate goal is to return to his hometown of Los Angeles and organize and direct a production company. 'It's my little Napoleonic complex,' he confides."[59]

But the success of *illumination rounds* among prize committees also worried Lang. He started to get requests to write similar pieces for other classical musicians, and feared that he might fall into a pattern of composing flashy crowd-pleasers. Instead, his second Yale project was the 1982 piano work *while nailing at random*, in which brutally pounding cluster chords seemingly plucked from the sound world of Karlheinz Stockhausen's *Klavierstücke* are occasionally interrupted by snippets of a muted chorale. He wanted to create something, he said a few years later, "unidiomatic for the instrument," and his music of the mid-'80s continued in this vein.[60]

The composers learned as much from each other as they did from their teachers. Bresnick's deliberate avoidance of what he has called "paternal authority" allowed for strong peer cohorts to develop.[61] Composers who attended the Yale program in the early 1980s described their relationship to their fellow students as a key component of their experiences. Given Druckman's professional preoccupations and Bresnick's relative youth, as Jeffrey Brooks put it, "Nobody was watching the store." He described his fellow students as "in charge of the asylum."[62] And because Bresnick and Druckman both avoided cultivating strong "schools" of hand-picked students, Brooks said, "the main identity we had was not with a teacher but with each other."[63] Scott Lindroth described the importance of being able to watch his friends grow as musicians, whether it was Gordon "trying to figure out how minimalism intersected with mainstream modernist styles," or Michael Daugherty navigating how to synthesize his love of jazz piano, his training in modernist electronic music at IRCAM, and his prior studies with Charles Wuorinen.[64]

Figure 1.4 David Lang, Michael Gordon, and Julia Wolfe, late 1980s. Photograph by Robert Lewis.

This feeling seems specific to Yale in the 1980s, as Martin Brody did not recall a strong sense of camaraderie with fellow students when he attended the school in the previous decade.

This mentality allowed the Bang on a Can composers to connect as a group, supported by a competitive but not cutthroat environment (Figure 1.4). "It was a really amazing class," Lang remembered. "We got that from our teachers. They were nice to each other, and they built this world where they had to figure out how to have a relationship that was not based on ideological purity."[65] He and Gordon would compose next to one another on the balcony of Lang's New Haven apartment, with one working on *illumination rounds* and the other writing *Thou Shalt!/Thou Shalt Not!*. "Everything I know about how to be courageous in a piece of music, I know from Michael," Lang said of this period.[66] And by the time that Wolfe arrived at Yale, her principal composition cohort was Gordon and Wolfe.

They Gave All-Night Marathon Concerts

Gordon, Lang, and Wolfe rarely mentioned Yale in interviews they gave in the early years of Bang on a Can—understandable for an organization that sought to distinguish itself from "academic music," even if the culture at Yale may have subverted uptown stereotypes. But there was one clear, and significant, exception. In prominent outlets in the 1990s, the Bang on a Can founders discussed the indebtedness of their very first marathon concert to one part of their Yale experience. "Martin founded an ensemble at Yale called Sheep's Clothing," Wolfe told *Village Voice* critic Kyle Gann in 1993. "They gave all-night marathon concerts, like happenings, in unusual spaces that people would check out at three in the morning. He's not at all stylistically biased. That kind of spirit shaped our thinking."[67] That said, not all of the Sheep's activities shaped Bang on a Can's thinking. Lang, Wolfe, and Gordon took certain lessons from the undergraduate collective, while also consciously overlooking others.

Sheep's Clothing originated with Martin Bresnick, an idea that developed from his years on the West Coast. Having arrived in the Bay Area for graduate studies at Stanford immediately following the Summer of Love, Bresnick immersed himself in the countercultural mindset that suffused institutions like Mills College and the San Francisco Tape Music Center. Around this time, the experimental composer Ivan Tcherepnin, who was teaching at Stanford, suggested to Bresnick the idea for an all-night marathon concert. In traditions such as Indian raga and Catholicism's Divine Office, music served a different function when performed at different times of the day, and Tcherepnin wondered what it might mean to hear avant-garde music at three in the morning.

Bresnick had this idea in the back of his head when he arrived at Yale's Department of Music in 1976. The principal outlet for new-music performance at the time was the Yale Contemporary Ensemble, which primarily focused on canonic modernist repertoire and works by Yale faculty and graduate students. Seeing few opportunities for the undergraduates he taught, in 1978 Bresnick offered a seminar on experimental music with a strong orientation toward performance. Some of the students in Bresnick's course sought to continue their activities outside the classroom setting, and Sheep's Clothing was born.

The Sheep staged their first all-night concert in spring 1978. The second marathon, in March 1979, opened at midnight with Frederic Rzewski's *Les Moutons de Panurge*—a 1969 open score that instructs musicians to work through a sixty-five-note melody in unison and subsequently improvise, with the added instruction "Stay together as long as you can, but if you get lost, stay lost"—and concluded with Terry Riley's *In C* at sunrise.[68] Attendees were invited to bring sleeping bags, and Bresnick told the *New Haven Register* that "we don't mind if audience members lie down or occasionally chat with one another."[69] The then-thirteen-member group played music by John

Cage and Karlheinz Stockhausen along with new conceptual works created by ensemble members. A kind of collegiate irreverence was at the heart of the enterprise—undergraduate Jenny Rycenga told the student newspaper that she hoped it would "become a Yale tradition, if that's not too sickening a thing to say."[70] The marathons drew audiences of several hundred. "It was by far the most exciting and best attended new music event that happened at Yale," Bresnick recalled.[71]

The all-night marathons became annual affairs, supplemented by other Sheep concerts and advertised with posters featuring Dada-esque newspaper collages and scribbled drawings. Much of the music created by the Sheep combined post-Cagean happenings with irreverent jabs at the classical tradition, as in Rycenga's String Quartet No. 3 ("The Lark"), which, according to the *Yale Daily News*, was composed for "five string players, beverages, hats, and four cats tied to chairs."[72] (The students also played a hefty amount of European modernist work by Olivier Messiaen, Stockhausen, and others.) Observers and participants frequently contrasted the feisty, liberal arts Sheep of Yale's undergrad music department against the purportedly dull denizens of the graduate music school. A *Yale Daily News* preview of the 1981 marathon noted that it was "certainly more fun than a Yale Composer's Concert," and "a celebration of modern music conspicuously full of that element most lacking in 'academic music'—a sense of humor."[73] Guest composers such as Tcherepnin, Pauline Oliveros, Daniel Goode, and Tom Johnson dropped by campus; students participants included a mixture of new-music veterans and novices.

Newbie Daniel Plonsey was a math major at Yale who played in the marching band, and was drawn into the experimental world through his roommate, Sheep member Chris Maher. By his sophomore year, Plonsey was creating text-based scores in which "musicians wander through the audience muttering things like 'B double-flat; how about that.'"[74] Evan Ziporyn, on the other hand, majored in music. He studied composition with Bresnick, played jazz saxophone and clarinet in student-organized concerts on campus, and was considered an accomplished enough undergraduate composer to be featured in School of Music concerts at Sprague Hall. But Ziporyn also took a stand against what he saw as the music school's staid culture, pontificating in the student newspaper about the isolation of academic composers from the public and criticizing the Yale Contemporary Ensemble's concerts for not attracting an audience.[75] In one column, he chastised a visiting composer because he "seemed unperturbed that only 12 people showed up to listen to him."[76] Instead, Ziporyn later said, "I really saw my musical life as being" in Sheep's Clothing.[77] He soon became a close friend to and collaborator with

Gordon, and then a mainstay of the early Bang on a Can marathons and founding member of the All-Stars ensemble.

Humorous, anti-academic, and aimed toward a broad audience might also sum up the philosophy of Bang on a Can, and it is perhaps unsurprising that Lang latched onto Sheep's Clothing soon after he arrived at Yale. Lang had already participated in the bohemian, West Coast culture out of which the Sheep were born. At Stanford he had realized Fluxus scores with his peers, and was apparently banned from using university instruments after a rendition of La Monte Young's infamous *Piano Piece for David Tudor #1*, which instructs performers to feed a bale of hay to a piano. "I had been infused with Cage's spirit," Lang recollected of his stint with the Sheep. "That lots of things can be music which are not about playing notes with an instrument, and I thought here was the great opportunity for me to push that as far as it could go."[78]

For an October 1982 performance in which Lang participated, the Sheep ambled around Yale's campus at midday, presenting short concerts in different locations that included sounds created by sirens, cats, gourds, and triangular math rulers (Figure 1.5). The performances concluded with the

Figure 1.5 Sheep's Clothing ambulatory concert at Yale, October 1982. From left, Craig Pepples, Jay Rozen, and David Lang. Courtesy of Jay Rozen.

ensemble revealing and crashing cymbals hidden beneath black coats. "I think they express in a fundamental way the freedom given by the University to its students," an undergraduate spectator told a student reporter.[79] In one of Lang's compositions, Bresnick recalled, "We just stood in a line, holding these branches with bells, and anytime anybody approached us as they came close, we would shake our little branches and the little bells would jingle. And we had deadpan faces; we never explained what we were doing or why we were doing it."[80] At this or another Sheep event, Lang handed out vegetables to the audience to use as musical instruments, and conducted the resulting orchestra.[81]

For Lang and a few other graduate student participants, the Sheep represented an outlet to dabble in experimental practices not offered in the School of Music. Lindroth described the Sheep antics as an "eye-opener," fondly reminiscing about one concert where he played Reich's *Piano Phase* at an andante tempo to better hear the music's gradual process unfold.[82] What served for the undergraduates as a musical way of life was, for these graduate students, fodder for side projects as they pursued more traditional musical endeavors—and conventionally notated scores—in their lessons with Bresnick and Druckman. Bang on a Can drew upon the Sheep's do-it-yourself spirit, irreverence toward convention, and concerts of extraordinary lengths that emphasized experiential immersion, but did not overtly take on one key component of the undergraduate collective's philosophy: its explicit political stance.

The Sheep's engagement with indeterminacy, text scores, and minimalist processes was partly inspired by a post-1960s leftist ethos that viewed participatory music-making—in which traditional boundaries between composer, performer, and listener were blurred or subverted—as a mode of political dissent. According to Plonsey, the Sheep were dedicated readers of Cornelius Cardew's *Stockhausen Serves Imperialism*, a 1974 book that included polemics shaped by the British experimental composer's immersion in Marxist-Leninist thought and the Maoist Cultural Revolution. In the book's title essay, Cardew denounced his former lodestars Karlheinz Stockhausen and John Cage as perpetuating falsely bourgeois notions of genius, in that they appeared "eager to propagate an ideological line—such as mysticism or anarchism or reformism—that is in so far friendly to imperialism in that it opposes socialism and the ideas that would contribute to the organization of the working class for the overthrow of imperialism."[83] The book also contained a history of the Scratch Orchestra, a collective founded by Cardew and colleagues that included amateur musicians and focused on graphic scores and improvisation. In the early 1970s, the Scratch Orchestra became increasingly Maoist and began investigating the possibilities of making a music that would communicate directly with the working class, from ambulatory concerts to performing at political rallies to mounting agit-prop theatrical productions. And like the Sheep, the Scratch Orchestra had originated in a college experimental music course.

There were also political influences closer to home. At the festival New Music, New York, mounted at The Kitchen in 1979, Tcherepnin—who had given Bresnick the inspiration for an all-night concert—had raised the question of whether the institutionalization of experimental music signified by the large scale of the nine-evening series represented an alliance with capitalism and the state: "Is not the stand being taken, viz. to 'establish' the Experimental music scene and provide an endowment for its sustenance also tying the participants into the system, which will eventually incorporate it? Isn't there an implicit complicity with Big Business and Government involved here?"[84] Bresnick himself shared these vocally anti-establishment views. He had joined anti-Vietnam sit-ins at Stanford as a member of the Students for a Democratic Society, participated in a Marxist reading group at Yale, and spoken at a 1980 Campaign Against the Draft rally on campus.

With Cardew as inspiration, the Sheep sought to distance themselves from bourgeois forms of music-making and dissolve traditional hierarchies. Although Bresnick originally served as faculty advisor, the group soon functioned as an empowered collective. As Rycenga told the student newspaper before the second all-night concert, "We even have the right to revolution in 'Sheep's Clothing.'"[85] Graphic notation emboldened the musicians to think of themselves as co-creators in the artistic process, and members of the group created their own scores to be realized collectively.[86] Reflecting back on the Sheep in 2017, Plonsey characterized their approach as a "democratic notion of music making, that everyone should be involved in every aspect of production."[87]

In undermining the conventions of concert culture, the Sheep also saw themselves as thumbing their noses at the mindset of Yale's School of Music. "We were really in reaction to what we saw of the graduate school composers," Plonsey recalled, describing the Sprague Hall concerts as "the most dry and unappealing events."[88] According to Ziporyn, Sheep Chris Maher had in this period theorized a "Marxist music" in which "no musical material could be owned," thus allowing "music—rather than an individual's musical career—[to] grow and develop freely."[89] In contrasting the free development of music against "an individual's musical career," Maher mirrors Cardew's critique of the imperial, bourgeois notion of genius with local implications, implicitly pitting the anti-professionalism of the undergraduate Sheep against the academic careerism of the graduate composers. Yet while radical politics were at the heart of the Sheep's self-definition, these nineteen- and twenty-year-olds criticized the Sprague Hall concerts not only because they were bourgeois but also because they apparently weren't very fun. Inviting privileged college students to listen to avant-garde music in their dorm common rooms in sleeping bags was not necessarily going to awaken the working class.

When Bang on a Can retold their relationship to the collective's activities, they didn't mention the Sheep's leftist antics. I once asked Lang about this curious omission. He described how he had flirted with campus politics back in his undergraduate days; when he arrived at Stanford, it was still a hotbed of student unrest, and administrative buildings had broken windows from anti-ROTC demonstrations in 1970. He participated in the gleefully impudent, student-run marching band—they put on a salute to Mao and a show about Patty Heart's kidnapping—but he soon became frustrated by such efforts. "I got really disaffected by the radical students at Stanford, who were childish," he recalled. His fascination with Russia had drawn him to Trotskyism, and he was more interested in politics as a form of rigorous intellectual analysis.[90] Cardew had visited Stanford when Lang was there, after the Scratch Orchestra had broken up and the composer had abandoned his experimental work in favor of composing folkish songs with Maoist texts. To Lang, they seemed simplistic. Cardew, he felt, "neutered himself to make the politics obvious, and that seemed like a loss."[91] The young composer wanted to engage politically in his music, while also allowing for ambiguity and avant-garde complexity. The result was works like *illumination rounds*, in which coolly precise instrumental dialogues symbolize the violent technology of tracer bullets. By the time he arrived at Yale, Lang had already tired of the kind of headily collegiate, partisan debates in which the undergraduate Sheep were immersed. He was less interested in subverting bourgeois music-making than in a more narrowly post-Cagean sonic experimentation.

And Sheep's Clothing dissolved soon after Lang began working with it. Gordon attended some of the performances, but did not join the Sheep, and Wolfe only heard the stories of their exploits. Bresnick had lost touch with the undergraduates once he moved from the music department to the School of Music, and the original cohort of Sheep graduated—the ambulatory performance in fall 1982 was one of their final outings. "This was the last sixties event," Bresnick said of Sheep's Clothing. "And never to be repeated, I think, in quite the way that it was."[92]

After Plonsey and Rycenga left Yale, they formed a group in the Bay Area called Composer's Cafeteria. As Plonsey described it, the collective modeled itself after the egalitarian approach of the Sheep, encouraging composers and performers to play each other's music and avoiding the exchange of money when possible. Thinking in comparison to Bang on a Can—which commissioned him in the late 1990s—Plonsey voiced a note of skepticism. "The world's gone further and further in this neoliberal direction in which everything that you can make money out of, you do make money out of. And it's virtually impossible to be a musician outside of that structure." In this context, he wondered, "Is Bang on a Can a resistance, or is Bang on a Can just another new-music ensemble that, by incorporating some guitar, bass, and drums, and some loud noises, is just another successful bunch of entrepreneurs?"[93]

If Lang, Gordon, and Wolfe's marathons were modeled after this last event of the sixties, their organization's broader ideological agenda was not. They had grown up in the idealistic 1960s, gone to college during the disillusioned 1970s, and started their careers in the individualistic 1980s. The Sheep adopted an all-pervasive ethos, in which collective music-making aligned with collective decision-making, in the hopes of modelling a utopian, egalitarian society. Though Bang on a Can is cooperatively curated by the three founders, the organization does not share the Sheep's radical setup. Nor did the three composers shirk what Cardew and the more militant Sheep might have criticized as the bourgeois profession of composition. Indeed, if they learned that professional mentality anywhere, it was at Yale.

You Weren't Just Staying in Academia

In December 1986, during a forthright, nearly three-and-a-half hour-long interview for Yale's Oral History of American Music project, David Lang told the story of what he considered to be his "best lesson at Yale."[94] Lang had presented his music at a colloquium, where a professor from another department had asked him a hostile question. Lang responded with "a put down which made all of the professors sort of alternately laugh and groan." In the composer's next meeting with Druckman, his teacher "spent a whole lesson telling me how I comport myself in a situation in which there are people who are more important than I am." This, for Lang, was the key pedagogical moment of his graduate studies. It was not a revelation about orchestration, counterpoint, or style; in fact, its significance was that "it had nothing to do with music. It had to do with career." And just as important as the message itself was its bearer: Druckman, an experienced professional who possessed what Lang described as "a very good idea of what the world is like."[95] Further, Lang continued, this kind of instruction was preferable to the typical composition lesson in which a teacher might look at a student's piece of music and say something like, "Oh yes, well, in a situation like this, a C-sharp in the bass is always the answer." Such musical minutiae were not what Lang looked for in his studies. "A lesson is to learn how people who you respect, how they live and how they act," he said. "In a way, jet setting around the globe is as much of a lesson in that case as how to listen to a piece of music because it's all part of the same thing."[96]

Lang had started telling this story to explain why he had chosen Yale over other schools: "I went there to have a career." This was not an unusual reason to attend a graduate composition program in the 1980s, as such programs were designed as a form of pre-professional training. But it was broadly understood that these graduate degrees provided a pathway to remain in the university system. When first arguing for the creation of a composition PhD at Princeton back in 1960, Milton Babbitt, with his colleagues Edward T. Cone and Arthur Mendel, stated in a memo that "It must be realized that university teaching provides the only means whereby the composer can exist within his profession; to deny his right to teach is to deny serious music its right to exist."[97] Or, as Feldman more sardonically put it a few years later, the academic system was geared toward "teaching teachers to teach teachers."[98]

But Lang had envisioned a different pathway when he chose to pursue further graduate studies. "If I'm going to go back to school and if I'm going to be a composer, my goal is not to be a composer teaching at a university," he said in 1986. "My goal is to be a composer whose music is played round the globe."[99] He picked Yale because his desire for a global career was reflected in the attitude of the graduate program. Babbitt had imagined the academy as a retreat from the marketplace; at Yale in the 1980s, Druckman conceived of the academy as a springboard to the marketplace.

Yale was not always that way. Prior to Druckman's arrival, it was the kind of school that produced composers like Gordon's NYU professor Brian Fennelly. In the mid-1970s, the department was largely shepherded by composers Yehudi Wyner and Robert Morris. Wyner was primarily active in the genre of chamber music, and Morris was a theorist and creator of electronic music; both fit the stereotypical profile of the academic composer. During this period, Martin Brody recalled, the general outlook on post-graduate life was that "the way to make a living was to get an academic job."[100] Composers had an "extremely ad hoc" relationship to the performance component of the School of Music, and Brody said that "It was a culture that was very much around the individual lessons." In this regard, Yale was not particular differently from Columbia, Princeton, or Iowa, with their reputations as outposts for the theory-heavy, uptown avant-garde. Or, in the skewering words of

Feldman, the vision of the composer as a figure "on his way to tenure" but "a drop-out in art."[101]

But the arrival of Druckman, a successful symphonic composer who publicly disavowed overly academicized thinking, signaled a major shift. And though Bresnick was not orchestrally oriented, he held a similar attitude. He had founded Sheep's Clothing to give the undergraduate composers at Yale performance opportunities, and had similar aims for the School of Music. As he later put it, "I've always pursued the notion that the performance of our composers should be the primary activity of our composition program."[102] In 1989, Druckman and Bresnick expanded the Sprague Hall series where *The Tree Watcher* premiered into the initiative New Music New Haven—in which School of Music performers played music by student, faculty, and guest composers—which continues to this day.

Multiple Druckman students have recounted how the composer would take phone calls from major orchestras, conductors, and publishers during their private lessons. At one point, his students apparently held an informal competition about how "good" their lessons were based on the reputation of who was calling their teacher to interrupt them.[103] Though these moments may have indicated a professor who prioritized professional obligations over pedagogy, Druckman's pupils saw such interruptions as a natural outgrowth of the composer's philosophy. Lang described Druckman's attitude as one in which "Your job as a composer is not just writing music in your studio, but it's actually being out in public and trying to change the world."[104] His classmate Michael Daugherty put it more bluntly: "Jacob Druckman liked to be written about in the *New York Times*. Jacob Druckman liked to be popular."[105]

"It was okay if you did something that made you famous," Daugherty continued. "I don't think other composers who were teaching at major institutions thought that way."[106] This attitude further attracted students interested in pursuing non-academic careers. When the precocious young composer Michael Torke attended Tanglewood's Festival of Contemporary Music in 1983, he noticed that many of the composers hanging out there had spent time in New Haven. "It seemed like in the early '80s, Yale was the place that a certain kind of composer went," he remembered.[107] Aaron Jay Kernis and Lang were at Tanglewood at the time, and apparently told Torke that "You've got to go to Yale. Jacob's the center of the universe."[108] So he did. Before arriving at Yale in fall 1984, Torke already had a reputation as a rising star. He had received the prestigious Tanglewood fellowship while still an undergraduate at the Eastman School of Music, along with awards from ASCAP and BMI. But he dropped out of the Yale program after only a year. Having received major commissions from the Brooklyn Philharmonic and New York Youth

Symphony—and having been courted by the publisher Boosey & Hawkes, with which he signed a contract in 1986—Torke found he had little time or patience for school and left to freelance in New York. In this case, it was less that Yale had created Torke's professional ambitions than that the school's orbit had, briefly, attracted this marketplace-oriented composer.

For those students without Torke's immediate success, Yale had its own professional rewards. By the early 1980s, Druckman had accumulated an enormous list of accolades. He had won the Pulitzer Prize, served as Composer-in-Residence at the Aspen Music Festival several times, and sat on the New York State Council on the Arts' Music Advisory Panel and the board of the American Music Center. He had been elected to the American Academy and Institute of Arts and Letters, and co-chaired National Endowment of the Arts panels. He served as president of the Koussevitzky Foundation, and had been a Resident in Music at the American Academy in Rome. With his deep institutional ties, the composition professor's recommendations carried significant weight.[109] Druckman's connections facilitated fellowships for Tanglewood's summer program, which were frequently awarded to Yale students, as well as the New York Philharmonic's Revson Fellowship, held by Lindroth and Lang, for which they assisted Druckman in organizing the Horizons festivals. Kernis, Lindroth, and Lang all won the prestigious Rome Prize, which provided a yearlong residency at the American Academy in Rome. Perhaps most famously, Druckman arranged to have an orchestral work by Kernis, his prize student, publicly rehearsed by the Philharmonic at the 1983 Horizons festival, which stirred a controversy that helped launch his career.

Some of these offerings represented typical benchmarks in a young composer's journey into a conventional academic vocation. Yet, when intertwined with Druckman's "being out in public" attitude and Bresnick's focus on performance, they facilitated a group of students in the early 1980s who emphatically described Yale as an outlier among universities. Daugherty recalled that "the attitude there was about reaching out to audiences," and, as Lindroth described, "It was an ideal bridge from music as something you study at school to, 'Okay, here's what we're going to do now in the world as artists.'"[110]

If that approach was appealing to Lang in a moment when he was set on his music conquering the globe, it was perhaps less so to Gordon, who, between his art-rock band and unruly postminimalist scores, was busy carving out a path as a downtown maverick in the mold of his hero, the composer-guitarist Glenn Branca. (In a 2018 tribute to the composer shortly after he passed away, Gordon wrote that "In my tiny corner of the universe, listening to Branca's music meant that your soul had been purified or purged and had knelt before God in humility and glory."[111]) Still, even if he was less interested in the orchestral career of a Kernis or Torke, Gordon remained cognizant of his colleagues' aspirations. In 1997, he described the atmosphere at Yale as a place of "focus," and said that it "had a lot to do with Druckman, which was you were there and you're a success or you're going to be a success."[112] He described his peers as ambitious, deliberately situated "on a career track," winning grants and prizes and currying favor with powerful senior composers. "I couldn't care less," Gordon said of these professional trappings. "It meant nothing to me."[113]

Hyper-aware of how he fit—or did not—among his cohort, Gordon was not particularly interested in the academy or marketplace. He never applied for a Tanglewood fellowship or Rome Prize. A 1989 article describing the accomplishments of recent Yale alumni noted that "If one were to look over the list of those who studied composition during the past ten years, one would find a remarkable record of achievement," including "Rome Prizes, Fulbright Fellowships, Guggenheim Fellowships."[114] Gordon's accomplishments were not quite so grand: his entry simply stated "Michael Gordon, MM '82—Founder Michael Gordon Philharmonic, State Council New York Commission on the Arts, Minnesota Composers Forum." In other words, in his seven years since graduation, Gordon had won no prizes and been awarded only two commissions. He was creating a different kind of path with the upstart Philharmonic, which toured Europe that year.

Julia Wolfe's entry in the article was more substantive: "Julia Wolfe, MM '86—two ASCAP prizes . . . commission with New York Youth Symphony, commission from the Rotterdam, Holland Arts Council."[115] Wolfe had readily absorbed the professional and practical components of her Yale lessons. After she took Bresnick's advice about reworking *On Seven-Star Shoes* into a woodwind quintet, the piece was quickly taken up by chamber groups, prompting further career validation from Druckman. Wolfe recalled that, following a New York City performance of the piece by the Quintet of the Americas, Druckman excitedly approached her about the fact that it was reviewed in a major newspaper.[116] "In contrast to the elite aims of the who-cares-if-you-listen perspective of Babbitt's famous manifesto," Wolfe later wrote, "Druckman was openly ambitious and prepped his favorite students in the nuances of career building."[117]

And then there was Lang, whose globe-trotting aspirations went far beyond writing woodwind quintets: "David Lang, MMA '83—Guggenheim Fellow, NEA, Revson Fellow, New York Philharmonic Composers Prize, composer-in-residence American Symphony Orchestra, works published by G. Schirmer and Margin Music."[118] As the only of the three composers to have already obtained a master's degree before Yale, he had been enrolled in Yale's Master's of Musical Arts, designed as a pipeline to the doctoral DMA. Yale's DMA program explicitly encouraged composers to pursue opportunities outside the academy. Upon completing coursework, exams, and a dissertation, doctoral candidates were meant to spend several years building a professional portfolio and then return to campus for a final examination and recital. In his 1986 interview, Lang described how this curriculum shaped his current professional agenda. Alternately castigating and praising Yale—he characterized it as a "very well connected professional school" that "has very high standards for its students" but also stated that some of "the classes are horrible" and "your teachers wouldn't really be around because of all of your teachers lived in New York and you were stuck in New Haven"—the composer went on to lay out, in precise detail, why the School of Music was nevertheless the right place for him:

> It was something that you did in order to have a career. It has an incredible connection to New York and an incredible reputation and they protect it which is the nature of the reason why I am, at the moment, why my doctorate is A.B.D., because the program that I was in was called the Master of Musical Arts which is the gateway to their doctorate, where you take all your courses and you write your dissertation and you do everything that you have to do in two years and then they kick you out into the world and then, in a few years, they see if you're successful and if you're still in music and if you are successful, then they invite you back to take a final exam. And that's why I'm A.B.D. I'm waiting to get famous. And on the one hand, I understand it perfectly, because they want to protect themselves. A place like Iowa had brilliant students finish their doctorates and then go out and become dental assistants or carpenters or something. There were no jobs. There was nothing for them to do. And their life was not sufficiently organized around being a musician so that they didn't keep it up.[119]

For Lang, Yale was nothing like Iowa, in which a traditionally academic curriculum purportedly prepared composers for life not as musicians but as dental hygienists. He and his colleagues had developed distinct personalities—Lang as outspoken whiz kid, Gordon as aloof art-rock rebel, Wolfe as open-minded liberal arts grad—but they had all found their way to Yale, and to each other. They had all sought further training that they hoped would be more sophisticated and rigorous than their previous studies, and would help them pursue some kind of non-academic career. Guided by the structure and pedagogy of his program, and Druckman's lessons in comportment, Lang was not biding his time as A.B.D. teaching counterpoint or writing articles for *Perspectives of New Music*. He was living in New York City, fresh off a fellowship working with the New York Philharmonic, and meeting up with Gordon and Wolfe at Lower East Side diners, brainstorming the first Bang on a Can marathon.

2
Horizons

A September 1985 snapshot captures David Lang in slacks, a crisp button-down shirt, and a tie, holding his blazer as he strides confidently next to his teacher Jacob Druckman outside Lincoln Center's Avery Fisher Hall (Figure 2.1). Though the outfit was standard issue for a professional composer in the 1980s, within a few years Lang was better known for his funkily iconoclastic attire, more in keeping with the Bang on a Can ethos—offbeat sweaters, t-shirts, even backwards baseball caps. Indeed, as if to confirm its highly unusual nature, in 2017 Lang tweeted about the 1985 photo: "Once, when I was 27, I wore a tie."[1]

But the young composer in the photograph looks comfortable in business casual, and other pictures from the period confirm that it was not an atypical outfit for the late-twenties Lang. At one point, Lang found his work at the center of the American classical music establishment—as a Revson Fellow and assistant to Druckman in organizing the New York Philharmonic's 1986 Horizons festival for contemporary music—quite rewarding. "I have benefitted greatly from seeing how such a complex organization is run," he wrote that year about the Philharmonic assistantship, "especially in light of the fact that, as a composer, I will be dealing with such organizations for the rest of my life."[2]

Within two years of that photograph being taken, Lang co-founded a very different kind of organization. Bang on a Can's renegade spirit might seem antithetical to the establishment culture of the symphony orchestra, and the three founding composers rarely mention the Horizons festivals when they discuss their past. Julia Wolfe's 2012 dissertation, a two-hundred page history of Bang on a Can, devotes only a single sentence to Horizons, and does not mention Lang's participation.[3] But Lang's work with Horizons is crucial for understanding the festival that he and his colleagues launched in 1987. When asked by the New York State Council on the Arts to describe their history in a 1990 grant application, Bang on a Can wrote: "As the Assistant Composer-in-Residence for the New York Philharmonic in 1985/86, David Lang had the opportunity to work with Jacob Druckman on the Philharmonic's contemporary music festival, Horizons '86. At that point, it became clear that what New York

48　Industry

Figure 2.1 David Lang and Jacob Druckman, September 1985. New York Philharmonic Leon Levy Digital Archives, ID 800-014-10-01-F26.

needed was a regularly occurring showcase for the works of contemporary American composers, and focusing on music of young composers."[4]

As it turns out, the orchestral world of the 1980s served as a significant, if unexpected, precedent for Bang on a Can: the Horizons festivals represented one of the most high-profile exemplars of an emergent rapport between contemporary music and the marketplace in this period, one that Lang, Wolfe, and Michael Gordon witnessed firsthand. The Philharmonic aimed its first Horizons festival, held in June 1983, toward a broad public. With its heavily advertised and provocatively interrogative theme, "A New Romanticism?" the festival incited significant reaction in the press, indicated to many the decline of the academic avant-garde, and became a surprising box office coup for contemporary music. Horizons '83 served as the flagship project for the Orchestra Residencies Program, an initiative sponsored by Meet the Composer. Funded by an innovative combination of public, foundation, and corporate support, in 1982 Meet the Composer placed six composers in residencies with US orchestras. The program soon expanded to other cities and yielded significant results. By 1989, the residencies were responsible for the performances of 700 contemporary works and 200 new commissions.[5] And Meet the Composer's grants created a nationwide system of funding with the explicit goal of placing contemporary music in dialogue with a non-specialist audience—a crucial structural and ideological component of new music's marketplace turn, and an approach that shaped Bang on a Can. Part of a cohort of young composers who saw the Orchestra Residencies Program as providing new symphonic opportunities, Lang attended nearly every performance in the 1983 and '84 Horizons, and helped organize the 1986 festival; Gordon and Wolfe, too, participated in some of the proceedings. Lang's work with the Philharmonic provided him with administrative experience and connections that benefitted his new organization, but the youthful composer's ambivalence about working in the highly institutionalized world of the American orchestra also shaped the maverick mindset of Bang on a Can.

The Marketplace Puts Composers Together with People

In his year with the Philharmonic, Lang lived in midtown Manhattan, and would stroll through Central Park every day and up to Lincoln Center for work. After he finished in the evening, he would visit the offices of Meet the Composer on West 57th Street, and hang out with the organization's founder John Duffy and his second-in-command Frances Richard. He learned quite a bit from the pair who had been, for the past decade, engaged in a massive endeavor to re-envision the role of the composer in American society. Meet the Composer had originated in the short-lived program Composer in Performance, sponsored by the New York State Council on the Arts and supervised by the Fluxus composer Benjamin Patterson. Launched in 1969, Composer in Performance subsidized classical and jazz composers to perform, conduct, and attend concerts of their music. As Patterson described it in 1970, the initiative sought to create "a new public image" for living composers—"The old image of an ivory-towered dabbler, attending a rare performance of one of his works must be replaced by one of [an] involved person absolutely essential to, and at the core of the development of a healthy musical culture." It would foster "meaningful composer-audience contacts—by presenting the composer in an active and recreative relationship with his works, performing or directing."[6] From its origins, Composer in Performance was intended to counteract the pervasive image of the American composer as an academic removed from concert life.

But by 1973, Composer in Performance had faltered due to mismanagement, and a number of prominent composers who had participated in the initiative subsequently petitioned the state council to relaunch it.[7] The prolific composer John Duffy, who had written scores for on- and off-Broadway plays and worked as a music director for several major theatrical organizations including the American Shakespeare Festival, was selected to supervise the new program, in part because of his experience outside the academy.[8] Renamed Meet the Composer, it was funded with a grant of $66,000 from the state and housed at the American Music Center, with an initial focus on counties throughout New York State. In 1978, Duffy and associate director Frances Richard incorporated Meet the Composer as an independent organization with its own board of directors and advisory council, and by the early 1980s it had established enough state, federal, and private sponsorship to grow nationally and create regional offices across the United States.

Meet the Composer's principal effort was its Composers Performance Fund, which provided grants to nonprofits to invite composers to attend concerts of their music and talk to audiences. As 1984 application guidelines stated, "The important ingredient is exchange between the composer and audience."[9] Such interactions would belie the idea that the music of living composers was inaccessible or obscure. "If you see the person who's actually written the music that you're going to hear, you're much more accepting of it, no matter what it is," the composer Charles Wuorinen recalled. "It becomes a social situation rather than some strange, esoteric experience."[10]

"Put into one sentence: Meet the Composer is helping create a marketplace for today's composers," Duffy wrote in a 1981 essay.[11] Praising an earlier history of composers "as craftsman/artists who functioned in society" such as Bach, Beethoven, and Puccini, he stated that Meet the Composer would seek to return composers to their former status, "to help create an environment for our composers to work and flourish in, to help them contribute to our society." The method to do so would be the marketplace, and programs such as the Composers Performance Fund. Only if composers were present at concerts and communicating with audiences would they build a market for their work. "In crass business terms, you display the wares," Duffy wrote.

The public-facing nature of Meet the Composer, in other words, would help justify composition as a paid profession. "The marketplace puts composers together with people," he continued. "By providing composers with wages it makes them professionals."

This market, Duffy described, stood in contrast to the established patron for composition in the United States, the university. "Composers themselves have been culpable in perpetuating their obscurity and near demise," he wrote. "Many have opted for teaching posts in academe. This cloistered existence, though financially secure, cut them off from the general public." Unlike the great composers of the past, these academics composed for each other and "small cadres of earnest worshippers ... Their work fed on itself rather than on audience response. Their music turned inward—beyond the pale."[12]

Grant-writing, a related form of "research work," had contributed to this isolation, allowing composers to fund their music without it necessarily having public performances. Though Duffy does not name Milton Babbitt or "Who Cares If You Listen?" it is clear that he is singling out the ideology of uptown as a culprit in the composer's retreat from the public. Meet the Composer's grants were instead tied to projects that had clear communal components. Duffy liked to cite the example of Corning Glass Works, which had collaborated with Meet the Composer to commission a piece for the opening of a new wing of the corporation's museum. And ultimately, he wrote, Meet the Composer would be a "self-destruct organization. "As we create a marketplace," he added, "there will no longer be a need for Meet the Composer. Composers will be in the streets—away from academe and the present day, lace curtain welfare system of grants. Like doctors, lawyers, corporate managers, and other professionals, composers will be working their field and contributing on a one to one basis to their fellow human beings."

It was a utopian vision, albeit one based in capitalist reality. Commissions were "jobs for composers," "jobs that will stimulate and develop an ongoing marketplace." Even though the Composers Performance Fund subsidized composers' attendance at concerts—not commissions themselves—Meet the Composer used the promise of its funding to push organizations to provide composers with compensation. "Most important of all was the whole idea that the composer has to be paid," Richard recalled. "We told them, 'If there's no fee, there's no commission.'"[13] Grants leveraged outside support; as a newsletter reported in 1979, in the previous fiscal year $123,000 Meet the Composer dollars had generated $773,000 sponsor dollars in New York State alone.[14] Composer Libby Larsen recalled that Duffy strongly instilled in her the idea that "a composer is a professional" and that a commission "is to be compensated."[15] In some sense, Duffy and Richard's calls for professionalism represented a push for worker's rights, advancing the idea that the American composer was a laborer deserving of a middle-class salary. Their means to do so, though, was an all-hands-on-deck approach that involved working within the system, lobbying the government for funding, partnering with corporations, leveraging matching funds from foundations, and developing splashy projects that would attract attention and support.

The organization created handbooks that put this philosophy into practice. In 1984, Meet the Composer issued *Commissioning Music*, a pamphlet for composers and patrons that included guidelines for potential commissioning fees. In 1989, it published *Composers in the Marketplace*, which provided an overview of copyright, performance, publishing, recordings, royalties, and promotion.[16] Their efforts shaped the work of other institutions; beginning in 1987, for example, the New York State Council on the Arts' program booklet for grant applications based its commission fee guidelines off research conducted by Meet the Composer.[17]

The final pages of *Composers in the Marketplace* offer a "case study" concerning a fictional composer named Eric, who resided in upstate New York but "decided he was tired of living in obscurity," of not having his music performed and not getting paid for it either.[18] With Philip Glass, Steve Reich, and Henry Threadgill as his models, Eric heads to New York City to write music for modern dance companies, starts an ensemble to play his work, and begins getting gigs downtown. His main collaborator, a choreographer, takes Eric's *Dance Piece #1* on a national tour, and it becomes the subject of a public television documentary. Eric finds himself schmoozing in Hollywood and scoring a feature film, nets a commission for a prestigious chamber music series and then a commercial publisher, and, finally, attracts the attention of "the resident composer of a major symphony orchestra" and finds orchestral fame. "He now had the money, the time, and the contracts to do what he loved above anything else," the case study concludes, "to compose music and to share it with people wherever they may be."[19] The case study then details the miscellaneous rights related to these variegated composition activities. From downtown collaborations to film scores to symphonies, Eric's imaginary career was clearly modeled after that of Philip Glass. Notably absent from the case study is any mention of the academy, or any underwriting from granting agencies or foundations. Eric's journey seems to provide a clear and stable career path toward increasingly larger audiences and financial support, thus allowing his creativity to flourish. The marketplace offered bountiful opportunity, if composers were only willing to put themselves out there.

From its origins, stylistic catholicity was at the forefront of Meet the Composer's concerns. "We want to show that composers as a community are a rich resource, and to get across to the composers that they, as a community, stand firmer and stronger if they stand together," Duffy said in a 1985 interview. "Composers need to mend the ideological and aesthetic differences that divide them. And then it will no longer be a mad scramble for crumbs and occasional prizes."[20] The profession would strengthen, Duffy believed, if composers stood in solidarity, and the organization thus advocated for transcending the bitter feuds between minimalists, serialists, neo-Romantics, and other camps that were pervasive in the 1970s and 1980s. Circa 1984, Meet the Composer's advisory board of forty-two composers included a broad representation of figures from different areas of the compositional world, including academics Milton Babbitt and Roger Reynolds, experimentalists Ornette Coleman and Muhal Richard Abrams, minimalists Philip Glass and La Monte Young, and orchestral composers Joan Tower and Libby Larsen.[21] In 1998, Tower fondly recalled these idealistic days: "We would all sit together in the same room: La Monte Young, Ned Rorem, Charles Wuorinen, Leroy Jenkins, Bernard Rands, all because John Duffy had this incredible vision and breadth."[22]

And Tower was invited into an institutional world from which women were frequently excluded.[23] In its 1984 application, Meet the Composer stated that it "gives priority to applicants who program the works of women and minority composers."[24] Its advisory board that year included nine Black composers and six female composers. Although that number might seem low, it was substantive in comparison to other boards and panels that adjudicated support for contemporary music.[25] And the presence of women and people of color made Meet the Composer feel distinctive—as Tania León fondly recollected, "Muhal [Richard Abrams] was sitting on that board, Leroy Jenkins was sitting on that board, I was sitting on that board."[26] African American composer T.J. Anderson wrote to Duffy in 1986 that "a cursory review of composers who are associated with Meet the Composer clearly demonstrates the program's attention to diversity of styles, race, religion, and sex."[27]

Even if panel meetings for awarding grants could become contentious—there was one incident in which a fistfight almost broke out over whether to award a grant to Glass—they were seen as more hospitable to a range of musical idioms than those of other organizations at the time.[28] León described Meet the Composer as "an inspiration, a mentor, a shoulder, and a faithful teacher supporting those unspoken dreams in my creative endeavors," and Ned Rorem wrote that "Meet the Composer has made the United States a finer and subtler land." Even Babbitt was impressed, heralding its "profound effects on the American musical climate . . . unprecedented and unparalleled in their effect and scope."[29] Such praise was inspired, in part, by Meet the Composer's dramatic expansion. By 1984, a decade after its founding, Duffy had developed the total annual budget from its initial $66,000 grant to over $1 million.[30]

What, You Don't Have a Resident Composer?

Much of that increase in funding can be attributed to Meet the Composer's most publicized and wide-reaching endeavor: the Orchestra Residencies Program. Within a two-week period in February 1981, Duffy received separate phone calls from Leonard Fleischer, a senior advisor for Exxon's arts philanthropy program, and Howard Klein, director of arts for the Rockefeller Foundation. By coincidence, both philanthropic administrators had been seeking potential avenues to strengthen the relationship between composers and the American orchestra. Klein had overseen a previous composer-in-residence initiative sponsored by the Rockefeller Foundation, but it was deemed a failure because of lack of interest among participant orchestras. A new partnership with Meet the Composer offered the opportunity to try again.[31]

Duffy was aware of how the relationship between orchestras and American composers had frayed by the 1980s. "Gone are the days of the Boston Symphony under Koussevitsky, the New York Philharmonic under Mitropoulos, the Philadelphia under Stokowski, the Chicago under Reiner, when the music of living composers was regularly commissioned and performed," he said in 1981. "Since the 1960s, the doors of the nation's orchestras have been virtually locked."[32] It had taken its toll. "Most younger composers felt that the orchestra was hopelessly out of reach, so instead they wrote electronic or chamber work," Duffy later told the *New York Times*. "That was not a healthy musical situation."[33] After brainstorming with Fleischer and Klein, Duffy sought the advice of Ezra Laderman, director of the National Endowment for the Arts's music division, who promised federal funding for the project.

Duffy, Fleischer, and Klein consulted with composer John Adams—who had recently achieved national acclaim as New Music Adviser to the San Francisco Symphony—and sent a questionnaire to several hundred composers requesting their input on how to structure potential residencies. A memo from Duffy to Fleischer, Klein, and Laderman in August 1981 argued that past residencies had failed because composers "functioned on the fringe."[34] They would instead seek to craft collaborative relationships between composers, music directors, and administrators. In the course of its research, Meet the Composer was surprised to learn that orchestra managers and conductors felt that they, too, would benefit from a resident composer program, which might "tap new audiences for orchestral concerts; increase subscription sales; revitalize orchestras."[35]

As plans developed, the major financial stake proposed by Exxon and the Rockefeller Foundation helped open doors with orchestra administrators otherwise uninterested in new music. Although public-private partnerships were at the core of American arts policy since the founding of the NEA, such a collaboration between corporations, foundations, and the federal government was also indicative of major shifts in this period. After abandoning an attempt to cut the budget of the NEA by 50 percent, President Reagan focused his arts policy primarily on motivating involvement from the private sector and rewarding corporate philanthropy. Exxon itself was awarded a National Medal of Arts by Reagan in 1986, a prize created in part to honor private arts patrons.[36] Duffy himself acknowledged the growing importance of private sector philanthropy, describing corporations in a 1985 interview as "our 20th century answer to Esterházy and the Medicis"; he later called the Exxon–Rockefeller–NEA collaboration a "model public-private partnership" and "a stirring case of American enterprise."[37]

In May 1982, Meet the Composer assembled a group of composers, music directors, and orchestra managers at the New York Philharmonic for a press luncheon to announce its plan. Beginning that September, six American orchestras would launch two-year composer-in-residence initiatives: John Adams with the San Francisco Symphony, Jacob Druckman with the New York Philharmonic, John Harbison with the Pittsburgh Symphony, Robert Xavier Rodríguez with the Dallas Symphony, William Kraft with the Los Angeles Philharmonic, and Joseph Schwantner with the St. Louis Symphony. (The Minnesota Orchestra, the seventh for the initial wave, announced its residency with composers Libby Larsen and Stephen Paulus in early 1983.) Each composer would write a major work for the orchestra; organize a new-music series as part of the subscription season; assist music directors in reviewing scores and tapes, advising on programming, and preparing rehearsals; serve as a liaison to the composer community; and act as advocate for new music to the orchestra and its audience. They were expected to devote themselves to the orchestra as a full-time occupation, and received a $40,000 annual salary. (This was a substantial income, equivalent to approximately $107,000 in 2020.) Orchestras agreed to premiere and record the commissioned piece, assist the resident composer in executing the contemporary series, provide rehearsal time for new works, and promote the efforts of the project.

The budget for the endeavor was considerable. In its first five years, Meet the Composer's total expenses for the residencies amounted to more than $2 million (the equivalent of around $5 million today). The Rockefeller Foundation

56 Industry

and Exxon each contributed $875,000; the NEA contributed $246,000; various other foundations and corporations contributed $91,000; and the orchestras themselves also contributed.[38] By 1987, Exxon had also spent an estimated $250,000 on a national promotional campaign. Across the country, magazines and newspapers printed full-page ads that showed a composer assiduously at work at the piano with the tagline "Sometimes, it's easier to compose a symphony than to get it performed" (Figure 2.2).

For the ultimate aim of the Orchestra Residencies Program, such advertising was essential. As Duffy wrote Fleischer, Klein, and Laderman in August

Figure 2.2 Meet the Composer advertisement. Printed in *Foreign Affairs* 61, no. 5 (Summer 1983).

1981, "All agree that project must be widely promoted." Citing the significant national press garnered by Adams in San Francisco, he added that "The hoped for result of the project and documentation of residencies is to encourage other orchestras to initiate residency programs."[39] If an orchestra chose to renew its residency past the initial two-year term, Meet the Composer's payment toward the composer's salary would be halved. Duffy hoped to encourage orchestras to gradually take on the financial burden of the project, with the eventual goal of permanently endowing composers as members of their staff.

In 1985, after the first round of seven orchestras, the initiative expanded to include the Atlanta Symphony with Alvin Singleton, Houston Symphony with Tobias Picker, Indianapolis Symphony with Christopher Rouse, and Seattle Symphony with Stephen Albert. "As you renew the original orchestras, music directors and management get to the point where they can't do without a resident composer," Duffy told *EAR Magazine* in 1986. "In fact, the word is now, 'What, you don't have a resident composer?'"[40] When the program concluded in 1991, 33 residencies with 29 different composers had been mounted at 21 orchestras. Duffy compared composers to "a Johnny or Bessie Appleseed": "People see on the program Leonard Slatkin, Music Director; Joan Tower, Composer in Residence; it immediately strikes them that the composer is part of the family."[41]

Not all families were happy. In Pittsburgh, John Harbison found himself in the middle of a conflict between music director André Previn and orchestra management, spoke out publicly, and was fired; in Indianapolis, members of the symphony put in earplugs to protest the loud dynamics of resident composer Christopher Rouse's music (one player in the ensemble even filed a complaint with the Occupational Safety and Health Administration), and he resigned. Charles Wuorinen arrived for a residency with the Louisville Orchestra in 1984 while the orchestra was on strike. The collaboration was called off, and he decamped to San Francisco to take over for Adams after his residency ended in 1985. But the project's measurable successes outweighed such momentary failure. Two works premiered during residencies, Bernard Rands's *Canti del Sole* and Shulamit Ran's Symphony, won Pulitzer Prizes. John Corigliano's Symphony No. 1, his Chicago Symphony residency commission, and Adams's *Harmonielehre* became national sensations among audiences, and their recordings climbed to high positions on the *Billboard* charts.[42] Meet the Composer's foundational agenda of providing grants in order to encourage matching funds had worked. Over the total ten years of the program, Meet the Composer ultimately provided $5.5 million, and the estimated contribution from participating orchestras was as high as $21 million.[43]

American composers saw the residencies as enacting a cultural transformation. Tower wrote that "I know of no other program that has had as much impact and as significant a long range consequence as the orchestral/composer/residency program."[44] Such changes recalibrated the careers of composers who had already achieved orchestral renown, such as John Adams. Adams's collaboration with the San Francisco Symphony as New Music Advisor began in 1979 while the composer was teaching at the San Francisco Conservatory, and his relationship with the orchestra developed as he was turning away from post-Cagean work in the Bay Area experimental scene and toward an explicitly Romantic musical language, as exemplified in the heralded 1981 premiere of the choral-orchestral *Harmonium*. But it was the subsequent Meet the Composer residency, from 1982 to 1985, that provided Adams with the institutional support for a career in the marketplace. Though administrative duties were considerable—when Druckman was at the Philharmonic, for example, he fell behind on a commission for the Metropolitan Opera that the company ultimately cancelled—residencies represented a rare opportunity for composers to receive a full-time paycheck to work outside the academy.

In a 1995 essay, Adams described his experience as "a bridge between a life as a part-time composer and a life as a full-time, totally engaged composer."[45] His income had previously come from teaching, and composing was "too often shunted off to the side." He continued, "Working nights, weekends, and summers, I not only had trouble meeting deadlines but also had a malingering suspicion that composing was just a hobby, an avocation, something you did in your off hours, like tying flies or coaching Little League. People would ask me what I did for a living and I'd twitch in discomfort over the way my life and work had become so necessarily compromised."[46] The annual salary that Adams received from Meet the Composer—he described it as a "three-year economic safety net," noting that it provided nearly twice the remuneration as his teaching position at the Conservatory—offered enough financial security to allow him to leave academia and pursue composition full time. Not every resident composer found a career outside the academy. Druckman continued teaching at Yale, for example, and Joseph Schwantner, who moved his family to St. Louis for the duration of his three-year residency, returned to Rochester to teach at the Eastman School of Music when it concluded. But the financial support, public exposure, and administrative experience provided by the Orchestra Residencies Program helped set Adams on the path toward becoming one of the most widely performed living composers at American orchestras.[47]

Musical Hothouse

It was no coincidence that the 1982 announcement of the initial round of orchestra residencies took place at the New York Philharmonic's headquarters. Within a year of that first press conference, eight composers-in-residence returned to Lincoln Center for a forum open to the public to discuss the Orchestra Residencies Program (Figure 2.3).

It was June 1983, and Exxon had paid for the composers to fly to New York to witness the beginning of a flagship Meet the Composer-sponsored project. The Philharmonic and its composer-in-residence Jacob Druckman had consolidated their season-long new-music series into a two-week mega-festival titled "Horizons '83: Since 1968, A New Romanticism?" The event coincided with the annual meeting of the Music Critics Association, which brought more than a hundred writers to town.[48] If Horizons won over the critical establishment and New York's audiences, it would cement the importance of the Orchestra Residencies Program nationwide.

Figure 2.3 Press conference for Orchestra Residencies Program, Lincoln Center, 1983. From left, Stephen Paulus, Libby Larsen, Robert Xavier Rodríguez, William Kraft, Jacob Druckman, John Duffy, John Adams, Joseph Schwantner, John Harbison. Photograph by Bial Bert, New York Philharmonic Leon Levy Digital Archives, ID 800-116-09-002.

Horizons succeeded far beyond initial expectations. Advance ticket sales had been relatively slow, and the Philharmonic had only opened one of the box office windows at Avery Fisher Hall. But a huge audience appeared, which stretched the ticket line outside into Lincoln Center's plaza. "There were 1,500 people lined-up around the square and we were frantically telephoning to get somebody to open up other windows," Druckman later recollected.[49] Such box office frenzy was the result of the deliberate question mark raised in the festival's subheading—"A New Romanticism?"—and the furor it provoked within the press.

Druckman theorized his curatorial framework for New Romanticism in an essay published in the glossy program book printed for the first Horizons festival. Despite what he described as an "ever increasing diversity and a constant acceleration of technical and aesthetic change" in contemporary composition, Druckman identified a "steady underlying rhythm" present in music history. "This great and steady shift seems to happen repeatedly between two distinctly different artistic climates," he wrote. "On the one hand there is the Apollonian, the Classical—logical, rational, chaste and explainable; and on the other hand, the Dionysian, the Romantic—sensual, mysterious, ecstatic, transcending the explainable."[50] For Druckman, the twentieth century had been dominated by an Apollonian framework that encompassed Stravinsky's neo-classicism, Schoenberg's twelve-tone method, and the "post-Webern generation" of Babbitt, Pierre Boulez, and Elliott Carter. But in the mid-1960s, he saw a New Romanticism emerging that instead embraced Dionysian "sensuality, mystery, nostalgia, ecstasy, transcendency." (One might go as far as calling it postmodernism.) New Romanticism was less of a cohesive aesthetic than a means of describing a wide swath of disparate musics that belonged to what Druckman called a "mysterious and fragrant garden of dreams."[51] Druckman also situated New Romanticism within his own personal trajectory—his turn away from overly academicized methods of composing. The composer's imagining of New Romanticism aligned with Duffy's agenda for Meet the Composer. It would offer not only an aesthetic rebuttal to the Apollonian music of the "post-Webern generation," but also an explicit reorientation toward the public.

Even if it resonated with the anti-academic and anti-serial posturing of composers like David Del Tredici and George Rochberg—who were widely known for having renounced modernism in the 1970s in favor of nineteenth-century tonality and expressive gestures—New Romanticism was not necessarily neo-Romanticism. Although the festival included the music of Del Tredici and Rochberg, Druckman's essay did not mention those two composers. Instead, he identified the emergence of what he called "the new aesthetic" in works by Krzysztof Penderecki, Witold Lutosławski, and György Ligeti; he saw Luciano Berio's collage-like, postmodern 1968 *Sinfonia* as a key example of New Romanticism.[52] With the *Sinfonia* as a centerpiece, the festival's six orchestral concerts ultimately featured twenty-five composers and a broad range of voices, including music by Donald Martino, Joseph Schwantner, Morton Subotnick, Tōru Takemitsu, and Frederic Rzewski.

"When we used the expression 'A New Romanticism' in the announcement, suddenly the press got very interested; some of them hating the idea and some liking it, and they began to fight with each other," Druckman later remembered. "We were getting incredible publicity that nobody could have bought, and nobody had any idea that it was going to happen."[53] He should not have been that surprised. The festival's organizing committee, led by Philharmonic managing director Albert K. Webster, had embraced Druckman's conception of New Romanticism to court such press attention, in the hopes it would generate buzz and ticket sales. Minutes for a November 1982 meeting note that "The direction and tactic of the press release and publicity for the Contemporary Festival was discussed. It was agreed that the sub-heading 'A New Romanticism?' would engage controversy and that this should be handled at its inception at the press conference in January."[54] In a meeting two months later, "Other marketing angles were discussed, i.e. Using 'romanticism' . . . The committee agreed that Jacob Druckman should speak out forcefully on the Romanticism theme; while it would provoke considerable controversy, it would also encourage interest in and press coverage for the Festival."[55]

Audience engagement was a point of recurring attention. An early planning document for Horizons '83 described it as a "musical hothouse" that "will attract the key forces in contemporary music—students, diligent contemporary music enthusiasts, new audience members, music historians and theoreticians."[56] And it noted further that "Appropriate avenues of publicity and announcements to the academic and music community will be fully utilized to attract the largest and widest possible audience." As per another committee meeting, the festival's goals included "Develop new audience" and "Serve as a catalyst for contemporary music reaching the people."[57]

A campaign budget approved in February 1983 proposed a total of $82,102 to be spent on 200,000 pieces of direct mail; a run of advertisements in the *New York Times*, *Village Voice*, and other periodicals; packages of radio ads for broadcast on four stations; and further promotions.[58] Promotional schemes were regularly discussed in committee meetings, although some were deemed too outlandish. One committee member suggested an advertising gimmick in which audience members could collect a $1 rebate from the orchestra for attending a performance, tied to the slogan "'You couldn't pay me to attend contemporary music'—'Oh, yes, we will!'" (The minutes coolly noted, in response, that "This might not be the best approach artistically."[59]) Widely distributed flyers proclaimed the festival as "Three weeks that could just change your mind about the meaning of new music."[60] Consistent through the planning phases was the concern that ticket prices be kept low in order to attract a broad public. Single tickets were ultimately priced at $8; a pass for all six concerts cost only $30; students and seniors received a 50 percent discount; and four symposia as well as six preconcert "What's the Score? Meet the Composer" panels were free.[61]

Significant press attention helped guarantee that the festival's opening night, on Thursday, June 2—a concert of works by Marc-Antonio Consoli, Peter Maxwell Davies, Takemitsu, and Del Tredici—was a splash. "We held the first notes for about twenty minutes and we still didn't get all the people in," Druckman later recalled.[62] Ultimately, an average of 1,800 tickets were sold for each of the six concerts in the 1983 festival, filling Avery Fisher Hall at an average of over 70 percent capacity.[63] Journalists consistently observed that such an audience for new music was extraordinary; the *Los Angeles Daily News*, for example, noted that "The turnouts at the three concerts I attended were remarkable."[64]

Many of the hundred-plus music critics already in town wrote about Horizons. Duffy alone had sent personal invitations to more than seventy writers to attend the resident composers meeting on the second day of the festival. Critics inevitably argued about the New Romanticism theme, speculating on its historical significance, discussing whether the works chosen by Druckman fit neatly within the curatorial framework, and often dismissing the larger concept entirely. As Samuel Lipman wrote in the *New Criterion*, "What is clear is that by using the word 'Romanticism' Druckman provided a legion of grateful music critics with a hook on which to hang yards of sophisticated discussion."[65]

In a reflection whose headline wondered "Is 'New Romanticism' Music of the Future?" *New York Times* critic John Rockwell described Horizons as a "healthy success," identifying Druckman's achievement in having "forced people into a consideration of just where music today may be heading."[66] Ten days later, *Times* critic Edward Rothstein described the festival as "the first major institutional acknowledgment that the 'advanced' compositional world had somehow changed its direction."[67] Rothstein's column used New Romanticism to paint in broad brushstrokes about the direction of postwar music, seeing a new "freedom to indulge in sentiment" having emerged among recent composers that combatted the "severe, serial hand" of the "European Darmstadt school." Riffing on Boulez's famous 1952 essay on Arnold Schoenberg, Rothstein wrote that "One is almost tempted to type out in bold letters 'THE AVANT-GARDE IS DEAD'—because the traditional progressive notion of music that the 20th century avant-garde represented is no longer tenable."[68]

Such reflections were typical of responses to New Romanticism, which was widely seen as a referendum on, and refutation of, serialism and the academic avant-garde. If it was not explicit in the reviews of the 1983 festival, this perspective was made emphatically clear in an essay by Milton Babbitt written for the 1984 festival's program booklet, in which the composer lambasted Druckman's conception of New Romanticism and its critical reception as a form of anti-intellectual populism. "It is written by the stars of journalism and in the words of the prophets of cultural history that music is entering a new era or reentering an old one (by the back door or trap door?)," Babbitt wrote, "and this birth or rebirth has been celebrated by appropriately Dionysian dancing on the tombs of those musics liquidated and interred for the mortal sins and aesthetic transgressions of intellect, academicism, and—even—mathematization."[69] Composers who had never abandoned tonality to begin with were also perturbed. "Everybody makes a fuss over somebody who quits smoking," Ned Rorem told the *Times*, "but never over the person who is smart enough never to have started."[70]

The heated reception accorded to two particular works at Horizons '83 served as representative of such seismic shifts. On separate nights of the festival, a combination of fervent applause and a chorus of boos greeted David Del Tredici's glitteringly Straussian cantata *All in the Golden Afternoon* and John Adams's emphatically tonal and repetitive *Grand Pianola Music*. In a festival crowded with compositional voices, the mini-scandals afforded to those representatives of provocative musical styles—neo-Romanticism in the case of Del Tredici, minimalism in the case of Adams—served to bring special attention to their work. One critic observed that "these reactions seem refreshingly healthy—and undoubtedly Del Tredici and Adams were well aware of the publicity value of a succès de scandale." [71] For those hoping that the festival would shake up the orchestral world, the divided response confirmed the necessity of Horizons. "Better a worked-up audience, fiercely booing and cheering the resolute tunefulness of a Del Tredici or an Adams than a snoozing crowd of regular subscribers at yet another orchestral run-through of the three B's," Alan Rich wrote in *Newsweek*.[72] Even Samuel Lipman, who called the Del Tredici work the "apotheosis of camp" and the Adams the "biggest unstaged Busby Berkeley musical in history" noted that "mingled cheers and boos of the audience added up to a mini-sensation."[73]

Some critics imagined that the boos emanated from disciples of Babbitt, academic atonalists disgusted by New Romanticism's throwback pandering. In the *Village Voice*, Gregory Sandow wrote that "This year, people who want forbidding music boo when they hear anything comfortable."[74] In fact, at least some of the dissent originated in a different source. A reply to Sandow printed in the *Voice*, signed "Charles Ruggles, Brooklyn Heights," revealed that "Those of us who booed David Del Tredici at the Philharmonic were not crying over the lost values of serialism."[75] Describing the work of Del Tredici as "hackneyed," the writer confronted the entire premise of the festival, noting that it "bore a weird resemblance to a proceeding one might expect to find during a totalitarian cultural purge, as composer after composer stood before the audience, admitting shamefacedly to past errors in their choice of aesthetic, but assuring the stern but understanding crowd that they had seen the light." Based on their chosen pen name—a portmanteau combining Charles Ives and Carl Ruggles—the author clearly valued neither the academic avant-garde nor the new Romantics, but the American maverick experimental tradition. Indeed, the author claimed, there was "another road," taken by "individualists for whom fame and financial recompense were secondary, if not irrelevant," such as Ives, Lennie Tristano, Conlon Nancarrow, and the jazz musician Blood Ulmer.

Their conclusion was strong: "Until Druckman and his cronies learn that music need not be simpering and precious to be taken seriously, until Philip Glass and Steve Reich remember that breaking into the concert hall isn't the point at all, and until critics realize that there are more important issues in music than discovering the latest first, those composers who choose to follow their own path will have to make do on their own." The author was clearly dissatisfied with the status quo of bourgeois concert rituals, the celebration of a seemingly backwards-facing New Romanticism as a new vanguard, and the impression that both neo-Romantics and minimalists had sold out to classical audiences. It should not be surprising, then, that the writer of this letter was none other than a former participant in Sheep's Clothing—the composer and clarinetist Evan Ziporyn. Ziporyn had been joined at Horizons '83 by Daniel Plonsey and possibly other Sheep who, "horrified" by Del Tredici's music, had "decided to revive the tradition of booing."[76] (The Sheep had once presented a concert with the title "We should turn towards the people without falling into the neo-romantic trap"[77]). It was not necessarily irate serialists, then, who objected loudly to New Romanticism, but a handful of disaffected leftist experimentalists.

Whatever the reasons behind it, such controversy kept the press engaged. An engaged press helped boost ticket sales, and healthy ticket sales were continually discussed by the press. The combination of critical and public interest made significant waves in the orchestra world, endorsing the Orchestra Residencies Program as a worthwhile endeavor. When Druckman and Webster announced at an American Symphony Orchestra League convention that the box office receipts for Horizons '83 were comparable to those for a Mozart or Beethoven festival, they received a massive wave of applause.[78] "We attracted a younger audience—a way of replenishing the audience," stated the notes for one post-festival meeting. "Box office success gives managers courage."[79] Horizons '83 "obliterates notion that no one cares about new music and there is no audience with publicity."

Rockefeller administrator Howard Klein wrote in a congratulatory letter to Webster that the festival "has given a shot in the arm to the entire program."[80] Meeting with Philharmonic administrators, Duffy said that "The NYP has been the 'flagship' of the program. No question that it is 'known for a fact' that the NYP has given other orchestras courage to follow our example."[81] In a five-year internal planning document created by the NEA, a section on the Endowment's Music division noted how most non-profit presenters "rely primarily on standard attractions to attract their audiences; they often find few incentives to present the new or the experimental." It added that "More efforts like the New York Philharmonic's 'Horizon' series of 20th century music are needed."[82] The festival resonated powerfully outside New York, representing a moment in which the aims of Meet the Composer intertwined with the curatorial ambitions of a composer-in-residence and the priorities of a symphony orchestra. New music was given a major opportunity to reach a large public, and—in part because of New Romanticism—it succeeded.

The Workings of the Entire Organization

In a 2000 essay, David Lang wrote that, along with attending every concert of the 1983 Horizons festival and the two subsequent festivals held in 1984 and '86, he "went to many rehearsals and attended almost every panel."[83] It was not just the Sheep who observed Horizons. Many of Druckman's Yale students witnessed the realization of this "musical hothouse"—the ticket lines that snaked out into Lincoln Center's plaza, the boos and applause that followed controversial music, the debates in the press and the boxes of Avery Fisher Hall around its New Romanticism theme. And for those emerging composers eager to participate in the new marketplace that the Orchestra Residencies Program revealed, one event in the 1983 festival was particular notable: the

Philharmonic's open rehearsal of *dream of the morning sky,* a new work written by Lang's Yale colleague Aaron Jay Kernis.

Kernis's piece had impressed Druckman, who proposed it be read by the Philharmonic under the direction of Zubin Mehta in a free open rehearsal attended by almost a thousand patrons.[84] The purpose of the rehearsal was to provide the audience with a sense of what the compositional process was like in writing for orchestra—the kind of composer-audience interaction encouraged by Duffy—and Mehta thus frequently interrupted the reading to discuss the work with Kernis. But the interjections quickly soured. "Not only did he start to talk about it, but he started to become mister composition teacher, and began to criticize," Kernis recalled a few years later.[85]

Further, it became clear to Kernis and members of the orchestra that Mehta was not fully acquainted with the score itself.[86] At various moments in their back-and-forth, Kernis defended himself against Mehta's concerns. Occasionally, the audience agreed with him, and burst into applause. The "mini-scandal," as Kernis called it, became a media sensation.[87] "The sight of the diminutive future Pulitzer Prize winner Aaron Kernis speaking the truth quietly but firmly to Zubin Mehta captivated the audience and became the story of the festival in the national and international press," Lang recollected.[88]

Despite dissenters like Ziporyn, the effects of Horizons on young composers were clear. The Orchestra Residencies Program had opened a new avenue by which to engage with the symphonic world, and Horizons '83 was its most high-profile exemplar. In a meeting after the festival, Druckman noted that "composers now see that they can write for full orchestra and expect to be performed."[89] Scott Lindroth, who had just graduated from Yale when Horizons began, said in 2014 of the new orchestral landscape that "When composers began to realize that this too might be available to them—and that it wasn't all about the Pierrot ensemble plus percussion—we were all very, very excited: there might be another way to move forward as a composer."[90] Lindroth was describing an ensemble configuration modeled after Arnold Schoenberg's landmark modernist score *Pierrot Lunaire,* one that had become a prototype for uptown groups like the Da Capo Chamber Players, further instantiated in the Rockefeller-funded ensembles that dotted the university landscape. The freelance ensemble recruited to Lang's alma mater University of Iowa for its Center for New Music in the '60s, for example, comprised a roster of flute, piano, percussion, violin, cello, and soprano—almost the exact instrumentation of *Pierrot Lunaire,* minus clarinet.[91]

But the Kernis case also pointed out the complications in such new opportunities. Even as composers had the chance to experiment with an instrumentation much larger than the Pierrot setup—and potentially win over audiences significantly larger than those of academic series like Yale's Sprague Hall concerts—they still had to contend with the very real apathy of music directors and other stakeholders in the marketplace. This, too, would be the conundrum that Lang faced as he worked directly with the Philharmonic as its Revson Fellow in 1985 and '86. His experience with the orchestral world prepared him for the administrative work of Bang on a Can, and provided him with professional connections that would benefit the upstart festival. But, perhaps more importantly, the highly institutional and conservative Philharmonic also made Lang jaded toward the symphonic scene, and fueled the renegade, entrepreneurial ethos of Bang on a Can.

The press narrative around the subsequent Horizons festivals of 1984 and '86 was one of decline. With its theme of "The New Romanticism—A Broader View," the second festival significantly expanded its curatorial framing. Ten concerts included five Philharmonic performances, the guest ensembles Group for Contemporary Music and American Composers Orchestra, and two miniature series designed to incorporate the uptown academic and downtown experimental scenes, neither of which had neatly fallen under the moniker of 1983's New Romanticism. Charles Wuorinen and Roger Reynolds curated three concerts focused on computer music, and *Voice* critic Gregory Sandow provided programming input for The New Virtuosity, the theme of two recitals featuring composer-performers like Diamanda Galás and Stuart Dempster.

For some critics, this broadening meant that Horizons was no longer distinguishable from other new-music series presented in New York: New Romanticism had lost its specific, vanguard edge. *Voice* classical critic Leighton Kerner chastised the "rather leaky umbrella-title" of the '84 festival. Although he observed that "slogans . . . have their legitimate uses"—noting the "triumphant figure" of a more than 70 percent capacity box office in the 1983 festival—the new festival was notably less popular, "which suggests that the financial benefits of escalating a slogan by removing a question mark can be undone by broadening whatever view that slogan entails."[92] Attendance fell from an average of 1,800 tickets sold for the six concerts in 1983 to an average of 1,500 tickets sold for each of the five Philharmonic concerts in 1984, and critics continually dwelled on this waning, with some raising concerns as to whether the next Horizons, planned for 1986, would go ahead.[93]

But Horizons did return once more in June 1986, with a festival the *Times* described as "the most ambitious in terms of budget ($800,000), number of concerts (seven) and overall scope."[94] And it was in planning for this undertaking that Lang gained intimate experience with the world of the American orchestra. The Revson Foundation had offered $30,000 to provide two consecutive, one-year fellowships for young composers to work with Druckman in planning Horizons. In a May 1984 press release announcing the initial search for potential Revson Fellows, Duffy noted that "Most young composers study orchestral writing in a vacuum and generally know little about the day to day administration of a complex institution like a major orchestra. The Revson Fellows will learn on the job from masters in the profession."[95] Lindroth served first in the position from fall 1984 to June 1985, attending Philharmonic rehearsals, discussing the conception and programming of the festival with Druckman and Mehta, working with musicians and staff, and sorting through piles of scores mailed to the orchestra.

For Lindroth, the new career trajectory offered by the fellowship was promising. "It is extremely difficult for a composer to get a foothold in the music field, and nearly impossible to gain intimate access to a major symphony orchestra," he wrote to the Revson Foundation's president at the end of his term. "The Revson Fellowship has completely changed this rather bleak outlook by providing me with the instant credibility necessary for me to meet and to associate with some of the finest composers in the world."[96] Lindroth noted in his fellowship report to Duffy, for example, that when he sent out his music with a cover letter on Philharmonic stationary, it was warmly received by corresponding orchestras.[97]

Lang had unsuccessfully applied for the Revson Fellow position in its first year. In his June 1984 application letter to Duffy, he noted that he was already at work on two orchestra commissions, *flaming youth* for the New York Youth Symphony and *eating living monkeys* for the Cleveland Orchestra.[98] For the second year of the fellowship, the search was expanded nationally; an ad in the American Music Center newsletter in 1985 stated "Composers aged 22–30 with experience in and knowledge of new orchestral music are eligible" and noted a weekly salary of $260.[99]

Despite the national search, the 1985–86 fellowship was awarded to Lang, affirming the significant professional prospects that Druckman offered his Yale students. Lang and Lindroth both attended a May 1985 conference of the resident composers at Exxon's offices in Manhattan, where they gained an insider's perspective on the strengths and pitfalls of an orchestral career. As notes from the meeting reveal, John Adams discussed the importance of receiving a salary for his work as a composer, and the success of his New and Unusual Music series in drawing a large public; Dallas Symphony composer Robert Rodríguez—whose residency was not renewed—spoke about facing a conservative audience and an administration either hostile or indifferent to new music; and St. Louis Symphony composer Joseph Schwantner, who had established a strong partnership with music director Leonard Slatkin, observed that "When artistic director has strong voice, program can accomplish a lot."[100]

Both Revson Fellows also sifted through what Lang described as "thousands of unsolicited manuscripts."[101] Lindroth created a system for reviewing the scores mailed to the orchestra, and Lang attempted to incorporate some of the submissions into the 1986 festival.[102] In an interim report to Duffy about his fellowship, Lang described preparations for Horizons '86 as having "allowed me to move freely through almost all departments of the Philharmonic." He talked about audience demographics with Webster, wrote a press release for the publicity department, "presented our programming proposals both at meetings of the general staff and at meetings of the Board of Directors," helped apply for grants, prepared program notes for an educational concert, edited scores in collaboration with Mehta, and spoke to a hundred schoolteachers at a banquet. In short, Lang wrote, "the Festival has allowed me to see the workings of the entire organization."[103]

Druckman even let his former student mostly take the reins in curating the festival, which introduced a new theme of "Music as Theater," inspired by the composer-in-residence's work on his Metropolitan Opera commission. The festival had a strong orientation toward the European avant-garde, including composers rarely played by the Philharmonic—all-Berio and all-Ligeti evenings, as well as Karlheinz Stockhausen's *Der kleine Harlekin* and Mauricio Kagel's *Pas de Cinq*—along with pieces by Philharmonic staples Druckman and John Corigliano and the world premiere of Morton Feldman's *Coptic Light*. Lang's vision was idealistic, but also savvy to institutional logistics. He carefully read the union books so that the orchestra could be split in half to rehearse a concert comprising Stockhausen's *Trans* and Louis Andriessen's *De Staat*. He was not yet fully abreast of classical music's institutional politics, though—the entire endeavor almost fell apart after Lang tried to program a piece by an avant-garde composer whose work was detested by a wealthy board member.

And with Lang's involvement, the festival also clearly welcomed a musical movement mostly overlooked by the two previous Horizons: minimalism. Meet the Composer had already requested in 1983 that Druckman feature music by Reich or Glass; instead, John Adams served as the festival's only minimalist.[104] In the wake of Horizons '83, Howard Klein wrote to Druckman that "We are in a remarkable period when some composers are actually in demand in concert and on recordings. A salute in the direction of Messrs. Glass, Reich, Adams, and others could be a good follow on."[105] It was not just the style of the music that the Rockefeller director advocated for, then, but also minimalism's significant audience draw. Horizons '84, despite its downtown programming, featured none of those composers.

But Lang convinced Druckman and the Philharmonic to mount the New York premiere of Andriessen's *De Staat*, a work beloved by the three Bang on a Can founders, as well as Arvo Pärt's *Tabula Rasa*.[106] And Horizons '86 devoted an evening to American minimalism too, also orchestrated by Lang: the Paul Dresher Ensemble performed the first act of that composer's *Slow Fire*, and Steve Reich and Musicians played the landmark *Music for Eighteen Musicians*. Lang had even reached out to Glass, but the potential collaboration fell through—it would take another thirty-one years for Glass's music to make its New York Philharmonic debut. In a *Times* profile in advance of the concert, critic Tim Page described Reich, nearing age 50, as increasingly "accepted by the musical establishment."[107] Rockwell's review of the performance, however, observed that the presentation of minimalist music in the hallowed Avery Fisher Hall was still a point of contention—he overheard an elderly concertgoer continually repeating to a friend about the Dresher, "That the Philharmonic should present such a work is just a crime."[108]

For young postminimalists, the presentation of Reich's music by the Philharmonic may have signaled a similar kind of institutional opportunity that Kernis's open rehearsal had for promising neo-Romantics. In May 1986, Michael Gordon wrote to Druckman that he had seen the listings for the upcoming Horizons festival and observed that "The only thing it's missing is me!"[109] He proposed that Druckman add the Michael Gordon Philharmonic to the Reich/Dresher bill as a program opener; it could perform Gordon's sinuous and assaultive piece *Strange Quiet*, the follow-up to *Thou Shalt!/Thou Shalt Not!*. Reich had apparently agreed to the idea. (In hindsight, Lang and Gordon both recounted that the former likely wrote the letter on behalf of the latter, who was reluctant to self-promote; and when one imagines a potential marquee, "The New York Philharmonic Presents the Michael Gordon Philharmonic," it seems like a specifically David Lang kind of mischief.)

Although nothing came of Gordon's suggestion, it's clear that Lang was not the only Bang on a Can founder with an interest in Horizons. Gordon and Wolfe recalled that they attended the Reich/Dresher concert, as well as the performance of *De Staat*. Wolfe, in fact, was in line to serve as a subsequent Revson Fellow around 1991—Duffy had advocated for her, and she may have been interviewed by Mehta. But the position was suspended shortly before the residency could begin.[110] "He changed everything for composers," she later said of Duffy and his work.[111]

Despite the following that Reich's music commanded, audiences for the 1986 festival dwindled further. The festival's seven concerts averaged around

1,200 attendees, which the *Times* wrote "appeared skimpy in Avery Fisher Hall."[112] The Philharmonic was beginning to lose interest in the project, which was increasingly becoming a financial burden. It dropped the symposia, preconcert lectures, and glossy program books that had helped contextualize the previous festivals.[113] Horizons '86 ultimately brought a close to the flagship of the Orchestra Residencies Program. "Not since Haydn and Esterházy has there been a residency so meaningful as those of the Meet the Composer program and never has it been done on such a grand scale," Druckman wrote to Duffy in October 1986.[114] Though David Del Tredici served as composer-in-residence at the Philharmonic from 1988 to 1990, no further festivals were mounted.

A Black Hole

What Duffy described as an "ideal public-private partnership" hit a major setback in 1986, when Exxon cut nearly all its art funding in order to maintain profits as the price of oil declined. Between 1982 and 1987, Exxon had contributed more than 40 percent of the Orchestra Residencies Program's $2,082,000 total expenses; Meet the Composer scrambled but made up the lost funding with support from various foundations.[115] The ten-year Orchestra Residencies Program concluded in 1992, leaving a mixed legacy. When the residencies began in 1982, participating orchestras had programmed twenty-four contemporary works in subscription concerts. In 1992, that number had grown to more than eighty.[116] New careers in the orchestral world, including those of John Adams, Joan Tower, and Libby Larsen, had been firmly established. Among US orchestras writ large—not only those participating in residencies—performances of twentieth-century works increased by 63 percent from the 1982–83 season to the 1990–91 season.[117] Lang said in September 1991 that, because of the initiative, "Young composers are now thinking that writing orchestral music is a good thing to do."[118]

At the 1991 conference summarizing the Orchestra Residencies Program at which Lang spoke, Libby Larsen asked the fundamental question: "Do we program risky music as a project, or do we change the orchestra's structure to include risk in our programming?"[119] Duffy wrote to Druckman echoing Larsen's words, and added that "If project, then it will end when the program ends. If structure, it's part of the rock foundation and will last as long as orchestras themselves."[120] In that October 1991 letter, Duffy was describing to its most prominent composer-in-residence his goal of creating endowed chairs for composers to serve as permanent members of American orchestras.

But Duffy's vision was never realized. "It was clear that there were very few orchestras that actually were going to continue this program and that had any interest—any real interest—in contemporary music," Joan Tower later recalled. "As soon as the program was over, it died."[121] Meet the Composer's next major effort would instead be a fund, sponsored by *Reader's Digest*, focused on commissioning new works for smaller orchestras as well as opera, dance, and theater companies. Reflecting back in 1996—when only six of the twenty-one orchestras that had participated still maintained composer positions—*New York Times* critic K. Robert Schwarz wrote that "As orchestras retrench, the composer-in-residence will become an increasingly endangered species."[122]

Meet the Composer transformed the marketplace, but the Orchestra Residences Program ultimately represented a project, not a structure. And some young composers saw firsthand that the orchestral world was not a permanent solution to finding success outside academia. For Lang in particular, there seems to have been a fork in the road after Yale: follow his teacher Druckman and his colleague Kernis down the orchestral career path, or join his best friend Gordon among the downtown rebels. He had fallen under the spell of Louis Andriessen's music, and began writing restricted, caustic works that heightened the "unidiomatic" language of *while nailing at random*; he called it his "anti-orchestration period."[123] (If it wasn't already clear by the music they wrote at Yale, none of the Bang on a Can composers were New Romantics.) After a summer studying at Tanglewood, Lang had been taken on as a kind of apprentice by the prominent German composer Hans Werner Henze. Henze briefly championed the young composer's music and convinced the Cleveland Orchestra to commission his first major orchestral work, the confrontational *eating living monkeys*, in which pealing brass and lacerating strings trade halting gestures, accompanied by the ringing of four desk bells—perhaps a throwback to Lang's role in *The Tree Watcher*. Henze conducted the Cleveland premiere in 1985. During the rehearsal period, though, Lang found himself making tea in the middle of the night for the senior composer.[124] It felt a bit ridiculous.

In later interviews, Lang characterized his experience at the New York Philharmonic in less sunny terms than in the reports he had written to Duffy. A little over a decade after the festivals concluded, he described the Horizons work as "very demoralizing and a very good indication of how narrow the world was, and how for any composer who was saying to himself or herself, 'Oh, the secret of my future will be to write one orchestra piece. Every orchestra will play it. I'll be world famous.' It just showed how impossible, or how narrow, or how unsatisfying that experience would be."[125]

In the mid-'80s, Lang would have breakfast regularly with Gordon and Wolfe at dairy restaurants on the Lower East Side. "We'd meet and we would just complain, just talk about the things we wished would be different," he recollected. "And I would come home from what I saw at the New York Philharmonic, and I would just say 'Look what I just saw, this is really horrible.'"¹²⁶ Where in his letters to Duffy he described helping create an orderly system for filing away the multitude of scores the orchestra had received, in 2016 he remembered a more troubling experience. "They led me to a walk-in closet—a small office—and there were 10,000 unopened envelopes of scores that people had sent to the New York Philharmonic," he recalled. "That they'd never opened. That hopeful composers, from around the world, and famous composers would send." He found it "horrifying." "My first thought was, 'It's disrespectful.' But my second thought was, 'It's also bad for the community: it's bad for people to think that what they do is they're writing music and then throwing it into a black hole.'"¹²⁷ Horizons, it seems, was a dead end.

Composers would instead have to create their own opportunities, he realized, and imagine a world outside of the symphonic realm. Around this time, Gordon had a piece of his programmed on a concert alongside a work by a much more well-known composer. Despite the difficulty of his piece, the ensemble devoted nearly all of its rehearsal time to the famous composer's music and performed Gordon's poorly. Such moments of disrespect were a principal topic over their breakfast conversations. Wolfe may not have had similarly negative professional encounters by this point, but her dispiriting confrontation with serial pedagogy at Michigan was not far in the past. Their encouraging experiences at Yale were more the exception than the rule. It seemed that young composers had to be obsequious and deferential, to wait their turn in a culture overseen by uncaring orchestras and old guard gatekeepers. They didn't want to wait to be chosen for one big break, only to be publicly chastised by the likes of Zubin Mehta. And they decided that griping about how things were run wasn't enough. They wanted to change them.

"We were all sitting around going, 'Well, here's a little taste of the way the institutional world works,'" Lang said in 1997. "'It's clear that that's not going to work for us. It's clear that that's not going to be something that supports young composers in general. It's clear that it's not going to be supporting the kind of music or musical environment that we wanted to live in.' After sitting around talking about that basically every day for about a year we said, 'Okay, let's do a concert. Let's see if we could create an environment that we did want to live in.'"¹²⁸ They started to make a list of pieces that they wanted to hear, in their ideal concert experience. Lang's programming for Horizons '86 was a kind of trial run, but this time they wouldn't be at the whim of moneyed donors or apathetic administrators. Eleven months after the conclusion of the final Horizons performance, Lang traded his Lincoln Center slacks and tie for more casual attire, and he and his two colleagues mounted the first-ever Bang on a Can festival.

But there was continuity, too. Even if the Orchestra Residencies Program was short-lived, the marketplace that Meet the Composer envisioned remained a crucial backdrop for Lang and his compatriots' subsequent efforts. Meet the Composer provided funding for orchestral neo-Romantics and do-it-yourself postminimalists alike. Its goal was not to foster one single kind of music-making, but to broadly cultivate a relationship between American composers and the public. When Lang, Gordon, and Wolfe were planning their first festival, they met with a very enthusiastic John Duffy. The first grant ever received by Bang on a Can was provided by Meet the Composer.

3
Festivals

It was an unassuming beginning. Around 2pm on a Sunday in May 1987, Michael Gordon tapped a microphone and announced, in a characteristic deadpan, "Hello. Welcome to the Bang on a Can festival. We're going to start with Phill Niblock's piece *Held Tones*."[1] For the next twenty minutes, in the loft-like space of the SoHo gallery Exit Art, flutist Barbara Held strolled through the audience while sustaining a single note, accompanied by Niblock's enveloping, buzzing electronics. Then Gordon's Yale colleague Scott Lindroth introduced his frenetic *Relations to Rigor* for chamber ensemble and tape, followed by the Dutch pianists Gerard Bouwhuis and Cees van Zeeland performing an arrangement of Louis Andriessen's *De Staat*.

Over the next ten-plus hours, visitors could drop in to hear composer and electric guitarist John King play *move*, in which rowdy distortion undergirds spoken word commentary on racism; Evan Ziporyn perform his languorously postminimalist, solo clarinet piece *Waiting by the Phone*; music by Jacob Druckman and Martin Bresnick, and a saxophone piece by Julia Wolfe's Michigan teacher Laura Clayton; works by Yale graduates Jeffrey Brooks and Aaron Jay Kernis; one of Pauline Oliveros's sonic meditations, led by the composer and performed by the audience; avant-garde monuments including George Crumb's *Black Angels* and a two-piano version of Stravinsky's *Agon* (the oldest work on the program, and the only one by a non-living composer); and a piece by each of Bang on a Can's three founders. Sometime in the very early morning, the marathon ended with John Cage's meditative *Ryoanji*, rendered by the S.E.M. Ensemble. Remarkably, the event mostly ran on schedule.

There was a makeshift stage at one end of the gallery, and a bar at the other. Throughout the afternoon and evening, an elevator opened onto the seventh-floor space, which was packed with people who came and left between performances. "It was like a party," bassist Robert Black, the most active musician in the festival—he played four pieces, spaced out over the marathon—recalled.[2] The audience was youthful, the atmosphere informal, beer readily available. Around four hundred people showed up to hear twenty-eight works by Bang on a Can's founders, friends, teachers, and heroes.

For its three artistic directors, the event's success seemed a minor miracle, and one that might just begin to redress their grievances about new music in the mid-'80s. In their grumbling conversations, Gordon, Wolfe, and David Lang had decided that the principal problem for young composers was not really the New York Philharmonic. It was, instead, a much smaller and more insular musical establishment—or, really, two musical establishments. They would take the subway up to Columbia University's McMillin Theatre to hear performances of atonal music by academic composers, and they would traverse their own lower Manhattan neighborhoods to hear heady drones and improvisations at small venues like Experimental Intermedia.[3] Those twin spheres of musical activity, uptown and downtown, felt isolated from one another, from a mainstream audience, and from their generation. Gordon, Lang, and Wolfe loved some of the music that they heard but not the culture that propagated it. They shared John Duffy's belief that composers should be in dialogue with the public. And so they had decided to start a new venture, in the mold of the all-night happenings of Sheep's Clothing—the first annual Bang on a Can festival.

"We had a little manifesto," Wolfe recalled in 2016. "Whether it was written down or not I don't know. Every piece was treated the same: if you were the big shot it's not like you got more rehearsal time than the person who's young and fresh out of school."[4] Bang on a Can was, in many ways, charting a familiar path: young avant-gardists who, fed up with the status quo, wanted to remold the world in their own image.[5] But rather than issue polemical essays describing their musical style or aesthetic ideology, Gordon, Lang, and Wolfe instead did what any entrepreneurial American composer who grew up in an era of proliferating arts institutions might. They started a non-profit, applied for grants, found a venue, hired a publicist, advertised prolifically, and put on a show. Their manifesto would be a concert.

This unwritten avant-garde manifesto had two principal aims, described by Gordon, Lang, and Wolfe in numerous interviews, which shaped what Bang on a Can was and what it meant. "When the Yalie triumvirate, fresh from New Haven, founded the Bang on a Can Festival in 1987, their goals were clear," a *Time Out New York* feature characteristically recounted in 1996. "First, to galvanize audiences that were ambivalent toward new music, then to erase the battle line between uptown and downtown composers."[6] The organization's scheme was two-fold: a marketplace-oriented agenda to build a non-specialist audience for new music that they felt was missing from both uptown and downtown scenes; and an aesthetic agenda aimed toward dissolving the uptown-downtown binary itself. These two goals had ideological and practical sides that contrasted sharply with Bang on a Can's institutional peers, and brought forward the organization's vanguardist vision.

We Were Going to Change Music

"We all moved to New York about the same time, and we thought we were going to change music," recalled Jeffrey Brooks about his cohort of Yale composers in the mid-'80s.[7] By 1986, all three Bang on a Can composers had completed their master's degrees—Lang would earn his Yale doctorate in 1989—and arrived in the city alongside other recent graduates from their program. Lang received a grant from the New York Foundation for the Arts that he used toward staging a concert at the Cooper-Hewitt Museum that summer. He needed to supply a pithy description of the event for a promotional brochure, and Wolfe came up with the line "A bunch of composers banging on cans."[8] Music by Lang, Gordon, and Brooks was performed—though no cans were banged, Wolfe played a metal pipe in Brooks's piece—the Michael Gordon Philharmonic played a set, and they packed the hall with their friends.

But Lang, Gordon, and Wolfe were eager to reach beyond their social circles for their next endeavor. They tossed around ideas for how to seek out new listeners. At one point Gordon suggested staging an impromptu concert on the Staten Island Ferry in order to capture the neophyte ears of unsuspecting commuters.[9] Eventually, though, they settled on replicating the format of Sheep's Clothing—an all-night, eclectic concert. The trio adapted Wolfe's jokey phrase into a title, and thus the Bang on a Can Festival was born. "We wanted to confuse people, twist people's preconceptions," Lang said of the name in 1987. "There have been a lot of new music festivals, but this is the first annual 'Bang on a Can Festival,' and we wanted to be different."[10] (For decades, it would also mean that the organization was frequently mistaken for the off-Broadway theatrical percussion group Stomp.)

The composers wanted to host the performance at an art gallery. They consulted a book of New York venues, settling on the Exit Art gallery at 578 Broadway in SoHo, founded by Jeanette Ingberman in 1982. The proposal they sent to Exit Art outlined a concert that would begin at 9pm and end at 9am:

> The Bang on a Can Festival is an all-night contemporary music extravaganza, featuring avant-garde music from the United States and Europe. It is our theory that, in a friendly environment, musics that existed previously in polarized settings can be better appreciated side by side. We will represent a large spectrum of music, from Louis Andriessen to Milton Babbitt, with an occasional nod to our experimental ancestors, such as Ives and Varèse. Special emphasis will be given to works of composers under forty.[11]

They promoted the fact that many composers would be on-hand to introduce their music, provided an ambitious draft program of more than thirty contemporary works to be performed, and outlined a budget of $10,300. Upon acceptance by Exit Art, most of the proposed ideas remained intact, with one important tweak—Ingberman would not sign off on an all-night concert, so the program was shifted to last from 2pm to 2am.

In that very first proposal, Bang on a Can described a "theory" at the heart of their enterprise: that bringing together music from "polarized settings"—specifically, the supposedly divided worlds of uptown and downtown—into a "friendly environment" would allow it to be better understood. This premise is baked into the mythology of Bang on a Can, and undergirded how Lang first described the festival's name—that even if New York was already jam-packed with contemporary music events, Bang on a Can would be *different*. But what was actually happening musically in New York, from which Bang on a Can attempted to differentiate itself? And just how sound were its claims to difference?

In the years after the first Bang on a Can marathon, the organization's founders would tell and retell the story of why the New York new-music scene of the time so badly needed a new festival. When Gordon and Lang first arrived in New York, they would trek to McMillin at Columbia, Merkin Concert Hall on 67th Street, and Carnegie Recital Hall to hear reputable ensembles like Speculum Musicae and the Group for Contemporary Music perform works by Elliott Carter, Charles Wuorinen, and Columbia graduate students.[12] And Gordon, Lang, and Wolfe would all hang out in their downtown environs to see improvised performances by John Zorn and Shelley Hirsch at the venue Roulette; pulsating drones from Ellen Fullman and Arnold Dreyblatt at Phill Niblock's Experimental Intermedia loft; and the multimedia spectacles of Robert Ashley at The Kitchen.

The trio liked much of the music they heard, but not the vibe surrounding it. The two musical universes—the one that housed ensembles performing precisely notated, atonal music on the Upper West Side, and the one that comprised composer-performers rendering their own quasi-improvisatory experimentations below 14th Street—felt divided, with their own attendant aesthetics, ideologies, and practices. Gregory Sandow at the *Village Voice* and John Rockwell in the *New York Times* regularly framed the concerts they heard within these competing worlds of uptown and downtown. Many composers saw the terms as mere inventions of the media. At a panel in 1979, Rockwell asked Wuorinen and John Cage to respond to the uptown and downtown labels, and Cage chose instead to impishly discuss his zip code.[13] But the labels stuck.

In this very period, the sociologist Samuel Gilmore was interviewing dozens of musicians in New York, conducting ethnographic fieldwork centered on understanding the discourses of uptown and downtown. He found that within contemporary music, there existed less "schools of thought"—aesthetic alliances around codified styles such as serialism—than "schools of activity"—subworlds and cliques that shared conventions. Uptown's school of activity, for example, comprised academic specialists who were best known to each other but not to a general concert audience, maintained close associations with groups like Speculum Musicae, and shared a "musical common practice" of composing fully notated works executed by highly trained classical performers.[14]

Like Cage, some of Gilmore's interviewees resisted the idea that they belonged to unified schools of thought, which they described as "fabrications," "put ons," and "fictitious," imposed by outside critics and scholars.[15] But those impositions were powerful enough that they lodged themselves in a young generation's imagination, shaping their own efforts at world-making. Gordon, Lang, and Wolfe understood uptown and downtown as representing both cultural norms and sonic characteristics—schools of activity *and* thought. At McMillin, they saw scholarly audiences, read dense program notes, and heard atonal music that reminded them of their pre-Yale academic years. At Roulette, they saw small crowds of experimental musicians, read no program notes at all, and heard eclectic improvisations. Wolfe frequently recalled that both communities had their own grayscale clothing: tuxedos uptown, black t-shirts downtown. "Neither side was really fun," she would say.[16] The uniformity of these uniforms provided a visual metaphor for what Bang on a Can perceived as a self-seriousness, and aesthetic conformity, endemic to each scene. "If you went to hear Speculum Musicae, there was invariably one composer doing great stuff in an ugly language, and the others were bad composers working in the same ugly language," Lang told *Village Voice* critic Kyle Gann in 1993. "Same thing Downtown: there'd be a free, sonic piece by a really good composer and a bad sonic piece right behind it. Pieces were being grouped by ideology, not quality."[17]

The composers connected this orthodoxy with the purportedly small audiences they saw. If a concert series were to invest in quality instead of ideology, and find some ways of having a bit more fun, it might reconnect with a broader mainstream. Even Yale seemed to them more diverse than New York—after all, as Lang once pointed out, composers writing in such disparate idioms as Gordon and Kernis had participated in the program.[18] Bang on a Can simply wanted to extend the pedagogical ecumenicalism of Bresnick and Druckman into the city. Aesthetically, too, Bang on a Can's generation "fell in the cracks," as Wolfe once put it.[19] At some point during their academic training, they had all individually settled on notation as their primary vehicle for musical expression, a practice they viewed as indebted to uptown. But they were also interested in the minimalism, and explicit engagement with world music and rock, that they heard downtown. A festival that brought together these diverse aesthetics and practices, along with their own music and that of a young generation they felt was ignored by the establishment, might make a bold statement.

Bang on a Can was not alone in perceiving some degree of stagnancy in this moment. In a 1985 column titled "What Happened to Our Vanguard?" Rockwell mused on the seeming lull in the current new-music scene, which he explained away with a wide range of scenarios: high real estate premiums, megafestivals like the Brooklyn Academy of Music's Next Wave that focused on big names over smaller acts, the NEA-stimulated regionalization of the arts, an absence of strong curatorship at The Kitchen, the uptown-downtown divide, the false promise of fame offered by the art-rock scene, and the prominence of mixed-media performance over "serious new music," among others. "All we need for a renewal of new music here will be one or two commanding young composers, plus two or three farsighted young (or maybe not so young) critics, three or four bold funders and presenters and club-owners, and a new, fashionable audience," Rockwell wrote, seeming to foreshadow the festival that would launch two years later.[20] And Bang on a Can did explicitly stake its claim to innovation on trying to attract a new, fashionable audience. Though the proposal to Exit Art omitted an explicit discussion of audiences, they were central to the festival, and an undercurrent of its creators' desire to create a "friendly environment" to bring together uptown and downtown. Describing the overarching intent of Bang on a Can in 1997, Lang stated that "Our mission in a sentence is to find new music for a new audience, to make a new environment where people will feel that they are not uncomfortable, where they can listen freshly and listen more carefully."[21]

Bang on a Can, too, positioned that mission as distinct from what they were seeing at concerts in the '80s. A 1994 fundraising letter described the typical contemporary music concert of the past as attended by "a small number of hard core new music professionals, all of whom were easily recognizable."[22] As one 1996 grant report put it of the first marathon, "They sought to appeal to an audience beyond the 'new music specialists.'"[23] "We went to new music concerts all the time," Gordon later said, "and there would be 50 or 100 people."[24]

Actual audience numbers, however, were a little more encouraging. In its three-concert 1984–85 season at McMillin, which seated 1000, Speculum

Musicae attracted audiences of 150, 500, and 250 attendees, respectively.²⁵ Auditing a March 1985 Speculum concert for the New York State Council on the Arts, the young composer Steven Swartz noted that "The audience was very academic-collegiate, and ranged in age from the undergraduate to the fully tenured."²⁶ The following year, Speculum moved to the more centrally located Merkin Concert Hall, with a more reasonable capacity of 450, where its concerts attracted between 100 and 250 attendees.²⁷ In 1986, Rockwell criticized the ensemble's 15th anniversary concert as "half-filled with the dusty-feathered birds that make up the uptown contemporary music establishment."²⁸ What he didn't mention, though, was that the performance's venue, Lincoln Center's Alice Tully Hall, had a capacity of around 1,200—if it was, in fact, half-full, that meant there were around 600 attendees.²⁹ When the Group for Contemporary Music performed at Carnegie Recital Hall, capacity 250, in its 1985–86 season, it averaged a little over 80 percent full over four concerts.³⁰ Typically, then, at least a couple hundred people, if not significantly more, would come out for uptown shows. Even if the audience did tend toward the collegiate, and the theaters sometimes looked half-empty, this was not a miniscule fanbase.

And concerts at Experimental Intermedia occasionally neared capacity—though Niblock's downtown loft space could only hold a hundred-or-so visitors. (Roulette was of comparable size, and The Kitchen a bit larger.) Along with dance and theater performances, Experimental Intermedia hosted over thirty "Composers Concerts" a year, attracting disparate crowds ranging from a dozen attendees to a full house. "It would be an understatement to call these concerts informal," one visitor wrote of a 1980 performance, noting that the seating area comprised scattered sofas.³¹ "The advertised price of admission, $2.50, is automatically discounted to $2 at the door. Cheap wine is available at no charge throughout the evening." Auditing a 1986 concert, Swartz noted that the audience was an "informal-dressed group, hirsute and thoughtful."³²

Experimental Intermedia had no problem with the fact that its audience was somewhat insular, as Niblock saw its primary work as that of a service organization for a specific community. "Concerts by Composers at E.I.F. are held in an environment sufficiently informal to encourage experimental and developmental work by a variety of new-music composers," the organization stated in a 1981 grant application. "The music and multimedia works are often composer-performed; the focus of the concerts is on composer development rather than audience development. Consequently, the audiences are generally small, familiar with the work, and supportive."³³ The previous year, the foundation described its purpose as providing a space for experimental work-in-progress to be heard "in an informal, sympathetic atmosphere."³⁴ Audience development, in some ways, was antithetical to this vision—a sympathetic atmosphere required listeners familiar with experimental music. Composers could develop best, according to Experimental Intermedia, when their work was shielded from a large listenership. Nor did uptown ensembles necessarily place attracting audiences at the forefront of their agendas. The Group for Contemporary Music, for instance, described its purpose as "dedicated to the control by composers over the destiny of performances of their works."[35] These institutions carved out niches for themselves to serve constituent communities and aesthetic visions, but were not overly preoccupied with reaching a broader public—nor was their approach toward concert presentation aimed at welcoming new listeners.

Elsewhere, large cultural institutions sponsored performances of new music that did attract blockbuster crowds. The Bang on a Can founders observed the musical hothouse of Horizons '83, with its unprecedented box office sales for a contemporary orchestral festival, although they also watched those audiences wane in later years. Across the river, the Brooklyn Academy of Music sold out a five-night run of Philip Glass's *Satyagraha* in 1981 attended by nearly 10,000 people, and a similarly popular revival of his *Einstein on the Beach* in 1985. With its focus on Glass, Laurie Anderson, and other prominent interdisciplinary experimenters, BAM's Next Wave Festival tapped into a young and diverse crowd who were not otherwise found at Carnegie Hall or Lincoln Center, which BAM director Harvey Lichtenstein characterized as a "SoHo audience."[36] By the late '80s, 80 percent of Next Wave's audience was under the age of forty, and 23 percent under twenty-five.[37]

Bang on a Can targeted a similar market. As Wolfe told *Time Out New York* in 1996, "We were trying to reach the people who check out new theater and new art but normally have no connection at all to new music."[38] The ideal listener, they frequently described, was the youthful urbanite generally curious about independent films, modern dance, and contemporary visual art, but, when it came to music, gravitated toward art-rock bands like Talking Heads rather than contemporary composition. If new music were presented in a fun, informal manner that did not necessarily bring along all of the trappings of the academic concert environment or the opaque non-rituals of the downtown loft, it might find success with that demographic. Thus, too, the festival's title. "We wanted to break down any serious, elitist, highbrow image," Wolfe said of the name Bang on a Can in 1994. "You would feel that you were coming to something that was fun and that would be open to anybody."[39] And to attract this non-specialist audience, the founders selected Exit Art in part because it did not have a history of presenting contemporary music: it could thus act, as they later described, as a "neutral location."[40] (For whatever reason,

Bang on a Can didn't acknowledge that contemporary art spaces had actually been a longtime, familiar home for new music.)

They hired publicist Lynn Garon, a well-connected figure who represented Steve Reich and his ensemble as well as Speculum Musicae. She met with the trio and appreciated their fervor. As Lang later recalled, Garon responded by crafting press materials that were "super hype-y," and "in-your-face."[41] In her release announcing the festival—billed as "Twelve continuous hours of new and newer music"—Garon described the event as an "eclectic supermix of composers and styles from the serial to the surreal." "Beethoven was once considered a brash young avant-garde composer; now we recognize his genius," she wrote. "Today, people are learning to spell Xenakis and Andriessen, enjoy the poetry of Druckman and the mysticism of Crumb, participate responsively with Oliveros, understand the pioneering role of Cage."[42] She netted the organization enthusiastic advance listings in the *Village Voice* and *New York Times*.

Gordon, Lang, and Wolfe ran a small ad with the full program run-down in the *Voice* and created a flyer that they sent to contacts in the worlds of art and dance as well as music, drawing on mailing lists they purchased from the Dance Theater Workshop. Ingberman's husband, the performance artist Papo Colo, created a poster for the festival—a grayscale image of two hammers, banging on cans that contained the program and a rolled-up page of frayed sheet music (Figure 3.1). The design established a pattern of gritty industrial imagery that Bang on a Can has continued to employ since. Tickets were priced at $10 for the entire twelve hours, with "re-entry encouraged."[43]

Bang on a Can hoped that attendees would listen closely to a piece, grab a drink and converse about what they heard, and dip back in for another intense musical experience. Composers and fans and newbies were meant to mingle, and apparently did. "It was as much a social event as it was a concert," Scott Lindroth recalled. "You were hearing things that you wanted to talk about, and for a concert that's going to go on that long, that it would allow that kind of fluidity of coming and going and paying attention and then not—that was so refreshing, and allowed you to really immerse in it in a way that you couldn't if it were a four-hour concert that was nothing but a concert. In that sense, it did facilitate a more heterogeneous community in the audience."[44]

Garon's press release touted that "With almost all of the composers on hand to introduce their work and interact with the audience in a relaxed gallery setting, a special ad-hoc chemistry is sure to evolve."[45] Such introductions were nothing new in the era of Meet the Composer—and Bang on a Can had pitched the idea for the festival to John Duffy, who gave his endorsement and a $1,500 grant. But Bang on a Can placed their own

Figure 3.1 Poster for the 1987 Bang on a Can festival.

spin on the concept, with the idea that casual, pre-performance chats by composers would fully replace the typical program note—they later called them "living program notes"—and draw in new listeners with their informality. The program itself was rudimentary, typical of downtown but not academia: three simple, stapled white pages that listed times, composers, works, performers, and funders. At the marathon, Lang told critic Tim Page that they avoided including bios of musicians because "We wanted our audiences to just *listen* to the music without thinking about where *this* composer went to school and what prestigious awards *that* composer had won."[46] As much as possible, Bang on a Can sought to minimize the intellectual trapping of the classical concert, in favor of immediate experience: listening without presumptions.

In their initial proposal to Exit Art, Bang on a Can had budgeted $3,000 of its total anticipated expenses of $10,300 toward publicity.[47] Musician fees accounted for $3,000, composer fees were $1,500, and other expenses such as the sound system and hall and equipment rentals accounted for the rest. Their income to offset expenses consisted of the $1,500 Meet the Composer grant, $4,000 from individual contributions—most of these donations were made by the founders' immediate family—and an estimated $4,000 from ticket sales and $500 from concessions.

With tickets priced at $10, Bang on a Can had to attract an audience of more than 400 to fully recoup costs. But local fire code restricted Exit Art to no more than 250 audience members at any given time. Bang on a Can ultimately had somewhere around 400 people in attendance, which means that their proposed model of re-entry—what they would later advertise in posters as "Come and go as you like or stay all 12 hours"—worked. Lang collected money at the door and passed it on to Wolfe, who ran it backstage to Gordon, who handed it to musicians as they completed their sets.

At least two music critics showed up. Tim Page of *New York Newsday* and Bernard Holland of the *New York Times* both praised the unpretentiousness of the proceedings and the eclecticism of the programming. Holland, who took in a chunk of the evening performances, described the festival as a "laid-back, supermarket approach to new ideas" with "every brand and generic name imaginable." "The elevators opened directly onto the performing space and overhead fans hummed away, but no one seemed to care," he wrote.[48] Page fondly compared the festival to "the days when small bands of listeners would climb five flights of stairs to listen to the early music of composers such as Reich and Philip Glass." He also noted that Exit Art, and Bang on a Can, existed in a very different SoHo from the loft days of those minimalists: "The floors were polyurethaned, there was an automatic elevator, the walls—painted the requisite loft white—were not peeling, and the temperature was comfortable."[49] Weaving together interviews with the founders alongside his own commentary, Page struck a tone for which Lang, Gordon, and Wolfe had likely hoped:

> I found a general openness, a willingness to pay close attention to divergent sounds and to examine each one for its own merits that has become increasingly rare in the polarized world of contemporary music. Not that an occasional judgment was not privately passed on—composers are composers, after all, and most of them have a personal esthetic, a "true faith" to defend. Still, the atmosphere was friendly and engaging; this was one new music festival that did not eschew the festive.[50]

Open-minded, friendly, festive, and *different* from other spaces in American new music. Bang on a Can had landed.

Fighting Against the World We Had Inherited

Along with describing what he heard in the early evening, Bernard Holland also mentioned a portion of the marathon which he did *not* hear: "The program was arranged with contrast in mind. Thus, as the organizers note with satisfaction, Milton Babbitt's 'Vision and Prayer' rubbed shoulders with Steve Reich's 'Four Organs.'"[51] Garon's press release did not single out these two works, although it did note that "This concert presents the full spectrum of new music; where else could you hear a concert with Niblock, Babbitt, and Reich?"[52] But at some point during the festival, Holland had apparently grabbed Lang to ask him a few questions, and the composer told him about the importance of programming Reich and Babbitt side-by-side.[53]

The trio had spent months of painstaking work figuring out the marathon's programming, and there were plenty of noteworthy curatorial moments. There was *De Staat*, a piece that captured their imaginations when they first heard it at Yale. They programmed a much-belated, posthumous US premiere of the two-piano arrangement of Stravinsky's *Agon*, prepared by the composer himself. They promoted the music of their teachers and graduate school colleagues. And they smartly spaced the music by more prominent figures throughout the marathon so that the audience would stick around to hear their obscure, younger friends—the majority of composers programmed were under the age of thirty-five. With twenty-eight works by twenty-eight composers, Bang on a Can's eclectic supermix had many potential highlights.

But only thirty-five minutes of music from the first marathon were emphasized to the *Times*, and further underscored in later interviews and grant applications. At around 11pm, Mimmi Fulmer sang Milton Babbitt's *Vision and Prayer*, a cryptically disjunct 1961 setting of Dylan Thomas poetry for soprano and tape. Immediately afterwards, the S.E.M. Ensemble performed Steve Reich's *Four Organs*, an unremittingly static, twenty-minute augmentation of a single dominant chord accompanied by the steady shaking of a maraca. For more than three decades afterwards, Gordon, Lang, and Wolfe would talk about this half-hour of music again and again, describing the Reich-Babbitt collision as the defining episode in the origins of their enterprise.

Why did the three composers care so much about the placing of these two works side-by-side? Why, in her dissertation-length history of Bang on a Can, did Wolfe emphasize the fact that Babbitt and Reich, despite having their music programmed together, avoided meeting one another at the festival—and why did she stress that "At that point, to our knowledge, no one had programmed the music of Milton Babbitt and Steve Reich on the same event"?[54]

In 1993, Lang griped to the *Voice* that uptown and downtown concerts tended to feature one great composer followed by a slew of mediocre imitators: that music was grouped according to ideology instead of "quality."[55] Bang on a Can attempted to reorient this approach by bringing together what the founders considered to be the "best" of each musical world, rather than a supposedly sycophantic devotion to narrow stylistic dogma. Placing Reich and Babbitt—representing the opposing aesthetics of minimalism and serialism—directly back-to-back made an unambiguous statement. And Bang on a Can also evaluated "quality" through very specific criteria. *Vision and Prayer* is an unusual Babbitt selection—a relatively minor work compared to, say, *Philomel*, his best-known piece composed for the exact same forces. *Four Organs*, similarly, is not necessarily an obvious choice for Reich's best music prior to 1987—*Drumming*, *Music for Eighteen Musicians*, or *Tehillim* might be more likely contenders.

Instead, Bang on a Can's curation of this first festival was guided, as Lang put it in 1997, by the question, "Was this a revolutionary piece for its environment?"[56] The answer was clearly yes for both *Vision and Prayer*—which was the first-ever work for live vocalist and synthesized sound—and *Four Organs*—whose unremitting, amplified austerity led to an infamous near-riot at Carnegie Hall in 1973.[57] These works were chosen precisely because they were early, lesser-known, and radical exemplars from the oeuvre of established composers. "Both of these pieces are very, very hard nosed and very unlistenable," Lang said.[58]

Programming early Babbitt and early Reich also drew attention to the fact that these once radical composers had *become* established. Later in the 1997 interview, Lang described his college-era first encounters with the early works of Reich and Glass, which he treasured because they were simple, clear, "obnoxious," and "really harsh."[59] But as those minimalists developed an increasingly expressive, ornate, and somewhat traditionalist language—while finding mass popularity—Lang had become disillusioned. "I was really angry because it was really nice to listen to," Lang recalled of when he first heard *Music for Eighteen Musicians*. "I started thinking, 'Is the point of this music to make music that's engaging and difficult and interesting, but present it in a way to make it possible to listen to it and think about it? Or is the point of this music to massage you and make you feel good about being alive?' I think by that time I had already sort of recalibrated myself to think that interesting things in music happened when music was ugly, or when music was difficult or when music was challenging."⁶⁰

Such is the typical stance of the young avant-gardist, critical of the establishment and claiming to understand the revolutionary significance of an elder generation better than those elders understand themselves. The Bang on a Canners wanted to restage past revolutions, and perhaps even redirect minimalism away from the kind of easy listening that Lang believed it had become. Yet Reich and Glass themselves didn't necessarily share this agenda. Wolfe recounts in her dissertation that when they asked Reich about playing *Four Organs*, he responded "Why do you want to do that piece?"⁶¹ When they invited Glass to perform his 1969 work *Music in Similar Motion* at the 1988 festival, the composer apparently balked, saying "Why do you want to play that piece, that's the fastest way to empty a hall I know!"⁶² In their initial proposal to Exit Art, Bang on a Can had even suggested programming John Adams's *Ktaadn* (1972), an obscure choral piece written in an early, Cagean idiom that the composer soon abandoned.⁶³ As with *Four Organs* and *Music in Similar Motion*, by trying to perform *Ktaadn*, they were trying to complicate, or even repudiate, Adams's 1980s image as a composer of accessibly tonal, postminimalist orchestral music.⁶⁴ The piece didn't end up on the 1987 festival, and Bang on a Can have been unsuccessfully petitioning Adams to let them perform it ever since. That said, the trio did give John Cage his choice of music for the marathon, writing him that "You could do whatever you like, from a solo performance to a piece involving musicians, actors, and dancers—a five minute piece or a five hour piece."⁶⁵

Bang on a Can's notion of "quality" was informed by their own rather idiosyncratic aesthetic priorities. "Maybe I'm a masochist, but I really like those harsh experiences," Lang said.⁶⁶ "I like the fact that here's an ugly sound, you know—listen to it." Leading up to the 1987 festival, the trio had been composing music cast in such severe idioms. The first marathon featured Lang's *frag*—written around the same time as *eating living monkeys*, and infused with the same blunt force as Louis Andriessen's music—in which a trio of flute, oboe, and cello constructs a dragging, unison melodic line out of hocketing pizzicato and staccato sixteenth notes. The Michael Gordon Philharmonic played *Strange Quiet*, the 1985 piece that had been pitched to Druckman for Horizons' 86, which builds from psychedelically hushed intertwined melodies to ecstatic rhythmic unisons. At Exit Art, Wolfe showcased a new work, *Williamsburg Bridge*, written for a nonet of winds and strings. Comprising a series of overlapping dynamic swells that accrue into a dissonant, teeming sound mass that then trails off, the work recalls the famous andante from Ruth

Crawford Seeger's *String Quartet 1931*; Wolfe herself cites György Ligeti as a main influence.[67]

"I think of my music as postugly music," Gordon told the *Voice* in 1993. "Academic music wasn't dissonant, because to have dissonance you need to imply consonance. Now that minimalism has simplified all those parameters, the disruptions can stand out. BoaC music tends to have dissonance not just in the pitch language, but in the rhythm, the structure, and the form."[68] The combative sound of Gordon's *Thou Shalt!/Thou Shalt Not!* and *Strange Quiet*—not to mention the provocations of *The Tree Watcher*—manifest this conception of post-ugly dissonance, a style that Kyle Gann would later dub "totalism." "Post-ugly" music might appear at odds with the composers' desire to attract a broad public, but this was exactly the point. They wanted to create an environment in which the harshest of musical languages would be heard, receptively and without prejudices. The *The Tree Watcher* scandal at Yale, or the booing of Adams and David Del Tredici at Horizons '83, were precisely the sorts of reactions they hoped to provoke—they wanted their new festival to inspire immediate and heated debate.

Performing *Four Organs* and *Vision and Prayer* side-by-side also brought uptown and downtown directly into dialogue. It was one part philosophical mission and one part, as Gordon later admitted, "us being pranksters."[69] After all, this was a cohort that spent time in graduate school conducting an orchestra made out of vegetables and writing music for amplified hotel bell. In the early years of the marathons, they applied for New York State funding to simultaneously commission an acoustic string quartet from Glenn Branca—an untrained musician who led noisily amplified, rock-esque ensembles—alongside an electric guitar quartet from their teacher Martin Bresnick. "Branca, as a 'downtown' composer searching for structure, and Bresnick, an 'academic' searching for more expressive music, seem to be chipping away at either side of the same wall," they wrote in the grant application.[70] "They are both very excited about the invitation to switch sides." There's an intellectual bent to such a project, a logical extension of their juxtaposition of Reich and Babbitt, but its crossing of musical wires also seems a bit mischievous. (The Branca commission was funded, and premiered at the 1991 festival; the Bresnick was not, though Bang on a Can later commissioned him for a work for their All-Stars.)

When the Bang on a Can composers retell the story of the first festival, they frequently note that Babbitt stayed until *Vision and Prayer* and left immediately afterwards, and that Reich only arrived after Babbitt's piece had concluded.[71] The two composers never crossed paths, never spoke, and apparently avoided one another. It was clear evidence that, as Wolfe once put it, they belonged to "separate camps."⁷² "There was a war going on," Gordon later said.⁷³ "The 'uptown/downtown' thing." But Wolfe also noted that this evasion was "more 'their' battle than ours. We didn't really inherit that battle because we were interested in both musics and that was of a different generation. In some ways we did because we were definitely fighting against the world we had inherited but we felt like we wanted to break down those barriers for us, so that's why we mixed the pieces."⁷⁴ Placing the clashing aesthetics of Reich and Babbitt next to one another was also about resolving them—imagining a new kind of new-music community that would merge the two disparate scenes of uptown and downtown, rendering those schools of activity and thought irrelevant. If Reich and Babbitt could not get along, Bang on a Can's generation would simply move past the hidebound tensions.

In 2018, during a Q&A following a panel at Bang on a Can's summer festival, I asked Reich about his perspective on the 1987 marathon. Gordon, Lang, and Wolfe had often told their story of programming *Four Organs*, but Reich had never publicly expressed his own opinion about it. And as it turned out, he had no particular memory of the event. He even seemed surprised to learn that Bang on a Can had programmed Babbitt's music to begin with, given its rarity on the organization's concerts today. "Milton Babbitt and I met a number of times," Reich answered diplomatically. "He's a very charming gentleman. He knows every popular tune ever written and can regale you with charming stories. He understands Schoenberg better than I do. Everybody has to do what they do, and let's just hope they do a good job, that's the main thing." Wolfe then mentioned that the two composers had belonged to different social circles, and Reich responded that the uptown-downtown binary was "good for 10–15 minutes" but that, after the passage of time, "the music is left, the music that people want to hear and that musicians want to play."⁷⁵ Reich appeared wholly uninterested in this definitive moment in Bang on a Can's history. And perhaps rightly so. "Neither one was really the answer for us at the time," Jeffrey Brooks said recently of Reich and Babbitt, but then qualified his statement with a laugh: "As it turns out, Steve Reich is pretty close to the answer, actually."⁷⁶

Bang on a Can's attempt to rethink the uptown-downtown binary invites comparison to the efforts of Meet the Composer. John Duffy brought composers of diverse styles and identities onto advisory boards and panels in the hopes that if they mended their ideological divisions, they would stand stronger as a profession. Bang on a Can, too, hoped that presenting an eclectic concert that seemingly resolved aesthetic differences would help contemporary composition shed its insularity. The 1987 audience cheered equally for *Vision and Prayer* and *Four Organs*, which Gordon, Lang, and Wolfe took as evidence that non-specialists in the crowd were unaware that they were supposed to cheer either serialism or minimalism, but not both. But Bang on a Can was not Meet the Composer; they were putting on a concert, not starting a professional service organization. They didn't attempt to sit Reich and Babbitt down together, as Duffy might have—not that they would have had much luck in changing the views of their elders—but were instead creating a narrative about themselves.

Reich and Babbitt both spoke before their pieces were performed—responding to applause and cheers, Babbitt introduced himself with the self-deprecating line "I'm delighted to hear that my reputation hasn't penetrated this far downtown"—and John Cage and Pauline Oliveros were also in attendance.[77] The celebrity of these composers lent considerable legitimacy to an upstart musical soiree hosted by three unknowns, and the event represented an opportunity for Gordon, Lang, and Wolfe to cultivate personal relationships with their heroes. In the mid-'80s, Gordon had struck up a mutually admiring correspondence with Reich after sending him the score to *Thou Shalt!/Thou Shalt Not!*, and Gordon and Wolfe had snuck into the after-party for the 1984 premiere of *The Desert Music* at BAM to meet the composer in-person. While working on his doctorate, Lang had written a fan letter to Oliveros, in which he stated that "The Schools of the '80s are still not teaching the lessons which should have been learned in the '60s, so I plan to keep on learning those lessons from you."[78] When Cage showed up to the '87 festival, he refused Lang's insistent offer to supply him with a complimentary ticket—Gordon recalled, "David says, 'You're John Cage, you're our guest!' John says, 'No, I'm not coming in, unless you sell me a ticket' "—and stayed for several hours, although he left before *Ryoanji*.[79] Babbitt wrote a warm thank-you note after the event, calling it a "singular achievement which deserves to become a permanent part of the musical culture of our time."[80]

Global Aspirations

"When we put the word *annual* into the description," Lang said in 2003, "we just laughed and laughed and laughed, because we thought no one would ever be crazy enough to do this more than once."[81] The three composers frequently recalled that billing their event the "first annual Bang on a Can festival" was more joke than aspiration, claiming that it was only when sweeping up and putting away folding chairs at 2am on the morning after Mother's Day that they started talking about hosting a second marathon. But they had actually been considering a sequel well before the first outing wrapped up. Nearly three months before the 1987 marathon, they had sent a grant application to the New York State Council on the Arts detailing plans for an expanded festival the following year.[82] In his review of the 1987 marathon, Tim Page wrote that "Whatever happens, however, the trio promises another 'Bang-on-a-Can Festival' next year." Lang told the critic that "We have global aspirations."[83]

Global aspirations translated swiftly into institutional action. By the end of that summer, Wolfe began soliciting letters of support from prominent composers for a fundraising package.[84] "I am all for Bang on a Can," John Cage wrote in June 1988. "I remember thinking before I attended their first marathon that the name was not very good. After two years I've changed my mind. Because of what they do (their devotion, the excellence of the performers, etc.) and how they do it, everything is great, including their name, Bang on a Can."[85] Cage also donated a couple thousand dollars to their efforts (Figure 3.2).[86] They met with a state arts council evaluator in the winter, who wrote in her review that "The Festival made a stellar debut last May, and the machinery is well in place for a second event . . . Printed materials are very nicely done, and press coverage was excellent."[87] And they gathered a few well-connected friends—a development director at the New York Philharmonic, the executive director of the New York Youth Symphony, and even, briefly, Abigail Disney, a philanthropist and heir to the family fortune—to create a board for fundraising purposes.

Figure 3.2 John Cage, David Lang, Julia Wolfe, and Michael Gordon, May 1992. Photograph by RJ Capak.

The second annual festival kicked off on May 8, 1988 with Philip Glass and Michael Riesman performing *Music in Similar Motion*. Glass donated his services; Gordon and Lang had worked for him as copyists in the mid-'80s. Oliveros led another of her sonic meditations—the audience was asked to make a sound, breathe, listen, breathe, and replicate a sound heard in the room, resulting in a twelve-minute collage of whistles, claps, stomps, and animal noises. Accompanied by his Philharmonic, Gordon sang an excerpt from his new project, a video opera about Vincent van Gogh. Visiting from Britain, Steve Martland introduced his pounding, dissonant two-piano piece *Drill* by castigating the Thatcher government. Guest ensemble California E.A.R. Unit performed minimal classics including Frederic Rzewski's *Coming Together* and Terry Riley's *In C*. Pianist Yvar Mikhashoff played Mario Davidovsky's *Synchronisms No. 6*, that year's nod toward uptown. Many of the sets were amplified and bracingly visceral—infamously, during composer Jack Vees's performance of his feedback-laden, Hendrix-esque electric bass work *John Henry*, a hunk of plaster fell off the ceiling onto the stage—which would become the standard Bang on a Can approach. Percussionist Steven Schick recalled that when he performed Morton Feldman's muted, gestural *The King of Denmark*, an outlier on the program for its quietness, some members of the audience thought he was simply setting up his equipment.

The concert took place at the RAPP Arts Center, a small multi-disciplinary organization housed on a rough block on the Lower East Side that would host three Bang on a Can festivals until they were abruptly kicked out (Figure 3.3). But the theater's shabbiness, traditional proscenium set-up, and location seemed an impeccable fit. "It was a perfect Bang on a Can setting, because it was a concert hall, and yet it was falling apart," Lindroth recalled. "It had the rhetoric of a concert but also, you're there in your jeans and t-shirt."[88] Kyle Gann, who had skipped out on the first festival, heralded the 1988 marathon in the *Voice* as "brilliantly curated" in "creating a forum for a mass of fine music that is rarely accurately perceived here because it needs a context that neither uptown nor downtown categories allow."[89] And he explicitly called for Bang on a Can to expand, picturing next steps in which they sought out a prominent funder, requested half-a-million dollars, and became "major league."

Though they didn't request $500,000 from a single sponsor, they otherwise realized Gann's fantasy of growth. "We'd go to meetings, we'd talk to people, beg people, we would look at other peoples' materials," Lang recalled.[90] "We'd go to a concert of Speculum Musicae, they'd go 'We're funded by the Ditson Fund.' We'd go, 'If the Ditson Fund is funding this, why can't they fund us?'" In their first few years, Bang on a Can received support from major organizations including the National Endowment for the Arts, New York City Department

Figure 3.3 Cees van Zeeland, Michael Gordon, Julia Wolfe, and Gerard Bouwhuis outside of RAPP Arts Center in 1989. Courtesy of Michael Gordon.

of Cultural Affairs, Mary Flagler Cary Trust, New York State Council on the Arts, ASCAP, Meet the Composer, Ann and Gordon Getty Foundation, and Philip Morris, as well as numerous private donors. And, yes, Columbia's Alice M. Ditson Fund.

In 1989, the festival branched out beyond the marathon to also include three concerts of music by Rzewski, Andriessen, Cage, Branca, and others (Figure 3.4). By 1990, attendance for a full week of concerts—evenings of music by Harry Partch, the Kazue Sawai Koto Ensemble, and Terry Riley as well as a marathon—reached more than 2,000: Bang on a Can had mailed 35,000

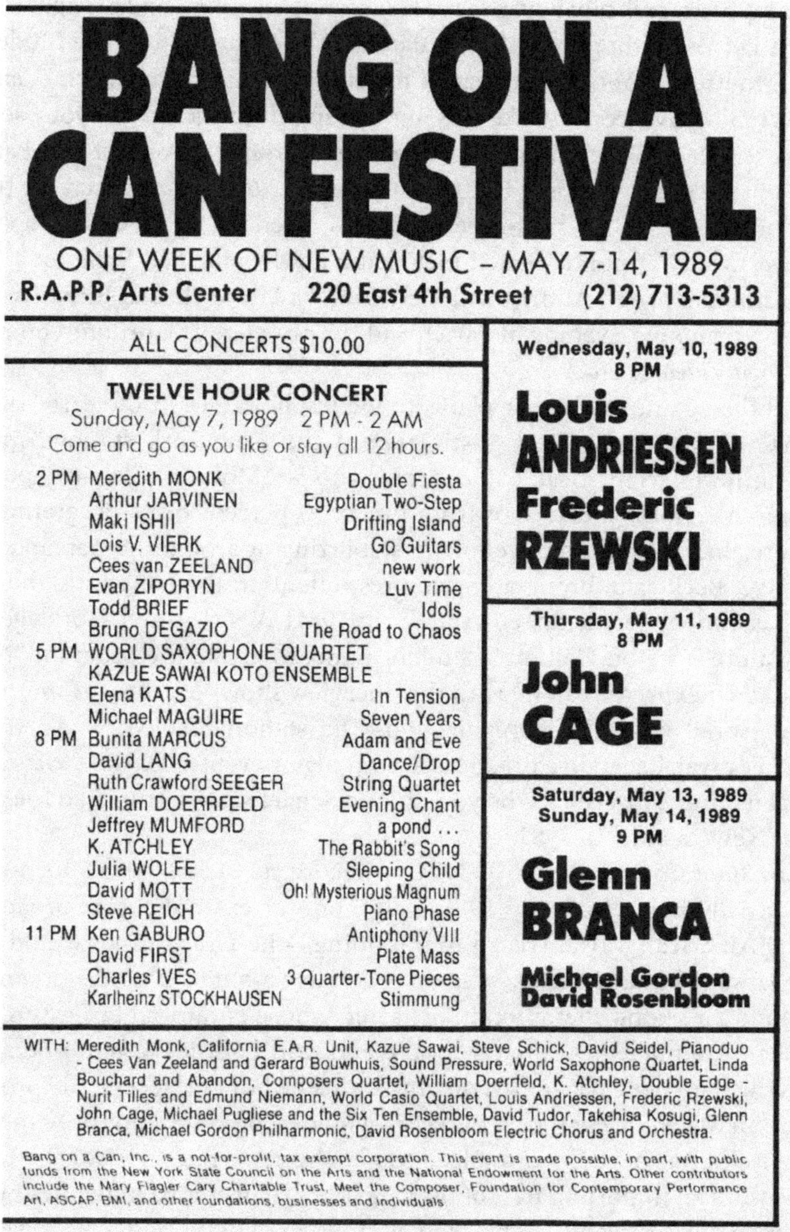

BANG ON A CAN FESTIVAL

ONE WEEK OF NEW MUSIC – MAY 7-14, 1989

R.A.P.P. Arts Center   220 East 4th Street   (212) 713-5313

ALL CONCERTS $10.00

TWELVE HOUR CONCERT
Sunday, May 7, 1989   2 PM - 2 AM
Come and go as you like or stay all 12 hours.

2 PM	Meredith MONK	Double Fiesta
	Arthur JARVINEN	Egyptian Two-Step
	Maki ISHII	Drifting Island
	Lois V. VIERK	Go Guitars
	Cees van ZEELAND	new work
	Evan ZIPORYN	Luv Time
	Todd BRIEF	Idols
	Bruno DEGAZIO	The Road to Chaos
5 PM	WORLD SAXOPHONE QUARTET	
	KAZUE SAWAI KOTO ENSEMBLE	
	Elena KATS	In Tension
	Michael MAGUIRE	Seven Years
8 PM	Bunita MARCUS	Adam and Eve
	David LANG	Dance/Drop
	Ruth Crawford SEEGER	String Quartet
	William DOERRFELD	Evening Chant
	Jeffrey MUMFORD	a pond ...
	K. ATCHLEY	The Rabbit's Song
	Julia WOLFE	Sleeping Child
	David MOTT	Oh! Mysterious Magnum
	Steve REICH	Piano Phase
11 PM	Ken GABURO	Antiphony VIII
	David FIRST	Plate Mass
	Charles IVES	3 Quarter-Tone Pieces
	Karlheinz STOCKHAUSEN	Stimmung

Wednesday, May 10, 1989
8 PM

Louis ANDRIESSEN
Frederic RZEWSKI

Thursday, May 11, 1989
8 PM

John CAGE

Saturday, May 13, 1989
Sunday, May 14, 1989
9 PM

Glenn BRANCA

Michael Gordon
David Rosenbloom

WITH: Meredith Monk, California E.A.R. Unit, Kazue Sawai, Steve Schick, David Seidel, Pianoduo - Cees Van Zeeland and Gerard Bouwhuis, Sound Pressure, World Saxophone Quartet, Linda Bouchard and Abandon, Composers Quartet, William Doerrfeld, K. Atchley, Double Edge - Nurit Tilles and Edmund Niemann, World Casio Quartet, Louis Andriessen, Frederic Rzewski, John Cage, Michael Pugliese and the Six Ten Ensemble, David Tudor, Takehisa Kosugi, Glenn Branca, Michael Gordon Philharmonic, David Rosenbloom Electric Chorus and Orchestra.

Bang on a Can, Inc., is a not-for-profit, tax exempt corporation. This event is made possible, in part, with public funds from the New York State Council on the Arts and the National Endowment for the Arts. Other contributors include the Mary Flagler Cary Charitable Trust, Meet the Composer, Foundation for Contemporary Performance Art, ASCAP, BMI, and other foundations, businesses and individuals.

Figure 3.4 Advertisement for 1989 festival.

flyers, tapped significant advance press and radio coverage, and brought in the Orkest De Volharding from Amsterdam and Le Nouvel Ensemble Moderne from Montreal.[91] Yet they managed to retain their informal spirit. "Isn't it great coming to a concert like this and getting to drink beer at your seat?" composer Dean Drummond was quoted remarking, at one of the Partch shows.[92] In 1991, they spent $270,000—a nearly 2,600 percent increase from their budget in 1987—on thirteen concerts, attended by 3,000 and spaced out over nearly a month, which included a newly launched Bang on a Can Orchestra that played Andriessen's *De Tijd* and a Music Theater Initiative that sponsored another evening of Partch and the premiere of Gordon's complete *Van Gogh Video Opera*.[93]

And they gained a further platform via public radio. In the early 1980s, WNYC director John Beck distinguished the New York station's music programming from local competitors with a "Modern Classics" policy. Twentieth-century music shot from under 20 percent of its programming to more than 85 percent, eventually stabilizing at around 65 percent. The initiative, Beck said, brought "more press attention than anything the station has done in ten or fifteen years."[94] In 1981, WNYC hired Tim Page, already a presence on Columbia student radio, to create the program "New, Old, and Unexpected" along with the interview show "Meet the Composer," co-sponsored by Duffy's organization. The station revived its American Music Festival, began live broadcasts from major events like Next Wave and Horizons, and conscripted the young John Schaefer, who launched the program "New Sounds" in 1982.

Bang on a Can convinced WNYC to record its early festivals for future airplay. Highlights from the 1987 marathon, for example, were broadcast during American Music Week programming—these recordings would also be repackaged as a series of Bang on a Can live albums. And the organization found a strong champion in Schaefer, whose curatorial tastes brought together minimalism, avant-garde jazz, and world music—a genre-bending ethos that had been part of the downtown scene but not necessarily present on the airwaves. "New music deserves wider recognition, not only in musical circles but in the marketplace too," Schaefer wrote in 1986.[95] "Radio exposure is an important part of that." In 1994, Schaefer narrated five hour-long shows featuring highlights from various Bang on a Can festivals, which also aired across the country. "It was huge, because we were just kids, and we did this crazy thing, and there it was, on the radio," Wolfe later told the *Times*.[96] Schaefer would become a regular Bang on a Can collaborator, co-hosting many of their concerts as part of his New Sounds Live broadcast series.

A Cornerstone of the New-Music Scene

As Bang on a Can ascended, attentive music critics framed the upstart festival against the decline of a longstanding one: New Music America. "These impresarios have an insight, a point of view, a vision that provides an unusually intelligent, coherent context for the music," Gann wrote in 1989 of Gordon, Lang, and Wolfe. "BoaC isn't splintered by the favors to repay, the factions to satisfy, that have diluted New Music America and made it so disappointing (if necessary) year after year."[97] Gann's rhetoric was heated, but keenly perceptive.

New Music America began as New Music, New York, a nine-evening affair at The Kitchen, prompted when John Rockwell suggested that the venue host the annual meeting of the Music Critics Association. Kitchen curator Rhys Chatham organized a parallel festival designed to celebrate the downtown musical universe. Billed as "a comprehensive review of current developments in new music" that would also serve as a "focal point of the effort to organize a better support system for composers and a distribution system to make this work better known," the series featured stars including Glass, Reich, and Meredith Monk and a wide swath of experimentalists from Alvin Lucier to George Lewis.[98] Feisty seminars debated the future of experimental music—one packed panel included the likes of Rockwell, Glass, Brian Eno, Robert Fripp, and Leroy Jenkins—and the young composer Beth Anderson issued leaflets firing off incendiary criticisms. (On *Drumming*: "After all these years, Mr. Reich is too fucking loud. Men hitting things."[99]) With many out-of-town critics in attendance, New Music, New York provided the Kitchen and its SoHo scene with international exposure.

Some musicians expressed concerns that the large-scale festival represented a dangerous institutionalization of downtown—this was where Ivan Tcherepnin raised the question of what it would mean to see experimental music enmeshed with big business and big government.[100] Nevertheless, a conference of arts presenters met in tandem with the festival, which birthed the idea that it should go national and travel to different cities each year as New Music America. Over the following years, festivals were held in Minneapolis, San Francisco, Chicago, Washington DC, Hartford, and other cities, and New Music America's bureaucracy swelled. For the 1985 festival in Los Angeles, parent organization New Music Alliance received 600 proposals, which were reviewed by a thirty-plus-person local screening committee whose reviews were then examined by a national advisory board, and the submissions were narrowed down to twenty-five presenters and thirty-seven events.[101]

In November 1989, New Music America returned to New York for its tenth anniversary—six months after Gann had critiqued the festival as splintered and diluted in comparison to Bang on a Can. Gann was not mistaken: the festival sprawled to almost a hundred events in twenty-three venues across New York City. Overseen by the Brooklyn Academy of Music, the events included Phill Niblock at Experimental Intermedia, Musica Elettronica Viva at the Knitting Factory, and Butch Morris at the Whitney Art Museum, among many, many other acts. Major support came from BAM's Next Wave, which was itself funded by a $350,000 grant from Philip Morris. The festival also received more than $100,000 in support from a consortium of major record label executives, who were hoping to capitalize on avant-garde music in the wake of Glass's and Laurie Anderson's recent commercial fame.[102]

New Music America's proliferation of events, however, meant that its audience was at times diffuse. Rockwell fretted that "Some of these festivals can fragment into a million shards, none of which seize the attention of mainstream critics and/or members of the public."[103] Rather than refracting a diverse international scene across multiple venues, Bang on a Can's marathons instead drew together many musics into one space. They had their own gripes about New Music America, too; when Lang submitted his music to the festival for consideration, he would partially cue up his tapes and mark a small dot on them, to know whether or not the jurors had actually listened to the recordings. Every year, the tapes were returned untouched and unheard. "It was clear that I had not risen to the level of someone who was worth evaluating," he remembered.[104] To avoid programming only familiar or favorite names, Bang on a Can instituted a blind evaluation process. Gordon, Lang, and Wolfe solicited tapes from the new-music community, which they would listen to together; only if all three agreed on a piece would they consider programming it for the festival. Bang on a Can regularly commissioned young and unknown composers that were selected from these nationwide calls.[105]

But a more significant difference between the two festivals lay in aesthetic orientation, curatorial purview, and how they ultimately defined "new music." In a 1982 profile of Glenn Branca, who taught his electric guitar symphonies to performers through oral instruction and unconventional notation, Rockwell described a "post-literate avant-gardism that has sprung up in the electronic era—an era in which the recording studio and electronics provide the 'permanent' documentation that written notation used to provide."[106] Post-literate avant-gardism was, broadly speaking, the ethos of New Music America: Cagean indeterminacy, experimental improvisation, and live electronics overseen by radically pluralist composer-performers.[107] Despite its institutionalization, the festival represented what composer and 1985 New Music America organizer Carl Stone described as "work that exists outside the commercial and academic mainstream."[108] Rockwell frequently noted that these tendencies meant that New Music America rarely included new music from the classical tradition. As he said in 1989, "Theoretically, NMA festivals would welcome Milton Babbitt and Elliott Carter and Charles Wuorinen, and for that matter William Bolcom and David Del Tredici; practically, they shy away from anything with a direct indebtedness to mainstream classical vocal and instrumental traditions."[109]

But Wolfe, Gordon, and Lang were not post-literate. Despite their renegade inclinations, they ultimately belonged to that mainstream lineage of Carter and Del Tredici. "We all fall into the category of composed music," Wolfe told Rockwell in 1990, "Music created by one individual that is written down." [110] This was yet another way in which Bang on a Can saw themselves as integrating uptown and downtown—they combined academia's notated scores written for virtuosic, classically-trained performers with the minimalist rhythms, cross-genre influences, and amplification of experimentalism.

Lang once complained that at the Knitting Factory—the downtown club that opened in 1987 and quickly became the home for improvisers such as John Zorn—musicians would be booed if they had music stands. In that scene, he recalled, "written music is something that gets in the way of you expressing yourself."[111] The three composers, however, had all decided that music stands were necessary. Lang had his Bay Area experimental phase and flirted with Sheep's Clothing, but ultimately dedicated himself to densely conceived chamber and orchestral compositions; Gordon gave up his rock band to focus on composing for his aptly-named Philharmonic, which played from fully-conceived scores; and Wolfe left her Michigan theater troupe for Yale because she wanted to compose in more large-scale musical forms. "If you weren't interested in improvised music, there was no place to go," Gordon told Gann in 1993 about when he first started out in New York. "The improvisers weren't the continuation of the scene around Reich and Glass, they came more from jazz and rock. Our generation, the postminimal generation, heard classical music, pop, jazz, folk, world music from different cultures. We were open to all these influences."[112] Downtown improvisers were certainly open to pop, jazz, folk, and world music from different cultures, but Bang on a Can mediated those influences through the traditional notation of classical music.

And Bang on a Can readily conscripted similarly minded allies such as the composer Lois V Vierk. Inspired by her study of Japanese gagaku, Vierk wrote cacophonous music for massed ensembles, such as the 1981 *Go Guitars*, in which five electric guitars assemble a grueling groove out of chromatic bends and twanging glissandos. ("The entire piece should be quite LOUD," she notes in the score.[113]) With a sound resembling that of Branca, and performances at Experimental Intermedia, Vierk might seem a quintessentially downtown figure. But she meticulously notated all of her pieces, and did not herself perform them. Downtown musicians, she recalled, were not interested in or even skilled enough to play from her scores; "I needed the musicians from uptown," she later said, "but they hated the music, or they didn't know about it."[114] Often citing Vierk as an example of the kind of composer who didn't have a clear home before their festival, Bang on a Can programmed *Go Guitars* on the 1989 marathon, as well as two more of her works in 1987 and 1991. That's not to say that Bang on a Can did not also feature improvisers and composer-performers—and the music of downtown guru Cage was a perennial highlight—but it was clear from their early years on that their broader stance was distinct from that of New Music America.

Gann praised Bang on a Can over New Music America precisely because their engagement with such a longstanding tradition as conventional notation seemed radical at the time. "In a scene that settled into automatic pilot around '84, BoaC reminds us every year that there are ways to make new music besides improvisation and computers," he wrote in 1990.[115] When first visiting the marathon in 1988, he had praised it for representing the "missing center" between uptown and downtown, and as he tracked festivals over the years, occasionally devoting two full weekly columns to what he saw, he described Bang on a Can as illuminating "widespread collective changes in how American music is made."[116] He first dubbed their aesthetic "New Dissonance" in 1990 and then more precisely theorized it as "totalism" in 1993. Emblematized in works by Gordon and Evan Ziporyn, the style, as Gann characterized it, drew the rhythmic structures of minimalism and the mathematical complexities of serialism into a discordant idiom.[117] Gann returned to the term again and again, aligning it with what he heard at Bang on a Can and consecrating the directors' uptown-downtown narrative. Writers from the *New York Times* and other publications soon picked it up.[118] Some critics, however, were not so sure that the festival's aesthetic vision could be so neatly summarized. "In the end, it is impossible, or would at best be wildly inaccurate, to try to say anything coherent about Bang on a Can," wrote critic Mark Swed in a review of the 1992 festival in *American Record Guide*. "Bang on a Can's value is its open door policy."[119]

As Bang on a Can settled into an institution with a clear mission, there was understandable skepticism among some downtowners about a changing of the guard. In a 1990 review of Bang on a Can in *EAR Magazine*, one of the principal media outlets for the downtown scene, David LL Laskin commended the festival's camaraderie, energy, and enthusiastic audiences, but also sounded a note of caution.[120] He praised an improvised trombone set by George Lewis—an impromptu performance after the composer's computer configuration failed to function—as a bludgeon against what he heard as an otherwise stale homogeneity across the festival as a whole, lashing out at the very things that Gann praised. There was "too much consonance (or timid dissonance), too much in the post-minimalist orbit, too many performers engaged with scores."

"Why," Laskin asked, "after 50 years of radical experimentation, do we find ourselves faced with the deadeningly conventional setup of performers sequestered up on a stage, behind the 'fourth wall,' hidden behind music stands (icons of text and often disembodiment, literally, from the point of view of the audience), reading what for the most part sound like conventionally notated pieces? Even John Cage's randomly composed *Six Melodies* sounded nice. There is a place for these devices, but there must be room for others, too. These are issues involving and questioning the entire community of composers, performers, presenters, and listeners."[121] Engaging with scores signaled a reversal of the anti-hierarchical practices—the scrambling of traditional boundaries between composer, performer, and listener—fostered downtown for decades. A historical shift was underway, one that Laskin saw as contrary to a half-century-old anti-institutional and anti-academic revolution originally led by Cage and his cohort.

Laskin added, though, that Bang on a Can was a worthy endeavor that "fills an important musical gap vacated, for the most part, by the itinerant, annual New Music America."[122] As it turns out, the New Music America held in Montreal that year was the festival's last hurrah. It had grown to such a size that few funders or producers were willing to sponsor it. In the wake of economic recession, the New Music Alliance decided to scale down the festival into New Music (Across) America, which would involve smaller events spread across multiple cities. This decision had been made at a meeting held in conjunction with the June 1991 Bang on a Can festival. Shortly after, *EAR* proclaimed that Bang on a Can had become "a cornerstone of the new music scene in this country" and was "taking over a role left vacant by New Music America."[123] One festival was buried, another consecrated.

This transitional moment signaled much more than a shift in aesthetics. As New Music, New York swelled into New Music America, it acquired the administrative heft of governing committees, local organizers, formal submission guidelines, and collaborative dialogues between multiple presenters, alongside ceaseless debate among participating musicians about what the festival represented, what its future should be, and what kinds of compromises it might make with capital and the state. Yet while Gann attacked New Music America for its entrenched interests and compromises between stakeholders that made a bloated and unwieldy artistic experience, its bureaucracy also offered a semblance of democratic representation for the downtown scene. The traveling format, rotating curatorship, and advisory board meant that the festival could serve a broad constituency of musicians who actively participated in its administration. Carl Stone, who co-organized the 1985 Los Angeles chapter of New Music America with Joan La Barbara, recalled that the bureaucracy was at times chaotic, and that each festival was largely planned by the local committee, but that "We wanted it to be democratic, in that there should be some kind of application process, not just the taste of the artistic director."[124] He also noted that the festivals maintained a "democratic fee" system, in which superstars like Glass and young unknowns were paid the same rate.

With their blind tape submissions, claims to stylistic inclusiveness, and an unwritten policy to treat luminaries and newcomers equally, Bang on a Can gestured heavily toward democracy. But it was entirely controlled by three artistic directors, with no rotation of curatorship. This tightknit management gave the festival a well-defined and powerfully articulated artistic agenda, which provided the early marathons with a freshness and ingenuity that was widely heralded in comparison to New Music America. Yet while Bang on a Can's programming was musically invigorating, the broad array of composers they promoted did not participate in how the festival was governed. Bang on a Can brought together the music of uptown and downtown—*Vision and Prayer* and *Four Organs*—but, unlike Meet the Composer, they did not necessarily bring together the actual people of uptown and downtown—Babbitt and Reich, who managed to avoid each other in 1987.

And for the founders, Bang on a Can's entrepreneurialism could serve as a defense against critique, even as the organization became increasingly established. "People now come to BoaC to stand at the back and complain," Lang told Gann in 1993. "They tell us, 'You're not representing our music.' We say, 'Well, when we started out, no one was representing our music. Go out and start your own festival.' The more festivals we have, the better."[125] (Gann himself would soon become one of the complainants.) Lang envisioned an industry comprising dozens of upstart new-music organizations that could represent many musical worlds. In the early 1990s, though, Bang on a Can was seen as the sole replacement for New Musical America, not one among an array of festival start-ups. And there was little opportunity for other composers to petition Bang on a Can, or to change the organization from within, as there was with New Music America.

But it was precisely the flexibility and nimbleness of Bang on a Can—the fact that it was a top-down organization whose scope was determined by only three composers—that helped them endure, and even expand, in moments of economic downturn. They did not need to serve multiple constituencies, negotiate the needs of different presenters, or satisfy different factions. New Music America began when a conference of arts professionals met to brainstorm ways to strengthen the support system for musicians nationwide; Bang on a Can launched from three young composers carping about their professional prospects at diners and in their kitchens. Such foundational differences guided the future of both organizations. New Music America invited participation, but it was doomed in part because of its administrative weight. Bang on a Can endured due to their agility and focused strategy, one that would be continually refined as the organization grew into the next decade.

4
Funding

A few weeks before Bang on a Can presented their fifth festival in June 1991, they found themselves without a venue. RAPP Arts Center, the multi-purpose Lower East Side space where the organization had held their past three marathons, was owned by the Church of the Most Holy Redeemer. That previous September, the center's founder and producer, Jeffrey Cohen, had had deliberately provoked the church by staging "The Cardinal Detoxes," a play about a real-life bishop who had killed a pregnant woman while driving inebriated. The Roman Catholic Archdiocese of New York attempted to shut down the play and even padlock the theater, on the grounds that Cohen had signed a morality clause in order to rent the space.[1] Although the church succeeded in evicting RAPP, it had agreed to honor existing contracts with organizations subleasing the venue, including Bang on a Can. In the spring, however, the Archdiocese stated that the center's auditorium was unsafe, in need of crucial repairs, and thus unable to host the festival.

"I did not want to get into this argument," Michael Gordon told a reporter for *Newsday*. "I've got a festival, there are thousands of people coming down, I sent out forty thousand pieces of mail. If there are violations in the building, it's the church's obligation to fix them."[2] But they weren't fixed, and Bang on a Can scrambled to seek alternative spaces, losing tens of thousands of dollars in the process.[3] Concerts of music by Glenn Branca and Arnold Dreyblatt were moved to La Mama, and performances of Harry Partch's *The Wayward* were relocated to Circle in the Square. David Lang stood outside RAPP, holding a sign directing audiences to the alternative venues. "We are starting again from zero," John Cage declared at the opening of the marathon, held at La Mama. "Our arts are coming alive."[4]

Legitimate questions of whether the arts might again start from zero—as in, zero government funding—floated about in Bang on a Can's early years. These questions were not entirely unrelated to "The Cardinal Detoxes" and similar battles between boundary-pushing artists and conservative religious leaders. Seemingly minor local incidents like the RAPP Arts Center's programming were framed within the so-called Culture Wars, a referendum on post-'60s society waged between left and right that, as Andrew Hartman writes, became "the defining metaphor for the late-twentieth-century United States."[5] Back in 1989, spurred by the religious right's attacks on avant-garde art it deemed obscene, congressional Republicans had battled to defund the National Endowment for the Arts and leave American artists to depend entirely on the free market to support themselves. As part of a compromise to hold onto its funding, the NEA required artists receiving grants to sign a pledge that their work was not obscene. Morality clauses were in the air.

In a 1989 article, Lang reacted to the congressional debates and their implications for the world of new music. "Artists like to feel that their work is challenging enough to be controversial," he wrote. "Photographers, painters, filmmakers and the like can imagine victimization at the hands of Congress as a badge of honor. They are Art-martyrs to the First Amendment."[6]

"With all of the excitement," Lang fretted, "it is disturbing that so little of this controversy is aimed at composers. Are we not controversial? Why isn't Congress rushing to censor the subversive power of modern music? It is possible that we are doing something wrong."[7] Taking a somewhat strident tone, Lang listed the reasons why contemporary music might have been overlooked by politicians, such as its abstraction and the traditionalist training of its composers. But Lang ultimately singled out one central culprit. "It could be that our natural inclinations toward good behavior have combined with a more recent phenomenon—a colossal loss of nerve," he wrote. As the academic avant-garde imagined in Milton Babbitt's "Who Cares if You Listen?" essay faded, he added, composers were looking to work with mainstream institutions and reach large audiences, and thus "there are a lot of people we can't afford to offend."

Lang's principal scapegoat was "polite music," "music that has purged itself of the spirit of exploration" that was "designed to impress an audience, not to provoke it." (He does not name musical styles, but he might have been thinking of the New Romantic fare at Horizons '83.) Lang's argument might seem to contradict Bang on a Can's audience-oriented aims, but it actually fit their agenda neatly, aligning with their programming of early Reich and early Babbitt at the 1987 festival: they wanted to attract audiences with, rather than despite, provocative and off-putting music. Lang does not dwell at all on the actual repercussions of new congressional oversight for living composers, nor on the perils of potentially massive cuts to federal arts funding. Instead, he uses the Culture Wars as a pretext to make his own point about the state of contemporary composition. "We need to work harder to challenge those standards, to chase the politeness out of the world," he concludes. "After all, Congress says we are dangerous. It is up to us to prove it."[8]

In one sense, Lang was right. Contemporary composition was not a target of conservative ire, although it seems unlikely that "the new politeness" was actually to blame. But new music was collateral damage in the Culture Wars, swept up in the developments that the religious right set into motion, and not just when the Catholic Church abruptly declared its venues uninhabitable. National politics barged in on, and ultimately intensified, new music's marketplace turn, as cuts to government subsidy through the 1980s and 1990s jeopardized one of its principal sources of support. Moreover, there was real controversy within new music. But it was less about aesthetics than institutions. When the New York State Council on the Arts attempted to implement hot-button cultural policy around multiculturalism, neoconservative composers and critics strongly protested, deploying rhetoric that aligned with the national debates. These disputes shaped which institutions survived a period of increasing arts austerity, one in which Bang on a Can flourished as some of their peers foundered. The Culture Wars formed a crucial context for Bang on a Can's growth—a remarkable ascent from a budget of $10,300 to more than $429,000 in their first decade—as the organization fitfully, but ultimately successfully, navigated a new political climate.

We Raise All This Money

The story of the struggles around arts funding in the 1990s begins back in 1965 with the founding of the National Endowment for the Arts, created as an independent agency alongside the National Endowment for the Humanities. As historian Donna Binkiewicz recounts, the Endowments served a Cold War agenda. Domestically, they provided cultural analogues to Lyndon Johnson's Great Society, a means for the arts and humanities to serve as social uplift; internationally, Binkiewicz writes, the programs helped "outshine the Soviets in cultural displays and by so doing entice developing nations away from the lures of communist culture."[9] The congressional act that established the Endowments declared that "An advanced civilization must not limit its efforts to science and technology alone but must give full value and support to the other great branches of scholarly and cultural activity in order to achieve a better understanding of the past, a better analysis of the present, and a better view of the future."[10]

The NEA's first annual budget was a mere $2.5 million (equivalent to about $20.6 million today). Unlike European systems of patronage, the Endowment was not designed to act as a primary means of support for artists and institutions. Instead, inspired in part by the postwar granting of the Rockefeller and Ford foundations, the NEA served as the central component of a patchwork system that included government funding—at the federal, state, and local level—alongside corporate, foundation, and individual donations. As the second chairman of the program, Nancy Hanks, would frequently quip, "In America we have this unique pluralism in arts support—federal—state—municipal—private sources."[11]

But the NEA did create a crucial national dialogue around the arts. With a newly established system of review, in which panels of peer artist "experts" assessed funding applications, the Endowment's adjudication of grants was widely viewed as a guide to how and what the private sector might support: the imprimatur provided by an NEA grant, or what was colloquially known as a governmental "seal of approval," provided prestige for further fundraising.[12] The NEA's participation in the so-called "arts boom"—the massive postwar growth in arts organizations, artists, and audiences in the United States—also structurally reoriented American institutions. As James Allen Smith writes, "Nonprofit organizations, increasingly professional in their work, would become the dominant mechanism for organizing cultural activity in the United States."[13]

In its early years, the NEA was plagued by various minor controversies, but its budget nevertheless expanded through the Nixon, Ford, and Carter administrations. Programs were divided by discipline, and adjudicating panelists selected from artists in those fields. The Music division grew consistently through these years, from a budget of $83,575 in 1966 to $15,280,425 in 1984.[14] Although first focused on assisting symphony orchestras and opera companies, the Music program steadily broadened its reach to become a crucial means of support for new music, funding fellowships to individual composers, consortium commissions, and, beginning in the mid-1980s, a composer-in-residence project. By that decade, additional funding came from a New Music Performance category that sponsored ensembles; the Inter-Arts division, founded in 1982 to support mixed-media works; and Opera-Theater's New American Works initiative. The NEA's Composer Fellowships were largely awarded to figures associated with the academy—74 percent of its awardees between 1979 and 1985 held academic positions, and half of those awarded came from only eight universities.[15] But national funding also began to reach more experimental composers, as the Inter-Arts and New Music Performance categories supported figures like Steve Reich and Pauline Oliveros.[16]

A challenge grant program, first established in 1976, leveraged federal support to spur investment in the arts from private donors. Through the 1970s and 1980s, large corporations such as Philip Morris and Exxon developed their own major arts initiatives, often in partnership with or taking cues from the Endowment. Total corporate support for the arts ballooned from

$22 million in 1965 to more than $500 million in 1983.[17] Corporate donations were the largest source of growth for arts funding during the Reagan era, and foundations provided crucial support as well. In the world of new music, this mixed approach was epitomized in the Orchestra Residencies Program, Meet the Composer's multi-million dollar partnership with Exxon, the Rockefeller Foundation, and the NEA, which was mentioned in a 1984 Endowment guidebook titled "Business and the Arts."[18] Similarly representative was the Brooklyn Academy of Music's Next Wave Festival, backed by hundreds of thousands of dollars from Philip Morris. (When the tobacco company was thanked before performances, audience members would loudly cough in protest.[19])

Corporate backing expanded under Reagan in part because the administration celebrated private funding while attempting to severely curtail government support. Running against the liberal social programs of the Great Society, Reagan's campaign platform focused on reducing the size of the federal government and encouraging market competition. Soon after his inauguration, newspapers began to report that the administration was considering significant cuts to the NEA and NEH. Reagan's Budget Book, which took much of its free market policy direction from the conservative Heritage Foundation, argued speciously that the two endowments had "resulted in a reduction in the historic role of private individual and corporate philanthropic support."[20]

The administration proposed a massive 50% cut to the NEA, galvanizing immediate pushback among arts advocates, including congressional opposition led by Representative Sidney Yates, the longtime Democratic champion of the NEA. Reagan launched a Presidential Task Force on the Arts and Humanities, co-chaired by Charlton Heston, in the hopes that it would investigate private sector solutions, but the Task Force argued for endowment funding to be perpetuated. Following months of congressional budget hearings, the administration abandoned its plan and instead made less substantive cuts to the endowments' budgets. By 1984, the budgets for the NEA and NEH were restored nearly to their 1981 dollar amount; when accounting for inflation, though, the real dollar value of the NEA decreased through the 1980s.[21]

Corporate support as well as state arts budgets, which expanded during the 1980s amidst economic growth, helped make up for those losses. And Reagan found other ways to advance his ideological commitment to free enterprise. Along with changing tax policy to allow corporations to write off large arts donations as charitable contributions, he launched a President's Committee on Arts and Humanities—comprising agency heads, celebrities, and CEOs— to promote private sector support, and helped create the National Medal of

Arts, which recognized both artists and corporate donors. As Chin-Tao Wu critically notes, the Committee set up the government to serve "as fundraiser rather than simply as funder," swapping out the Endowment for "the personal aura of the President, and removed from the arena of open democratic debate."[22]

The American Music Center's newsletter maintained a "Washington News" column that kept composers up-to-date—and irate—about the Reagan administration's decisions. A 1981 article reported that "Reagan's presidential assault on the arts could have serious long range consequences for new music performance and composition throughout the country" and called for composers to "rebuff the Reagan/Stockman 'plan' for arts support in this country with all possible effort."[23] The next year, the newsletter featured an editorial by the AMC's president declaring that "No one who is paying attention needs to be told that the status of American music is changing and not for the better," and reprinted a speech by composer Ezra Laderman, a past director of the Endowment's Music division, arguing that "it is of the utmost importance that we insist on the fiscal health and continued effectiveness of the NEA."[24] (Laderman cited the Orchestra Residencies Program as an exemplar of how the NEA's "stamp of approval" and "catalytic funding" could enlist corporate support.[25]) This was the political backdrop for new music's marketplace turn, as a Reagan-era NEA, under the direction of chairman Frank Hodsoll, advocated for public-private partnerships like the New York Philharmonic's Horizons festivals—splashy, well-publicized, and undergirded by corporate philanthropy.

Public funding was still strong—but waning—in Bang on a Can's early years, and the George H.W. Bush administration continued Reagan's work of advocating for institutions to seek out non-governmental support. Bang on a Can's initial $10,300 budget combined a $1,500 grant from Meet the Composer—which packaged together public, corporate, and foundation support—with ticket sales and individual donations from family and friends. The festival's beginnings were somewhat ramshackle, an all-volunteer endeavor mostly organized in Lang, Gordon, and Wolfe's kitchens. Wolfe recalled a meeting around 1990 with Gayle Morgan, the director of the Mary Flagler Cary Trust's music granting, in which the founders told her that "It's incredible, we raise all this money and it all goes to the artists! We're not skimming off money for anything else, it's all going to the performers!" As Wolfe tells it, Morgan retorted, wisely, "You are not going to survive. You're going to burn out: you have no structure to keep things going."[26]

The trio took such administrative advice readily, and learned lessons quickly. That year, the Cary Trust awarded Bang on a Can a "special grant to strengthen administration," which they used to hire a part-time administrator and launch a more aggressive fundraising strategy.[27] They put together an information packet attached to grant proposals that provided detailed budget information, a list of "festival highlights," and statements of purpose reiterating the organization's origins, their support of composers, and their successes in building audiences. These efforts went far beyond applications by comparable organizations like Experimental Intermedia and Speculum Musicae.[28] Bang on a Can received increasing support from the National Endowment for the Arts: its first direct grant in 1989 was for $3,500, and it was awarded $6,000 in 1990, and $6,600 in both 1991 and 1992. The supercharged, feisty rhetoric that they brought to their PR permeated their fundraising efforts as well. "Have there been any significant changes or developments in your organization since it was last reviewed by the Council?" asked a form question on a 1990 New York State Council on the Arts funding application. "It's bigger, it's better, and it's badder," Bang on a Can responded.[29]

The work quickly paid off. Bang on a Can's most remarkable leap in funding took place between 1990 and 1991, when the organization's annual income ballooned from around $85,340 to $216,685—a more than twentyfold increase from the budget of their first festival, hitting a level they maintained through the early 1990s.[30] The largest factor in that increase was $130,750 provided by fifteen different foundations, including $20,000 from the Cary Trust, $10,000 from John Cage's Foundation for Contemporary Performance Arts, $25,000 from Pew Charitable Trust, $20,000 from Lila Wallace, and a whopping $25,750 from three Meet the Composer programs (Figure 4.1).[31]

In 1992, they hired Rebecca Sayles as executive director—particularly necessary as Wolfe and Gordon spent much of that year living in Amsterdam—and began renting a small office space. The following year, Gordon, Lang, and Wolfe founded Red Poppy Music, an independent publishing company to represent their music.[32] And in 1994, Bang on a Can received a major, three-year expansion grant from Chamber Music America, a program designed to help organizations transition from volunteer to paid management, that allowed them to hire two full-time staffers. The role of director went to Bette Snapp, who had previously worked for major music publishers, maintained her own promotional firm for composers, and begun serving as Bang on a Can's publicist in 1990. Karen Sander, a young administrator who had previously worked for the Metropolitan Opera's education department, became the organization's manager.[33] (Sayles had left the organization before these hires.) "I thought Bang on a Can was slightly miraculous as its audience had such a good time at contemporary music concerts," Snapp said in a press release

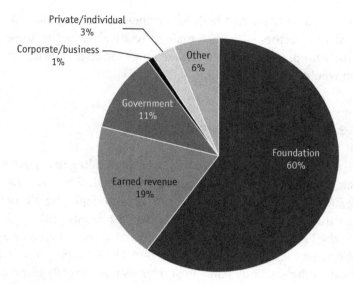

Figure 4.1 Bang on a Can's income in 1991 (total of $216,685)

announcing her new position. "The potential for growth is just enormous. My job now is to be able to make the visions happen."[34]

And she did. The new staff, as a foundation funding request put it later that year, "have begun the process of transforming our energy and passion for Bang on a Can into a 'grown up' organization that will have the structures to thrive and grow. Already they have put in place a computerized accounting system, a database, a fundraising plan and are working with a consultant to develop a long range plan."[35] The letter characterized the moment as "our transition from a volunteer organization to a professional one."[36] Sander assisted in the day-to-day activities of the organization, from grant-writing to concert production to organizing tours for the new All-Stars ensemble. "All of us were like, 'Let's go for it,'" she said about fundraising in this period. "Let's take whatever opportunities there are."[37] The small administrative team spent long nights at Lang's loft refining the language of their annual appeal letter to individual donors, and hosted letter-stuffing parties to send them out. This was the kind of activity that most composers were not only not particularly good at, but also highly uninterested in devoting time to. But the Bang on a Can trio seemed to pursue fundraising with the same single-minded devotion they gave to every aspect of their organization's development. "Everything we thought about," Sander recalled, "from how we're going to write the fundraising letters to having an equal amount of passion and discussion about who's going to be on the next show."[38] Money wasn't everything: they only invited people who knew and believed in their artistic mission to serve on their board of directors—which remained relatively small in these years—limiting their fundraising potential in exchange for assurance that their creative vision would not be compromised.

Test the Magic of the Marketplace

While Bang on a Can expanded, a battle over the funding of art in the United States was unfolding. In 1989, right-wing religious leaders became enraged over *Piss Christ*, a photograph by Andres Serrano depicting a crucifix submerged in the artist's urine, shown in a North Carolina exhibit indirectly funded by the NEA. Having already protested what they perceived as an immoral, liberal arts intelligentsia when the film *The Last Temptation of Christ* was in theaters the previous year, conservatives now directly targeted a government agency for promoting blasphemy. Worried about similar controversies, the Corcoran Gallery in Washington preemptively cancelled a large-scale exhibit of photographs by Robert Mapplethorpe, who had died of AIDS earlier that year, which included several explicit depictions of gay sex acts as well as images of nude children. Serrano and Mapplethorpe became lightning rods for an uproar among Republicans in Congress, who debated whether the Endowment should be defunded or significantly restricted; a newly galvanized and well-organized evangelical movement accused the Endowment of promoting profanity and pornography. As Senator Alphonse D'Amato put it while tearing up a reproduction of the Serrano on the Senate floor: "This is not a question of free speech. This is a question of abuse of taxpayer's money."[39]

Evangelical conservatives deployed emerging right-wing radio and television outlets, as well as massive mailing lists, to disseminate hyperbolic tales of an Endowment that directly subsidized child pornography and dipping crucifixes in urine. "The enclosed red envelope contains graphic descriptions of homosexual erotic photographs that were funded by your tax dollars," stated one mailer, which announced the launch of a new Christian Coalition, and included bluntly exaggerated summaries of the most controversial Mapplethorpe photographs. "Your hard earned tax dollars paid for this trash."[40] The Endowment was now wrapped up in the Culture Wars, caught in the onslaught with everything from public school and college curricula to hip-hop lyrics and Scorcese films.[41] Arts funding became a pawn in the religious right's assault on George H.W. Bush's presidency. When paleoconservative Pat Buchanan, who frequently railed against the NEA, later ran against Bush in the 1992 Republican primary, he declared in his convention speech that he was launching a "war for the soul of America," one "as critical to the kind of nation we will one day be as was the Cold War itself."[42]

Back in the summertime skirmishes of 1989, though, the leader of the unfolding Culture Wars was the right-wing senator Jesse Helms, from North Carolina. Helms introduced an amendment to restrict federal funding for "obscene or indecent" art including "homo-eroticism" and "material which denigrates the objects or beliefs of the adherents of a particular religion."[43] Outright homophobia undergirded the right's objections to the Endowment, and the same politicians and religious leaders calling Mapplethorpe a pervert also heatedly opposed government intervention in the AIDS crisis. Despite fierce resistance to the "Helms amendment" from the arts world, gay activists, and the congressional Democrat majority, a fall 1989 appropriations bill nonetheless restricted the NEA and NEH from funding work "considered obscene," including "depictions of sadomasochism, homoeroticism, the sexual exploitation of children or individuals engaged in sex acts" that "do not have serious literary, artistic, political or scientific value."[44] It was amidst the passing of this policy that Lang penned his article on the "new politeness."

To execute the new amendment, John Frohnmayer, Bush's NEA chairman, created a so-called "loyalty oath" that grant recipients were required to sign pledging that their work would not violate the new obscenity guidelines. Famous artists such as the theater producer Joseph Papp refused NEA funding on principle. Frohnmayer took it upon himself to overturn a panel recommendation to support four controversial performance artists, most prominently Karen Finley, who became known as the NEA Four when they sued the Endowment. The anti-obscenity guidelines, loyalty oath, and NEA Four's court case forced figures in the world of new music to respond. Pauline Oliveros and her collaborator Ione accepted Endowment funding for a music-theater project but they wrote to *EAR Magazine* that "we added the following language to the contract: 'We comply insofar as this clause is constitutional.'"[45] They added: "We decided that returning the money was just what Jesse Helms et al would want us to do. We ultimately decided that we could be more effective by taking the money to do work that deals with the issues that oppress us most—racism and sexism."[46]

Meet the Composer, which had lobbied against Helms's efforts, accepted its NEA grants so as to not endanger large-scale projects such as the Orchestra Residencies Program. "This unreasonable interference in our activities will not deter us from our mission," Duffy wrote to Frohnmayer in protest. "We shall not compromise trust in the hundreds of composers and musical organizations who participate in our programs. We will not investigate their morality, probe their politics, question their integrity, nor dismiss their commitment to the furtherance of American musical arts."[47] A group of experimental composers that included Oliveros, Laurie Anderson, and James Tenney gathered at a Telluride conference in July 1990, formed a legal defense fund for musicians, and issued a manifesto stating that "We abhor censorship in all forms. We commit ourselves to achieving massive increases in the level and breadth of support for art in our society and in all societies."[48] Congress did not renew the anti-obscenity pledge in 1990, instead passing a less stringent requirement that the Endowment's granting consider "general standards of decency and respect."[49] And Bush would sack Frohnmayer in 1992 as Buchanan pressed him to take a more aggressive stance on the NEA during his campaign for reelection.

The principal discussion in the endless media coverage and editorials surrounding this node of the Culture Wars focused on censorship and freedom of speech. But infusing the Endowment debates was also the question of whether artists deserved government support. In a 1989 press release denouncing the NEA's funding "for pornography and anti-Christian bigotry," the American Family Association proclaimed: "Let the NEA and the artists they support meet the same test as other artists in our society—the demand of the marketplace. The NEA will still receive their millions from private grants, and if the 'works of art' have merit they will succeed in the marketplace."[50] During the Senate debates, Helms asked why the government was "supporting artists the taxpayers have refused to support in the marketplace." He asserted, "No artist has a preemptive claim on the tax dollars of the American people; time for them, as President Reagan used to say, 'to go out and test the magic of the marketplace.'"[51]

Opponents of the conservative view rightfully argued that government funding gave artists necessary independence from commercialism and thus the opportunity for a critical stance of the kind that Oliveros and Ione described to *EAR*. As one San Francisco-based poet put it, "The marketplace can give us Teenage Mutant Ninja Turtles but it takes public support to give us Sesame Street; corporate sponsorship can give us evenings at Lincoln Center, but it takes public support—as well as the grit of the artist—to bring us frank expositions of race, sexuality, politics and other controversial subjects."[52] In another *EAR Magazine* piece, David LL Laskin contrasted stories of Chinese and Indonesian musicians, who faced direct government censorship and oppression, with the condition of American artists: "American hegemony tends to shy away from such police tactics; rather, with popular culture and democratic ideology as filters, Americans 'freely' choose the self-enforcement of the marketplace—a more subtle, and perhaps more insidious, method of control."[53]

At the same time, though, there were those in new music who placed some of their faith in the free market—in rhetoric if not in action. "The healthiest thing for the arts is for them to be profit-making," Duffy told Laskin in a 1991 *EAR* interview, echoing, and perhaps also escalating, the arguments he made about the role of the marketplace a decade earlier. "Composers should come to a certain point where they earn a living from their work and they don't have to rely on government or private support."[54] Although Duffy noted that many composers created work that "doesn't easily satisfy the public," and would continue to require non-profit support, he singled out Philip Glass, Steve Reich, and Laurie Anderson as model artists who "earn their living from writing and performing their own music."[55] Laskin countered that though Glass might compose film scores, his operas and much of his other work were still "supported by the non-profit sector" and "hooked into the classical establishment." Even the most successful composers, Laskin argued, were "not making a living in the capitalist world; they're surviving on the non-profit world."[56]

Questioning Duffy's approach, Laskin wondered about the role of the artist in societies "where money may not exist." Uninterested in such anticommercial utopianism, Duffy responded bluntly: "We don't live in a tribal society. We live in a capitalist society. We live in a society where people earn a living, sell their wares, where they deal with the marketplace in one fashion or another. How can one best function in that situation?"[57] Duffy did not share the skepticism or hostility toward the corporate world that Laskin and his downtown comrades harbored. Having once described corporations as contemporary Medicis and Esterházys, Duffy told *EAR* that "People in corporations are not all monsters. They care."[58]

Still, Duffy's free market aims were more aspirational than practical. As Laskin pointed out, Glass and Reich might appear to be prototypes for what an artist's career looked like if they were supported by the free market, but in reality they were not. This was, after all, why Meet the Composer itself existed, to push composers toward the marketplace while supporting them through more traditionally non-profit means. Duffy told *EAR* that composers should be self-sustaining, but he also told the *New York Times* that NEA support was crucial to the flourishing of American music; a large slice of Meet the Composer's funding came from the federal government.[59] Duffy wanted composers to flirt with the magic of the marketplace but, unlike Helms, he vociferously defended the necessity of government funding.

Despite receiving increasing sums of public support, Bang on a Can at times expressed similar enthusiasms. As federal support for the arts waned, various non-government funders developed programs to help guide arts organizations through the new climate, such as the Arts Forward Fund, a new initiative launched in 1991 by a consortium of private donors to help applicants seek new avenues for self-sufficiency and long-term stability. When Bang on a Can applied for Arts Forward funding in 1992, they tailored their application toward these new norms, imagining a bright future in the marketplace. In the grant letter, Sayles articulated an ambitious, hypothetical vision for the organization:

> We believe that the wave of the future is a restructuring of non-profits away from the patron-artist relationship. Most non-profits traditionally look at themselves as organizations that lose money in all of their activities. This attitude has to change! Our goal is to have 50% of our revenue generated from non-traditional funding sources.[60]

Suggested "profit-making areas" included concerts by the All-Stars, recordings, radio and television appearances, and even commercial licensing of the organization's name. (The idea was floated, perhaps in jest, of "Bang on a Can Potato Chips.") "Injecting a for-profit mentality into our operations," the letter continued, might even include partnerships with airlines, hotels, and travel agencies to create packaged tours for festival attendees.

These ideas seem less like a realistic description of future plans than a bit of hype for grant-writing purposes. There would be neither Bang on a Can chips nor tour packages, nor even an actual "for-profit mentality" guiding their activities. The application does not appear to have been successful, and the All-Stars and their recordings became Bang on a Can's most dedicated marketplace efforts, ones that were aimed toward growing their audience internationally and increasing their earned income—non-profit revenue generated from sales and services, rather than from grants or donations. But Sayles's letter evinces an organization that could see itself aligned with the ethos of Duffy rather than that of Laskin. Even if this agenda were designed to appeal to a specific granter, it would be hard to imagine Experimental Intermedia or Speculum Musicae, not to mention Bang on a Can's leftist precursor Sheep's Clothing, dreaming up branded snacks and airline partnerships. At times, Bang on a Can seemed to imagine that capitalism was less of an impediment to artistic creation than a potential tool for institutional growth.

Encouraging Diversity

Not all of Bang on a Can's peers experienced such growth. Other new-music institutions struggled in response to a changing set of conditions tied to another component of the Culture Wars. Buchanan, Helms, and their rightwing coalitions were representative of the paleoconservative movement, populists who railed against the NEA because of its purported elitism and denigration of Christianity. In protesting the Endowment, they were joined by a faction of neoconservatives, who instead defended elite notions of high art and saw the NEA as a politicized entity that threatened the Western canon. Whereas paleoconservatives wanted to destroy the Endowment entirely, neoconservatives such as art critic Hilton Kramer and music critic Samuel Lipman wanted to rebuild it according to their own ideological aims. As *Time Magazine* put it in 1989, "Neoconservatives want to keep the NEA because they would like to run it. Paleos like Helms don't greatly care whether it exists or not; if attacking it can serve a larger agenda, fine."[61]

With their control of radio and mailing networks, and significant congressional representation, paleoconservatives represented the true political threat to the Endowment. But neoconservatives played a key role in setting the terms for debate around government funding for the arts. Further, whereas paleoconservatives affected the world of new music obliquely, through their general attacks on public support, neoconservatism had a more direct presence in contemporary composition, as personified in Lipman and the composers Charles Wuorinen and Milton Babbitt. Neoconservatives campaigned on behalf of high art and against government-funded multiculturalism, and shaped a debate around the funding of new music by the New York State Council on the Arts in the early 1990s, refracting the national conversation around arts funding and changing the landscape of New York's new-music scene.

A gifted pianist who had given the New York premiere of Elliott Carter's Piano Concerto, Samuel Lipman studied political science at UC Berkeley, served on faculty at the Aspen Music Festival, and became music critic for the conservative journal *Commentary*, where he wrote lengthy essays on the decline of classical music. A champion of what he saw as the heroically American, midcentury modernism of Aaron Copland, Lipman had strongly negative words for more recent developments in composition: the avant-garde was "self-indulgent chaos and nihilism," the New Romanticism of Horizons '83 was "unbuttoned vulgarity," postmodernism was the "aesthetics of the cafeteria," and minimalism was "no more than a pop music for intellectuals."[62] Nearly a decade before the Helms attacks, Lipman had ghostwritten an essay on the NEA and NEH in *Mandate for Leadership*, the massive tome prepared by the Heritage Foundation to guide Reagan's first presidential administration, in collaboration with Michael S. Joyce, executive director of the conservative Olin Foundation. Writing that the Endowments had recently begun to "reveal a tendency to emphasize politically inspired social policies at the expense of the independence of the arts and the humanities," Lipman and Joyce argued that the NEA had neglected its commitment to high art and instead served as a fount for entertainment, seeking out large audiences without care to the quality of the work it supported and facilitating "greater employment of advertising and marketing techniques which cheapened when they do not actually compromise artistic content."[63] The agency, they continued, had created an overbearing arts bureaucracy preoccupied with serving "politically powerful groups" and "high-flown welfare and employment schemes."[64] Rather than "art for the sake of social service," the Endowment should exclusively support "high culture" that was "concerned with permanent values beyond current tastes and wide appeal."[65] Echoing the Heritage Foundation's central goals, art should exist "in a free market place of aesthetic ideas," and the NEA should have a lighter footprint to "lessen the predominant role of government in our lives."[66]

Such were the underlying parameters of Lipman's continued critiques of the NEA throughout the 1980s and into the Culture Wars moment of the 1990s. Populism, multiculturalism, affirmative action, and bureaucracy endangered serious culture, and the NEA perpetuated these insidious liberal ideas. Though *Mandate for Leadership*'s recommendations on the Endowments would not be taken up directly by the Reagan administration, Lipman was added to the National Council on the Arts, the citizen board that advised the NEA, in 1982. His ideas received a prominent outlet in the pages of *The New Criterion*, an arts journal launched by Lipman and *New York Times* critic Hilton Kramer that same year with $300,000 of support from the Olin Foundation.[67] The foundation stood at the forefront of conservative "dark money" spending, an ostensibly neutral non-profit that in fact advanced pro-corporate and anti-regulation interests through its advocacy for the emerging jurisprudential movement of law and economics. In the first issue of *The New Criterion*, Kramer argued that criticism had failed its duty to protect the separation between an "independent high culture" and commercial entertainment, and had lost its aesthetic disinterestedness due to post-'60s politics.[68] As Kramer put it in 1983, "Something had to be done to rescue the cultural scene from over-politicization by the left."[69] With a circulation that had by then reached 7,500, the journal served as the cultural arm of a broader attack on liberal values.

Lipman never saw eye-to-eye with Helms, and did not condone the defunding of the NEA. Nevertheless, the Culture Wars represented an ideal opportunity for the *New Criterion* crowd to articulate its own critique of government support. In the midst of the Mapplethorpe debates, Lipman contributed an editorial to the *New York Times*, titled "Say No to Trash," where he argued that NEA support should be diverted toward "the championing of the great art of the past, its regeneration in the present and its transmission to the future."[70] A direct mail campaign for the *New Criterion* in 1990 asked potential readers: "Are you offended by the claim—recently supported by the Rockefeller Foundation and the National Endowment for the Arts—that the Western tradition of classical music (Bach, Mozart, Beethoven, et al.) is now to be considered nothing more than the narrow 'ethnic' interest of a remnant of European immigrants . . . Are you apprehensive about what the politics of 'multiculturalism' is going to mean to the future of our civilization?"[71] "There is only one magazine that tells you what is right," it proclaimed.

By that point, "multiculturalism" had become a buzzword in the American arts world: promoted by foundation and government administrators, detested by conservatives, and made an explicit if only partly realized goal for arts institutions. In these contexts, multiculturalism was typically understood to signify the advocacy for art created by minority groups as well as outreach by traditional institutions to minority communities.[72] Amid the Culture Wars, it became a lightning rod for debates over how the New York State Council on the Arts should adjudicate its funding. Established in 1960 as a public funding body for the arts in New York State, NYSCA preceded the NEA and served as a model for some of its programs. As far back as the 1970s, it robustly sponsored contemporary music, funding venues such as The Kitchen and festivals like New Music, New York. It had also launched Composer in Performance, the precursor to Meet the Composer. Like the NEA, NYSCA faced cuts through the 1980s that were largely staved off by mobilization from the arts community. Under the direction of James Jordan—the cousin and long-time manager of Ornette Coleman—NYSCA's Music division increasingly supported new music, including adding a priority for programming living composers to its guidelines in 1985, and running statewide tours intended to grow audiences for new work.[73] Jordan maintained a strong commitment to funding experimental jazz and the work of Black composers, and shared Meet the Composer's marketplace ideology, seeing public funding as a means for new music to reach new listeners. He was a third interlocutor in that 1991 conversation between Duffy and *EAR*'s Laskin, where he asked, "Can you sell experimental music? I think you can. But you have to sell its humanity, its spirituality . . . It's the marketing that sells, whether it's experimental or not."[74]

In this period, NYSCA attempted to address the issue of multiculturalism, partly in response to political pressure. In 1987, it launched a program to diversify audiences for large cultural institutions like the New York Philharmonic via funding for outreach.[75] But in a series of public hearings conducted by the New York State Black and Puerto Rican Legislative Caucus, the "new audiences" initiatives were critiqued for subsidizing established institutions at the expense of smaller organizations within minority communities. The caucus organized a task force which produced a 1989 report, "Towards Cultural Democracy," lambasting NYSCA for excluding people of color from its staff and panels, and for awarding grants primarily to "Eurocentric" institutions; its minority-aimed Special Arts Service Division, for example, was continuously underfunded and required lobbying simply to stay afloat.[76] NYSCA's panel review system was itself suspect, as its "experts" were typically only familiar with Eurocentric art forms and perspectives: "People of color are always out numbered on panels and have little or no input in that decision-making process."[77]

"This is not a purely symbolic debate," sociologist Samuel Gilmore wrote of multicultural arts funding in 1993. "Rather it is a battle over the current and future allocation of scarce artistic resources."[78] Public agencies were continually and rightfully pressured by their constituents to wrestle with how to allocate arts funding across different ethnic and racial demographics. As they attempted to do so—often poorly and unfairly, as the critics in "Towards Cultural Democracy" argued—they also faced critique from *New Criterion* neoconservatives who felt that the organizations were abandoning the "permanent values" of the supposed canon of high art in favor of serving political interests. The terms of this debate mirrored contemporaneous political battles over affirmative action, in which liberals argued for the necessity of acknowledging racial difference and conservatives instead made a case for purportedly "meritocratic" colorblindness. And what unfolded at NYSCA reflected national trends in arts funding. In the final years of the 1980s, as Gilmore points out, NEA programs in multiple categories steadily increased grants awarded to minority-based initiatives (though, in proportion to the agency's total budget, such efforts still remained paltry).[79] In 1990, Frohnmayer described multiculturalism as an NEA priority, and language around it was incorporated into grant-making guidelines.

NYSCA's advocacy for multiculturalism led to an uproar in the world of new music, most vociferously voiced by Charles Wuorinen. The composer had co-founded the Group for Contemporary Music, among the first of the uptown ensembles that arose during the Cold War funding boom, which prioritized exacting performances of modernist repertoire. Wuorinen had a forbidding reputation as a stalwart and fiercely combative advocate for serial composition. In numerous interviews and profiles, he consistently articulated a pessimistic, neoconservative worldview that echoed that of Lipman, expressing concerns about populism, pluralism, and the decline of "serious culture" as emblematized in the rise of minimalist music. In a 1988 profile in the

New York Times, on the occasion of Wuorinen's fiftieth birthday, writer Joan Peyser focused on the composer's concerns that minimalism was overtaking twelve-tone music, driven by the tendency of institutions such as NYSCA to prioritize audiences over art.[80] Like Lipman and Kramer, Wuorinen traced the plight of the present moment to the late '60s: "That was the turning point. Art became capitalized, a Good Thing, something to be brought to everyone. With that came the promoting, the merchandising, the marketing—the change from art to entertainment."[81]

In Peyser's account, Wuorinen warned that the Group for Contemporary Music's next season might be scrapped in part because of NYSCA: the composer "says the council's money is going to organizations specializing in Minimalist music and that members of its music committee have told him of their wish to help promote the work of women and blacks."[82] Wuorinen attempted to resist such efforts, steadfastly refusing to take any political considerations into account when programming his ensemble's repertoire. The late '80s were a turbulent time for the Group—its administration had significant turnover, Wuorinen was busy with his Meet the Composer residency at the San Francisco Symphony, and the ensemble lost its longtime home at the Manhattan School of Music.

Grant application materials held in the New York State Archives further clarify both NYSCA and the Group's positions. Reviewing the ensemble's 1986–87 application, a Council administrator noted concerns about the ensemble's failure to program women and minority composers.[83] (In the preceding years, the Group perform no music by women composers, and only one work by a Black composer.[84]) Wuorinen and the Group's staff met with James Jordan in fall 1986, and in a response to Jordan and NYSCA that November, the ensemble's executive director wrote that the Group had received few scores by women or minority composers in the past, but it would issue a public call, emphasizing that women and minorities would be encouraged to apply. Still, he noted, "We will continue to select the most worthy ones for performance without respect to gender or ethnic background." [85]

The peer panel that voted on the funding application later that month was not convinced: "That the Group has received only one score from a woman and none from minorities in the past two seasons had more to do with the history of not performing the works of women and minorities, creating an unwelcome atmosphere."[86] Its annual funding was cut substantially, from $16,000 to $10,000. (There were other issues raised by NYSCA: the previous year, the state had funded a Group tour that did not actually take place.) Other organizations faced similar scrutiny. Panelists reviewing an application from Speculum Musicae discussed the "insularity of its programming, and the lack of evidence of any real effort to include women and minorities," and its funding was cut by $3,000.[87] In a 1985 review meeting, administrators from Experimental Intermedia told a NYSCA officer that they would feature more women and minority composers going forward.[88]

Beginning with its 1990 handbook, NYSCA's guidelines included a new policy advocating for applicants to increase the diversity of their staff and program for culturally diverse audiences. To evaluate these new criteria, NYSCA asked questions "relating to participation in and service to traditionally underserved populations."[89] It was not seeking any specific answers, but it wanted to see a given applicant demonstrate good-faith effort. "We don't punish those who don't program women, minority, and American composers," Jordan told *EAR* in 1991. "We reward those who do."[90]

Predictably, the Group refused to play ball. In June 1987—a little more than a month after Bang on a Can hosted their first festival—the ensemble held a board meeting in which it decided that "affirmative action programs had no place in artistic endeavors," and "that The Group must continue to maintain the integrity of its programming, despite the consequences of NYSCA funding or lack of it."[91] Its NEA funding had been cut back, too, and its New York seasons shrunk. The Group did, however, perform music by Michelle Ezikian and Barbara Kolb in 1987 and 1989. After skipping attempts at NYSCA funding for two years, it applied again in 1990 for a modest $5,500 for a three-concert, free series comprising music by Wuorinen, Milton Babbitt, Olivier Messiaen, and other composers—all white men. Responding to one of the new application questions—"Do you include artists who are representatives of minorities and special constituencies in your programming?"—the Group reiterated what had now become familiar rhetoric, that it was interested in programming minority composers "of merit" and that its artists "are selected on the basis of ability."[92] The peer panel reviewing the application debated whether to reduce requested funding based on its failure to address past concerns over diversity, and the state ultimately awarded $5,000. But the Group presented only one of its three proposed concerts and in 1991–92, the ensemble's thirtieth season, it ended its live series entirely, instead dedicating its resources exclusively to recording. "The State Council of New York attempted to tell me what I should program," Wuorinen told an interviewer around this time. "That's why the Group for Contemporary Music doesn't exist anymore, except on paper. The Arts Council wanted affirmative action." He added that "They were taking artistic control from us and I wouldn't have it."[93]

But multicultural programming was not the only issue at play. When evaluating the Group, NYSCA panelists had also "questioned its ability to even draw free audiences."[94] Although a new series at the Guggenheim Museum had attracted a couple hundred attendees, one of the ensemble's other concerts drew an audience that a NYSCA auditor described as "pocket-sized." Such panel concerns stemmed partly from a new, music-specific priority included in that same 1990 Council guidebook: "Applicants are expected to try to reach as wide and diverse an audience as possible."[95] Alongside the questions around diverse programming, applications began to ask, "What efforts are you making to expand the outreach of your organization?"[96] Jordan's marketplace orientation—his belief that experimentalism could be sold—became ingrained in cultural policy.

Its consequences provoked immediate uproar. In a January 1991 *New York Times* column titled "For Contemporary Music, Times Are Hard," critic Allan Kozinn interviewed directors of several longstanding ensembles, including the Group, the Downtown Ensemble, and Parnassus, all of whom faced significant cuts to their funding from several sources, including NYSCA. "What worries the musicians most is that some financing agencies are starting to take audience size into consideration when making grants," Kozinn wrote.[97] Parnassus director Anthony Korf told the *Times* that NYSCA stated that his organization's funding would be reduced from $11,000 to $9,000 because its audience had shrunk. (It was then reduced to $7,000 due to emergency budget cuts.) "You can't apply market economy values to something like contemporary music," he said. "The value of Parnassus and groups like us is not how many people we entertain in a night. It's that we are helping composers who are living and writing today, and who need the outlet."[98] He blamed his loss of audiences, and thus funding, on the "trendiness" of minimalism and "derivative" neo-Romanticism—repertoire his ensemble avoided. Wuorinen characteristically griped that "We have reached the stage, under the impulse of cultural populism, where we are incapable of measuring or acknowledging artistic merit except in terms of commercial success. We don't distinguish between the committed, passionate audience and the trend-seeking yuppie audience. We just count bodies and measure sales."[99]

As Jordan and NYSCA attempted to push new music toward multiculturalism and audiences, Bang on a Can had little to fear. When Kozinn reviewed their 1991 marathon that June, he reflected back on his interviews with Korf and Wuorinen, and noted an opposite trend. The festival had attracted a packed crowd to La Mama's 300-seat auditorium despite the last-minute relocation and, the critic wrote, "The audience was everything a presenter of classical music could hope for: predominantly young, open to a broad range of styles, and enthusiastic but discriminating."[100] Bang on a Can had already taken a public stance against Wuorinen's viewpoint: back in 1988, Lang had penned a letter to the *Times* rebuking the Peyser profile, accusing Wuorinen and his academic compatriots of shutting minimalism out of the musical establishment and "rooting out dissent with the ardor of holy warriors on a serial jihad."[101] Without explicitly mentioning his organization—though he signed the letter "Artistic Director, Bang on a Can Festival"—Lang also made a clear pitch for its necessity: "There is a substantial audience ready to cheer good music of any style or school, if it is presented properly." Chastising the downtown scene, too, for its dogmatism, Lang noted that "Only by encouraging diversity can music hope to stay vital."[102]

Lang, in fact, served as a NYSCA panelist in these year, from 1989 to 1992. He would have sat out of any reviews of Bang on a Can's applications because of a direct conflict of interest, but the organization found increasing state support anyway. It had easy answers to the questions that the Group had protested. In a 1990 NYSCA application, Bang on a Can described in detail their marketing and publicity to reach diverse audiences, and noted that "our commitment to women and minorities has been, and remains, very strong," providing a list of more than twenty women and minority composers featured in the past four years.[103] Gordon, Lang, and Wolfe had embraced this work out of genuine enthusiasm, not for the purposes of raising money. But their priorities also aligned with those of public and private funders in this period, and thus made Bang on a Can an appealing candidate to foundations that supported similar multicultural initiatives. That year they successfully applied for funding from a Meet the Composer/Reader's Digest fund to commission three new string quartets by women composers, which the organization pitched as helping rectify the fact that "women composers are under-represented" in standard repertoire.[104]

In a 1991 funding request to the Jerome Foundation, Gordon wrote that "In the past five years we have presented on our marathon concerts works by 82 emerging composers, of which 34 were by women and composers of color," and that all of their commissions for 1992 were by women and people of color.[105] He then noted that during their process for evaluating works submitted for performance at their marathons, following an initial blind review to see if the music fit the "artistic vision of the Festival," there was a second review with a number of considerations including "whether the composer is an emerging, woman, or minority composer."[106] This clear acknowledgement that the organization took gender, race, and ethnicity into account would have been anathema to Wuorinen and Lipman, who saw such efforts as a form of social engineering that jeopardized their notions of an individualist meritocracy. Bang on a Can presented Black experimentalists such as the AACM founder Muhal Richard Abrams, from whom they commissioned a new string quartet, and violinist-composer Leroy Jenkins, who performed on the festival—figures who were often overlooked by white new-music organizations. Both were championed by Duffy and Jordan, and served on Meet the Composer's advisory board and the same NYSCA panels as Lang.

State program reviews and panel comments on Bang on a Can applications were consistently positive. The year that Parnassus's funding was slashed, Bang on a Can's increased by $1,000 to $13,000. "Once again the dynamic organizers of Bang on a Can disprove the common perception that serious new music is impossible to sell," a NYSCA staffer wrote in his evaluation of Bang on a Can's 1991–92 funding proposal, an endorsement that seemed aimed at those who had complained to the *Times* earlier that year. "It is rare to find an organization which programs the works of women and minorities in representative numbers in a way that is natural to the goals of the organization," he continued.[107]

But concerns over audience numbers and multiculturalism were not what ultimately jeopardized New York's new-music institutions in the 1990s. That decade began with massive reductions to NYSCA's allocations, in response to the 1990 economic recession, which caused a deficit crisis in New York State. In 1991, Governor Mario Cuomo requested a 56 percent cut in NYSCA's budget, prompting outrage in the arts community.[108] Jordan told *EAR* that the proposed cuts were the "worst shape we've been in during the last 20 years," and Duffy urged readers to fight back.[109] The budget was cut by 44 percent and, by 1992–93, the state arts budget was at its lowest level since the early 1970s; total granting in music had dropped from $6.5 million in 1989–90 to $2.4 million in 1992–93.[110] New-music institutions across the board faced major state cutbacks (Figure 4.2).

Through the Reagan years, state arts budgets had increased as the NEA's declined. Now New York musicians faced shrunken federal and state funding.[111] These cuts compromised attempts toward fostering diversity. "If you're giving an organization $10,000, you can say, 'In return to that we expect you to have a social face,'" Lang recalled. "If you're cutting them from $10,000 to $1,000, you can't say, 'Oh by the way for this $1,000 we'd like you to change your organization' . . . That social action, at least from government organizations, was ascendant as the funding was ascendant, and when the funding got cut a lot of steam went out."[112] In its 1995–96 NYSCA grant application, when asked how its programming reflected "efforts to broaden and diversify its audience," Experimental Intermedia did not mince words: "Frankly, we have to state that continued federal, state, corporate and foundation arts funding cuts have stripped most organizations to the bone. We continue our open invitation to and interest in minority artists, but there are no funds with

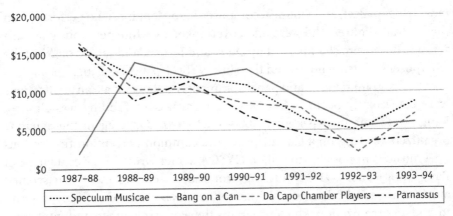

Figure 4.2 Total annual funding from the New York State Council on the Arts

which to explicitly address these issues beyond what is possible in regular programming."[113]

But some prominent composers would remember the culprit of this moment not as the recession, or a state government that deployed arts cutbacks to balance its budget, or even the paleoconservatives fighting at the national level. Invited by *The Musical Times* in 1994 to respond to the prompt "Music: the next 150 years?" Milton Babbitt took a bleak outlook, lambasting "pervasive and invasive populism" that threatened the future of what he perennially called "serious music."[114] His principal target was not Jesse Helms, but the NEA itself. According to Babbitt, the Endowment "has imposed through its appointed panels a censorship of egalitarianism, regionalism, sexism (some may wish to term this 'reverse sexism') and racism (some may wish to term this 'reverse racism') which has had far broader and harsher effect than the publicized attacks and threat of censorship by a yahoo legislator and his fellow protectors of the public morality."[115]

Arguing that the "NEA's ideological correctness has trickled down to other public and private benefactors"—presumably referring to NYSCA, although Babbitt does not name the Council—the composer echoed Kozinn's article, citing Wuorinen's story about the Group for Contemporary Music's funding woes and its cessation of live performance. Babbitt praised the Group as a pioneering ensemble that produced "revelatory" performances.[116] And he repeated Wuorinen's claims that the ensemble's funding was jeopardized by its small audiences and failure to program music by minority composers. Instead, Babbitt argued, "There is apparently little concern that the most threatened minority groups are the composers and performers who have been on the programs and on the stage."[117] New music itself, in other words—rather than new music by women and minorities—deserved affirmative action.

The rest of Babbitt's essay is largely unsurprising. He goes on to discuss failures in education, the fragmentation of musical society, and the threatened position of the serious composer amidst a landscape of charlatans, all part of the narrative of declension he had been promulgating for decades since his infamous "Who Cares if You Listen?"[118] Since the 1930s, and especially during the Cold War, Babbitt held steadfastly to the belief that popular culture—which anti-Communists saw as a dangerous form of social domination—threatened the position of the individualist, modernist American artist.[119] But Babbitt's harangues against the NEA supplied a newer addition to this philosophy: the composer's anxieties now extended to race- and gender-conscious public funding initiatives, which he saw as yet another form of social control, and an encroachment on the vital independence of organizations like the Group. He had thus praised the ensemble's curation of works "not for the 'kinds' they instantiated, but for what they individually were."[120]

Like Wuorinen and Lipman, Babbitt believed that Helms and the paleoconservatives were less of a threat to serious music than liberal multiculturalism. His claims of the NEA's reverse racism and reverse sexism in panel adjudication echoed conservatism's "colorblind" opposition to affirmative action and other social programs that attempted to address inequality. Babbitt and Wuorinen had both benefited from Cold War–era foundation and university patronage, and their approach toward modernist music's individuality, and distaste for what they saw as a politically correct government bureaucracy that threatened it, was steeped in rhetoric of that time. If they saw themselves as heroically embattled figures during the Cold War, they assumed an even more embattled position during the Culture Wars.

At the same time, Babbitt's rhetoric should not be taken as representative of the actual state of public funding. Both neo- and paleoconservatives inflated what they disliked about the arts bureaucracy into a grand critique that assumed that the NEA and NYSCA exclusively funded the multicultural, the popular, and the obscene. Just as Mapplethorpe's photographs were an outlier that was not representative of what the NEA largely supported—as its advocates continually argued—public funding of new music did not necessarily strongly favor multiculturalism or minimalism over Babbitt's academic colleagues. Federal support for minority artists was largely concentrated in NEA programs like Expansion Arts, which had a much smaller budget than the Music division. And funding for non-academic composers came primarily from the Inter-Arts initiative, and for ensembles through a Music category shared with traditional chamber and jazz groups.[121]

By contrast, the NEA's Composer Fellowships clung to unwritten, more conservative criteria. In 1987, musicians Sylvia Glickman and Tina Davidson launched an official complaint after their Endowment proposal for a consortium commission of all-female composers was denied funding. In researching their case, they found that women had only received 9 percent of Composer Fellowships over the past eleven years, and that in 1987 only 3.26 percent of Endowment music funding was awarded to female composers, totaling two grants.[122] They noted that very few peer panelists were women, and even fewer were women composers. "The Endowment, by ignoring women composers' excellence, effectively bars them from other funding sources, performances and continued artistic growth," they wrote.

The NEA did not, then, support "reverse sexism" with regards to promoting women composers, nor did it necessarily promote the minimalists that Wuorinen loathed. Postminimalist composer Paul Dresher, who had served two years on Composer Fellowship panels, wrote to the acting director of the NEA's Music program in 1994 that the fellowships awarded by the Endowment "uniformly represent only a very narrow part of the spectrum of American compositional activity" and that "almost all the panelists are aesthetically aligned with a narrow spectrum of the overall range of compositional style."[123] Most panel judges, he noted, were academic composers, who tended to select fellow academics. "The reaction to works outside the academic mainstream was often one of distinct defensiveness or outright dismissal," he added of his experience adjudicating panels, particularly with regard to

> works that referred in any way to popular culture (i.e. it had a "good" beat, or used electronics), more popular forms of composition, such as styles influenced by or in the lineage of Steve Reich, John Adams or Phil Glass, or non-European derived styles. Similarly, works that depended on long time durations, performance environment, improvisation or chance procedures did equally poorly.

Minimalist- and pop-influenced music, it seems, was still frowned upon by the NEA; academic composers closely policed the boundaries of the prestigious fellowships, perhaps wary that public funding might go to more "popular" composers who could instead find success in the marketplace.[124] (By contrast, Dresher cited Meet the Composer's excellence in assembling aesthetically diverse panels and rewarding grants more equitably.)

But the fellowship and consortium programs would not have much time to take these critiques into account—to become actually multicultural, or stylistically pluralistic, as Babbitt and Wuorinen feared. The yahoo legislators soon had their say.

When Things Are Tough All Around Us We Dream

The election of President Clinton in 1992 seemed to put the congressional battles over arts funding on hold. Controversies that flared up—as when an artist in Minneapolis hung blood-soaked paper towels above his audience, as commentary on the AIDS crisis—continued to rile Helms and the religious right, but did not result in new legislation. Perhaps responding belatedly to Lang's call for contemporary music to become more controversial, Bang on a Can staged a festival at The Kitchen in 1993 that seemed to respond directly to the cultural moment. It opened with a concert titled "A Political Songbook," curated by the trio Bermuda Triangle, which featured songs about Rodney King and the KKK, as well as a guest trio of teenage rappers, and raised money for the AIDS charity God's Love We Deliver. (The conservative-leaning *Times* critic Edward Rothstein was skeptical, describing the evening as "politically correct politics in a seeming self-parody."[125]) Along with more typical Bang on a Can fare, including a John Cage tribute and the usual marathon, the festival also featured a Chinese shadow puppet play by composer Bun-Ching Lam, an evening of guitarist-composers and spoken-word poets, and a rageful indictment of societal indifference to AIDS by composer Ben Neill and the late artist David Wojnarowicz. Wojnarowicz, an outspoken gay activist who died of AIDS in 1992, had become infamous during the Culture Wars for authoring a scathing essay attacking a homophobic New York cardinal, as well as Helms and other Republicans. That piece was printed in the catalog for a 1989 art exhibit about AIDS, causing conservative uproar and leading John Frohnmayer to briefly cancel the show's NEA funding. Surveying the Kitchen concerts, Kyle Gann found some of the performances compelling, but his *Voice* review framed the festival as "souped up ... with visual art, poetry, and politics, hoping to lure people who don't include new music on their usual beat."[126]

Everything changed following the 1994 midterm elections, when Republicans campaigned successfully on Newt Gingrich's Contract With America, a legislative plan calling simultaneously for massive tax cuts and balancing the budget. Lacing together Heritage Foundation-inspired reductions in the size of the federal government with the religious crusading of the Culture Wars, the Contract sought both "the end of government that is too big, too intrusive, and too easy with the public's money" and the "beginning of a Congress that respects the values and shares the faith of the American family."[127] Unsurprisingly, it proposed eliminating both arts and humanities endowments. The power of a Democratic presidency to halt this "zeroing out" of the NEA's budget was limited in the face of the first Republican majority in both congressional chambers in forty years. Sidney Yates, the longtime chairman of the House Interior Appropriations Subcommittee and staunch defender of the NEA, stepped down, and a Republican took his place.

Those in Congress who had fought against Reagan-era cuts and Bush-era obscenity clauses were now in the minority, and arts lobbying only went so far. Ultimately, in 1995, Congress slashed NEA funding by 40 percent: by 1996, the budget shrunk drastically from $162 million to $99.5 million, and the Endowment cut nearly half of its staff.[128] Of equal significance was the Endowment's structural transformation. Shortly before Congress began debating the scope of the Endowment's restructuring, the NEA had sponsored a meeting of new-music constituents, where an advisory panel recommended that they continue direct support of composers. In a letter to Jane Alexander—Clinton's NEA chairman—composers Carl Stone and Randall Davidson, acting on behalf of the American Music Center, made clear the stakes of abolishing individual fellowships:

> There is no art without artists. Direct support to artists makes possible research and development in the arts, not only for artists themselves but for the future of art. The resulting work of individual artists can sometimes be messy or controversial, but it is necessary. Direct support, in addition to the financial remuneration, provides a recognition unlike any other and allows the artist to retain control of his or her creative endeavors.
>
> The argument that individuals can always be properly supported through institutions and through alliances with institutions reflects a lack of understanding about the creative artistic process. Funding artists through organizations, to the exclusion of direct funding, is not enough. Artists' work with institutions, particularly those which meet the Endowment's application restrictions, is only one type of creative work, and may not always be the most vital, interesting, and risk-taking.[129]

But Congress mandated the elimination of nearly all fellowships awarded to individual artists, including the Composer Fellowships.

It was a massive blow to American artists, who could now only receive funding through institutional grant applications. In an attempt to make the most of a dramatically shrunken Endowment, and also to insulate it from additional congressional attacks, Alexander dissolved the NEA's discipline-specific framework and replaced it with four thematic categories: Creation and Presentation, Heritage and Preservation, Education and Access, and Planning and Stabilization. Arts organizations could submit only one application to the Endowment per year, and had to choose the category to which their funding attempts belonged. "The elimination of the discipline-specific programs has hurt the fields, since we've lost access to much of the intelligence at the agency," argued Marc Scorca, the director of Opera America, in 1996. "Now the NEA is more about these four themes and less about art."[130]

The massive cuts quickly rippled through the world of new music. Phill Niblock has recalled that Experimental Intermedia largely stopped receiving NEA funding in this period.[131] The organization's budget had plummeted since the mid-1980s, when its annual income hovered around $200,000: in 1997, it brought in only $67,198.[132] And though Paul Dresher's cohort had been largely shut out of the Composer Fellowships, his ensemble had been funded regularly through the Music, Theater, and Inter-Arts programs. After the restructuring, however, they could only apply to one NEA division per year and Endowment funding, he said in 2016, had "been spotty since then."[133] The downtown composer Scott Johnson characterized the 1980s as a "new music boom" and the subsequent decade, by contrast, as a "turn to the right" in which "the public funding dried up … The nineties were much tougher."[134]

The Contract With America directly shaped the future of Bang on a Can. In 1995, the organization had received more than $30,000 from the Endowment: $11,380 to support their second album with Sony Classical; $13,000 toward presenting the marathon that year; and a $6,000 advancement grant "for a 15-month period of management assistance and strategic planning, culminating in the creation of a written multi-year strategic plan."[135] At the time, they were still participating in the Chamber Music America expansion grant. Having won the NEA grants, Bette Snapp submitted to CMA an ambitious, three-year plan that outlined a mission to broaden activities including the festival, All-Stars touring, commissioning, and recording, as well as renewed strategic efforts to increase government, foundation, individual, and corporate support.[136]

The following year, however, the organization received no funding from the Endowment. The advancement grant had helped them pay for a consultant who advised on board development and management, and sessions with administrators from the Brooklyn Academy of Music on fundraising and the Kronos Quartet on touring, to prepare for their tenth anniversary season.[137] But it was only Phase I of the NEA's advancement program. In Phase II, typically awarded the following year, organizations were given $50,000 to implement the strategic plan they had developed during the initial research phase. The congressional cuts, however, eliminated the advancement initiative entirely, and Bang on a Can never received the $50,000 they had been expecting in 1996.[138]

In a fundraising plea to individual donors, the artistic directors wrote that public cuts had led to a loss of "about a fifth of our budget."[139] The challenge, however, was not insurmountable. "When things are tough all around us we dream," they added. "It's a Bang on a Can thing. Just as arts funding is collapsing, we're mounting new projects to build a new audience for a new kind of music." A July 1996 memo lists more than a dozen corporations and foundations from whom they intended to seek support, each with a detailed "plan of attack" outlining proposals and meetings.[140] For the anniversary season, Bang on a Can's budget of $429,000 included $179,000 of foundation and corporate support, with a $50,000 grant from the Rockefeller Foundation as well as their first major corporate sponsorships: $15,000 from Philip Morris toward the festival, and $15,000 from AT&T to support a national All-Stars tour.[141] Twenty-thousand people had attended forty-seven concerts featuring music by fifty-six composers, and Bang on a Can had netted an impressive $203,000 from earned income.[142] And in 1997, they received a windfall of public funding that compensated for the previous loss: a grant of $93,500 from the NEA's new Planning and Stabilization category.[143] Intended to be fully matched by outside donations, the Endowment grant was dedicated toward the organization's long-term health, paying for a cash reserve; small stipends for Gordon, Lang, and Wolfe; and a new staffer for All-Stars booking and management.[144]

In the graph shown in Figure 4.3, note the significant rise in Bang on a Can's total income, even as federal and state music granting continuously declined. The principal source for Bang on a Can's early growth is a large increase in foundation funding, but in the second half of the 1990s, earned income becomes both the organization's largest stream of revenue and source of growth—due to the work of the All-Stars.[145] The organization's remarkable growth in these years of diminishing public funding can be attributed to their ingenuity and entrepreneurial drive, whether in their ability to attract audiences, to make a strong case to granting institutions with whom their priorities aligned, or to market themselves to new patrons.

The All-Stars ensemble, the partnership with Lincoln Center, and the forays into the record industry all speeded and were aided by this expansion. But Bang on a Can's growth was also clearly shaped by structural changes in the funding landscape during the Culture Wars. Granting organizations, including NYSCA and the NEA, were eager to subsidize the long-term development of arts institutions that could demonstrate that they could withstand the climate of public austerity. The administrative director of Speculum Musicae told Kozinn in 1991 that "I have been writing to lots of foundations and finding that many of them want a broader appeal and greater national visibility than we can give them."[146] By contrast, Bang on a Can had found that broader appeal, dedicating significant resources to fundraising from

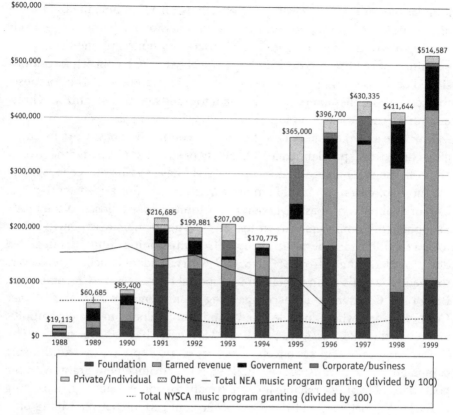

Figure 4.3 Annual income, Bang on a Can

foundations, corporations, and individuals, and marshalling the facts, figures, and rhetoric attesting that they could subsist in this new reality. "The artistic force still remains with its founding trio who appear to have a marvelous combination of street smarts, idealism and sophistication that keep this often colorful and at times wacky series of events afloat," wrote a NYSCA staffer in reviewing Bang on a Can in June 1999.[147] "Fundraising and clever marketing continue to produce new audiences and contributors. Staff salutes this remarkable organization and is pleased to recommend increased, multi-year support."

Bang on a Can's tenth anniversary season marked the launch of a new, long-term initiative responding to the transformed NEA: the People's Commissioning Fund. The program would pool small individual donations to fund new pieces for the All-Stars, with an explicitly populist spin. Works would no longer be commissioned by distant government agencies, elite foundations, or singular wealthy patrons, Bang on a Can imagined. "Our audience members and supporters become commissioners themselves, actively shaping a world where emerging composers can flourish," one description explained of the proto-crowdfunding project. At a PCF concert, a commissioned composer might introduce their new piece, and then "The composer thanks the commissioners and asks them to stand and be recognized. Three-quarters of the audience stands."[148]

"Imagine a revolutionary new program to commission new work by emerging composers," proclaimed a 1997 glossy postcard announcing the project and soliciting members and donations. "Yes! I have passionate feelings about the future of new music! No! I am not a materialist! I don't need another tote bag, or umbrella, or toaster! I want opportunities to get closer to the music I support, the composers who write it and the performers who play it! I want to be a founding member of The People's Commissioning Fund!"[149] Suggested donation tiers ranged from $50 to $5000, with attendant benefits from access to open rehearsals to an invitation to a special dinner with PCF composers. Bang on a Can started an accompanying promotional mailer, The People's Commissioner, which included news updates, letters from the community, and fun extras like crossword puzzles and Steve Reich's recipe for stir-fry.[150]

The program was first conceived as part of a comprehensive fundraising campaign under the auspices of the 1995 NEA advancement grant, with the goals of establishing a reliable income stream for commissioning, increasing individual donations, and building closer connections between Bang on a Can and their constituency.[151] They secured challenge funding from NYSCA for marketing, and additional matching funds from the Mellon and Jerome foundations soon afterwards: an emblematic public-private partnership.[152] By 1999, total membership had reached 300, in part because the previous fall, Bang on a Can had hosted a large benefit.[153] Held in honor of Duffy—"We see the People's Commissioning Fund as our way of carrying on John Duffy's legacy," the organization wrote—the benefit was overseen by an outside consultant, who helped assemble a large fundraising committee and conscripted celebrity performers and chairpersons.[154] There was a party at Philip Glass's home, and the gala itself was held at the Angel Orensanz Foundation, a beautiful nineteenth-century synagogue on the Lower East Side, with a concert featuring excerpts from one of Duffy's operas as well as performances by Glass, Cecil Taylor, DJ Spooky, the All-Stars and composer Pamela Z, and even Sonic Youth's Thurston Moore.[155] Photos from the event, which raised around $30,000 in donations, depict a wide range of attendees including Steve Reich, John Corigliano, Billy Taylor, Joan Tower, and Alvin Singleton (Figure 4.4).[156] "I feel enormous joy to stand in solidarity with Michael, Julie

BANG ON A CAN BENEFIT CONCERT HONORING JOHN DUFFY, SEPTEMBER 13, 1998
left to right, seated front: Pamela Z, Julia Wolfe, Paul Miller (DJ Spooky), Steve Reich
standing, center: Lisa Moore, Billy Taylor, Cecil Taylor, John Duffy, Fran Richard, Maya Beiser
standing, rear: Christine Williams, David Lang, John Corigliano, Michael Gordon, Mark Stewart, Evan Ziporyn, Joan Tower, Alvin Singleton, Steven Schick, Thurston Moore, John Schaefer.

Figure 4.4 Bang on a Can benefit concert honoring John Duffy, 1998. Photograph by Peter Serling.

and David and to pass on to them the baton," Duffy wrote in a supportive statement. "In doing so, I remind myself and others that what we commission and perform today is our legacy to future generations."[157]

A flyer described the first three PCF-commissioned composers as "art rocking Virgil Moorefield, computerized performance artist Pamela Z, and radical improviser Dan Plonsey."[158] Z had performed her intricately layered music for voice and electronic processing at the 1996 marathon; Moorefield, a percussionist and electronic musician, led his own amplified ensemble in microtonal, quasi-improvised music the following year. Plonsey was new to

Bang on a Can but quite old to the founders, as an early member of Sheep's Clothing. These were composer-performers who, a decade earlier, might have participated in New Music America's post-literate avant-garde, but whom Bang on a Can instead conscripted to write for their All-Stars. Bang on a Can designed the initiative for "awarding commissions to rebel composers who live in the cracks between different musical worlds," the same philosophy that had motivated the commissioning of Glenn Branca and Muhal Richard Abrams to write string quartets earlier in the decade.[159] "I didn't have a lot of experience composing chamber music," Pamela Z recalled. "The Bang on a Can People's Commissioning Fund was a really key part of my growth as an artist" (Figure 4.5).[160]

Bang on a Can explicitly framed the PCF as a post-Culture Wars project, one that emerged from a landscape defined by harsh cutbacks to public funding. In a thank-you letter to their first pool of donors in 1998, the artistic directors wrote that "A year ago, faced with the NEA's decision to no longer fund the creation of new work by individual artists, we imagined that a group of music lovers would collectively form a commissioning group to fund new work."[161] And in an invitation to the second PCF benefit in 1999, Gordon similarly wrote that "Institutional funding for individual artists has been under attack for years, and with NEA's ongoing cutbacks the situation has become

Figure 4.5 Poster for People's Commissioning Fund at the Knitting Factory, 1998.

even more grim. In 1997, we decided to take matters into our own hands, and began appealing directly to the people to support new work."[162] One proposal pitched the PCF as "New Music for the People."[163]

The commissioning fund's name evinces a potentially utopian political vision—indeed, one Bang on a Can fan apparently suggested it retitle the project, as it initially sounded "too socialist."[164] And given that anyone could participate in the process by donating as little as $5, it would seem to offer a more democratic approach than past alternatives. Further, it had a potentially broader mission in terms of whom it selected to award. Given Dresher's 1994 complaint, it is unlikely that those supported by the PCF would have received NEA Composer Fellowships in the '90s; Lang later contrasted the PCF against established commissioning organizations like the Koussevitsky Foundation in that it supported less conventionally credentialed composers.[165]

For several decades prior to 1996, though, the American people as a whole had funded the creation of new work by individual artists, including composers, through the National Endowment for the Arts. By virtue of paying taxes—NEA chairman Jane Alexander frequently remarked that each citizen's contribution to the arts cost the equivalent of two postage stamps—the people commissioned new art, and were invested in the democratic governance of a national system for arts patronage.[166] This had been, quite literally, new music for the people. But the 1990s was the era of welfare reform and school vouchers, of public goods refigured into private enterprise. With their commissioning fund, Bang on a Can attempted to salvage some vestige of the NEA's support for individual artists, in the wake of its destruction by free market conservatives and the religious right. They were adapting to a landscape in which the American people would no longer support individual artists via a central, nationalized, democratically controlled organization, one in which peer panels adjudicated grant recipients and elected officials shaped bureaucratic decisions. The PCF anticipated the default mode of American arts funding in the twenty-first century: patching together income streams from many small sources, scrambling for grants, crowdfunding online, and attempting, more and more, to petition individual patrons to open their wallets. "Today the NEA is a shadow of its former self," wrote Donna Binkiewicz in 2004, "merely adding small amounts of federal money to an arena of cultural philanthropy dominated by private institutional patronage."[167] At the close of the century, the marketplace was no longer a rhetorical position—an ethos that could be embraced or defied—and no longer a choice. It was an imperative, and its "magic," as Reagan and then Helms put it, could no longer be resisted.

5
All-Stars

In August 1994, onstage at Seiji Ozawa Hall on the grounds of the Tanglewood summer music festival, the Bang on a Can All-Stars played a new piece by Julia Wolfe titled *Lick*. Archival video captures a few minutes of the performance: attired in funky clothing—guitarist Mark Stewart and saxophonist Evan Ziporyn in brightly-colored button-downs, cellist Maya Beiser in a gossamer red dress—the sextet bops incessantly along with Wolfe's propulsive music. Stewart and pianist Lisa Moore aggressively nod their heads, while Ziporyn conducts the beat with his saxophone and Robert Black placidly plucks his bass. If percussionist Steven Schick weren't consistently switching from snare drum and toms to vibraphone, he could almost be mistaken for a headbanging rock drummer—a wholly appropriate approach to *Lick*.[1] In a note printed in the Tanglewood program, Wolfe described a new source of inspiration among her recent works: "That body energy of pop music came into my music and it's still here and definitely in *Lick*. I'm totally excited about it. Motown, funk, rock. This is the music I grew up on—listening, dancing to it. There's a certain kind of freedom to it."[2]

"I really thought about the All-Stars when I wrote it because I wanted to see them lock in with this intense energy," she added. "It's definitely over the top."[3] The work opens with a series of fits and starts, as the ensemble plays brash, accented eighth notes that alternate with rests and are occasionally interrupted by the sudden entrance of a solo instrument. A steady state eventually emerges, as soprano saxophone plays an insistent, sixteenth-note line—with the indications "ecstatic," "more ecstatic," "even more ecstatic"—atop a constantly shifting backing groove. In an extended section toward the middle of the nine-minute piece, the saxophone bleats out whole notes in a high register as the piano hits fistfuls of cluster chords and the electric guitar shreds.

Perhaps it was during *Lick* that Tanglewood's artistic director, the distinguished pianist Leon Fleisher, very publicly covered his ears and scowled. Or perhaps it was elsewhere in the evening: when Schick assayed David Lang's junk metal tour-de-force *the anvil chorus* or Beiser traversed Michael Gordon's gnarly *Industry*; or when a subset of the group played Louis Andriessen's honking, canon-infused quartet *Hout*; or when the full sextet premiered a new commission by their British friend Steve Martland, the tenaciously driving *Horses of Instruction*. Nearly all of the loudly amplified works that the All-Stars performed might have annoyed a classical music traditionalist such as Fleisher. "There was no doubt in his mind that not only were the barbarians at the gate, they had opened the gate," Stewart recalled. "They had let them in."[4]

Tanglewood's Festival of Contemporary Music had long been a home for the uptown avant-garde, under the direction of composer and conductor Gunther Schuller, who steadfastly refused to program minimalist music. But in 1994, the Dutch conductor Reinbert de Leeuw became its new artistic director, and invited Louis Andriessen to serve as composer-in-residence.[5] In turn, Andriessen welcomed the barbarians, inviting the All-Stars and curating a mini-marathon that included works by Wolfe and Lang. The *Times* described that year's festival as the "the end of a long 12-tone reign by Northeastern academic composers."[6]

Around the Tanglewood campus hung posters that featured a birds-eye-view photo of the All-Stars gazing dreamily up at the camera (Figure 5.1) and declared, in bold type, "Unstoppable! Sexy! LOUD!" "What we did decide to do in 1992 was make our own ensemble from some of the most brilliant performers over the existence of the festival," Bang on a Can wrote in the concert's program book. "Soloists, new-music virtuosos, pioneers who knew how to swing. We call them All-Stars."[7] The rhetoric that Bang on a Can deployed to describe their new ensemble mimicked how it sounded—self-assured, pop-inspired, far from Tanglewood's classical norms. And the 1994 concert was one of their first high-profile gigs.

Only a few years earlier, the *New York Times* had interviewed directors of several longstanding new-music groups about their declining funding and winnowing audiences. Characteristically against the grain, Gordon, Lang,

Figure 5.1 Bang on a Can All-Stars, mid-1990s. Photograph by Peter Serling.

and Wolfe designed an ensemble to take their ethos on the road, building a larger audience and opening a new source of revenue for Bang on a Can. And the sound and image of the All-Stars facilitated a major pivot in Bang on a Can's identity, from emphasizing how they bridged stylistic divides *within* new music (as epitomized by the uptown–downtown binary) to instead emphasizing how they blurred genre boundaries *between* contemporary classical music and rock. But a clear division of labor between composers (the Bang on a Can directors) and performers (the personnel of the All-Stars) also led to some tensions. Freedom resounded in the body energy of *Lick*, but not always in the institutional practices of the group that performed it. This attitude grew directly from the artistic philosophy of the three founding composers, and how they carefully positioned their new ensemble toward the marketplace.

Ensemble Conception

Bang on a Can built a reputation for presenting a great variety of guest ensembles at their festivals, from the downtown S.E.M. Ensemble, Los Angeles's California E.A.R. Unit, and Philadelphia-based Relâche to the Dutch ensemble Orkest De Volharding, the London group Icebreaker, and the Toronto-based Sound Pressure. As Kyle Gann wrote in 1988, "The most patent sign of Bang on a Can's timeliness was the wild cheers that greeted good performances of the most mediocre works, as though new music audiences are starved for excellent execution."[8] The following year, Gann's review of the festival identified the importance of an "ensemble conception"—one that combined the reedy timbres of early Philip Glass with the mallet percussion of Steve Reich and Pierre Boulez—to an emerging aesthetic current he heard there (and which he would later name totalism).[9] In a *Times* review of that same 1989 marathon, John Rockwell noted "the uncommon high quality of the Bang on a Can performances."[10] The directors frequently assembled ad hoc ensembles of local and visiting freelancers to perform the music they wanted to program. Although a formally named "Bang on a Can Orchestra" played at the 1991 festival, for example, it was essentially a pickup group put together to play Andriessen's *De Tijd*.

Back in 1983, after working through the musical material of his *Thou Shalt!/Thou Shalt Not!* on the piano, Gordon gathered various instrumentalists to read drafts and eventually settled on an sextet comprising violin, viola, electric guitar, bass clarinet, electric organ, and percussion, which he dubbed the Michael Gordon Philharmonic.[11] Unlike many downtown ensembles, and unlike Sheep's Clothing, Gordon's Philharmonic did not engage with indeterminacy, graphic scores, or improvisation. The Philharmonic was a byproduct of a mostly-existing work, rather than a group formed to create brand-new music in real time. This set the Philharmonic apart from Gordon's minimalist forefathers, who frequently created music through collaborative and oral processes. Even Steve Reich's canonical 1976 *Music for Eighteen Musicians* developed in cooperative rehearsals; a score for the work did not exist until composer Marc Mellits transcribed one in 1996.[12] Though Gordon played electric organ in his ensemble, the Philharmonic otherwise established a setup conventional to classical music, in which the composer completes a notated work to be executed by a team of performers (Figure 5.2).

And the Philharmonic maintained a performative, if restricted, relationship to rock music. Though the ensemble's full-throated, amplified aesthetic is clearly indebted to Andriessen's orchestrations in works like *De Staat*, its band-like set-up also gestures sonically toward the late '70s hybridity of No Wave and the noisy, massed electric guitars of Glenn Branca and Rhys Chatham. *Thou Shalt*'s instrumentation, its score describes, should include a "portable rock-type organ" and a highly distorted electric guitar.[13] When he introduced his Philharmonic at Bang on a Can's 1987 festival, Gordon told the audience that "The thing that attracted me to this group is that it's half of a string quartet and half of a rock band."[14]

Figure 5.2 Michael Gordon Philharmonic in 1986. Photograph by Elliot Caplan.

But while the Philharmonic was meant to gesture toward the pop world, at the very same time that he was completing *Thou Shalt*, Gordon was also concluding his career as an actual rock musician. His art-rock band Peter and the Girlfriends broke up shortly before the Michael Gordon Philharmonic played its first concert. "It really wasn't what I wanted to do ultimately," he later recalled of the transition. "A band is a band. I think writing music is kind of a different experience. You really have to be a collaborator in a band. And it's really a pop idiom."[15] The composer neatly separates his work in a band from his work with his own ensemble. "Writing music," for Gordon, is about executing his own specific musical vision in a notated musical work, not writing songs in a cooperative medium. In these ways, the Michael Gordon Philharmonic anticipated key aspects of the All-Stars: the group resembled a rock band in sound and image, but not in collaborative practices.

We Have Put Together a Touring Package

After debuting with *Thou Shalt*, the Michael Gordon Philharmonic continued to serve its founder as a vehicle for his music. The ensemble also expanded its repertoire to works by Jeffrey Brooks and Evan Ziporyn and appeared on Bang on a Can's early marathons. So if Gordon had his Philharmonic, and his two colleagues had access to skilled freelance performers to play their music at the festivals, what motivated Bang on a Can to start an in-house band?

Soon after the success of the 1987 marathon, the founders had fielded calls from administrators in other cities to present some version of Bang on a Can outside New York. The logistical challenge of mounting an entire marathon of mixed instrumentation works in an unfamiliar city was daunting. A small ensemble, performing a standardized concert representative of the festival's spirit, provided a more manageable solution. As Wolfe put it in 1999, "Well, 24 pieces and 10 groups and, I mean, it was an unwieldy thing to relocate. And just little by little it dawned on us that if we had an ensemble, we could take the aesthetic on the road."[16] In a December 1991 grant application, Bang on a Can outlined a new endeavor to be inaugurated in the following months: the "Bang on a Can All-Stars." The group would serve as "a mixed ensemble of five to sixteen virtuosi, specializing in the music of our time" that would "become a foundation of future Bang on a Can Festival events," including the organization's New York season along with national and international tours.[17] When the ensemble debuted at the May 1992 Bang on a Can festival, it comprised a larger ad hoc group from which different instrumental combinations were drawn.[18] In this regard, the first iteration of the All-Stars was not markedly different from the other pickup bands put together for previous festivals. Even before that concert took place, however, Bang on a Can began to envision a smaller and more stable roster. In a February 1992 pitch to perform on the Chamber Music Chicago series, they described the All-Stars as "six of our finest festival musicians."[19] But it took additional performances until the sextet iteration of the All-Stars actually arrived. The group's first concert outside New York was held at the Toronto chapter of New Music Across America (the successor to New Music America) in October 1992, and featured nine or ten musicians. A month later, at the Walker Arts Center in Minneapolis, the sextet version of the All-Stars made its debut, comprising percussionist Steven Schick, bassist Robert Black, cellist Maya Beiser, clarinetist and saxophonist Evan Ziporyn, pianist Lisa Moore, and guitarist Mark Stewart. When Bang on a Can first invited the six musicians to collaborate, they asked them to wear Converse All-Stars sneakers and jeans, but the performers declined. Moore recalled to the writer K. Robert Schwarz, a freelance critic who wrote frequently about Bang on a Can in the 1990s, that "A few of us said, 'Well, wait a minute, I don't have a pair of blue jeans and, number two, if I wanted to wear a uniform I would have joined an orchestra.'"[20]

Of the six, Ziporyn had the longest association with the founders. He had performed alongside Lang in Sheep's Clothing as an undergraduate at Yale, maintained a close relationship with Gordon in the Michael Gordon Philharmonic, and was invited to play at and organize pickup groups for the early marathons. Black had worked with Gordon at Buffalo's North American New Music Festival, and was subsequently invited to perform on the first marathons, where he played solo bass works such as Tom Johnson's *Failing*. A classmate of Lang at the University of Iowa, Schick performed music by Feldman and Xenakis at the 1988 festival. A native Australian, Moore had specialized in contemporary music as a pianist at the University of Illinois and SUNY Stony Brook, and first worked with Bang on a Can as a last-minute substitute at the 1989 marathon (at the time, she also performed with the Da Capo Chamber Players). Stewart—who studied cello and contemporary music at Stony Brook, but also played electric guitar on the side—attended early Bang on a Can festivals as a fan and was first hired to play guitar for a piece on the 1991 marathon. Beiser, a cello soloist who grew up in Israel, studied at Yale at the same time as Wolfe. She met the trio through Black, developing a close relationship with the founders and commissioning them to write pieces for her, including Gordon's solo *Industry*. With the exception of Schick, the other five members of the sextet had performed in the initial large ensemble iteration of the All-Stars.

The principal reason for the sextet configuration, the Bang on a Can founders frequently stated, was to gather the most talented players who had performed at past festivals in a single supergroup. They placed a strong emphasis on the individual virtuosity of the musicians, which was not just hype—the players were extraordinarily well-versed in executing the dense scores produced by Bang on a Can's cohort, and had begun to master the difficult rhythmic demands of music that relied on ever-changing, ever-disrupting postminimalist grooves. But there were other motivations. The trio was also thinking carefully about how the ensemble should sound, and how it might represent Bang on a Can on the road.

In 1995, Gordon told Schwarz that "We didn't want it to be clarinet, flute, violin, cello, percussion, and piano"—a reference to the "Pierrot" ensemble, the prototype for the uptown avant-garde—and that "the group had to have an electric guitar in it, because electric guitar is the great instrument of the 21st century."[21] And as Lang described it in 2016, the finalized sextet resulted from a strategic debrief among the directors, following the first couple All-Stars concerts. "We went, 'I don't think we're going to be able to get where we want to go with an ensemble that doesn't have a sound,'" he recalled. "'We're not going to be able to make our way with an ensemble that has a conductor. We're not going to be able to make our way with an ensemble that plays music that other people play.'" Lang invoked the Kronos Quartet as a model, for being "relentless about commissioning music for themselves so that it's *their* sound." He continued, "If we set the ensemble so that it had its own unique instrumentation, it would have its sound. If we made music specifically for it, it would have its own repertoire that nobody else would have."[22]

In a 1993 funding application to the Robert Sterling Clark Foundation, Bang on a Can outlined another component that shaped the creation of the All-Stars. The Clark Foundation provided grants to help organizations boost their earned income, with the goal of helping arts organizations become self-sufficient in an era of precarious government support. Bang on a Can applied "to support a new program we have designed to increase the percentage of earned income in our budget," which at the time only accounted for 13 percent of their revenue.[23] The organization hoped to raise their earned income to 30 percent of their budget by the 1995–96 season, and eventually to 50 percent. The application's pitch was similar to the "for-profit mentality" that Bang on a Can had outlined in the Arts Forward grant letter the previous year. But rather than promote a line of potato chips, the organization described more overtly artistic efforts to seek new sources of earned revenue.

The letter added that since the festival "is already well-promoted and well-attended we do not foresee many possibilities for growth in this area." Instead, it outlined four spaces in which they hoped to significantly improve earned income: radio broadcasts, recording, guest curating for other organizations, and "packaging the festival for presentation and performance venues around the world":

> It has become clear that the greatest potential for earned income lies with the touring program; each year more presenters express interest in importing Bang on a Can. What attracts these presenters is that Bang on a Can represents the full spectrum of the vibrant New York music scene. In response to their requests, we have put together a touring package that closely resembles the electric mix of composers and styles that is the trademark of the festival.[24]

That "touring package" was the All-Stars. Ticket sales at the New York festivals could only raise so much money—a traveling ensemble opened up a new stream of revenue via contracted fees from outside presenters, even if it still relied on fundraising and grant writing to stay afloat.

Although the All-Stars' work was already underway at this point, Bang on a Can was requesting grant funding toward enhancing its marketing, including research into suitable venues, creating new promotional materials and a Bang on a Can logo, employing additional administration like concert management, and advertising in major trade publications. The Clark Foundation awarded $25,000 toward the initiatives, and the All-Stars served as Bang on a Can's principal method for boosting their earned income.

The clearest precedent for the All-Stars' image and business model was the Kronos Quartet, founded in 1973 by violinist David Harrington. By the 1990s the string quartet's dedication to contemporary repertoire as well as jazz and world music, hip outfits, theatrical lighting and amplification—they toured with sound-and-light engineers—and chart-topping albums on Nonesuch had made it an icon for how a familiar chamber configuration could defy classical norms. Kronos's organizational strength might also have inspired Bang on a Can: its 1992 budget of $1.2 million dwarfed other groups dedicated to contemporary music, and 72 percent of its revenue comprised earned income.[25] In 1995, as part of Bang on a Can's Chamber Music America expansion grant, the organization worked directly with Kronos's managing director Janet Cowperthwaite on "developing a comprehensive booking and marketing plan for the Bang on a Can All-Stars." They beefed up mass mailings and attendance at industry conferences, and consulted with her again a few years later to specifically discuss the issue of earned income.[26]

The Kronos Quartet was infamous for its cover of Jimi Hendrix's "Purple Haze," which closed out its first album on Nonesuch in 1986; by 1995, the

All-Stars were encoring their sets with Ziporyn's arrangement of Nirvana's "Lithium."[27] And Kronos's pop culture marketing provided a clear model for how Bang on a Can packaged their ensemble. When the group performed in Minneapolis in 1992, the Walker Arts Center printed traditional bios for each of the six musicians. A few representative, brief excerpts:

- "Maya Beiser has been praised as 'Israel's most exciting and promising young cellist.'"
- "Robert Black has worked with and commissioned over 35 of today's leading composers."
- "Evan Ziporyn teaches composition and non-western music at MIT."[28]

Such demure professionalism is typical of performer biographies in the classical and new-music worlds, which tend to list career accomplishments, conservatory pedigree and university appointments, and pull quotes from prominent press outlets. By contrast, the paragraph-long All-Stars bios printed in the 1994 Tanglewood program provide scant information about the performers' professional experience or training, and are written in an extemporaneous, self-expressive first-person perspective:

- Beiser: "When I started to play new music, I realized that the total experience of making music means that I can't separate my physical and emotional presence from my playing."
- Black: "I'm not conscious when I'm playing. I get into another mental state."
- Ziporyn: "When I am breathing correctly and my fingers are moving nimbly and my mouth is not too tired—when I'm getting exactly what I want—the clarinet becomes an extension of my body."[29]

These were the result of Bang on a Can's collaboration with the writer Deborah Artman for the organization's Lincoln Center partnership. In advance of their first Lincoln Center concerts in 1994, Artman interviewed composers and performers to craft personalized program notes and bios that mimicked the informality of Bang on a Can's pre-performance introductions. And such rhetorical flourishes extended beyond the program books. Bang on a Can coined "Unstoppable, Sexy, and Loud" as a promotional mantra for the new group. A mid-'90s press kit described the ensemble as "a coming together of the most brilliant and provocative performers": "All-Stars we call them, each a giant, a warrior, a fearless combatant for the music of our time."[30] It was the logical extension of the hype-driven advertising that had suffused Bang on a Can since their first marathon.

The efforts paid off. In 1995, managing director Karen Sander attended two major booking conferences to promote the All-Stars. Within a year, they had booked international tours to the United Kingdom, the Netherlands, Australia, New Zealand, and Italy. "This year Bang on a Can reached an unprecedented point, where our earned income was more than a third of our income overall," Bette Snapp reported to Chamber Music America that year, as part of an interim update for the expansion grant it had received.[31] In fact, 40 percent of the organization's total revenue of $396,700 in the 1995–96 season comprised earned income.[32] "We are working hard to sustain this growth," she added.

They had sent promo mailings to hundreds of European presenters, put together a commissioning consortium to fund new works for the All-Stars, and aggressively pursued domestic and international booking. "We see the Bang on a Can All-Stars as an important part of our organizational stability," the memo continued.[33] "They continue to increase our level of earned income, and they are also important for our artistic stability. The presence of a permanent ensemble, with a stable and growing repertoire means that every year the music we champion reaches a broader audience worldwide." Among Bang on a Can's multiple income streams—including government and foundation grants, private donations, and corporate funding—earned income represented the most significant, and consistent, source of growth through the late 1990s.

Not a Bad Band by Art-Rock Standards

All of this impressive growth was predicated not just on how the All-Stars were described, but also on how they sounded. Rock and popular music had always been part of the story that Bang on a Can told about themselves. Gordon took to the makeshift stage of Exit Art at the 1987 marathon to describe his Philharmonic as quasi-string quartet, quasi-rock band. Other music performed on the early festivals was strongly inflected by popular music, picking up on a tradition of genre-crossing that had crystallized in the postliterate downtown of Branca, Chatham, and New Music America as well as the influence of Louis Andriessen and his pupils like Steve Martland.[34] Bang on a Can had cultivated other forms of genre hybridity, whether in music by composers such as Ziporyn and Lois V Vierk—influenced by gamelan and gagaku, respectively—or in the presentation of non-Western groups like the Kazue Sawai Koto Ensemble and improvisers like the World Saxophone Quartet.

And the creation of the All-Stars facilitated a deeper connection to popular music for its founders. In the three-and-a-half-hour interview that Lang gave for Yale's Oral History of American Music project in 1986, he extensively discusses early influences including Dmitri Shostakovich, Harry Partch, and Lou Harrison, but popular music never comes up.[35] Less than a year later, though, Lang completed *are you experienced?*, a piece for amplified tuba, large ensemble, and narrator heavily influenced by rock. The bizarre work opens with Lang stating, deadpan, "I know you were looking forward to hearing this piece, but something terrible has just happened." He goes on to say that the listener has been struck on the head, lost consciousness, and will experience a sequence of hallucinations. What follows is a series of rhythmically pulsating, surreally narrated episodes interspersed with virtuosic tuba freakouts, which blend into a haze of distortion evoking the Jimi Hendrix song for which the work is named. Lang's subsequent music of the early 1990s, such as the ensemble work *cheating, lying, stealing* (which became an All-Stars staple) and the clarinet piece *press release* (inspired by James Brown), also centers on rhythmic grooves indebted to pop.

In a 1991 interview with K. Robert Schwarz for a profile in the *New York Times*, Lang attributed much of his music's aesthetic force to the aggression of punk rock, recalling how he played rhythm guitar in high school and had a spiritual awakening in 1978 when he first heard The Clash.[36] "I wouldn't trust any young composer who grew up in America who didn't have a background in pop music, who didn't listen to that music as his first music," Lang declared to his interviewer. Schwarz described the composer as "dressed in black, with close-cropped hair and an informal manner," seeming "more like a member of a downtown rock band than a classical composer." The polemical profile may have burned some bridges. "Every notion advanced by the composer David Lang, and abetted by his interviewer," wrote the elder composer Ned Rorem in a long screed to the *Times*, "is either specious or puerile."[37] And indeed, Lang seems far from his blazer-and-tie New York Philharmonic days. In placing Bang on a Can at the center of his musical life, he began to more closely resemble his best friend Gordon, a downtown renegade rather than orchestral conformist. "Especially since Bang on a Can, I really have made an effort to try to sew all the disparate pieces of myself together," he said in 1997.[38]

Wolfe's music underwent a similar progression. She had strong ties to folk and popular music going back to her teenage singer-songwriter years, and her Yale piece *On Seven-Star Shoes* did include a "funky" bass clarinet line.

Like that of Lang, Wolfe's post-Yale music fell deeply under the Andriessen spell. Her 1989 piece *The Vermeer Room* comprises Andriessen-esque, hard-edged smears of sound, taut brass and wind swells alongside rolls of metallic percussion, and the 1991 string quartet *Four Marys* leans more overtly toward her youthful influences, mimicking the sound of a mountain dulcimer with glassy and sneering glissandos. Wolfe moved to Amsterdam in 1992 on a Fulbright, and Gordon joined her. Though she never took formal lessons with Andriessen, she did absorb some of his wisdom over doubles ping-pong matches.

As she described in the *Lick* program note, after the All-Stars were formed Wolfe began to incorporate the sounds of Motown, funk, and rock into her work. In 1993, she wrote *my lips from speaking*, for the six-piano group Piano Circus, an unruly fantasia on the opening riff of Aretha Franklin's "Think." *Lick* came next. Wolfe later described it as a "turning-point piece" in which she "let loose" and embraced the music she had danced to as a teenager.[39] More pop-infused scores soon followed.

In contrast to those of his colleagues, Gordon's aesthetic trajectory was much more of a straight line. He continued to write rock-influenced scores for his Philharmonic, such as the 1988 *Four Kings Fight Five*, which set up intensely polyrhythmic battles between groups of instruments. The approach culminated in 1992's *Yo Shakespeare*, which creates a joyfully toe-tapping tapestry from the simultaneous interweaving of three distinct rhythmic patterns.

With amplification and electric guitar—the instrument of the twenty-first century, as Gordon called it—the All-Stars indexed the new aesthetic priorities of their founders, while also evincing a broader shift in the programming vision of Bang on a Can. Just as rock wasn't at the forefront of Lang and Wolfe's music in the 1980s, rock wasn't quite at the forefront of Bang on a Can's early thinking about what they presented. When the founders gave interviews in the late '80s, they emphasized the festival's support for music across different stylistic categories, but seemingly entrenched in the world of contemporary composition, as emblematized in their juxtaposition of Reich and Milton Babbitt in 1987. As Lang told Tim Page that year, "We wanted to combine the musics of different composers who don't usually share programs."[40] The early years of the organization had focused on overcoming the uptown–downtown binary, representing what they initially described as an "eclectic supermix of composers and styles from the serial to the surreal."[41] "Serial to the surreal" encompassed the breadth of that initial vision: from academic twelve-tone music to Cagean performance hijinks.

But that vision broadened in the 1990s, driven by the All-Stars. "In the late seventies and early eighties, there was such promise for pop music," Gordon states in "Bang on a Can Conversations," part of the program-note interviews prepared by Artman for the All-Stars' second concert at Lincoln Center in 1994. There had been, he continues, "the potential or hope that rock music could be interesting and classical music could break out of its cerebral confinement. Much of the music in Bang on a Can follows up on that impulse to merge and synthesize."[42] The composer goes on to describe the genesis of the All-Stars, connecting the ensemble specifically to this notion of genre hybridity: "In classical music, you'll have this really great violinist, he sits in a chair, he wears a tux. He's not sexy, but he's the most amazing musician. There's no visual element, no show. In rock bands, it's all show. The All-Stars explore the question: what is presenting music?"[43] The group's creators continually positioned it as drawing together the stereotypical best of both worlds, by combining classical virtuosity—"the most amazing musician"—and pop sexiness—"it's all show."

Critics seized upon the new narrative. Reviewing a Lincoln Center concert for the *Times*, Allan Kozinn wrote that "the All-Stars are not a bad band by art-rock standards."[44] And in praising their debut Sony album *Industry* in the same paper two months later, Schwarz proclaimed the All-Stars to be "a fiercely aggressive group, combining the power and punch of a rock band with the precision and clarity of a chamber ensemble."[45] That pull quote soon became one of Bang on a Can's marketing refrains, repeated in publicity materials and printed on posters.[46] *Serial to the surreal* gave way to *rock band plus chamber group*.

And there were more subtle programming changes. During the 1994 Tanglewood concert, Lisa Moore had performed Mario Davidovsky's *Synchronisms No. 6* for piano and tape. (Although Andriessen's presence loomed over the festival, Davidovsky also served as composer-in-residence that summer.) The Pulitzer Prize-winning 1970 piece, part of a series of pioneering works for solo instruments and electronic sounds, was emblematic of Davidovsky's severe, high modernist language. It had been performed by a different pianist at Bang on a Can's 1989 marathon, and another of the *Synchronisms* made its New York debut at the 1992 festival. Given his longtime association with Columbia University and the Columbia-Princeton Electronic Music Center, Davidovsky served as a metonym for uptown, and his music's presence on Bang on a Can's programs echoed the 1987 performance of Babbitt's *Vision and Prayer*. Gann described Davidovsky's *Synchronisms No. 10*, at the 1992 marathon, as the festival's "one annual offering to the uptown deities."[47] The music of Babbitt, Davidovsky, and Elliott Carter tended to serve a tokenistic function for Bang on a Can, gesturing toward their purported transcendence of uptown and downtown—one short work every marathon or so, and no uptown music released on their recordings.

But beginning around 1995, uptown repertoire stopped showing up at all. Postwar modernism was instead represented in festival and All-Stars programs by European composers such as Karlheinz Stockhausen and Iannis Xenakis. There did not seem to be a single precipitating incident: the organization's programming began to change in the mid-1990s, as they adjusted to their new home at Lincoln Center, released commercial albums on major labels, and toured with the All-Stars. But the founders did allude to unidentified tensions. "It's really unfortunate that those uptown composers really are not only alienated from Bang on a Can but really vehemently against it," Gordon said in 1997.[48] "One of the reasons why we got discouraged about the 'uptown' world is that after ten years of doing this, they still won't talk to us," Lang had said a few months earlier. "There's only so much you can do to argue with a fundamentalist. I think that's really been one of my big disappointments."[49]

At the same time, Bang on a Can did not quite seek to unify the worlds of uptown and downtown, as Duffy's Meet the Composer had. It shouldn't be too surprising that the uptowners never took a liking to the organization—Lang had publicly chastised Charles Wuorinen in that 1988 letter to the *Times*, and much of the festival's programming and marketing would have been loathed by those who shared Wuorinen's sympathies. And Bang on a Can had received positive press and funding just as uptown groups were scrambling for resources. Lang also gave another reason for the drop-off in uptown programming: "That whole issue of 'uptown' versus 'downtown' isn't very interesting anymore."[50] After all, Bang on a Can had successfully presented the music of uptown and downtown side-by-side in their early programs, fulfilling one of their foundational goals. The 1990s would instead be about bringing together contemporary classical and popular music, fused in a single ensemble.

That's not to say that Bang on a Can ever stopped talking about their origins. The Babbitt–Reich juxtaposition was baked into the organization's mythology, and the familiar tale the founders told about arriving in New York and finding both uptown and downtown alienating showed up in Lincoln Center program books and Sony Classical liner notes.[51] But those liner notes, a quasi-manifesto written by the three founders for the *Industry* album, also added that "We had the simplicity, energy and drive of pop music in our ears. We'd heard it from the cradle."[52] That part of the story was new: transcending the uptown–downtown binary became the stepping stone toward transcending the classical–pop binary.

Michael Blackwood's 1997 documentary *New York Composers: Searching for a New Music*, which profiled the Bang on a Can founders alongside several peers, strongly registers this shift. "How do you get something that has this elemental power of pop music, and yet combine it with this fantastic sense of structure, and the responsibility of putting notes on paper that you get with classical music?" Lang asks in the first few minutes of the documentary.[53] Gordon distances himself from classical music, and describes how a new piece he wrote for the All-Stars, *I Buried Paul*, is based on the infamous "Paul Is Dead" Beatles conspiracy. Wolfe namechecks Led Zeppelin and Beethoven as major influences and states that her generation embraces "the sound world" of rock and the "immediacy" of minimalism. At no point do the three composers mention uptown or downtown on-screen. When the film came out, Bang on a Can was preparing *Music for Airports*, an acoustic arrangement of Brian Eno's epochal ambient record for the All-Stars—a rock crossover project that would help them reach new audiences.

The Need for Control

New audiences couldn't be reached, though, merely by virtue of a pop-oriented repertoire. Nor was the marketing of the All-Stars—the heady descriptions of new-music warriors, the promotional photographs, the visceral bios—just empty hype. Chamber music series, arts presenters, and music festivals don't book acts exclusively on their administrative savvy and attractive press kits. It matters how well they perform. And the six All-Stars, highly trained soloists working in an ensemble context, quickly crafted a cohesive artistic identity, such that today, the name "Bang on a Can" is just as often associated with the sextet as it is with its parent organization.

The members of the All-Stars found the early years of performing together—developing a collaborative rapport and a new repertoire—musically invigorating. "We just had this great chemistry," Maya Beiser remembered. "From the moment that we met, it was just fire."[54] "We like playing with each other, and it's a real joy to work together," Robert Black told Schwarz in 1995.[55] "There's an opportunity here to reach out to larger audiences and get a little exposure for the music." Bang on a Can's office would mail the players scores and parts, and they would assemble in New York for all-day rehearsal sessions. Absent a conductor, the group felt like a collective effort; it was just the six of them in the room, and they made their own decisions about how to play and what they played. "We were given no input into what we were trying to achieve musically, either on a large conceptual level or in some kind of orientation session at rehearsal," Ziporyn recalled of the band's early years. "We just showed up—the six of us—and got to work."[56]

New commissions for the group by experimental composers such as Nick Didkovsky and Henry Threadgill, which often omitted dynamic markings or other traditional notational devices, demanded thoughtful interpretation. Given Ziporyn's long-term relationship with the directors and the fact that the All-Stars frequently played his music, the reed player often served as de facto leader in rehearsal. He devoted many hours to realizing arrangements, copying out parts, and co-producing All-Stars albums in studio. The performers' assertion of artistic agency was recognized by critics: as Tim Page, who had reviewed the 1987 marathon, wrote in *Newsday* of a Lincoln Center show in 1994, the All-Stars "present new music the way it should be presented—with passion, precision, dynamism, stylistic authority, and a welcoming informality." He didn't actually care for much of the repertoire, but was won over by the fact that "the players *themselves* cared so much."[57]

The works that Bang on a Can's founders created for the new ensemble were deeply indebted to its sound. Wolfe credits the over-the-top energy of *Lick* to the over-the-top energy that the All-Stars brought to their repertoire as a whole. Schick painstakingly assembled the collection of junk metal that gave Lang's *the anvil chorus* its idiosyncratically resonant timbres, and the feral wail of Beiser's cello is crucial to Gordon's *Industry*. "It was about composers sketching out a framework, and then performers completing it by whatever means necessary," Ziporyn described.[58] And the composers increasingly hand-tailored their works for the individuality of the performers. Wolfe has written that in her *Believing*, she composed "wild, frenetic, improvised screaming on the bass" as "quintessential Robert Black-isms."[59]

In 1995, Schwarz asked Gordon what he thought of the *Times* likening the All-Stars to an "art-rock band." The composer replied that the designation was "condescending," because "anyone that's really familiar with rock"—as Gordon certainly was—"knows that this is not art-rock." Instead, he noted, "These are 20th century composers, living composers, writing very specific music down for highly trained classical musicians to play."[60] When asked whether the ensemble improvised, Gordon responded that, regarding the All-Stars repertoire, "98 percent of it is all written down."[61] This had long been the approach of Bang on a Can's founders, who saw themselves as writers of notated music to be executed by classically-trained musicians. Describing his lack of interest in jazz or improvisation back in 1986, Lang said that "I think that that says a lot about why someone becomes a classical composer because you really decide that the need for control is very strong, that an idea that is promising when it begins deserves to be fulfilled."[62]

Aspects of that spirit spilled over into the administration of the All-Stars, in a manner that made the group peculiar within the larger history of new music. In the past, if a composer founded or co-founded an ensemble—as Charles Wuorinen did with the Group for Contemporary Music, and Glass and Reich did with their own groups—they typically also performed within or conducted it. American new-music groups in the 1980s and 1990s usually included a mixture of composers and performers playing together, whether downtown with the S.E.M. Ensemble or uptown with the Da Capo Chamber Players. Speculum Musicae did not include composers within the ensemble, but its performing members ran it as a cooperative entity.[63] The Kronos Quartet was driven by the vision of its founding violinist, David Harrington. More broadly, even if American new-music ensembles had administrators or boards, they were largely self-governed entities. Performers managed themselves.

Abroad, more overtly political models had emerged for how to run an ensemble. While living in Amsterdam in 1992, Wolfe wrote *Arsenal of Democracy*, an abrasively antiphonal work, for the Dutch group Orkest De Volharding, who had visited Bang on a Can's festival in 1990. In a program note, she described the ensemble as "loud and tough" and "organized in a socialistic framework—everyone has equal say, everyone arrives at consensus decisions."[64] Louis Andriessen had co-founded De Volharding in 1972 as a political street band, one that prized itself on self-determination and the working rights of its performers. De Volharding had emerged from the "Movement for the Renewal of Musical Practice," a grassroots association of Dutch musicians who, inspired by the militant socialist activism that swept through the Netherlands in the late 1960s, sought to replace their country's authoritarian orchestral establishment with a more democratic culture of small ensembles.[65] "The music must be the property of the guys who play," Andriessen said in 1973. "It should not be that as the composer you are the employer and they are the employees."[66]

A similar framework was deployed by the British group Icebreaker, for whom Gordon had written *Yo Shakespeare*. Founded by flutist James Poke and composer John Godfrey, Icebreaker had its own manifesto that declared itself a "radical alternative to more mainstream forms of contemporary music which it often finds sterile"—an attitude not unlike that of Bang on a Can.[67] But Icebreaker also picked up on De Volharding's democratic approach. The ensemble gave composers a list of rules, ranging from "Icebreaker's music is loud" to "The group always plays without a conductor." It even had final say over the titles of all works written for it (and banned "generic titles such as 'sonata'"). Bang on a Can, then, had first-hand experience with new-music ensembles that were governed by their performers. But just as they had overlooked the collectivism of Sheep's Clothing, Bang on a Can decided against these models in favor of an alternative setup.

In a 2016 interview, Lang described the management of the All-Stars as "completely top-down." "I don't think we have ever turned down an idea that was brought to us by a player," he added. But he also described the dynamic bluntly: "It's not like we're fascists, or something. But we are fascists, I guess, because we are in control. We are the artistic directors, and we do the programming, and the band exists primarily to suit the needs of the organization."[68] Such frankness is typical of Lang, and "fascist" might be a bit of an exaggeration when it comes to running a new-music outfit. But, inadvertently and revealingly, Lang's comment echoes an important debate that emerged around the ensemble dynamics of Steve Reich, one of Bang on a Can's strongest role models.

Even after Reich turned away from working with electronics in the 1970s, his compositions for live musicians in this period were continually critiqued as "machine-like" because performances appeared or sounded hyper-controlled. During a tour of West Germany in 1972, reviewers also criticized his work for purportedly manipulating its listeners, with one critic describing Reich's *Drumming* as "musical fascism."[69] But Reich himself was at pains to instead emphasize his music's connection to the body. He told an interviewer that "The extreme limits used here then have nothing to do with totalitarian political controls imposed from without, but are closely related to yogic controls of the breath and mind."[70] Reich did yoga with members of his ensemble, and drew a "body logic" directly into *Music for Eighteen Musicians*, which opens with overlapping pulses structured as a series of musical breaths.[71]

Critics in the 1970s saw the clockwork precision of Reich's ensemble as machine-like and implicitly totalitarian. By contrast, the All-Stars did not receive such critiques. Indeed, the mid-'90s All-Stars would seem to bely any notions of "machine-like." In the Tanglewood video of *Lick*, the performers appear deeply self-expressive, as they bob their heads and sway to Wolfe's music; their individual bios were vividly personal and explicitly corporeal ("The clarinet becomes an extension of my body"); and though Ziporyn indicated downbeats with his instrument, the sextet lacked a conductor or other visible hierarchy. "The whole idea of tapping your foot is a no-no in classical music," Moore said in 1995. "One of the reasons why I love Bang on a Can is that you can actually tap your foot."[72] In the rehearsal room and on stage, the All-Stars were a group of hip, individualistic collaborators defying classical conventions; behind-the-scenes, however, a different picture emerged.

At first, All-Stars gigs were intermittent, and they were a lot of fun; when touring began to pick up, it felt surprising to the members of the sextet, and occasionally glamorous. Bang on a Can's office handled the organizational work—booking shows, making travel plans, finding rehearsal spaces—giving the performers the rare opportunity to focus primarily on their craft. In 2018, Mark Stewart described the management of the group as a "great blessing." "I want the full weight and irony and all attendant things to accompany these words: there's nothing like great leadership," he said, adding that the artistic and administrative guidance of the directors gave him "the freedom to do what I do and be what I am in this band: I can apply all my energy to the tasks."[73] Though they weren't running the ensemble themselves, they could also devote themselves to their own projects—Ziporyn led a gamelan group, Schick had a percussion ensemble—that would perform regularly at Bang on a Can's Lincoln Center marathons. And they were helping contemporary music reach a new audience, playing sold-out concerts around the country and then around the world.

But as that audience grew, as touring increased, strains soon emerged. The ensemble was amplified, but did not yet have a dedicated sound engineer. Though individual members had prior experience working with amplification, they were essentially left to their own devices to address balance issues in rehearsal and performance, with a different engineer at each venue. "It's frustrating not being in control," Moore said in 1995. "If you're trained as a classical musician, you're in control of your sound, and you've spent years learning how to balance against other instruments. And then all of the sudden you're given a microphone and a monitor, and that's all that you're hearing."[74] "Sound checks were just nightmares," Black recalled, describing the early tours as "a free-for-all"; Ziporyn characterized them as "very guerrilla."[75]

Tensions rose in the wake of a March 1996 tour to Australia and New Zealand. As part of the Adelaide Festival, the All-Stars performed five entirely distinct programs in five different spaces, over eight days.[76] The All-Stars didn't want to play the same show every night—they wanted to avoid the repetitive drudgery of a symphony orchestra—but the over-programmed tour and hasty sound accommodations went too far, and seemed to some members like an affront. For Bang on a Can, however, the relentless pace of Adelaide, and other prestigious international appearances, emblematized the group's growing success and justified its existence. As a contemporaneous grant report boasted, "During the 1995–1996 season, 15,000 people experienced Bang on a Can concerts from Amsterdam to Adelaide and New Zealand to New York. Bang on a Can was involved in twenty-nine concerts on three continents, presenting works by fifty-two composers."[77]

Conditions soon improved after two new hires. In January 1996, sound engineer Andrew Cotton worked with the All-Stars for a tour of England. "They were used to long, drawn-out sound checks, trying to explain everything to people, and people were not getting it," he recalled.[78] With a background collaborating with popular and jazz groups as well as contemporary ensembles like the London Sinfonietta and Steve Martland Band, Cotton grasped the challenges of live-mixing amplified musicians who blended aspects of classical and rock. He put together a stage plan that was fixed for each concert—cutting down significantly on messy movements of percussion between pieces—and provided each musician with a monitor and mix. "They seemed surprised at how painless the soundchecks were," Cotton added. "I couldn't work out what the big deal was." After the difficulties in Australia, Cotton was hired as the group's main sound engineer, beginning with a gig at the Settembre Festival in Turin. He has remained with them for more than two decades, and is frequently described as the "seventh" All-Star. And in 1997, Bang on a Can hired Kenny Savelson to help manage the All-Stars and their tours as production associate. "That turned us into a much more professional organization," Ziporyn recalled of these changes.[79]

Another issue raised by the sextet's performers was that of repertoire. Schick recalled that the All-Stars were not involved in repertoire decisions, and mostly remembered playing concert programs that they received from the directors. "Most bands form organically because they want to play with each other," Moore recalled, yet the All-Stars were "a very composer-dominated group." In particular, she had been dismayed by changes in the group's repertoire during the *Music for Airports* project, a live reimagining of the groundbreaking 1978 Brian Eno album that invented the label "ambient music." Gordon came up with the idea: Lang, Gordon, Wolfe, and Ziporyn divvied up the four sections of Eno's record and arranged them for the All-Stars, transforming the original's wash of tape loops into a careful collage of instrumental color. The project, tied to the release of a *Music for Airports* CD on the Philips imprint Point Music, dominated the All-Stars' touring between 1998 and 2000, and Eno's work was typically paired with music by the four arrangers (Figure 5.3).

Previously, the All-Stars had regularly programmed works highlighting individual performers, like Tom Johnson's *Failing* for solo bass or Frederic Rzewski's Piano Piece No. 4, but these were squeezed out by the *Airports* repertoire. Eno's ambient music did not provide as challenging or engaging work for the performers as the ensemble's other, more virtuosic fare. Mark Stewart recalled that the All-Stars were originally predicated on celebrating the individuality of the performers, but "That piece basically said, 'Yeah, that's not

Figure 5.3 *Music for Airports* at Lincoln Center, 1998. Photograph by Stephanie Berger.

so important right now,'" likening his role to that of helping install a work of visual art.⁸⁰ Even though Maya Beiser found *Airports* artistically compelling and a "spectacular project" as an album, she described touring the ambient work as "not that interesting for the performers," adding that "it's not a virtuosic part for anybody."⁸¹ But she also acknowledged that it was easily the ensemble's most popular repertoire, the "big hit of the Bang on a Can All-Stars." "All the presenters really wanted it," she added. "They were going to sell tickets, and people were really into it." In a 1998 pitch to a potential presenter, Savelson wrote that "*Music for Airports* is a well-known piece with a wide cult following—its inclusion on our touring program has proven to be a great way to introduce Bang on a Can to new markets—particularly due to its crossover appeal to both contemporary classical and popular music audiences."[82]

An agenda for a June 1999 Bang on a Can office meeting records the emerging dissatisfaction:

> The group is tired of the programming. I've talked with several of them about this and it's not just 'Airports' but the repetition of Cheating, Believing, Lick, Tsmindao, IBP, etc.[83] No one is really against performing any one of these works (incl Eno) but performing all of them together over and over is becoming tiresome. Programming a wider variety of the rep while continuing to include all of these piece & Airports would be welcome.[84]

But a wider repertoire was not the point of the *Airports* tour, whose concerts typically included the above-mentioned works by the founders and Ziporyn on the first half, and the Eno on the second half. The programs were designed to introduce Bang on a Can's core efforts to new listeners, with *Airports* as the hook. The All-Stars were never exclusively a vehicle for the music of Gordon, Lang, and Wolfe, but they were also always a narrower endeavor than Bang on a Can's marathons. The turn toward rock through the 1990s, as *Airports* came to epitomize, evidenced a further kind of narrowing, the consolidation of the organization's vision into a touring package to broaden their audience. Because of the Eno project, by June 1998, Savelson was discussing with the founders the possibility of hiring a booking agent from a major entertainment management firm, to expand further beyond arts presenters to commercial venues like clubs and "help increase our fan base."[85] (Ultimately, that plan did not come to fruition.)

Though Gordon, Lang, and Wolfe had founded the All-Stars to explicitly bring together six virtuoso soloists—or, as Wolfe once put it, "the top, phenomenal players" of the festival—it is revealing that they chose to emphasize the non-virtuosic *Music for Airports*. "Each year more presenters express interest in importing Bang on a Can," the organization had written back in 1993 of their creation of the All-Stars. "What attracts these presenters is that Bang on a Can represents the full spectrum of the vibrant New York music scene."[86] But it turned out that a full spectrum was less attractive to presenters and listeners than a sole ambient work by a famous rock musician, and Bang on a Can followed suit. From the perspective of the office, it seemed totally normal for the musicians to tackle a single, popular program for a few seasons before moving on to new material. After all, being an All-Star was not a full-time gig, and the musicians could always place their creative energy into their other projects. But for the performers who lacked control over administrative decisions, the routinized repertoire in these years served as a point of contention. The All-Stars programming broadened again after the *Airports* tour, and has encompassed numerous projects since the late 1990s and a bevvy of new works created for the ensemble through the People's Commissioning Fund.

"The All-Stars were always an unnatural organism," Lang said in 2019. "We liked these people because of their independent energy, and because of that there always was the tension that they would feel caged."[87] It was chamber group and rock band, six individualistic soloists and a collaborative sextet, overseen by a trio of composers. Rather than spell the ensemble's undoing, these contradictions anchored a residency at Lincoln Center and a series of CDs—Bang on a Can's two principal projects of the late 1990s—that helped its parent organization thrive in the marketplace.

6
Lincoln Center

Back in the fiery and fun early days of the All-Stars—four years before the *Airports* tour, two years before Andrew Cotton joined as sound engineer, five months before their Tanglewood debut—the ensemble played a sold-out gig in New York. It was March 1994, and the program included a mix of chamber and solo works by Frederic Rzewski, Tom Johnson, Evan Ziporyn, David Lang, Michael Gordon, Eleanor Hovda, and Mary Wright. The nearly 300 people in the audience knew that something unusual was taking place. And the critics were there too, paying close attention. Writing for the *New York Times*, Allan Kozinn found the All-Stars visceral and their program compelling. But the big news, he wrote, was not what the group played, or how it played, but where it played—Walter Reade Theater, on West 65th Street, part of the Lincoln Center performing arts complex:

> Professional worriers of different stripes are no doubt poring over the schedule of the eighth Bang on a Can series, searching for portents. For some, Lincoln Center's adoption of the post-Minimalist downtown festival, with its informal atmosphere and its occasional nods to rock-and-roll, is a sign of Western civilization's imminent collapse; or at least, of Lincoln Center's shameless abandonment of the artistic high ground in pursuit of trendiness. The alternative fear is that Bang on a Can, having allowed itself to be absorbed by Lincoln Center, will surrender its quirkily omnivorous character and be sucked into the bland mainstream.[1]

Was such hyperbole necessary? Were these two organizations—one, the home of classical music titans like the New York Philharmonic and Metropolitan Opera, the other, a grassroots new-music festival—so radically different that a partnership could seem so portentous? After all, Lincoln Center presented all kinds of different ensembles on its Great Performers series, and it had been hosting the downtown avant-garde with its Serious Fun! festival since the late '80s. And Bang on a Can, which had been rotating venues for their New York concerts every year since they got kicked out of RAPP Arts Center, had already hosted their 1992 festival uptown, less than two blocks away from Lincoln Center, at the Society for Ethical Culture.

But perhaps the rhetoric wasn't so hyperbolic. When Bang on a Can first showed up at Lincoln Center for two All-Stars concerts and a marathon in spring 1994, it represented a genuine, seismic shift (Figure 6.1). Longtime observers like Kozinn, as well as critics and musicians in the downtown scene, had viewed the organization as an anti-establishment, funkily communal festival, and they expressed significant concerns about Bang on a Can's direction as they both consolidated and expanded in the mid-'90s—not only with the Lincoln Center collaboration, but also with their founding of the All-Stars and march into the record industry. And this was not a one-off. For the second half of the 1990s, Bang on a Can held most of their New York concerts at Lincoln Center, as part of the center's embrace of contemporary music under the direction of administrator Jane Moss.

The partnership emblematized a new development in contemporary music's turn toward the marketplace: in the 1990s, some of classical music's most mainstream organizations looked to new work in the hopes of reaching new audiences. Whereas the Philharmonic's Horizons festivals of a decade earlier had been prompted by Meet the Composer, an outside organization, Lincoln Center's embrace of the new came entirely of its own volition, after it had witnessed the appeal of grassroots endeavors like Bang on a Can as well the success of a more established rival, the Brooklyn Academy of Music.

Figure 6.1 The Bang on a Can All-Stars at Walter Reade Theater at Lincoln Center, April 11, 1994. Photograph copyright Jack Vartoogian and FrontRowPhotos.

New music's marketplace stance had been an ideology held by composition professors at Yale, a rhetorical position promoted by Meet the Composer, a goal of upstarts like Bang on a Can, and a necessity of the diminished landscape for public arts funding. Now, it would be held by leaders of one of classical music's most powerful institutions.

And even if some saw an ostensibly hopelessly mismatched pair, it is easy to imagine how Bang on a Can provided continuity with Lincoln Center's more traditional offerings. The All-Stars represented an amplified, rock-inflected take on the conventional chamber ensemble, and the marathons presented an eclectic, informal take on the conventional concert experience. Indeed, Kozinn wrote of the March '94 concert that "neither Lincoln Center nor Bang on a Can seemed any worse for the encounter."[2] But Bang on a Can framed the Lincoln Center partnership as a radical gesture, and continually considered and re-considered its implications for their future. In the midst of an arts funding crisis, Lincoln Center offered the possibility of new support for the festival, as they focused on building outwards from New York with their touring ensemble and recordings. But most importantly, it gave Bang on a Can the opportunity to place themselves, and the composers they represented, in a highly prestigious location and in front of a larger audience. As Bang on a Can collaborated with Lincoln Center, the organization prioritized their marketplace aims—their desire for expanding their reach—over the anti-establishment image that they had previously cultivated. The festival was more like Lincoln Center than many realized.

We Want to Attract a New and Perhaps Younger Audience

"The nation's postwar cultural boom resonated most loudly and philanthropically in the project that brought New York's Lincoln Center for the Performing Arts into being," writes James Allen Smith.[3] Part of a massive urban renewal endeavor on Manhattan's Upper West Side initiated by Robert Moses in the mid-'50s, the cultural complex opened in 1962 with a starry gala at Philharmonic Hall. The Ford and Rockefeller Foundations guided the project, working closely with other foundations and corporate donors, and Lincoln Center received a significant portion of its initial funding from government sources. Within its first decade, the center's constituents included the New York Philharmonic, Metropolitan Opera, New York City Opera and Ballet, and Chamber Music Society. It established the multipurpose performing arts center as a national model, in which real-estate capital was enmeshed with high art, with imitators like Washington's Kennedy Center.

A major question in the early years of the center was whether it would primarily serve as a campus for its constituents, supporting the work of the Philharmonic and Met, or whether it would become a programming force in its own right. Center president and composer William Schuman leaned toward the latter approach, and started the Great Performers recital series in 1965, which featured the likes of Birgit Nilsson, Duke Ellington, and Joan Baez, as well as the Mostly Mozart summer festival beginning in 1966.[4] Great Performers soon started presenting rock concerts, but curbed its popular music fare in 1976 when it became too expensive to compete with other presenters, and focused on series featuring American orchestras, art-song recitalists, and visiting chamber groups.

With a considerable number of seats to fill in multiple venues, Lincoln Center continually sought new ways to expand its audience as well as overhaul its public image, which was typically associated with the conservative work of its high-art residents. In 1981, a producer for the center's Out of Doors festival—which featured bluegrass, B-Boys, a Hispanic Music Day, and mimes for its tenth anniversary that year—told the *Times* that "We want everybody to know that Lincoln Center is not a cultural fortress, a place only for people in tall hats and ropes of pearls with the price of a box at the Metropolitan Opera."[5] Neocons detested such efforts, as well as the premise of the arts center itself. Charles Wuorinen called it the "Lincoln Shopping Center," emblematic of a commercialization of the arts that substituted marketing hype for genuine education in serious culture. "The Lincoln Center impulse, for all its nobility of purpose, is basically one of enlarging the audience—the number of bodies," he told an interviewer in the late '80s. "If there aren't 3,500 people who want to hear the Beethoven symphony you turn around and sell it like toothpaste."[6]

New music was not a main priority for Lincoln Center in its first two decades, though there were occasional attempts, such as a nine-day Celebration of Contemporary Music in 1976, a Bicentennial collaboration between the New York Philharmonic and Juilliard that reached large audiences with concerts, lectures, and open rehearsals. But it was in some sense an outside project, initiated and partly funded by Paul Fromm and his foundation, and it did not return for a second year.[7] Projects like Horizons revealed that, if heavily marketed, new music could attract both traditional classical subscribers and new listeners to Lincoln Center. But without the financial and logistical support of organizations like the Fromm Foundation or Meet the Composer, such offerings required sustained attention from classical presenters who were often eager to fall back on traditional programming with a clearer economic model.

But across the East River, another performing arts center soon offered a prototype for the avant-garde as a sustained audience success. Under the direction of Harvey Lichtenstein, the Brooklyn Academy of Music's Next Wave Festival presented new work by Philip Glass, Twyla Tharp, Laurie Anderson, Robert Wilson, and other countercultural icons in lengthy, sold-out runs. Lincoln Center wanted its own Next Wave and, in July 1987, it launched Serious Fun!, a two-week festival of experimental music, theater, and dance. Billed as "eclectic, offbeat entertainment," the proceedings were overseen by an outside curator, Jed Wheeler, who ran a management firm that represented Glass and many other downtown figures, and had previously booked tours of Next Wave's productions.[8] BAM was dark in the summer, so Serious Fun could compete without directly siphoning off its audience.

This was not Mostly Mozart, nor was it Fromm's contemporary festival. Lincoln Center billed Serious Fun as bringing downtown uptown, providing acts normally seen at The Kitchen with the resources, air conditioning, and more than 1,000 seats of Alice Tully Hall.[9] And it had an emphatically populist air. Wheeler coined the name because he wanted a catchy alternative to "avant-garde."[10] "We're not selling an esthetic," he told the *Times*. "We want people to be entertained."[11] With a budget of $300,000 and major funding from the Fan Fox and Leslie R. Samuels Foundation, the first festival included a Robert Wilson production, the World Saxophone Quartet, the Lounge Lizards, Douglas Dunn and Dancers, and a group of Norwegian opera singers backed by a rock band. Nathan Leventhal, the president of Lincoln Center, described it as part of a broader "revitalization."[12] (That same summer, the center launched the three-concert series Classical Jazz, which served as the prototype for Jazz at Lincoln Center.) "We would like to expose our traditional Lincoln Center audiences to a form of art they would not otherwise be likely to see," Leventhal said to the *Times* about Serious Fun. "More important, we want to attract a new and perhaps younger audience to Lincoln Center."[13]

And it appeared to work. "Our marketing surveys showed that the average age of 'Serious Fun!' patrons was 35," Leventhal told the *Times* in 1988. "That's 20 years below the average for Lincoln Center as a whole."[14] The *Times* noted that the first festival had "sold a respectable 63 percent of the available seats."[15] The second festival included composers who had already seen success at BAM and in the record industry: a chamber opera by Michael Nyman, an evening of songs by Laurie Anderson, Philip Glass in live concert with Allen Ginsberg—along with many of Wheeler's other clients, Glass was a mainstay of the festival. It also presented a new commission by downtown electric guitar maven and former Kitchen music director Rhys Chatham.

In a *Times* profile, Chatham described how when he first began working at The Kitchen there was a small, loyal audience, but now the space sold out regularly. "What New York needs now is three kinds of spaces," he said. "We need small places for musicians, artists and dancers no one knows—places where they can show their work, and where critics will come and put out the word. We need intermediate spaces, for those who have gained some recognition. And we need big spaces like the Brooklyn Academy or Alice Tully Hall, for artists who can attract larger audiences and who need to reach people who have not yet heard their work."[16] Gentrification, he noted, had eroded the neighborhood artist enclaves of the 1970s. "Now everyone is dispersed," he added. "So in a way, it doesn't matter where we play. It could be the Kitchen, or it could be Lincoln Center. People who want to hear the music will come."[17]

Other attempts among Lincoln Center's constituents to program new music were less successful. In 1989, cellist Fred Sherry, known for his work with ensembles Tashi and Speculum Musicae, became director of the Chamber Music Society of Lincoln Center. He placed a strong emphasis on contemporary work, especially the music of uptown composers like Milton Babbitt and Elliott Carter. Within three years, ticket sales had declined more than 30 percent, and Sherry resigned. The drop in sales was partly attributed to the promotion of contemporary work, although there were additional factors—Sherry had dismissed many older musicians and brought in younger ones, and there was competition from new presenters nearby.[18] He was replaced by the clarinetist David Shifrin, who returned to more conventional fare and put contemporary music on its own series.

The kind of modernist repertoire played by Speculum Musicae, it seemed, was not going to attract audiences in the way that the downtown explorations of Serious Fun would. Further, whereas Serious Fun was a new venture seeking a new audience, Sherry's curation represented a major change for an existing institution with a built-in subscriber base: the conservative chamber music audience may have felt that new music was being forced down their throats. The issue, then, wasn't only what style of new music was being presented, but also what kind of listenership it was aimed toward.

Amidst Leventhal's revitalization, Lincoln Center was also hunting for a new director of programming. After fourteen months of searching, in September 1992 it announced that it had appointed Jane Moss. The forty-year-old Moss was, in many ways, an unusual choice. She had been an administrator for two theater organizations and worked as an arts consultant, but had no experience programming or booking concerts. And her introduction to the music world was quite specific: Moss had worked as executive director of Meet the Composer in the late 1980s, succeeding Frances Richard as John Duffy's number-two, where she oversaw the Reader's Digest Commissioning program, as well as new initiatives for choreographer and jazz commissions. "Going to Meet the Composer was a very significant shift for me," she said in 2019. "It sort of changed my direction in life."[19] She recalled that the "grounding in contemporary music as my first music outing definitely affected how we looked at things at Lincoln Center."[20] Duffy told the *Times* that Moss "sees the creative and performing arts as part of the larger fabric of society, and she has very broad musical interests."[21]

A lengthy *Times* profile of Moss, by a somewhat skeptical Edward Rothstein, situated her arrival as a crossroads moment: "Nearly every arts institution is now undergoing serious self-examination about its purpose and future, facing issues related to multi-culturalism, public financing, future audiences, and the relationship between art music and other traditions."[22] When Moss's position was announced, Leventhal was emphatic that "our core curriculum is classical music," and Moss took pains to emphasize that her new position stood for "evolution, not revolution."[23] The specter of the Culture Wars hovered over Rothstein's profile. "The notion that art and truth and beauty in and of themselves are of inherent value and need to be supported—I think those days are gone," she told the critic.

Multicultural programming would be considered, though based on artistic merit rather than "political correctness"; classical offerings would need to be given more context, as knowledge of the repertoire could not be assumed; ticket prices should be brought down. Moss explained that each art form and genre at Lincoln Center had a narrow constituency, but that her goal would be for their audiences to overlap, and move outside their comfort zones. Sprawling festivals like Serious Fun were the model, in their combination of the familiar and unfamiliar and emphasis on the "event." It is not hard to see how Bang on a Can might fit into such a vision. It is also not hard to see how her comments might anger conservatives—an administrator at the power center of American classical music announcing that high art could no longer sustain itself on its own merits. Samuel Lipman, never a fan of Lincoln Center, had already denounced Serious Fun and other non-classical offerings as having "nothing at all to do with high culture" back in 1991.[24]

At a press conference in May 1993, Leventhal announced that Moss would oversee a newly consolidated parent organization called Lincoln Center Productions, which handled more than 300 performances each season, including the Great Performers, Mostly Mozart, jazz, Out of Doors, and Serious Fun series.[25] (This constituted only about a fifth of Lincoln Center's total activities: the Met and Philharmonic had their own staffs and programming.) Moss and Leventhal had realized that Great Performers had become a financial liability, as it required costly name-brand musicians to fill seats, and audiences were declining. "I was hired as a change agent," Moss recalled.[26] "What was happening in the classical music world was that the old formulas were not working the way they used to." Lincoln Center Productions would instead shake up the series by presenting concerts at Alice Tully Hall and the smaller Walter Reade Theater, with an emphasis on repertoire- and composer-driven programming as well as emphatic attention to contemporary music.[27] A New Works Fund commissioned a collaboration between John Adams and Peter Sellars, string quartets by Elliott Carter and John Corigliano, a piano quartet by Charles Wuorinen, and a piece by Wynton Marsalis—an eclectic mix perhaps emblematic of the curatorial oversight of a former Meet the Composer administrator.[28] Moss also launched the Discovery series, dedicated to contemporary music and featuring the Kronos Quartet and Los Angeles Philharmonic's New Music Group. And she was unabashed about playing into trends. In October 1993, Discovery presented the Orchestra of St. Luke's performing Henryk Górecki's Symphony No. 3, in the wake of the blockbuster success of Nonesuch's recording of the piece, featuring soprano Dawn Upshaw and conductor David Zinman. The concert also included music by Arvo Pärt, and a press release noted that such spiritual minimalism was "currently at the peak of its popularity."[29]

Moss collaborated with Wheeler on the 1993 Serious Fun festival, but brought the curation in-house the following year, where it took on more of an international focus—and alienated some of its downtown regulars.[30] It was then subsumed into a new endeavor, the Lincoln Center Festival, which was explicitly oriented toward large-scale, international productions, and launched in 1996 under the direction of former *New York Times* critic John Rockwell. A *New York Magazine* cover story titled "The Culture Titans" profiled the competition between the Lincoln Center Festival and BAM's Next Wave, as they battled for the same youthful audiences and for the right to produce new works by avant-garde darling Robert Wilson. The first Lincoln Center Festival brought in 14,000 newcomers, with a Wilson production of *Four Saints in Three Acts*, plays by Samuel Beckett, and collaborations between Merce Cunningham and John Cage as well as Alvin Ailey and Jazz at Lincoln Center.[31]

And Moss added, as a capstone to her first season curating Great Performers, a three-concert series featuring Bang on a Can. "Bang on a Can is probably the most unusual new-music event in the city," she told *New York Magazine*. "Unusual because its artistic directors have managed to bridge both the downtown and the uptown music scenes."³² She described the collaboration as an "off-shoot" of Serious Fun. "It's about a younger, different audience. And the marathon is a different kind of concert-going experience; it encourages people to come and go and mingle in the lobby. Bang on a Can achieves another goal of mine, which has been to experiment with different kinds of concert formats."³³ It was part of her bigger attempt to revamp the center's image. "I'm very eager to broaden people's perception of Lincoln Center," she later told the critic K. Robert Schwarz, "to say that it's not just this high culture palace that you have to get dressed up for."³⁴

Bang on a Can's merging of uptown and downtown might have seemed "unusual" to Moss. But it is also possible to see the festival as a more conventional alternative to Serious Fun's emphasis on the interdisciplinary avant-garde. Bang on a Can predominantly represented composers who wrote fully notated music for chamber ensembles, albeit noisily amplified ones. In this regard, Bang on a Can offered an aesthetic vision much more closely aligned with the orchestras and chamber groups typically featured on Great Performers than Serious Fun, which tended toward downtown composer-performers like Laurie Anderson and Diamanda Galás. Despite their marathon lengths, unpretentious attitude, and loud, rock-inspired music, they would register to audiences, and perhaps donors, as a hip revamp of Lincoln Center's chamber music norms—evolution, not revolution.

I Would Rather Be Blowing up Lincoln Center

In early 1993, they got the call from Moss. They wondered if it was a joke, or perhaps a mistake. But they began considering it, weighing the pros and cons. The ensuing debate—described in hindsight by the founders in numerous interviews—represents a rare moment of dissension among Gordon, Lang, and Wolfe that they have discussed publicly. The stakes were clear. As then-managing director Karen Sander put it, looking back at that moment, "Is this going to ruin Lincoln Center, and is this going to ruin Bang on a Can?"³⁵

Around this time, the trio had been invited to curate a Bang on a Can-style marathon at the Holland Festival, and Wolfe recalled her amazement at the "many elegant dinners" they had with Dutch administrators during the planning process, marveling over the Netherlands' robustly funded arts bureaucracy.³⁶ Though there was something appealing about planning a festival over lavish meals rather than takeout in their tiny Manhattan office, Wolfe also found herself missing "the craziness of New York, the energized desperation."³⁷ Something about the constant hustle of applying for grants and soliciting donations and participating in American capitalism appealed to Bang on a Can's scrappy mentality. And Moss's request came at an opportune time. "We were really, really burnt out, because it was just the three of us really doing most of the work," Wolfe recalled.[38] In 1993, they had a single part-time employee, and had not yet hired any full-time staff. Lincoln Center could help with the heavy lifting.

But there were doubts. "There was a big fight because at first we said no to ourselves," Lang recalled. "We said, 'No way we're going there. That's the palace of culture.'"[39] Moving to a major arts center would seem to contradict their DIY spirit, their iconoclastic ethos, their explicit rhetoric around why new music had become so calcified, safe, and boring. In a 1993 grant proposal, Bang on a Can had specifically pitched their festival as breaking down the very boundaries that were erected by traditional presenters: "Art in our society has become dangerously institutionalized. The desire to localize and stabilize certain art forms has led to the creation of such institutions as Lincoln Center, the Museum of Modern Art, Carnegie Hall, and the Brooklyn Academy of Music."[40] What would be lost if they joined such efforts?

"It caused a lot of soul-searching," Lang told *Billboard*.[41] "We're known as the festival with the beer stains on the floor and the scruffy, East Village, downtown attitude. So the idea of going into a place that's clean, with paper towels in the bathroom, is unbelievable luxury." He was the most ambivalent about the project: the prodigal son was not eager to return to the site of the Horizons festivals. "I am the person who feels like I would rather be blowing up Lincoln Center than playing at Lincoln Center," Lang said in 1997, still skeptical about the ongoing collaboration.[42] Of the trio, he had the most conventional credentials, and had done the most work in such traditionalist environs—not just Horizons '86, but his attendance at Tanglewood back in 1983, and commissions for the Cleveland Orchestra and Boston Symphony. The New York Philharmonic had even played *eating living monkeys* at Avery Fisher in 1991; his music tended already to show up, at least occasionally, at Lincoln Center. Lang remained the most "establishment" composer of the trio, even as he refashioned himself as a punkish renegade in the 1990s. He wanted Bang on a Can to preserve their subversive streak, and he fretted about how the festival's independent spirit might be compromised by moving to a large-scale institution.

Gordon had no such qualms. He had spent his early years playing in dive bars and splitting door money with his art-rock band, carrying his own gear to Michael Gordon Philharmonic shows, and, with Wolfe and Lang, setting out music stands and cleaning toilets at the RAPP Arts Center, mailing thousands of flyers only to get kicked out of the venue at the last minute.

He was ready for a break. As Lang described it, Gordon felt "entitled" to the palace of high culture.[43] Wolfe, too, was excited about the prospect. All over Lincoln Center's plaza were three-sheet posters, held in standalone glass cases, that advertised big names like Yo-Yo Ma and Emanuel Ax. She wanted to see posters that advertised Bang on a Can, and their world music offerings, and women like Annie Gosfield. Gosfield and other downtown composers, including Glenn Branca, were apparently excited about the opportunity to storm Lincoln Center. Bang on a Can might sacrifice the funkiness and intimacy of spaces like RAPP, but the larger venue meant that they would be able to accommodate everyone who wanted to come to the marathons, and they would no longer be at risk of last-minute eviction. After a year at La Mama, a year at the Society for Ethical Culture, and a year at The Kitchen, they would have a permanent home, just as they were expanding outside of the city with the All-Stars. They would lose some of the grit, but they also wouldn't have to clean the grit off the bathroom floor at 2am.

And so Lang came around. They told Moss yes, and planned for a long-term partnership. Leading up to the spring 1994 series, they gave numerous interviews that built anticipation in the press, and outlined the collaboration as both unexpected and necessary. "Lincoln Center is a symbol in our country for culture and we feel that the music we're presenting should have the same status as *Swan Lake* or *La Bohème*," Gordon told the Associated Press.[44] In Bang on a Can's imagining, Lincoln Center was an arch-conservative institution that housed Tchaikovsky's ballets and Puccini's operas. Whereas Moss emphasized that the Bang on a Can partnership extended the work of Serious Fun—and was designed to push against the stereotype of Lincoln Center as a "high culture palace"—Bang on a Can's directors did not mention Serious Fun, nor Discovery, nor the jazz series, nor Midsummer Night Swing. They instead described Lincoln Center as entirely bereft of new and unconventional musics. "If we did not go there and play the music we wanted to play, there would be an entire year of Lincoln Center that would go by with no young composers, with no women composers, with no minority composers, with no alternative composers of any kind," Lang said.[45] He wasn't wrong—the center's existent new-music programming didn't represent the diversity of their younger generation. The framing was clear, though. Bang on a Can didn't need Lincoln Center; Lincoln Center needed Bang on a Can.

"Lincoln Center is the definition of classical music in our culture," Lang told Schwarz, for a *Stagebill* preview of the 1994 events.[46] "By inviting us, Lincoln Center is putting this music on the map. And this music *deserves* to be at Lincoln Center. It's the music of the next generation, and only if it gets to Lincoln Center will it survive and thrive." *Only* if it gets to Lincoln

Center: they were enshrining the institution with the same kind of power that, not so long beforehand, they saw as dangerous.

Ideological Differences

These two organizations, Bang on a Can and Lincoln Center, were, in theory, worlds apart—or at least according to the rhetoric espoused by Gordon, Lang, and Wolfe. But there were no big blow-ups in the collaboration, no radical disagreements as the institutions worked together for several years. The partnership was symbolically fraught, but proceeded largely without conflict, with the exception of a few significant points of difference as they learned each other's habits, and as the palace of culture accommodated itself to the renegades.

When they reminisced about the early years of Bang on a Can, the three directors tended to speak most frequently about the RAPP Arts Center. It had been home for three—nearly four—festivals, and represented the clearest instantiation of the organization's do-it-yourself determination. They had to put on a concert in a grungy neighborhood, set up the hall themselves, hand out tickets, run the stage and sound system, sell beers and t-shirts, and clean everything up at the end of the night. During the marathons, Gordon ran the stage, Lang ran the door, and Wolfe handled everything else.[47] It was DIY par excellence.

Lincoln Center was not. Not only did Gordon, Lang, and Wolfe not handle their usual tasks, but they weren't allowed to, by union regulations. "You've got nine guys doing what Michael did by himself," Wolfe said, describing the Lincoln Center stage setup.[48] And that was just with regards to moving equipment around. Lincoln Center had its own publicity, promotional, and box office apparatus: they would be mailing brochures and program booklets, releasing press releases, selling tickets. Lincoln Center even wanted to print program notes—exactly the kind of thing that Bang on a Can had avoided in the past because it felt too intellectualized, too conventional, too staid. This was when Bang on a Can brought in the writer Deborah Artman, who interviewed musicians involved in the concerts and created first-person program notes and bios. Bette Snapp and Karen Sander were also hired as full-time staffers right around this time.

"Now that we have begun collaborations with more mainstream institutions (i.e., Lincoln Center, Sony), we must actively maintain our identity and image," Snapp wrote in a grant report to Chamber Music America in 1995.[49] They had done so in the past with strategic attention to the written materials produced around the festival. Having spent years fine-tuning their organizational voice, Bang on a Can was emphatic about how Lincoln Center presented their work to a new public. Leading up to the first run of concerts in spring 1994, Gordon supplied information about the programs to Lincoln Center as well as past festival postcards, to give clear direction as to layout and style for advertising; Sander provided meticulous notes regarding promotional imagery and ad copy for the April marathon.[50] "We still do our own style of marketing," Snapp told an interviewer.[51] "The literature is written informally with the idea that you can come to hear some new, bold, brash, exciting music which is at the cutting edge."

Minor tensions emerged, as Lincoln Center tried to grasp this cutting-edge approach. Preparing a press release for the 1995 series, Bang on a Can faxed over an initial draft that included the following passages:

> The Bang on a Can All-Stars take the stage on Monday, March 13 with their radical arrangement of Philip Glass's mesmerizing 1967 masterpiece TWO PAGES. Brazilian jazz giant Hermeto Pascoal sends the audience reeling with the New York premiere of QUIABO...
>
> ... Young upstarts Michael Maguire, Lois V Vierk, Juliet Palmer and Norman Yamada shake the house with a gritty lower-Manhattan attitude...
>
> ... On Monday, May 1 the All-Stars are back in the Walter Reade, celebrating Mayday with the transcendental politics of Bang on a Can guru Martin Bresnick...
>
> ... New Yorkers Nick Didkovsky, Annie Gosfield, and David Lang find three different ways into a heavy beat...[52]

In a version of the document held in Lincoln Center's archives, a press representative appended handwritten questions and corrections. Next to "radical arrangement," they wrote "Explain"; "sends the audience reeling" and "shake the house" were criticized as "editorializing"; "transcendental politics" was circled, with the note "What does this mean?"; below "find three different ways into a heavy beat," they asked "again what does this mean—alone it doesn't make sense."[53] And it wouldn't have made much sense, from Lincoln Center's perspective. These were two very different visons for what a press release should accomplish: Bang on a Can sought out punchy, imagistic, captivating language; Lincoln Center wanted straightforward, formalized information to pass on to the reader.

But the kinks were mostly worked out. For another release prepared by Lincoln Center that season, Sander wrote to the press representative that "You guys did a wonderful job capturing the Bang on a Can spirit." She had faxed over her own handwritten corrections, asking their staff to call her if they had any "questions/comments/ideological differences."[54] Ideological differences aside, Gordon, Lang, and Wolfe were given total creative control over what works would be programmed, and what outside groups would be brought in to play: Moss wanted the festival to retain its independent curatorship. Marathon tickets were priced at $15 for a full day of music, consistent with past festivals and lower than Lincoln Center standards, though some downtown Bang on a Can fans apparently had trouble getting advance tickets before it sold out—because Lincoln Center needed a credit card, and they didn't have one. Bang on a Can convinced Moss to fill Alice Tully's lobby with folding chairs and tables with umbrellas for the marathon. People could mingle, talk, eat, drink beer.[55] In 1995, they even conscripted design students from Cooper Union to reimagine the lobby as a "giant cafe/art exhibit."[56] And the three directors settled into familiar roles at the performances. Attending an All-Stars concert in March 1995, K. Robert Schwarz observed that Gordon and Lang were still handing out programs and raffle tickets, and Wolfe handled onstage introductions. "Attitude is informal, casual, in attitude and dress, like rock band," he noted.[57]

There were occasional mishaps. The come-and-go mentality didn't jibe with Lincoln Center's box office approach. At first, they didn't allow any newcomers into Alice Tully once a marathon had sold out, even though some ticket holders had departed. "We'd have a 'sold out' show with a house that was three-quarters full," Wolfe recalled.[58] The 1997 marathon ran longer than anticipated, and Gordon and production associate Kenny Savelson had to negotiate backstage with crew chiefs to figure out how much overtime they could afford to pay the union stagehands. They ended up having to cut a piece by Lang.[59] Gordon apparently announced from the stage that the union was shutting them down; Lincoln Center wasn't pleased about that.[60]

"In these lean times, often the only way small presenters can survive is by sharing resources and collaborating with other organizations," Sander wrote in 1995.[61] Lincoln Center handled expenses from the hall, marketing, and stage labor; a 1994 letter estimated the costs at between $50,000 and $60,000.[62] Bang on a Can paid for everything else, estimated at $250,000 for that first year: fees, travel, and accommodations for artists; rentals for instruments, music, and rehearsal space; sound and tech crew; and some additional advertising and PR. Lincoln Center kept what they made at the box office, and gave Bang on a Can a straight fee in return.[63] So whereas administrative pressure was partly relieved, Bang on a Can's relentless fundraising continued apace.

Controversial Move

The real problem with the Lincoln Center partnership, it seemed, was the press. There was a lot of it, a wave attracted by the high profile of the performing arts complex along with a new round of qualms from Bang on a Can's veteran attendees. Edward Rothstein concluded his overview of the 1993 Kitchen festival—an exegesis on the meaning of "totalism"—by declaring the upcoming collaboration "wrong for both parties." Lincoln Center risked making Bang on a Can "seem more established, more absolute, more conclusive."[64] In the *Voice* a couple weeks later, Kyle Gann called it "a big step up—for Lincoln Center."[65] If there was a controversy brewing, Bang on a Can did not shy away from it. In a February 1994 pitch to a *Newsday* critic, Snapp wrote that "New York's funkiest annual downtown new music extravaganza, the Bang on a Can Festival, makes its controversial move 'uptown' this year to Lincoln Center."[66] The press picked up the hype, playing into the narrative about opposite worlds colliding. "Will Bang on a Can manage to retain its cutting edge in a performance space with upholstered seats and clean restrooms?" the *Star-Ledger* asked. "Will Lincoln Center succeed in wooing the cooks out of the Kitchen?"[67]

Reviewers in 1994 took note. Allan Kozinn laid out the high stakes of the partnership in his *Times* piece on the opening concert in March, but nevertheless found the All-Stars persuasive in their new setting.[68] Gann, however, was more concerned. He fretted that the All-Stars instantiated a "Lincoln Centerization of BoaC's ensemble concept"—they had not yet fully solidified as a group, and seemed overly focused on a prosaically "note-perfect" approach representing the "classical mainstream." Gann feared that the festival might "blend into Lincoln Center's faded woodwork," that it was losing its "long-underground roots."[69] Kozinn found the May marathon at Alice Tully entirely enjoyable, and consistent with Bang on a Can's history, writing that "virtually every contemporary style was represented," and noted a predominance of American works as well as a mixture of international music.[70]

Gann, however, seemed to be hearing an entirely different concert. He opened his review by noting his historical championing of the festival, because it represented "the first institutional recognition that my generation has something important to say."[71] The 1994 marathon program, by contrast, demonstrated that "Michael Gordon, Julia Wolfe, and David Lang had told the best minds of my generation to get lost." The organizers had become too preoccupied with providing a kind of "historical review of new music's pioneers" in their first foray to Lincoln Center—the marathon was bookended by works of John Cage and Philip Glass, and also featured music by Meredith Monk,

Karlheinz Stockhausen, and Ralph Shapey. The younger unknowns that Gann considered a hallmark of the festivals seemed absent. Though the organization had reviewed four hundred tape submissions that season, he pointed out that only a handful of works presented on the marathon seemed to have been selected from the call.

In his fervor for the totalist generation, Gann never quite understood that the festival's directors had consistently emphasized the importance of historical review to their curatorial vision, with the back-to-back programming of Babbitt and Reich serving as a foundational moment. But his piece echoed the kinds of critiques that Gordon, Lang, and Wolfe had made of the new-music world nearly a decade earlier: that institutions were programming music because of the reputation of its creators, and shutting out the misfits. "What emitted a self-serving odor was the coincidence of the move to Lincoln Center, the curators expanding their own presence on the program, and decimating that of their peers and colleagues," Gann added.[72] (This wasn't quite fair: the '94 marathon included a work each by Gordon and Lang, and none by Wolfe—less music by the founders than in previous years.) Gann compared the festival's quality to New Music America "in their waning years"—the ultimate dig, given that it was only a few years earlier that he had heralded Bang on a Can as a necessary replacement of New Music America. It's harder to gauge what elder downtowners thought of the proceedings, as *EAR Magazine* folded in 1991, in the midst of the economic downturn and NYSCA cutbacks.[73]

The issue was not Lincoln Center's interference. After all, Bang on a Can had total creative control over what music they wished to program or who they wanted to invite. Along with the All-Stars, they brought in Britain's Icebreaker, Montreal's Le Nouvel Ensemble Modern, and the Netherlands Wind Ensemble. But the spring 1994 concerts did feel different. At the most basic level was a rethinking of what Bang on a Can offered to their New York audience. Rather than the tightly programmed and sprawling series of events that had become the norm in the early '90s, the Lincoln Center run comprised only three concerts spread over three months: two All-Stars performances at Walter Reade Theater in March and April, leading up to the marathon at Alice Tully in May. This meant no all-Feldman or all-Partch evenings, no multimedia indictments of AIDS, no concerts of heated political song. Lincoln Center mandated that the marathons be truncated to only eight hours—and, given union regulations, they had to run on time.

Whether or not they paid Gann any mind, Bang on a Can did rethink their approach to the Alice Tully marathons after 1994. The high-minded rhetoric about why they were at Lincoln Center in the first place—to give an otherwise unavailable spotlight to young and alternative composers—was not always coming across in practice. The 1994 program had included Harrison Birtwistle's *Secret Theatre*, a large-scale classic by a British modernist composer that Lang had been particularly keen to hear live and described, flatteringly, as a "very big ugly piece."[74] But afterwards, Lang realized that music like *Secret Theatre* was designed for spaces like Lincoln Center; it would be much more radical to hear it at a downtown club. Instead, he and his colleagues decided that the marathon should be "even more committed to the music from composers who don't have a place to go."[75] The turn away from Birtwistle aligned, partly, with Bang on a Can's broader shift away from uptown composers like Mario Davidovsky and Elliott Carter right around this time. They had programmed Carter's violin and piano *Duo* at the 1993 marathon, yielding whoops from the audience; as Wolfe put it, "It was more exciting to hear Elliott Carter at The Kitchen than in Lincoln Center."[76]

"We've always put famous names close to unknowns to ensure a steady stream of people coming in and out," Lang told *Stagebill* in 1995. "Now that we've introduced ourselves to Lincoln Center, we have more confidence that the whole event is more of a draw. I actually feel like we could program composers no one has ever heard of and people would still come. The populist part of me says we need even more obscure names than those we've already had."[77] Nevertheless, the local critical response worsened. Though he had praised the previous year's run, Kozinn wrote that the "ramshackle, freespirited festival" had instead become a mere "concert series," with the All-Stars at the center. In *Newsday*, the young critic Justin Davidson was more skeptical, longing for the festival's early days and describing the May marathon as a "more doctrinaire extravaganza" in which composers "plumbed different depths of the same shallow ideas" in a "sumptuous display of dullness."[78]

And Gann embarked on a new line of critique: defending downtown against Bang on a Can. With Lincoln Center's time constraints, the marathon programming had "stagnated into a narrow and arbitrary chunk of what's going on."[79] A set by the percussionist Bobby Previte and his sextet was limited to only six minutes, hobbled by an "Uptownish, concert-oriented approach to time limits." Gann had a point. The marathon format was never an ideal one for much downtown music—it was perhaps better served, in Bang on a Can's early years, by the festival's ancillary concert events—and longform, improvisatory work that thrived in informal spaces like the Knitting Factory did not necessarily translate well to Alice Tully Hall. (This is what Rhys Chatham recognized, when he told the *Times* about the need for different kinds of venues in New York.) But it was also an odd attack from a critic who had once heralded Bang on a Can as a bulwark against the staid composer-performers of New Music America

"No festival is going to feel like home to all types of music," Gann wrote.[80] "But in the early years, BoaC marketed itself as a kind of wild and woolly East Village phenomenon. Even today, a proportion of BoaC's audience is Village musicians who got hooked on the marathon habit, some of whom wonder why this Eurocentric Uptown festival still benefits from a Tompkins Square cachet. BoaC slept with Downtown, and Downtown might be forgiven for having overestimated the seriousness of the commitment. Perhaps it was equally naïve to hope that BoaC's excitement, diversity, and unpredictability would survive the efficiency, professionalism, time limits, and Eurocentrism of Lincoln Center."

Did Bang on a Can betray downtown? If we take Gann's position on the organization, that their primary importance was in providing a wild-and-woolly outpost for his fellow Village totalists, then the answer might be yes. But if we look at Bang on a Can as a group of Yale graduates with close institutional ties to classical music's establishment, whose primary aim was to build a larger audience for contemporary music, and who were inveterate skeptics of both the uptown and downtown scenes, then Lincoln Center seems like a natural next step. The composer Arlene Sierra, a little more than a decade younger than the Bang on a Can founders, had studied at Yale after them, and was unconvinced by their whole enterprise; attending the first Lincoln Center marathon with a cynical eye, she recalled, "I didn't see them as the young rebels, I just saw them as establishment in a different way."[81]

Since 1987, Bang on a Can had global aspirations. And they had always been, in some small but crucial ways, a "Eurocentric Uptown" festival. Even as they placed their main focus on maverick American composers, the founders had also prized themselves on an internationalism that championed the European postminimalist Louis Andriessen—Gann had never taken to Andriessen's music—as well as Continental modernists like Karlheinz Stockhausen and Iannis Xenakis. As it happens, the Lincoln Center concerts in 1995 had fewer musical representatives from US uptown circles than any of the previous Bang on a Can marathons that Gann had attended.

Perhaps as a response to the critics, Bang on a Can presented an all-American marathon in 1996. Leading up to the event, they spoke frequently to the press about the call-for-tapes process—how it had become even harder to discover new unknowns now that the organization had heard and presented so much music. They idyllically recalled past discoveries, like the piece *Three Black American Folk Songs*, which they programmed in 1992 after hearing a tape submitted by Rocco Di Pietro, an obscure composer who taught music in prisons. Wolfe told *Time Out New York* that Lois V Vierk had sent in an anonymous tape so that her work might be programmed again—and it was.[82]

Filmmaker Michael Blackwood attended a tape review session, documented in his *New York Composers* film (Figure 6.2), and around the same time, they invited *Times* critic James R. Oestreich to sit in on the adjudication process. In a longform feature, Oestreich documented how the trio listened to more than two hundred tapes submitted that year: Wolfe handed out the tapes, Lang controlled the audio, and Gordon organized the delivery of Chinese food.[83]

They would listen and sort tapes into different piles; some pieces might be dismissed, but the directors could change their minds later and petition one another. Oestreich noted that around a third of the marathon's final program comprised tape submissions. "What we're primarily interested in is whether a piece adds something to the world that wasn't there before," Gordon said.[84] One wonders if a rotating system of curatorship could have enlivened the review process: other composers might have had a radically different conception of what was fresh and new than the likeminded Gordon, Lang, and Wolfe. The decisive factor in what Bang on a Can programmed was whether the music was something that the directors wanted to listen to live—what about what other musicians wanted to hear?

Figure 6.2 Still from Michael Blackwood, *New York Composers: Searching for a New Music*, 1996.

But this was neither New Music America nor an NEA peer review panel. Bang on a Can ran the show. That did not necessarily mean that their curatorial efforts were exclusively self-serving, as Gann critiqued them, but it did mean that the festival's aesthetic vision was guided by the same composers, year after year. In some sense, it was bound to become tiresome to well-versed listeners. Some of the directors' contemporaries complained about feeling shut out of their burgeoning project. And despite Bang on a Can's attempts, as the marathons became shorter in the late 1990s, their vision seemed to narrow rather than expand.

In hindsight, some of the critiques of the Lincoln Center collaboration do seem inflated—as if the writers are riffing more on the concept than its execution. The air of nostalgia feels too thick to be taken too seriously. Wolfe recalled that some critics seemed to believe that Bang on a Can should remain "perfect and precious"—that the festival should never grow beyond its neighborhood vibe to match the actual ambitions that its creators had when they first envisioned it.[85] But what is clear from these years of controversy was that there were real stakes in where Bang on a Can performed, how they performed, and what they performed. A wide swath of musicians and observers were actively invested in the direction of the organization, and, because it was entirely self-run, their method of input was to murmur about their resentments or voice them in the *Voice*. The Culture Wars did not hover over the Lincoln Center marathons as overtly as they did over the politicized multiculturalism of the 1993 Kitchen festival, but the partnership represented a symbol for a shifting musical culture, a rare example of high-profile success from a once-underground organization just as government funding was drying up, controversial voices were being silenced, and large institutions were becoming more fiscally and politically conservative. It is not hard to imagine why former loyalists would be upset. Bang on a Can was never as self-promotional as some made them out to be—they were always a communal project, one that advocated for older and younger musicians alongside the founders' peers—but they did consolidate in these years, as they sought new audiences in new partnerships with venues and record labels.

Those who were programmed registered these differences, and what Bang on a Can had meant. "The festival's changed a lot," the composer Daniel Goode told *Time Out New York* in 1996. A co-founder of the Downtown Ensemble who had been a guest of Sheep's Clothing back in the day, Goode had music played at Bang on a Can in 1991 and '92, and a thirty-five minute work of his was presented on the 1996 marathon.[86] "When it was downtown, it was a nice community event. I got positive reviews in the *Times* and other good feedback. The best feedback, of course, was being invited back. But now that it's at Alice Tully Hall, a larger and more curious audience has found it. Now it's reached the point that appearing there has international implications."

A Mandate to Get a New Audience

Did a larger and more curious audience find Bang on a Can, when they moved Lincoln Center? That was certainly a main goal for both organizations. Bang on a Can sought the resources of a major presenter to expand their reach. When Lang said in a 1997 interview that the mission of Bang on a Can was to "find new music for a new audience," he was discussing the Lincoln Center partnership specifically.[87] It was a chief factor in Bang on a Can saying yes to Moss. Wolfe told K. Robert Schwarz that "it satisfies what we wanted from the very beginning, which was to reach a bigger audience, to make this music part of what everybody thinks about, part of the culture."[88] And Lincoln Center sought the hip ethos and built-in constituency of the festival to reach beyond its typical subscribers. In a separate interview for the same piece, Moss told Schwarz that Bang on a Can "acts as a bridge that will allow us to bring a new, younger audience to Lincoln Center."[89] As Lang put it, "Jane Moss had a mandate to get a new audience."[90]

That new audience was not so new for other large institutions in this period. For Lincoln Center and Moss, the model was still BAM's Next Wave. In a 1986 essay, BAM president Harvey Lichtenstein noted that 80 percent of Next Wave's audience was under the age of forty, and 23 percent under twenty-five.[91] "It's a very mixed crowd, basically a young crowd, with a lot of painters and individuals who are not part of the Lincoln Center or Carnegie Hall crowd," he wrote. "The SoHo audience is our audience."[92] Just as Serious Fun had been and the Lincoln Center Festival would be, Bang on a Can provided another opportunity for Lincoln Center to reach the young, the arty, the SoHo crowd. That was, after all, the same kind of listenership that Bang on a Can had been explicitly cultivating from their very first marathon—young New Yorkers with a taste for avant-garde art and modern cinema and reading *The New Yorker*, but who gravitated more toward art-rock than contemporary classical.

And it makes sense why Moss's mandate drew her to Bang on a Can. Back in 1991, Kozinn had pointed out in the *Times* the seeming miracle of the scrappy festival attracting large, excited crowds.[93] The 1991 marathon had packed La Mama with 300 people, and the larger festival attracted 3,000 attendees.[94] The statistics continued to be compelling: the 1992 events at the Society for Ethical Culture reached an audience of more than 2,500, and the 1993 festival at The Kitchen had comparable numbers.[95] When interviewed for Michael Blackwood's documentary, Philip Glass said that "With the Bang on a Can festival, we're really talking about outreach, we're talking about going and finding audiences and including people, and developing larger audiences for this music that go way beyond the academic soirees that used to happen."[96] Audience development, for prominent observers such as Glass, represented a key takeaway from Bang on a Can.

Though the marathons tended to sell out, their audience fluctuated year-by-year according to the size of the space. With a capacity of over 1,000, Alice Tully Hall offered the largest seating yet for any New York marathon.[97] But there were fewer events at the 1994 Lincoln Center series than at The Kitchen the previous year, and thus a smaller potential audience maximum. Walter Reade Theater had a capacity of 268, and both of the All-Stars concerts there sold out.[98] The first Lincoln Center marathon at Alice Tully did well, with a little under 850 in the audience.[99] Subsequent Alice Tully marathons sold out, with more than thousand in attendance in '95 and more than 1,200 in '96.[100]

More specifics are available about the audience that Bang on a Can cultivated at Lincoln Center, because the organization conducted their first-ever audience survey at the 1996 marathon. They had used funding from their NEA advancement grant for a consulting session with BAM's executive vice president, Karen Hopkins, who recommended that they gather information about their audience that could appeal to corporations for future sponsorship. Hopkins, who would become president of BAM in 1999, was a corporate fundraising wizard: she had used data about the BAM audience's youth and education to attract major sponsors, including the pivotal $500,000 grant from Philip Morris in 1986.[101] Notes from a meeting record Hopkins telling Bang on a Can that "We need to know what magazines they read, what liquors they drink and most of all age, sex, race, how they found out about Bang on a Can, how often they've come, how long they've been coming, what they think of different venues, anything we can find out about how much money they have and how they spend it, ticket prices, etc."[102]

A survey was created and handed out to audiences at Alice Tully in 1996—if they answered the ten questions, they would be entered to win a $100 gift certificate to Tower Records. The survey asked about prior experience with Bang on a Can, CD purchasing habits, and how attendees heard about the festival; gender, age, and education; where those surveyed were visiting from, and habits including recycling, Internet usage, smoking, and drinking scotch (Figures 6.3–6.5). Approximately 375 people responded—a little more than 30 percent of the recorded audience.[103]

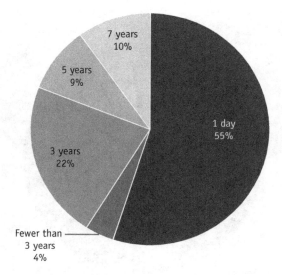

Figure 6.3 Survey responses: "I have been coming to your events for..."

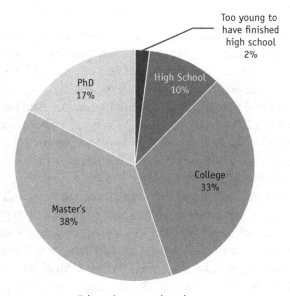

Figure 6.4 Survey responses: Education completed.

Their audience was clearly youthful—68 percent of those surveyed were under forty. Thirty-eight percent of the audience identified as musicians; 55 percent said they were involved in the arts. Eighty-eight percent of those surveyed had a college degree, and 55 percent had obtained a master's or

184 Industry

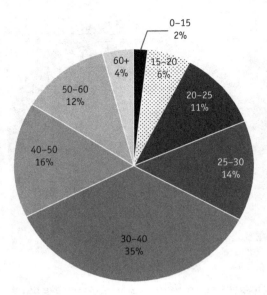

Figure 6.5 Survey responses: Age.

PhD. This would suggest that Bang on a Can was reaching the kind of nonspecialist, artsy, educated crowd they had always discussed as their ideal constituency. Respondents frequented Tower Records to buy CDs in a range of genres, with a strong preference toward classical music (47.9 percent)—and less toward rock (16.8 percent) than one might expect, given the festival's aesthetic orientation. (The survey had stated "When I walk into a record store I head straight for," and listed a series of musical genres, but some respondents appear to have selected multiple answers.) A little more than half of those surveyed were men. Attendees were mostly from the local area, they recycled, they used the Internet, and they didn't drink scotch or smoke all that much.

When Bang on a Can summarized this data to pitch to potential corporate donors—the principal target was Philip Morris, for a major sponsorship of the tenth anniversary season—they described "Bang on a Can's audience" as young, educated, in the arts, local, online.[104] They ultimately received a modest subsidy of $15,000 from the company. But the response to the first question on the survey complicates whether this can properly be described as *the* Bang on a Can audience. After all, 55 percent of those surveyed were attending their first-ever Bang on a Can event. Even well into the Lincoln Center partnership, the majority of respondents who showed up to the marathon were entirely new to the organization. (That said, it is possible that veteran Bang on a Can fans were not the type to respond to surveys.) And 22 percent had been attending for three years—the duration of the Lincoln Center collaboration.

Seventy-seven percent of "Bang on a Can's audience" surveyed, then, was really "Bang on a Can at Lincoln Center's audience." Only 10 percent had been attending Bang on a Can since their beginnings.

Back in 1995, Kozinn recounted in his review of the marathon that, toward the end of the evening, Gordon asked the audience "how many listeners had attended the marathon in its early days, downtown. Fewer than a dozen hands were raised."[105] The Lincoln Center events did much more to attract a new audience to Bang on a Can, it seemed, than they did to attract Bang on a Can's audience to Lincoln Center. Gann may have been right that in carving out a new niche for themselves uptown, the organization had abandoned not just their original spirit but also their earliest attendees. Lang had told *Stagebill* that the '94 Lincoln Center season was a success, with an enthusiastic audience, but noted that "They were different people. Lots of downtown people swear they never go above 14th Street, and I think a lot of them held to their word."[106]

None of this was news to Moss. Statistically speaking, she told *Musical America*, far more regulars at Mostly Mozart went to Serious Fun than Serious Fun regulars went to Mostly Mozart: "For all of the ways in which the classical-music audience is characterized as being stodgy and old-fashioned, it actually is, in its own way, more adventuresome than the Serious Fun audience."[107] Even if BAM's chic listeners did find their way to Lincoln Center for Serious Fun or Bang on Can, they would not necessarily provide Lincoln Center's other programming with long-term audience renewal. They wouldn't be settling into subscriber mode. As the media meta-narrative had it, Lincoln Center in the '90s was the moribund palace of high culture that needed an injection of the new. And importing Bang on a Can's upstart presence, innovative programming, flashy marketing materials, casual atmosphere, and sold-out marathons certainly fulfilled Moss's mandate. For the Lincoln Centers of the world, the recent popularity of contemporary music—as evidenced by BAM, by New Romanticism, by spiritual and non-spiritual minimalism, by Bang on a Can—offered the promise of new audiences. The classical record industry was banking on the same thing. New work was not just artistically necessary—Moss always emphasized that she considered creative programming more important than tickets sold—but could also rejuvenate classical music's dying audience. Savvy administrators saw new music's marketplace turn unfolding and brought new institutional resources to its aid. For Bang on a Can, that meant three-sheet posters, mailings, brochures, press outreach, even a TV spot in 1995 on the local evening news about All-Stars percussionist Steven Schick. (Schick is filmed shirtless, performing Vinko Globokar's *Corporal* on his own body; "That's right, you can't beat Steven

Schick when it comes to beating himself," the WCBS correspondent quips.[108]) "Our marketing was doubled up with Lincoln Center's marketing and its huge mailing list," Snapp said in 1995. "Often people come off the street from word-of-mouth or when they see the festival banner outside the Center."[109]

But what the survey suggests is that, along with lending their imprimatur and administrative support, traditional classical institutions also lent to new music *their own* audience. On their own substantive, entrepreneurial efforts, Bang on a Can had attracted a large and loyal following in their early years, larger than many of their new-music peers. It was not just Bang on a Can's longtime listeners who came out to Lincoln Center in droves, though, but also those reached by the center's own mailing lists. When audiences packed Alice Tully Hall, some of those present may have been regular attendees of Mostly Mozart. What is not entirely clear is whether those first-timers to Bang on a Can during their Lincoln Center run were also first-timers to Lincoln Center itself—in other words, were they new to classical music as well as contemporary music? In a draft of their 1996 survey, Bang on a Can included a question about how often their audience attended other institutions such as BAM, The Kitchen, Roulette, Dance Theater Workshop, the Knitting Factory, and Lincoln Center.[110] But the question was either stricken from the final survey, or its results were not recorded.

Now What?

Bang on a Can's tenth anniversary celebrations sprawled beyond Lincoln Center. "Bang on a Can's 10th Birthday!!!!!" proclaimed the poster, which depicted a cake on fire. "You Say It's Your Birthday! It's Our Birthday Too, Yeah!" It included a run-down of the season's programming: Interstate Bang on a Can, an eleven city All-Stars tour; the ensemble's two Walter Reade concerts; World Orchestra Day, a free concert featuring Evan Ziporyn's Gamelan Galak Tika, pipa player Wu Man, a flamenco group, and a bagpipe ensemble from NYU; the Alice Tully marathon; the debut of the People's Commissioning Fund; and a concert by the SPIT Orchestra at The Kitchen.[111] (Bang on a Can launched the forty-piece orchestra in 1995, to perform music by the likes of Glenn Branca and Lois V Vierk, with the slogan "Out of the Museum/Into Your Face." But it wasn't financially sustainable; this turned out to be its final outing.[112]) They made a greater push toward incorporating fresh voices: whereas the 1996 marathon included ten composers new to Bang on a Can's marathons (out of a total of twenty-three programmed), the 1997 marathon featured nineteen new composers out of twenty-eight total.

In *Fanfare* magazine, critic Justin Davidson previewed the anniversary activities at length, describing how the organization's "principal struggle is that of all revolutionaries who come to power: keeping the fires of rebellion stoked."[113] He noted the organization's professional staff, their $400,000 budget, the fact that all three founders now had young children, the gradual fading of their early eclecticism, and the directors' attempts, nevertheless, to maintain an irreverent spirit and program music that was weirder than ever. "We keep joking about how we wish someone would start a festival called I Hate Bang on a Can," Gordon told the critic. Lang added, "We may have to do it ourselves." One day, they said, they hoped to start a summer program for young musicians called Banglewood. The headline of the article was "The Revolutionaries Won. Now What?"

Lincoln Center's mid-'90s programming revamp did not solve all of its problems. Ticket sales did not improve significantly, and subscriptions continued to decline. "Every aspect of the live classical music experience must be reassessed and freshly conceived for a rapidly changing world," an internal report noted in 1996.[114] Lincoln Center was not banking exclusively on new music, although it was an important part of Moss's vision; Bang on a Can occupied only a sliver of each Great Performers season, and in the coming years, Moss beefed up her focus on repertoire-based programming and introduced several initiatives, including a series devoted to American popular song and New Visions, dedicated to multimedia productions by Peter Sellars and Bill T. Jones. But Bang on a Can's 1997 marathon was their final one at Lincoln Center. Moss recalled that the decision to part ways for the marathons—the All-Stars still gave occasional concerts at Alice Tully—was simply business-as-usual for arts presenters. "We always need to be mixing it up," she said. "We had a good run of it, and it was time for both of us to move on."[115]

At a staff meeting that August, Bang on a Can discussed whether "the strongest future for the Marathon is at Alice Tully or an 'alternative' independent site (preferably close to a coffee shop and/or record store)."[116] They considered the Brooklyn Academy of Music as an option, but it was unlikely for 1998, as "it will require diplomacy and the question of future affiliation which we want to avoid at this time." They outlined a potential plan: a self-produced marathon at a new venue in 1998, a Lincoln Center marathon in 1999, and, in 2000, finding a "future home based on the experience we have this year away from Lincoln Center."

In the coming months, they explored several options, including Webster Hall, Irving Plaza, and the Knitting Factory.[117] But no clear solution emerged and, for the first time in eleven years, Bang on a Can did not hold a marathon. There was, instead, the sold-out debut of *Music for Airports* at Alice Tully followed by US and European tours, the inaugural People's Commissioning Fund concert at the Knitting Factory, the benefit in honor of John Duffy and, in November, an All-Stars concert of Terry Riley's *In C* and *Airports* at the World Financial Center downtown.

As it turned out, the marathon would not return to Lincoln Center. The All-Stars gave a concert at Alice Tully in March 1999, but the festival that May was held at the Henry Street Settlement on the Lower East Side, and it harkened back to the early '90s: five well-attended concerts that included new works for conventional and non-Western instruments played by women; a performance by the DJ and tabla player Talvin Singh; an evening of Xenakis's complete percussion music; and a performance by the Fred Frith Guitar Quartet. The run opened with an eight-hour marathon packed with young composers and premieres, which was sold out with a capacity crowd of 450.

And for the first marathon of the new millennium, Bang on a Can looked to BAM. There were some concerns: at an October 1999 staff meeting, Lang talked about how they "don't want to lose the aesthetic of old marathons, what the org. used to be. Generosity to the new music community, attention to the new, emerging composers who get a real boost from BoaC. BAM marathon has a different slant. We're becoming a big, int'l organization instead of a little grassroots mom and pop store. But there's a way we can still promote the original values."[118]

What Bang on a Can "used to be." Lang himself recognized that something had changed. Gann and Kozinn and Davidson were not just imposing their own nostalgia on an institution that had clung to its original values during its years at the palace of culture: Bang on a Can knew that something had been lost in their continuous expansion, from grassroots to big league, from local to international, from eclectic supermix to a more consolidated vision. But the gains were clear, too. The Lincoln Center years had given them an influx of new audience members, a wave of national press, a stable home from which they could grow their touring and recording enterprise. It is less that Lincoln Center really changed Bang on a Can—as the partnership's early observers feared—than that Bang on a Can said yes to Lincoln Center because they were in the midst of changing themselves. The revolutionaries were ready to win, and did, and then worried about what they had sacrificed in the process.

Held in December 2000, Bang on a Can's eight-hour "Millennium Marathon" was the final event of BAM's Next Wave Festival—which otherwise featured Philip Glass's Symphony No. 5, the Lucinda Childs Dance Company, and a new Robert Wilson production—and was broadcast live on the radio and online. "We are targeting a young, curious New York City audience and plan to create an event which will be an engaging survey of contemporary music compelling for people with no background or prior knowledge," they wrote in one grant application about the new collaboration. "In the year 2000, musical boundaries around the world are falling away. The vision Bang on a Can was founded upon—that contemporary music doesn't have to be partitioned into camps and disciplines, that any audience, not just specialists, can appreciate and participate in their musical world—is becoming more and more of a reality."[119] They had reached out to big acts like the bands Sonic Youth and Tortoise, but the marathon ultimately featured Bang on a Can stalwarts like Steve Martland, Phil Kline, and Vierk; newer collaborators, including Iva Bittová, Hassan Hakmoun, and Tan Dun; and the strong presence of the All-Stars as well as Gamelan Galak Tika.[120] It was a showcase for regulars and unknowns.

More than 1,500 people showed up, and a WNYC live broadcast reached another ten thousand.[121] The program book advertised the People's Commissioning Fund and the upcoming debut of Bang on a Can's in-house record label, Cantaloupe Music.[122]

7
Record Labels

"The classical-record industry has made a startling discovery," wrote the *New York Magazine* critic Peter G. Davis back in March of 1994. "There's money in new music."[1] For an industry increasingly concerned about sales as the market for CDs slumped in the early 1990s, such a discovery was not just surprising, but momentous. Davis noted the unforeseen, smash hit success that ignited the revelation: Nonesuch's 1992 recording of the Polish composer Henryk Górecki's Symphony No. 3 which, by the time of the article, had sold 200,000 copies. Following the unexpected rise onto the pop charts of this fifty-five minute "Symphony of Sorrowful Songs," Davis pointed out, major classical labels had attempted to respond. BMG launched the imprint Catalyst and Philips initiated the line Point Music, both dedicated to contemporary composition. Surveying this new landscape, Davis also highlighted the work of Emergency Music, a hip new line created by the label Composers Recordings, Inc. to combat what the critic described as CRI's previous reputation as a "stuffy outfit run by composers from academe."

"The motivating spirit behind Emergency Music emerges most glowingly on two discs (a third is imminent) containing fourteen works performed live at Bang on a Can new-music festivals," Davis observed.[2] He praised Bang on a Can's "easygoing, undoctrinaire manner that does not preclude rigorous formal discipline or an underlying seriousness of purpose," concluding his article with "No wonder the records are selling." Within a year, Bang on a Can jumped from CRI to the majors, signing a contract with Sony Classical as the label joined its colleagues in an attempt to cash in on the Górecki moment.

Like the All-Stars and Lincoln Center partnership, recordings helped Bang on a Can expand their audience and influence. And though they made only a minor sales impact in comparison to Górecki, Bang on a Can's history on CD coincided with major shifts in the relationship between new music and the record industry in the 1990s. In an interview, the producer Joseph Dalton, who had worked at CBS Masterworks before overseeing Emergency Music as label manager of CRI, described the "record industry" and the "new-music world" as entirely separate spheres.[3] One included corporations like CBS and BMG that were financially invested in selling recordings of standard classical repertoire, whereas the other comprised non-commercial labels like CRI and

New Albion that issued albums of contemporary works to a specialist clientele. Through the 1980s and early 1990s, the borders between these two institutional worlds had been fixed. But in the midst of the Górecki moment, these boundaries were blurred, as major labels began investing in new composers, new compositions, and new institutions like Bang on a Can in the hopes of turning new profits.

The intrusion of major record labels added a new wrinkle to contemporary music's marketplace turn. Thus far, non-profit arts organizations from Bang on a Can to Meet the Composer to Lincoln Center had sought to establish a dialogue between new music and broad audiences. By the mid-1990s, though, the classical record industry was investing in new music in the hopes of reaching not just a public but also a lucrative market, and Górecki's Third joined the Three Tenors and other crossover projects in taking aim at substantial profits. Bang on a Can got caught up in this transition of contemporary music recording from a non-profit service in the 1980s into a potentially profit-making enterprise in the 1990s. It seemed like a perfect moment for the ambitions of David Lang, Michael Gordon, and Julia Wolfe—not to mention John Duffy and his advocacy for the arts to be profit-making—who asserted their institutional identity through their CRI and Sony albums, their *Music for Airports* project, and the launch of their indie label Cantaloupe Music. And just as they were striving to do so, just as Górecki's symphony was topping the *Billboard* charts, Republicans in Congress were calling for American artists to embrace the free market. The record industry's support would appear to be a logical test of their argument. It should not be terribly surprising that it didn't work out.

No One Really Profits from Contemporary Music

In 1983, the director of the NEA's music program described the state of recording contemporary American music as a "national scandal." "Even in the profit-making sector of the serious-music recording," he noted, "no one really profits from contemporary music, except, perhaps, the art of music, and eventually the audience."[4] In the previous two decades, there were a few moments in which recordings of contemporary music commanded popular support and sales, whether through surprise hits like Morton Subotnick's 1967 Nonesuch album *Silver Apples of the Moon*, or in larger initiatives like Columbia Records' Music of Our Time series.

Music of Our Time was an unlikely affair, curated by the experimental electronic composer David Behrman. Columbia launched the imprint with a

1967 promo LP that included the likes of Karlheinz Stockhausen, John Cage, and The Byrds, framing it as an explicit dialogue between rock and the avant-garde and aiming it toward the counterculture.[5] "The Establishment's against adventure," read one of the ads.[6] "So what? Let them slam doors. And keep it out of the concert halls. Nothing can stop great sound makers like Ives, Riley, Stockhausen, Varèse, or the Moog Synthesizer."

It was the tail end of the era of Goddard Lieberson, the canny and risk-taking president of Columbia, who had committed the label to releasing music by Anton Webern, Arnold Schoenberg, and other unpopular modernists in the 1950s, subsidized by profits from Eugene Ormandy and Leonard Bernstein orchestral recordings. But Music of Our Time, as one executive put it, was designed to "make the breakthrough to the young people" and find commercial success.[7] Records by Terry Riley, Luciano Berio, and Harry Partch did make it onto *Billboard*'s classical charts. The series' most significant new-music release was a 1968 recording of Riley's *In C*, which helped bring the work its canonic status and draw widespread attention to minimalism. But the record on the imprint that made the real sales breakthrough was *Switched-On Bach*, the infamous collection of music by Johann Sebastian Bach played on a Moog synthesizer by Wendy Carlos. As *Switched-On Bach* stayed at number one on *Billboard*'s classical charts for 153 weeks, it became an emblem of crossover success, ultimately subsidizing Music of Our Time's otherwise unprofitable releases. When a less adventurous executive took over for Lieberson in 1971, and Columbia became more attentive to profit margins on individual records as the classical market broadly fell into decline, the series was scuttled.

"Since then, those record companies were first seduced by greed and then paid the price for that greed in the partial collapse of their markets," wrote the critic John Rockwell about Music of Our Time in 1983. The slump in sales of popular music around 1979, he added, meant that "the companies retrenched, cutting back still further on their peripheral operations."[8] So the NEA administrator's description was largely accurate—recording new music in the United States was seen as a non-commercial affair, functioning less as a generator of profits than as a service to the field of composition. Rockwell described the early '80s as a period of "fragmentation," of the proliferation of independent efforts that reached discrete markets, leading to a "dizzying variety of music" but little ability for mainstream consumers to find it.[9]

The most prominent of these specialist labels, Composers Recordings, Inc., was founded back in 1954 and functioned as a non-profit service organization for American music. Composers or ensembles could submit proposals to CRI's editorial committee. Typically, the label would produce and release albums only if the applicant already had financial backing to subsidize the recording, and such support frequently came from foundations, public arts agencies, universities, and the composers themselves, which accounted in part for CRI's reputation for representing "academic" composers. Like that of its peer New World Records—first initiated with a $4.9 million Rockefeller Foundation grant to issue an anthology of American music during the Bicentennial—the larger goal of CRI was to establish a permanent catalog of American music. It claimed to never delete recordings from its collection, and would always keep them in stock and available.[10]

For composers less closely associated with the academy, indie labels like Mimi Johnson's Lovely Music, Foster Reed's New Albion, and Philip Glass's Chatham Square similarly maintained a non-commercial approach directed toward a specialist clientele. Johnson, who oversaw the avant-garde management firm Performing Artservices, told an interviewer that Lovely Music—which released albums by fringe figures such as Robert Ashley, Peter Gordon, and "Blue" Gene Tyranny—typically sold around a thousand copies of a record in its initial year of release.[11] Reed, the director of New Albion, told the *Times* in 1987 that "We're not trying to compete with the big companies." He described the label, which primarily recorded minimalist and experimental composers like Pauline Oliveros and Ingram Marshall, as "a musical answer to the small, excellent publishing houses or the SoHo art galleries."[12]

These efforts gained a larger platform through the New Music Distribution Service, a catalog representing a variety of experimental music labels—including Glenn Branca's Neutral Records, which released an LP by the Michael Gordon Philharmonic in 1987. Founded by composer and pianist Carla Bley in 1972 as a free service to distribute records by a group of independent jazz labels, NMDS expanded into a ramshackle non-profit enterprise that, by 1982, carried more than 240 labels and 2,000 recordings.[13] "Independent record production and distribution may be the only way for musicians to maintain artistic and economic control of their work," stated a 1981 ad for the catalog printed in a New Music America program. "NMDS is a service, not a business. We deal with all independent record producers equally, regardless of how much or how little the records sell."[14] The advantage of NMDS was its reach, providing retail access to specialty stores as well as Tower Records. "We want to stay away from commercially oriented material," label manager Taylor Storer told the *Times*.[15] Funding for NMDS came from government grants and private foundations, which freed them from the need to focus on profits: "We are not concerned by poor sales; we have records here that sell only one copy per year." A successful album distributed by NMDS might sell 5,000 copies over three years.[16]

In the early 1980s, it was widely understood that labels like CRI and distributors like NMDS served a genre that was otherwise not financially viable.[17] "There is virtually no future for the American composer in the commercial recording world," composer William Schuman had told *High Fidelity* in 1979. "CRI is one answer."[18] But in the following years, two labels also established a new model for contemporary music to achieve mainstream success, and even profitability. In 1978, the Munich-based experimental jazz label ECM, under the direction of producer Manfred Eicher, released the first recording of Steve Reich's *Music for Eighteen Musicians*. Deutsche Grammophon had actually recorded the album but didn't really know what to do with it, and let it go to ECM.[19] It sold more than 100,000 copies.[20] The producer Robert Hurwitz, working under Eicher at the time, described the record as "a genuine breakthrough for new music" that "proved to many of us that contemporary music could appeal to more than just a small, specialized audience."[21]

Two years later, Eicher found himself mesmerized by Arvo Pärt's *Tabula Rasa*, which he heard on the radio while driving. He subsequently created the ECM New Series imprint in 1984 to release Pärt's music and that of other living composers, including Reich, Meredith Monk, and John Adams. Capitalizing on the popularity of ECM's jazz roster, Eicher recorded superstar pianist Keith Jarrett performing Pärt's *Fratres* for *Tabula Rasa*, the record that launched the New Series. As Tim Rutherford-Johnson writes of that album, "This was a package designed to have an appeal beyond the typical contemporary music recording."[22]

Eicher's ECM set the stage for the transformation of Nonesuch in the 1980s, which became a prototype for supporting contemporary music across the rest of the industry. Founded in 1964 by Elektra as a budget classical label, Nonesuch expanded through the 1970s under the direction of Teresa Sterne. Sterne oversaw an eclectic output including the Explorer Series devoted to world music, crossover hits like Joshua Rifkin's recording of Scott Joplin rags, and electronic works commissioned for the medium including Subotnick's *Silver Apples* and Charles Wuorinen's Pulitzer-winning *Time's Encomium*. The new music represented on Sterne's Nonesuch was not markedly different from that issued by CRI, with records by Wuorinen, George Crumb, and Elliott Carter.

Sterne, however, was dismissed in 1979, victim to the same profit-driven forces that had ended Music of Our Time. Warner purchased Elektra in 1970, and its new distribution method—requiring record stores to place bulk orders—oriented toward the pop approach of quickly recouping investments, rather than the slower model typical of classical and jazz recordings. When sales weakened in the late '70s, executives were no longer tolerant of Sterne's adventurous vision, and replaced her with the label's marketing director.[23] "Nonesuch is in business, and it is losing its credibility in its marketplace," a Warner executive told the *Boston Globe*. "We can't make records that sell only outside the Russian Tea Room."[24]

In 1984, new Warner management installed Hurwitz as Nonesuch's director. He had started his career at Columbia Records and then worked as head of American operations at ECM. Though Hurwitz had been a Speculum Musciae fan in his twenties, and wrote liner notes for a Columbia recording of Elliott Carter's Third String Quartet, he soon found himself infatuated with minimalism and turned away from uptown, advocating that Eicher release music by Reich and Adams. He brought Adams with him to Nonesuch as an exclusive artist, and quickly signed contracts with Reich, Philip Glass, and the Kronos Quartet, signaling an aesthetic shift from the label's past curatorship. Some composers previously supported by Sterne felt shut out by Hurwitz's new approach—Wuorinen criticized his work as guided by a "populist impulse," and Subotnick observed that Hurwitz never reissued *Silver Apples*, which is notably absent from the label's history on its website.[25]

Hurwitz took full creative control of the label's curation, releasing a limited output of twenty to twenty-five albums per year by artists including the Brazilian singer-songwriter Caetano Veloso, the World Saxophone Quartet, and the soprano Teresa Stratas. For contemporary music specifically, Nonesuch's mid-1980s recordings of Reich's *The Desert Music*, Adams's *Harmonielehre*, and Glass's *Mishima* established the label's reputation as maintaining an unusually strong balance of critical and commercial success. In 1986, the *Times* dubbed it "one of America's most innovative classical labels—and by far the most ambitious classical label operating with major-label distribution."[26] And the label's eclectic output found a large audience. Nonesuch sold more than a quarter-million copies of the compilation *Le Mystère des Voix Bulgares* in 1987, which ignited a craze for Bulgarian folk music in the wake of 1980s global pop sensations like worldbeat.[27]

Nonesuch and ECM were among the first to realize that minimalism had serious sales potential. But others were also taking note. In 1982, Glass became the first composer since Stravinsky and Copland to sign an exclusive contract with CBS Masterworks—the direct successor to Columbia Masterworks, renamed in 1980. But even after reissuing *Einstein on the Beach*, the label did not provide Glass with full-service treatment. Despite the composer's petitioning, it declined for several years to record his second opera, *Satyagraha*, and even rejected his film score *Koyaanisqatsi*.[28] Glass's first project with the label was instead *Glassworks*, conceived as a Walkman-friendly cassette and released under a new crossover imprint targeted toward what *Billboard* described as the "progressive rock" market. It sold more than 200,000 copies.[29] His 1986 album *Songs from Liquid Days*, a crossover collaboration with lyrics by Paul Simon and Suzanne Vega and vocals by Linda Ronstadt and The Roches, reached more than 250,000 units in sales. (CBS apparently tried to convince Glass to replace Simon, who had left the label for Warner Bros., with its own Billy Joel.) Though Glass was technically exclusive to CBS, he had signed on as a keyboardist, not a composer. He could therefore release his film scores with Nonesuch, and decamped to the label fully in 1993.[30]

The industry increasingly paid attention to new music's commercial appeal. Spurred by the president of Elektra, a consortium of record companies subsidized the 1989 chapter of New Music America to the tune of $100,000.[31] "Why should we promote the avant-garde when we're not likely to ever sign [its artists] or make money from them?" asked Nancy Jeffries, the A&R vice president at Virgin, in an interview with Tower Records' *Pulse!* magazine.[32] "If the avant-garde is ahead of us, and then we catch up a little bit, and then they move ahead a little more, it enables all of us to keep moving forward—which is really good for the business." They were playing the long game, one that would help them discover artists who might one day prove profitable: "Maybe for every Laurie Anderson there's a Suzanne Vega." (Of course, Anderson had major sales potential of her own: her *O Superman* had unexpectedly shot to no. 2 on the UK Singles chart in 1981.) This new dynamic perturbed some of the indie labels who had championed new music before it got popular. As Nonesuch was gearing up to release an album by Ingram Marshall—a New Albion stalwart—Foster Reed told *Pulse* that "They'll sell more of them in six months than we've ever sold, because they've got access to that major label national distribution pipeline and they have a major label's financial backing for advertising."[33] But the support of Nonesuch and the industry meant that these recordings could also reach a mainstream listenership.

Shepherded by a new label manager named Joseph Dalton, even the traditionalist CRI began to look to Hurwitz's Nonesuch as a potential model. A contemporary music aficionado who had moved from Dallas to New York in 1987 to take an internship with the Brooklyn Academy of Music's Next Wave Festival, Dalton had worked in A&R at CBS Masterworks, where he had the opportunity to write liner notes for two Glass albums, and edited *EAR Magazine*.[34] A fan of Nonesuch, Dalton was frustrated with CBS's lack of commitment to contemporary music in the late 1980s—the executives who had first signed Glass had left, and Dalton knew that the label had run out of ideas of what to do with him. The position of managing director at CRI opened up, and in 1990, at the age of twenty-seven, Dalton moved from a major label to a non-profit (Figure 7.1). "At my first interview, I told them I came to New York

Figure 7.1 Otto Luening and Joseph Dalton at CRI's fortieth anniversary celebration at the New York Public Library for the Performing Arts, October 7, 1994. Courtesy of Joseph Dalton.

because I was attracted to the works of Laurie Anderson, Philip Glass and Steve Reich," Dalton later told the *Times*. "And I saw their backs tighten, but when I met with some of the businessmen on the label's board, I said, 'These people are on major labels, and they sell.' It was clear to me pretty quickly why things weren't happening at CRI."[35]

Dalton oversaw CRI's transition from the LP to CD medium and, along with catching up with a backlog of unreleased recordings, he launched several new imprints, including Emergency Music. With edgy album covers and repertoire focused on New York's downtown scene, Emergency Music was explicitly designed to counteract CRI's academic reputation. And Bang on a Can helped shape its direction. Dalton invited Lang to join CRI's editorial committee. While planning to launch the imprint, Dalton consulted him on his attempts to shift CRI's image away from its previously—as the composer described—"stodgy background."[36] Lang also helped Dalton brainstorm the name Emergency Music, a pun on the idea of "emerging" composers. Promoted to coincide with that year's Bang on a Can festival, the imprint's first wave of releases in spring 1992 included musicians closely affiliated with the organization: a CD by accordionist Guy Klucevsek; portrait albums by Lang,

Gordon, Conrad Cummings, and Aaron Jay Kernis; and *Bang on a Can Live Volume 1*, with recordings from the organization's early festivals.

In an April 1992 press release—which described the imprint as "a dramatic new series of pop-influenced music by young, emerging American composers"—Dalton proclaimed that "Emergency Music represents the rebirth of CRI. The music and the marketing are as urgent and vital as the state of the arts in America today. This is post-modern, post-minimalist, post-NEA music."[37] Postmodern and postminimal line up neatly with the repertoire represented in the new initiative. In the midst of the Culture Wars—and during a period of cutbacks to the New York State Council on the Arts—"post-NEA music" suggested a vision for contemporary music that did not need public funding, one that could survive on its own commercial merits in the free market. Dalton was echoing John Duffy's comments to *EAR Magazine* in 1991, that a certain kind of new music might flourish, and leave government support behind, by taking on a "profit-making" attitude. When Dalton left CRI in 2000, however, he told the *Times* that he frequently argued with board members who wanted to run the label "like a business," even though he had spent much of his time at CRI writing grant proposals. The label was "nonprofit" not because it was "struggling and poor," but because it was "dedicated to something that will not survive commercially."[38] "Post-NEA" was rhetoric, not reality. Not even a hip imprint like Emergency Music could actually sustain itself in the market.

But it is not hard to see why Dalton repositioned the stuffy, quasi-academic label toward the marketplace, and Bang on a Can aided in his efforts. *Live Volume 1*'s cover featured a stark image of a hammer, a direct link to the poster for the 1987 festival (Figure 7.2). "Postminimalism, New Tonality, New Dissonance, New Formalism—critics and scholars are searching for a name to describe today's musical trends," read a blurb for the album. "The name is Bang on a Can."[39] "Musically, New York was in a slump in 1987, and the first Bang on a Can festival caught the city sleeping," Kyle Gann wrote in the CD's liner notes. "No one realized that the decade had been pregnant with a new musical ear, and no one expected a new style to emerge full-blown at an audacious, oddly named little festival never heard of before."[40]

Bang on a Can produced all three albums they released on CRI in 1992, '93 and '94, selecting what performances would be included on each CD. The live recordings attempt, in a new medium, to conjure some of the spirit of the festivals. *Live Volume 1* opens with ambient noise from the 1988 marathon before All-Stars bassist Robert Black performs Tom Johnson's *Failing: A Very Difficult Piece for String Bass*, in which the composer asks the bassist to "fail" on stage by performing while simultaneously describing the act of

Figure 7.2 Cover to *Bang on a Can Live Volume 1*, 1992.

performance aloud. ("Most of the time, I am required to play a tricky chromatic melody at a fast speed, and by now, I am probably beginning to fail in one way or another," Black says about halfway through the work, while playing a jagged line). *Failing* offered a humorous introduction to the album that aligned with festival's playful ethos and—given Johnson's reputation as an influential new-music critic for the *Village Voice* in the 1970s—oriented the recording toward the history of downtown. Its spoken word component also provided a clear reference to Bang on a Can's "living program notes," the informal introductions that composers regularly gave at the festivals. The other works featured on the first release, including Gordon's *Strange Quiet*, Wolfe's *The Vermeer Room*, Evan Ziporyn's *LUV Time*, and Allison Cameron's *Two Bits,* are aesthetically diverse but maintain an overall orientation toward postminimalism. Subsequent albums continue to represent Bang on a Can regulars like Lois V Vierk and Jeffrey Brooks, but also provide a strong sense of the marathons' eclectic supermix, from the eerie, cascading chamber music of Bunita Marcus's *Adam and Eve* to a noisily polystylistic improvisation from

Knitting Factory stalwarts Shelley Hirsch and David Weinstein. Notably absent from all three live albums was music by uptown composers like Milton Babbitt and Elliott Carter, despite the symbolic importance of their presence on the early marathons. Given the predominance of such figures in CRI's recorded catalog, this curatorial decision provided a clear message that Emergency Music was distinct from the label's past.

Although there was some pushback against Emergency Music from more conservative members of the CRI board and editorial committee—Dalton had to convince them that his new initiatives were not abandoning the label's traditional repertoire, but instead expanding its vision—the new series garnered favorable reviews, and the first Bang on a Can record was frequently singled out for praise. In a 1992 feature for the *New York Times* illustrated with a portrait of Lang, K. Robert Schwarz described Emergency Music's first releases as a "genuine philosophical shift" and "esthetic reorientation" of CRI.[41] And in his 1994 *New York Magazine* article, Peter G. Davis wrote that, with Emergency Music, Dalton had "committed to a brasher, more streetwise sort of music that the old CRI would never touch."[42]

As Many Followers as Madonna

Although no precise figures are available, the Bang on a Can live compilations were apparently some of CRI's fastest-selling records—not that they reached the kinds of numbers seen for a major label release.[43] For a typical CRI album, Dalton recalled, a thousand copies would be printed, and "You'd give away a hundred of them, sell a couple of hundred, and you've got stock for the rest of your days."[44] The biggest hit during Dalton's tenure, the 1996 anthology *Gay American Composers*, sold around 7,000 copies, and the label's overall bestseller was a Harry Partch record that sold 25,000 units over several decades.[45]

But just as Dalton was changing the image of CRI, the Górecki moment unfolded. Nonesuch released its recording of the composer's Symphony No. 3 in April 1992, and it quickly began its ascent on the classical charts. Although the symphony had been recorded three times already, Hurwitz had decided to pursue a new recording with the young soprano Dawn Upshaw and the London Sinfonietta after hearing it performed in 1989. "I think a lot of people might like this," Hurwitz recalled thinking, "and we might sell twenty-five or thirty thousand copies."[46] That turned out to be a dramatic understatement.

The symphony had attracted a cult following in Britain and the US in the 1980s, and Nonesuch's 1992 album achieved massive sales success on both sides of the Atlantic. It reached number three on the U.S. *Billboard* classical charts over the summer, which prompted the new UK radio station Classic FM to place the album in regular rotation in September 1992 during its first week on air, and its growing popularity in Europe drove further high sales in the states.[47] "It obviously touched a nerve in the public that no one could ever anticipate," Hurwitz said.[48] Warner Classics UK quickly shifted its marketing strategy and sent copies of the disc to tastemakers including Mick Jagger, Enya, and the archbishop of Canterbury. The album peaked at no. 1 on American classical charts in March 1993, and remained in the top position until November. More remarkably, by February 1993, it had reached no. 6 on the British pop charts, and sales were averaging approximately 10,000 per day. In total, Górecki's plaintive symphony sold nearly a million albums.

Observers at the time situated the Górecki hit as part of "holy minimalism," an emerging aesthetic comprising meditative, spiritual works by European composers including Pärt and John Tavener that had sold strongly in recordings by ECM, Nonesuch, and Virgin. Foster Reed, who called the holy minimalists the "God Squad," told an interviewer that "You couldn't have created a Third Symphony from a marketing point of view, so now everybody who's in the market is saying, 'Let's make this for the market.'"[49] Rutherford-Johnson places holy minimalism within the same trend as the album *Chant*— the 1994 recording of medieval music by Benedictine monks that went double platinum—in appealing to a young demographic as "exotic yet unthreatening" in a manner that "contributed to a chic, design-oriented, aspirational lifestyle."[50]

For the classical record industry, the implications of Górecki's sales extended far beyond just those composers considered holy minimalists. The hope was that contemporary composition could broadly inject new relevance, and new profits, into a struggling industry. "Górecki had unwittingly demolished the iron curtain between high art and mass consumption," journalist Norman Lebrecht wrote in April 1993. "A symphony, he demonstrated, could attract as many followers as Madonna."[51] Such a potential following manifested at a crucial moment for classical label executives, as portfolio management techniques were deployed by major labels in the 1980s and 1990s that, according to Keith Negus, "exposed certain genres of music and artists that were previously less conspicuously subject to monitoring." "For many years, within most major companies, the classical division was allowed to run at a loss, supported with revenues generated from the sales of pop and rock," Negus writes. "The introduction of separate budgets and the redefinition of classical as a separate 'profit centre' have placed pressure on the classical division to follow other departments by balancing (or concealing) an investment in long-term acts with short-term revenues."[52]

Dale Chapman connects these developments to pervasive neoliberal financialization in the record industry, in which "the primacy of shareholder value"—an explicit concern with demonstrating profits to analysts and investors—dominated corporate culture.[53] This new corporate agenda, Chapman reveals, helped facilitate a boom for the "young lions" of neoclassical jazz like Wynton Marsalis. Just as Lincoln Center welcomed Bang on a Can shortly after it welcomed Marsalis's jazz series, then, major labels began speculatively investing in new music shortly after they had speculatively invested in neoclassical jazz.

Through the 1980s, the classical industry had met requirements for short-term profitability by converting their back catalogs from LP to CD so that collectors would repurchase albums in the new medium, which brought in immense amounts of revenue. But the strategy had a limited lifespan. "Never before have so many recordings been available," the critic Sedgwick Clark wrote in *Opera News* in August 1992, while also noting that "Never before have record stores been so clogged with what a fellow collector calls 'dumpster bait.'"[54] The huge number of reissues combined with new recordings of standard repertoire continuously pursued by major and budget labels had overcrowded the market, with a total of 400 to 500 classical releases per month. By 1993, reissue catalogs were mostly exhausted, new recordings were too expensive to produce, and classical sales began to slow. The transition from LP to CD also spelled doom for the New Music Distribution Service. One day in 1990, a truck from Tower Records pulled up to the organization's office to return all of the vinyl that it had stocked from NMDS, for full credit. Faced with huge deficits, the distributor suspended operations permanently.[55]

Portfolio management meant that labels had to seek new sources of classical revenue quickly as the reissue market fell into decline. Labels looked to marvels like the Decca recording of a 1990 arena concert of arias sung by the Three Tenors—Plácido Domingo, Luciano Pavoratti, and José Carreras—that, with more than 14 million in sales, became the most popular classical album of all time.[56] Frequently panned by critics for their middlebrow attempts to reach mass audiences by recording popular fare, such industry-led projects were known as "crossover." New profits were implicitly intertwined with these new ventures. As Clark wrote, "Opinions vary, but all agree that something must be done to expand classical's traditional 4 percent of the industry pie."[57] Back in 1986, *Billboard* had launched a separate "Classical Crossover" chart to distinguish between traditional classical recordings and what it called "nonclassical material performed by a recognized classical artist" or "specially arranged classical material recorded by a nonclassical artist."[58] And whether or not they were defined as crossover, major classical records in the 1990s were frequently accompanied by marketing strategies drawn from pop. The most notorious case was a 1996 recording of Bach violin partitas by Lara St. John with a cover that featured the twenty-something violinist covered only by her instrument from the waist up. The album sold a substantial ten thousand copies.[59]

And while sex sold, so too did contemporary music. "The outsize success of Górecki's Symphony No. 3 on Elektra Nonesuch continued to haunt classical A&R mavens in 1993," *Billboard* noted in December of that year.[60] These mavens began to launch imprints closely modeled after Nonesuch—new music, intended to reach new audiences—including Philips's Point Music, BMG's Catalyst, and Sony's attempted Alternative Contemporary Music Line. Deutsche Grammophon signed a contract with the young American composer Todd Levin. London Records invested new resources in its contemporary label Argo, which recorded orchestral superstars (and former Bang on a Can classmates) Aaron Jay Kernis, Michael Daugherty, and Michael Torke as well as the British ensemble Icebreaker (which released a CD of Michael Gordon's *Trance* in 1996).

It even paid off for the non-commercial indies. New Albion got a distribution deal with Harmonia Mundi USA in 1995. "No one with a business perspective would have done what I did, because there was no market for it," Reed told *Billboard*.[61] "When we started, it was before the new regime at Nonesuch and before there was an ECM New Series." The Górecki moment, he noted, had changed things: "People realized that contemporary composition didn't have to be dry and pedantic—it could be emotionally involving and invigorating to listen to." Sales were up, too, at New Albion—its most popular release, Somei Satoh's contemplative *Toward the Night*, sold 15,000 records, and an album by Harold Budd had reached almost 10,000 copies.

At the major labels, it was Music of Our Time all over again, but on an industry-wide scale and with more fretting over immediate profits. The avant-garde was no longer a long-term investment, as that Virgin A&R executive described it in 1989, but a short-term money grab. Those savvy about contemporary music gained new power in the industry—Point Music was curated by Philip Glass, Catalyst was overseen by critic Tim Page, and Sony's line was conceived by composer Martyn Harry—and aimed for Hurwitz's careful balance of artistic integrity and market achievement. But these initiatives ultimately did not last, as each failed to meet the Górecki-esque sales expectations of label executives in a moment of extreme speculation.

Tim Page's brief tenure at Catalyst was a typical story of these times. Page had worked as a freelance critic for the *New York Times* before being appointed chief music critic at *Newsday* in 1987—where he reviewed the very first Bang on a Can festival. He also maintained a strong presence on New York radio as a supporter of new music and proponent of Reich and Glass in programs he hosted for WNYC. In his writing, Page had closely tracked the plights of the record industry in the early CD era—a 1988 *Newsday* column worried that the glut of reissues of albums by Maria Callas, Jascha Heifetz, and Arturo Toscanini "might ultimately mean the end of the classical record business as a creative force."[62]

In January 1992, three months before Nonesuch released the Górecki Third, Page pitched to the president of BMG Classics the idea for a cross-genre imprint on the label. He proposed a series of albums including reissues of 1930s recordings of the Philadelphia Orchestra, a recital by the violinist Maria Bachmann, a string quartet composed by Glenn Gould, Southern gospel music, and "a good recording of Henryk Mikolaj Górecki's third symphony."[63] (Not yet aware of the forthcoming Nonesuch release, Page had played an earlier recording of Górecki's symphony on his radio show and praised it in newspaper columns in the late '80s.) The critic saw the potential imprint as a canny blend of art and commerce that could succeed in the marketplace just as standard repertory was entering a slump. "If I am ever privileged to help shape a record company, I will do so as an enlightened businessman," he wrote. "There would be no huge expenditures on thorny, abstract new orchestral works that don't mean anything to anybody except a handful of other composers. On the other hand, there is a lot of new music out there that not only has quality but the potential for genuine mass popularity. And I am convinced that it is new music—and new approaches to old music—that will be the salvation of the classical record industry."[64]

As Nonesuch's Górecki recording began to climb the charts, BMG signed off on Page's idea, and Catalyst was born. Though Page's initial proposal was wide ranging in genre and era, the label's executives decided instead that Catalyst should focus exclusively on twentieth-century art music. "The line had long been that classical music sells terribly, but it's especially terrible if you do new music," Page recalled. "The Górecki suddenly changed these addlepated, old brains to 'Well, classical music sells terribly. But if you do new music, it's going to sell like rock 'n' roll!' "[65]

"I wanted to basically be like what Nonesuch was, but with my own sensibility rather than Bob's," Page added, referring to Hurwitz.[66] Catalyst releases included Bachmann's recital album, named for Arvo Pärt's *Fratres* (a nod to holy minimalism), and two CDs by the percussionist Evelyn Glennie; records dedicated to composers Silvestre Revueltas, Einojuhani Rautavaara, and Alvin Curran; and *Memento Bittersweet*, an album of works by composers with AIDS. "We're not just trying to be groovy," Page told the *Chicago Tribune* in August 1994. "This may sound a little pretentious, but we're trying to make records that are intellectually interesting."[67]

Despite critical acclaim and strong sales, Page's project was short-lived. He resigned from BMG in May 1995, and authored a scathing article for Tower's *Classical Pulse!* outlining the circumstances behind his departure and the misguided excesses of his supervisors. The actual article printed in the April 1996 issue of the magazine is a relatively tame retrospective on Page's tenure and an overview of his favorite albums on the imprint. But the initial draft instead opened with a description of a meeting with BMG executives in Salzburg—the label had flown Page to Austria, even though both Page and the executives were based in New York—where he pitched them a CD of contemporary works performed by the pianist Bruce Brubaker:

> The tape is never played. The glowing reviews are never read. Instead, Brubaker's press photo—a standard tux-and-piano number with a by-no-means-unattractive man at the center—is passed around, to the marked furrowing of brows. "It's so . . . conservative," says the man in the gray suit. "I don't like his haircut," whines the whippet-thin trendoid with the coif, between sips of Diet-Pepsi. "He should be wearing contacts instead of glasses," says another executive, after a ruminative pause long enough to prove he'd given the matter thought.[68]

Recapturing the sales magic of Górecki was seen as a top priority. Unlike the marketable asceticism of holy minimalism, Catalyst foregrounded sex appeal, with suggestive album covers that included Glennie wearing a jean jacket and tights, Bachmann in a black jumpsuit gazing out at the listener through mesh netting, and composer Steve Martland shirtless. As the *Chicago Tribune* noted of Catalyst and similar initiatives, "Artists are dressed for a video shot on MTV."[69] BMG spent enormous amounts of money on advertisements in rock publications like *Rolling Stone* without providing Page sufficient resources for A&R. He remembered that one executive criticized the *Memento Bittersweet* project because it "might make BMG appear to be a 'gay' label."[70] Evidently, executives reconsidered this critique—after *Memento Bittersweet*'s impressive sales, BMG went on to release *Out Classics*, a compilation of music that included excerpts from Tchaikovsky's *Nutcracker* and Britten's *Peter Grimes*, with a cover depicting what the *Times* described as "the naked upper torso of an impossibly hunky young man, his body glistening with droplets from a recent workout."[71] Even though he saw himself as an "enlightened businessman," Page's decisions were frequently undermined, and he was pressured to release albums of which he did not approve. "I remain convinced there is a way to serve both Art and Mammon, without repeating past formulas and without descending into ephemeral trend-chasing," Page wrote in *Classical Pulse!* "Who will give this to us?"[72] But Górecki had become the new Madonna, and the expectation was that other recordings of new music could follow in its footsteps.

An Artistic—But Not Commercial—Success

At the height of the CD boom, the consumer electronics giant Sony, which had co-developed the CD format with Philips, entered the entertainment industry by purchasing CBS Records in 1988 and Columbia Pictures the following year. Sony president Norio Ohga was a former opera singer and classical music buff, and paid close attention to the conglomerate's music holdings. In 1990, Sony Classical was launched as a successor to CBS Masterworks under the direction of Günther Breest, a Deutsche Grammophon producer who had worked closely with Herbert von Karajan. Breest modeled Sony Classical after his former home, relocating the main headquarters of the label from New York to Hamburg, expanding production to focus on reissues and new recordings of the classical canon, and engaging in bidding wars over major conductors like Claudio Abbado. Breest was largely uninterested in contemporary music, or the adventurous legacy of Goddard Lieberson.

While these changes were unfolding, the young British composer Martyn Harry found a job as an assistant in the marketing division of Sony Classical's Hamburg office, promoting new releases, where he noticed "huge amounts of money being squandered on producing far too many CDs" of standard repertoire.[73] As Górecki began to climb the charts, Harry saw its sales figures as confirming that contemporary music might represent a more viable path forward for the industry. "When ECM and Nonesuch were basically signing exclusive contracts with composers, it really felt in the early/mid-'90s as though composers were the new Simon Rattle," he recalled. "Or the new Karajan." Breest had hired the Decca producer Michael Haas, who invited Harry to envision a potential new-music series on the label. Sony was chasing a trend, but Nonesuch and ECM had already signed all the popular minimalists, holy and otherwise, so Harry had to find new artists and a distinctive identity for the imprint. He created a six-CD proposal for an "Alternative Contemporary Music Line" that included albums by composers Valentin Silvestrov, Howard Skempton, Giya Kancheli, and Geoff Smith, as well as a record featuring Bang on a Can.

A friend had tipped Harry off to David Lang's music, and he had been considering recording an all-Lang CD. In November 1993, Harry heard the

All-Stars play at the Huddersfield Contemporary Music Festival in England in one of their earliest tours. "I was just completely blown away by that gig," he said. The All-Stars made a persuasive case in concert: Harry was "struck by the incredible energy of the individual performers." The group hadn't yet fully solidified, but there was a compelling sound to the ensemble and repertoire—whether in Gordon's snarling *Industry*, Louis Andriessen's groovily dry *Hout*, or Lois V Vierk's menacing *Red Shift*—and "creativity was bursting from all corners." "It was so different from anything that was being marketed commercially, in this sort of Philip Glass/Górecki kind of way," Harry recalled. They didn't look or sound like holy minimalists, less ascetic and sorrowful than sexy and loud. He wanted to use the All-Stars for the Lang album, and met with the composer. Lang recalled that he responded, "Why do you want to put out my music? I represent this organization: you could put out my whole organization."[74] And thus Bang on a Can were signed.

Although Breest's backwards-gazing Hamburg office was skeptical toward contemporary music, the hip image of Bang on a Can appealed to Sony's marketing division in New York. "They wanted something really distinctive that they could sell, and I think they were really convinced," Harry noted. "Bang on a Can made quite an impression."[75] Gordon, Lang, and Wolfe had recognized that the Górecki moment provided an opportunity to advance their agenda. A 1995 grant proposal stated that "With the recent success of contemporary works such as Górecki's Third Symphony, Sony Classical has recently launched a new series of recordings, designed and packaged to bring lesser known new music to a larger audience. This is also a principal mission of Bang on a Can."[76] A major label contract opened up a new source of earned income for Bang on a Can—not just from advances and royalties, but also from the visibility and promotion that Sony could provide, which helped them unlock further touring opportunities. (That said, little money ultimately came in from royalties, and any advances from Sony went toward funding the recording sessions.)

Harry had been interested in releasing a separate recording of music by Louis Andriessen, and when he became aware of the close ties between Bang on a Can and the Dutch composer, he conceived a CD along the lines of "Louis Andriessen meets Bang on a Can." The All-Stars recorded in a London studio in summer 1994, with additional musicians from the British ensemble Icebreaker and two Dutch pianists brought in for Andriessen's *Hoketus*, the centerpiece of the album. But while the Alternative Contemporary Music Line was being planned, institutional strife was unfolding at Sony. Breest's overspending and the label's dwindling sales led to his ouster. Peter Gelb, who had worked as Vladimir Horowitz's manager and president of the production company CAMI Video before joining Sony when it purchased CAMI in 1993, was installed as Breest's replacement in spring 1995.[77] Sony Classical had been bleeding money, and its parent company would no longer tolerate big losses. "Traditionally, classical music companies don't make money, and they generally are, at a major level, supported as a prestigious thing by pop companies," Harry recalled. "Sony Music decided that Sony Classical would now have—as a financial area—to break even."[78]

"While Breest was said to be disillusioned by pressures to compete in the classical industry with too many crossover projects, Gelb says his perspective is to link tradition with a policy of 'diversity and eclecticism,'" *Billboard* wrote of the shakeup.[79] The article further noted that "Due in April is 'Bang on a Can All-Stars,' a spinoff of a New York festival of avant-garde music that draws from elements of pop." The A&R mission of Sony had caught up with the Górecki moment. "I was certainly aware of it," Gelb recalled of the Górecki, "and very envious of its great success."[80] Gelb's Sony Classical would be markedly different from the CBS Masterworks that had frustrated Dalton and squandered its relationship with Glass. "There's been a negative trend in the past few years—the decline of sales of standard repertoire—so we have to be flexible and creative in balancing the most adventurous with the traditional," Gelb told *Billboard* later that year. "We know that the 500th re-recording has less potential than a recording of new music."[81]

Although Harry's initiative was prioritized in this moment, it also complicated his plans for the potential Alternative Contemporary Music Line. Gelb closed the Hamburg office and moved the Sony Classical headquarters back to New York. The executives and staff that Harry worked with in Hamburg were laid off, and he was relocated to the label's London branch. Keeping with the European tradition of small imprints on larger labels, the original plan for the Alternative Contemporary Music Line was to resemble Catalyst, as a fully conceived sublabel with cohesive design and promotion. But the New York office ruled against an imprint in favor of Bang on a Can's album and the others being issued as standalone records, marketed and released separately. During this chaotic transition, the concept of "Andriessen meets Bang on a Can" was dropped in favor of the title *Industry*—named for Gordon's cello solo—and the record's design became more explicitly oriented around Bang on a Can. The repertoire comprised Andriessen's *Hout* and *Hoketus* as well as Wolfe's *Lick*, Gordon's *Industry*, and Lang's *the anvil chorus*.[82]

The careful attention that Gordon, Lang, and Wolfe had paid to their organization's image and marketing materials paid off—Sony seemingly wouldn't have that much to do. For promotional materials, Sony used images that Bang on a Can's longtime photographer friend Peter Serling had already taken of the group, looking dour and confrontational, on the stark roof of a New York building (Figure 7.3). The design for the 1995 album, which featured a grayscale cover depicting two hulking, spherical oil storage tanks, aligned neatly with the image that Bang on a Can had cultivated since their origins. (Dalton noted that "The first disc on Bang on a Can on Sony looked like it belonged in the Emergency Music series: the packaging was a black-and-white, grainy, urban feel."[83])

While Tim Page expressed skepticism toward the "attitude"-focused marketing that label executive "trendoids" demanded from him at Catalyst, Bang

Figure 7.3 Ad for Sony album in Lincoln Center program book, 1995, featuring *Industry* album cover and Peter Serling's photograph.

on a Can seemed totally comfortable thinking along such lines. As with the Lincoln Center program notes, Deborah Artman interviewed the four composers on the album to create first-person descriptions of their music for the liner notes. "In the 70s, like others who were marching in the streets, I wanted to make a revolution," Andriessen says of his *Hout*.[84] Artman also spoke with Gordon, Lang and Wolfe as a trio, yielding a quasi-manifesto describing the by-then-standardized mythos of Bang on a Can: "When we came to New York in the 1980s, things were very polarized . . . So in 1987 we decided to make a happening . . . We didn't want to be restricted by boundaries, and we didn't want the listener to be restricted either."[85]

Critics saw Bang on a Can's jump to Sony as paralleling its move uptown to the auspices of Lincoln Center. "Some purists are even wondering whether success hasn't spoiled the Bang on a Canners as they eagerly reach out and embrace the musical Establishment," Davis wrote in *New York Magazine* in April 1995.[86] *Billboard* described Bang on a Can as "invading the mainstream."[87] And longtime observers pointed out that the Sony repertoire emblematized the shifts in Bang on a Can's curation with their All-Stars ensemble and Alice Tully programming. In a strongly positive *Times* review, K. Robert Schwarz wrote that "the Bang on a Can esthetic has narrowed, or at least solidified" since the CRI albums, and *Industry* provided a "unity so tight that the release almost amounts to a manifesto."[88] The critic noted that though other writers had used the term "totalism" to describe the sound of this music, it might more accurately be called "Bang-on-a-Can-ism." And the record, he wrote, even provided a kind of a sonic antidote to holy minimalism: "In an age that revels in the soothing, spiritualized Minimalism of Arvo Pärt, Henryk Górecki and John Tavener, *Industry* emerges as a bruising, bracing slap in the face."

Schwarz appeared to be taking his cues directly from the Bang on a Can founders. "This disk is very different from what is now considered commercial in the classical music department," Gordon told Schwarz in March 1995.[89] "What is considered commercial now is Górecki, and Eastern European feel-good mysticism, along with Philip Glass, who has always been very successful in the classical music department, and the Kronos Quartet." (Essentially, a summary of the Nonesuch roster.) Instead, he stated, the Sony record was "picking up on the Bang on a Can spirit—of new, more challenging, aggressive, fresh music" and added that "it's not easy listening." Gordon went on to note that contemporary music was reaching a new phase of broad popularity, in which major labels saw it as "a much bigger market than traditional chamber music." "We're entering a completely different period in terms of the relationship between contemporary music and the audience," he told Schwarz. He called it "the popular avant-garde."

Unfortunately, Bang on a Can's avant-garde turned out to not be as popular as Gordon had imagined, at least in terms of record sales. "We thought *Industry* was going to be a gold record," Evan Ziporyn recalled.[90] And why not have high hopes? The CD-buying public was clearly interested in new music, the All-Stars had built an international presence, and the marathons in New York had been selling out for years. But *Industry*, released in April 1995, never made it onto *Billboard*'s classical charts. Grace Row, a young producer who worked assiduously in the studio for both of Bang on a Can's Sony albums, recalled that, despite initial enthusiasm, the CD was "a challenge for our marketing department," and felt that it largely slipped through the cracks at the label.[91] Bang on a Can had tried unsuccessfully to convince Gelb and the marketing division to attend one of their concerts, in the hopes that it would help the label better understand what the organization was about. The classical charts that season were topped by the soundtrack to the Beethoven biopic *Immortal Beloved*, a Three Tenors live album, and *Chant*. Any new work in the top ten came from film—Michael Nyman's music for the *The Piano*, John Williams's score to *Schindler's List*. "Monks, tenors, and Beethoven are dominating classical record sales," wrote *Billboard* critic Heidi Waleson that fall.[92] "But labels are looking ahead to the next thing," she added—including new music. Still, she noted, there were risks: "Forays into this area are fraught with peril, of course. Neither DG's Todd Levin recording or Sony's Bang on a Can made a huge impact this year."

Sony had committed to two CDs, with the option to renew for two more. The second Sony album began as a disc devoted to the music of Lang and Brazilian avant-garde composer Hermeto Pascoal, and then came to include a more mixed repertoire. Titled *Cheating, Lying, Stealing*, the CD featured the titular Lang work alongside music by Frederic Rzewski, Nick Didkovsky, Evan Ziporyn, Lois V Vierk, and Pascoal (arranged by Ziporyn). Neither Sony record was, strictly speaking, "post-NEA music," as government funding supported both albums: a grant for $4,500 from the New York State Council on the Arts for *Industry*, and a grant for $11,380 from the NEA for *Cheating, Lying, Stealing* (though that amounted to only about 11 percent of the recording's budget).[93] The NEA funding arrived in 1995, right before the Republican majority in Congress forced the Endowment to end its support for individual artists, which included the music grant category for recording projects.

Collaborating with Grace Row on both albums, the All-Stars increasingly embraced pop-style studio technology, utilizing multitracking and post-production effects. They even recorded the second CD in the iconic New York studio The Hit Factory. Released in 1996, *Cheating, Lying, Stealing* did not make it onto the charts either. By January of the following year, it had sold around 6,000 copies.[94] "Bang on a Can was not a commercial success, but it was an artistic success," Gelb recalled.[95] Lang recounted that they met with Gelb after the second album came out, and he told them that their records weren't making any money.[96] And like Page, Harry soon found himself navigating a climate in which his notion of successful sales did not align with that of senior label executives. "The powers that be within Sony were really looking for hundreds of thousands of units," he said.[97] *Cheating, Lying, Stealing* was one of Harry's final records with the label.

Another kind of music, ultimately, satisfied the profit benchmarks set by Sony. In a September 1996 *Billboard* editorial, Gelb wrote that "After 50 years of being bludgeoned by inaccessible new music, the tides of new music are changing." Describing the audience-friendly works of Pärt, Tavener, and John Adams, Gelb added that "New music can be both artistic and accessible. I'm convinced that it is possible to maintain the character and integrity of classical music while broadening its scope and appeal."[98] Sony's strongest efforts in this area, however, were not in recording the works of Adams or the holy minimalists, but instead in investing in film soundtracks. "What I did and other companies did were to look for new music sources—but most new music, of course, doesn't sell," Gelb later said.[99] "The most profitable direction that I embarked on was trying to combine the composers who were either writing for movies or who were not writing for movies but could theoretically write for movies." Exploiting Sony's multinational, multimedia holdings, Gelb commissioned new works designed to succeed in both film and music—corporate synergy par excellence. He signed the Chinese composer Tan Dun to record his *Symphony 1997*, brought Yo-Yo Ma to the project as a soloist, and recruited Tan to write the score for the Columbia Pictures (and Sony-owned) film *Crouching Tiger, Hidden Dragon*, which also featured Ma. Gelb paired the composer John Corigliano with the director François Girard to create the soundtrack for the film *The Red Violin*, complete with a complementary concerto for the violinist Joshua Bell. Such an approach ultimately yielded a smash hit album that most would not necessarily see as a successor to Górecki's Third—the soundtrack to the 1997 film *Titanic*, which would go on to sell more than 30 million copies.

Higher Sales Potential

With Sony no longer an option, Bang on a Can looked to other labels in the still-bullish market for new-music recordings. In 1996, they put together an all-Reich CD for Nonesuch, with Ziporyn playing *New York Counterpoint* and members of the All-Stars and the SPIT Orchestra as well as Gordon performing *Four Organs* and *Eight Lines*, which was also included as part of a ten-CD box set of the composer's music. Gordon had a solo record, *Weather*, released on Nonesuch in 1999.

And Bang on a Can issued their most famous recording in 1998: *Music for Airports*. The project fell under the direction of Point Music, the Philips imprint founded in 1992 as a partnership with Philip Glass's Euphorbia Productions, led by longtime Glass collaborators Kurt Munkacsi and Michael Riesman. Point had early sales successes with recordings of Glass's "Low" Symphony—inspired by Eno and David Bowie—and Gavin Bryars's *Jesus' Blood Never Failed Me Yet*, in a newly expanded version featuring Tom Waits. The imprint also found clear commercial triumphs in crossover "symphonic rock," including albums devoted to orchestral arrangements of Pink Floyd and Led Zeppelin that sold in the hundreds of thousands.[100] Philips had been subject to what one journalist called a "brutal restructuring plan" in the early 1990s; it raised further profits and cut costs by closely integrating with its PolyGram record group and, like Sony, aligning its film and music operations.[101]

In 1997, Point increased staff and expanded its annual release schedule as part of a global restructuring of Philips, which included a shift in focus that *Billboard* described as "an eye to the creative marketing techniques that pop labels have practiced and that major classical labels have been slow to implement."[102] Glass had brought Wolfe to Point a couple years earlier, to work with Riesman on her 1996 album *Arsenal of Democracy*. In conversations with Point about Bang on a Can's future, the idea of a live arrangement of *Airports* came up, and the label liked it. Reimagining a canonic experimental album made sense for Bang on a Can, and reimagining music by a rock icon in a quasi-symphonic context made sense for Point. "Point is trying to redefine what 'classic' music is," Glass told *Billboard*. "For both Bang on a Can and I, Bowie and Eno's music is certainly classic—and suitable for interpretation in a 'classical' sense."[103]

Along with making a case for re-recording an iconic electronic album with live instruments, Bang on a Can also contextualized the project, which was co-produced by Ziporyn in the studio, as a pivot from the angular and aggressive repertoire of the Sony albums.[104] "It is the most ethereal thing in our bin," Lang said to a *Los Angeles Times* reporter, when the All-Stars toured *Airports* on the West Coast. "At least on some level, it might look like it's a stretch, but I think our mission from the very beginning has been to try and find a home for people and music who have no other home."[105]

214 Industry

Released in February 1998, the *Airports* project also represented Bang on a Can's next step in building a national platform for their recorded output. Promotional materials that announced the first *Airports* tour—eight US dates in the spring, beginning with the premiere at Alice Tully Hall—stated that the record should be filed under "new age, Brian Eno." Samplers would be given away at record stores along with "New Age bookstores, coffee shops, airport terminals, and other lifestyle outlets"; there was the possibility for promotional partnerships with commercial airlines, "including in-flight program advertising and program sampling"; there would be large-scale ad and publicity campaigns, and a video press kit.[106] (The five-minute promo video, which intersperses footage of the founders talking about the project with goofy vintage film of airplanes, including an excerpt from the 1933 classic *King Kong*, feels a little misguided.[107])

In April, the All-Stars visited London's Stansted Airport to play a promotional gig for PolyGram personnel and press—*Music for Airports* live in an airport. Eno himself turned up. A couple months earlier, he had written a long, supportive fax to Bang on a Can, having only heard the album just around when it came out. In the letter, Eno described a previous attempt to transcribe his electronic works for acoustic instruments that was largely unsuccessful, but wrote that he found himself unexpectedly moved to tears when listening to their *Airports* rendition. "When I made *Music for Airports*—almost exactly twenty years ago—I never imagined it would have such a long life, or such unexpectedly beautiful offspring," he added.[108] At Stansted, he described his original album as "merely a demo awaiting this first proper performance."[109]

In May 1998, representatives from Bang on a Can and Point discussed how to boost sales by looking beyond chain stores like Tower and HMV in order to reach new listeners. "In the first Mktg Meeting Point's central pitch was to pull BOAC out of the Classical Cellar and into the New Age Market for its higher sales potential," a memo describing the meeting reads; by then, the record had sold around five thousand copies.[110] Bang on a Can was eager to reach new markets. "Someone in the rock world who might listen to noise bands or Eno or alternative rock wouldn't necessarily find us," Wolfe told the *Los Angeles Times*. "This is a bridge."[111]

Though the record and live tours garnered favorable reviews, some saw *Airports* as more gimmicky than Bang on a Can's previous efforts. Having already soured to the Lincoln Center appearances, Kyle Gann took an especially cynical approach to the endeavor's Alice Tully premiere, calling it "either foolhardy or sublimely ironic," and describing the performance as souped-up, New Age-y, and possibly even "a mammoth publicity stunt."[112] And further, yoking Eno's record into the concert hall, with its new "silences of devout beauty," changed its aesthetics: "Suddenly, *Music for Airports* was no longer ambient, but a solemn hymn of Buddhist spirituality. Górecki and Pärt, eat your East European holy minimalist hearts out." The slap-in-the-face idiom of *Industry*, a rejoinder to the soothingly commercial appeal of spiritual minimalism, seemed far away. Other press, though, was more enthusiastic; in the *Times*, the pop critic Jon Pareles declared that "Bang on a Can did well by *Music for Airports*, finding a remote grandeur behind its self-effacement."[113]

Airports sold around 15,000 copies domestically—a strong showing for a contemporary record—and spent six weeks on *Billboard*'s New Age chart, peaking at no. 18 in March 1998.[114] Bang on a Can had pitched eleven records and a four-year partnership to Point, including multiple All-Stars albums, solo CDs by the three founders, and a collaboration with the short-lived SPIT Orchestra.[115] But it soon became a struggle to secure even a second record with the label. In a memo to Point that fall, Bang on a Can wrote about "a huge and growing movement among rock artists right now to expand the entire idiom in a more open, creative direction," with experimenters like Tortoise and The Flaming Lips pushing boundaries, and noted that their listenership was a logical target for a rock-oriented All-Stars record.[116] "There are many indie rock bands that are making instrumentally rooted music that sell 20,000 records and will never sell to the audience that already knows BOAC but we believe we can penetrate their audience," they wrote. "It's almost a new millennium, and all signs indicate that people are not only receptive to a new musical vision, they're craving it."

But Bang on a Can did not want to do an *actual* rock record; they didn't want to repeat *Airports* by picking another famous musician and remaking a canonic album, creating a more avant-garde version of symphonic Led Zeppelin. In November 1998, Bang on a Can made their big pitch to Point, writing to the label they had "truly broken into new markets, and are poised to go much further." Responding to a previous Point suggestion to record an album of minimalist music, the letter argued that "it's a worthy idea, but it's not us, and it won't sell." Noting that numerous recordings of works by Glass, Reich, and Adams already existed—including Bang on a Can's own recent Nonesuch CD—the letter stated that a minimalism-focused recording would represent a step backwards for the organization, "surrendering all our distinctiveness, all our reputation for constant innovation and genre-crossing that has sustained us for the past decade."[117]

The letter instead described a CD titled "Y2K" that would embody "music for a new millennium," naming bold precedents like *Introducing the Beatles* and Ornette Coleman's *The Shape of Jazz to Come*. "The sound: performer-oriented (i.e., with the personality of the band), multi-cultural (i.e., using samples), energetic," they wrote. "Another key is the production and packaging: rock-oriented, and conceived of as an album, not as a composer collection (i.e., the tunes are listed as tunes first with the composers in parentheses)—that is, marketed as a whole product by a band with a voice, rather than as a compilation of interesting commissions."

"We need to do exactly what the Eno did: take people by surprise in such a way that they end up broadening their concept of who we are, without being able to put us into a preexisting bag," they continued. Potential repertoire would include Gordon's *I Buried Paul* and Wolfe's *Believing*—both inspired by Beatles songs—a new piece by Lang, and works by Steve Martland, Phil Kline, Arnold Dreyblatt, and Eno. "Y2K would be sexy, loud, filed most certainly in the rock section, and attractive to both cutting edge and more mainstream listeners of electronica, rock, classical, alternative, world, jazz and everything else."

The letter is long, detailed, and ambitious. It also documents some of the strain between Bang on a Can and Point, mentioning the months of pitching various ideas that fell flat. Bang on a Can clearly believed their work could succeed amidst the inflated expectations of the record industry, but was also trying to prove to a major label that they could do so, without resorting to Pink Floyd or Minimalism's Greatest Hits. At the same time, the letter reveals how Bang on a Can's artistic vision had changed since their CRI years, as they moved further away from eclectic supermix compilation into tightly-conceived and coherent package for the marketplace. As Bang on a Can attempted to introduce themselves to a twenty-first century rock crossover audience, their originary narrative of merging uptown and downtown had no real role to play.

The Y2K concept became the 2001 record *Renegade Heaven*, with the proposed works by Wolfe, Gordon, Dreyblatt, and Kline, along with a piece by Glenn Branca, performed by the All-Stars. The album was recorded in The Magic Shop, a New York rock studio, and heavily utilized post-production techniques overseen by Ziporyn and producer Damian LeGassick. Its back cover and inside booklet foreground the titles of individual tracks and placed their composers' names in parentheses. Its title offered the patina of holy minimalism, responding to the trend with what Bang on a Can called "edgy spirituality."[118] And its sound returned to the grittily confrontational aesthetic of the Sony albums, from Wolfe's snarling headbanger *Believing* to Dreyblatt's just-intonation, roughhewn *Escalator* to the microtonal howl of Branca's *Movement Within*. It is easy to imagine the record's appeal to, say, Sonic Youth fans; it's much harder to imagine its appeal to those buying symphonic Led Zeppelin or *Chant*. *Times* critic Allan Kozinn named it one of his favorite records of the year, with music that "straddles the gulf between art rock and concert music."[119]

Renegade Heaven, however, was not released on Point. It instead represented the first recording issued by a new independent record label, Cantaloupe Music, founded by Gordon, Lang, Wolfe, and Bang on a Can's executive director Kenny Savelson.[120] "That was right in the moment when the record industry—the major label industry—started to bleed," Savelson, who served as executive producer on *Renegade Heaven*, recalled.[121] In 1998, to placate investors, Philips sold PolyGram to the Canadian liquor company Seagram, which merged its label holdings—including Philips Classics and Point as well as US distribution for Deutsche Grammophon and London Records—with Universal Music Group, which would command a quarter of the global market.[122] A single senior vice president oversaw all crossover releases at the group, regardless of label. She told *Billboard* that she was enthusiastic to do "whatever it takes to reach the most mainstream audience possible."[123] Point and Andrea Bocelli were now both part of the same crossover department—Bang on a Can was competing for attention with the likes of André Rieu.

The following year, under the broader Universal ownership, Philips Music Group (inclusive of Point) was absorbed into the classical label Decca.[124] Budgets were slashed, personnel were cut, corporate shakeups abounded. And then began a dramatic decline in industry profits writ large: in 1999, the file sharing platform Napster started to drastically affect CD sales, ushering in the age of downloaded music. Bang on a Can's pitches to Point for a second album unfolded in the midst of all this, as the label drifted between corporate owners who needed more sales, and more profits, than ever.

At a 1999 retreat, Bang on a Can staff discussed whether they wanted to move to another label, such as Nonesuch, or if they wanted "total autonomy."[125] Autonomy was risky. As physical sales tapered and blockbuster stores like Tower struggled to stay afloat, independent and non-commercial new-music labels were cut out of brick-and-mortar distribution networks. Dalton left CRI in 2000, and the label folded in 2003.[126] But major labels were risky, too. "These once-healthy companies have collapsed, merged, or become a shadow of their former selves, issuing just a few classical recordings," wrote *Chamber Music Magazine* in 2001. "And those they do release had better be hits. BOAC's biggest success, Eno's *Airports*, only sold 15,000—a smash for a not-for-profit, yet a small blip for a multi-national entertainment conglomerate."[127]

"It's no secret that over the last five years or so, the record industry has been constantly going through shifts," Gordon told *Billboard* in 2001.[128] "Companies are being bought and sold, and it seems to us that there's more emphasis on profitability and very big records. When we started with Sony six years ago, no one said to us, 'We need a record that's going to sell 100,000 copies.' Now, for a lot of big labels, that's where you start the conversation. And that's not what we're about or what we're interested in."[129] The Górecki moment had ushered Bang on a Can into the industry mainstream, but there were clear limits. The same forces that ousted Page and Harry for not meeting the sales demands of label executives also left Bang on a Can to their own devices.

Though older labels like CRI didn't last, indies were coming back in vogue. There was an entirely new marketplace on the Internet, one that rendered big stores like Tower obsolete. In 2001, Glass's producer Kurt Munkacsi collected all of the composer's master recordings and began reissuing them on a new label, Orange Mountain Music, which soon grew to release other new-music albums as well. New Albion also quickly established a strong web presence. It made a lot of sense for Bang on a Can's founders to start their own label—they had started their own festival, their own ensemble. Cantaloupe Music would serve as a boutique operation. It would focus on growing long-term relationships with a small roster of composers, pursue a limited release schedule with distribution from Harmonia Mundi, and build a web infrastructure to grow its online audience, while helping new audiences discover new music. In other words, it would do what CRI and New Albion had done for decades—a return to normalcy after the Górecki bubble.

***

This episode of collision between contemporary music and the record industry complicated the institutional landscape for contemporary music. When John Duffy opened up a new dialogue between new music and the public—and argued for American composers to enter the marketplace—he could not have imagined a climate in which label executives wanted such composers to sell a million records. When the New York State Council on the Arts stipulated that they would prioritize funding organizations that made audience outreach efforts, they wanted to see ensembles and venues attract hundreds of listeners to their concerts. And when Bang on a Can moved to Lincoln Center, it was to fill the thousand seats of Alice Tully Hall for their marathons. Finding hundreds of thousands of consumers, as the record industry demanded, was unfathomable.

In his August 1997 interview for Yale's Oral History of American Music project—conducted the same month that the All-Stars were in the studio recording *Music for Airports*—Gordon reprised what he had told K. Robert Schwarz a couple years earlier during the *Industry* press campaign. "The marketplace has opened up," he said. "One of the ideas that I like to think about, and it drives me—I think it has driven Bang on a Can—is the idea of the popular avant-garde."[130] He compared the moment to when the aristocratic system of patronage began to break down in the nineteenth century, and a ticket-buying public emerged, and virtuosos like Paganini and Liszt filled big concert halls. No longer did young composers have to take teaching jobs to make a living. Glass, Reich, and the Kronos Quartet had opened up new career possibilities, he noted, and Bang on a Can had seized on them. The record industry was paying attention. "It's a whole different thing," he said. "Interest is going up and the audience is becoming more aware." Gordon wasn't exaggerating. Audience numbers, sales figures, sold-out concerts, and a sense of excitement among musicians and listeners back up the composer's claim that he was living in an unprecedented era for contemporary music in the United States. And equally important to all of that data is the clear significance that Gordon placed on the idea that the avant-garde could be popular. He believed in it, and he was not alone in doing so. The ethos suffused the era.

That didn't make that much of a difference, though, when it came to recording. Gordon and Bang on a Can, Tim Page and Martyn Harry, believed that new music could find a substantial non-specialist audience, but their encounters with major labels demonstrate the hazards of that approach. Górecki was a flash in the pan, the sole contemporary disc that tapped into what the industry called the "massive passive." Philip Glass albums might have reached impressive numbers; orchestral Pink Floyd covers could, too, and the *Titanic* soundtrack could sell much more, but that didn't matter much to Bang on a Can. Though they wanted to promote music that was more consciously challenging than holy minimalism and crossover, the in-roads that Bang on a Can made in the industry reflected the same material conditions that buoyed Górecki and the Three Tenors. Even if the organization was prepared for this moment—they had the setup, savvy, and sound to appeal to Sony and Point—the market they had cultivated in their marathons and other activities was much, much smaller than that sought by major labels. Even *Music for Airports* was still more of an artistic than commercial success.

"Post-NEA music" was not a sustainable vision. Duffy argued that "the healthiest thing for the arts is for them to be profit-making," but none of this behavior seems particularly healthy. The popular avant-garde had limits to its popularity; there were good reasons why new music was primarily a non-profit enterprise. In the spring of 2017, sitting in his office as general manager of the Metropolitan Opera and thinking back on his work with Sony, Peter Gelb said that "Unlike my job here at the Met—which is to create art, not profits, because profits are impossible—in a for-profit company you have to create profits, or else you go out of business."[131] Even for those who hoped that contemporary composition might prosper in the marketplace, the actual free market of the 1990s—as embodied in the revenue-hungry record industry—did not serve as an accommodating long-term home. As they entered the twenty-first century, Bang on a Can did not abandon their marketplace philosophy. But after public funding was decimated and the record industry went bust and the Internet opened a new array of opportunities, they would move forward largely on their own.

Epilogue

Aaron Copland was once asked what he felt that he had accomplished in his career as a composer. He responded, proudly, that he "helped to make art possible in America." Recalling the conversation in a 1956 speech, Copland added that, "Come to think of it, that is what all artists in America do."[1] He lived through the beginnings of modernist music in the United States, the Depression- and World War II-era wave of populist Americana, the academic and bohemian postwar avant-gardes, and the rise of minimalists and neo-Romantics. Amidst shifting economic circumstances and ideological backdrops, generations of composers made their art possible. The enterprise of American composition has always been a do-it-yourself affair, or at least do-it-yourself until you can convince an institution to pick up the bill. And like much art in the United States, it mostly has, and mostly will, lose money; it has mostly been non-profit, and will likely remain mostly non-profit.

Reaganomics aside, the 1980s was a decade of promise for new music. Steve Reich, Philip Glass, and Laurie Anderson became famous; festivals like New Music America gave experimentalism a significant platform; Meet the Composer's residency program convinced symphony orchestras to support contemporary work; the Brooklyn Academy of Music sold out avant-garde productions; money seemed to flow easily from corporate coffers and the government. During this marketplace turn, this institutional drive to make contemporary music culturally relevant to a broad public, Bang on a Can seized their moment and carved out a niche for themselves. Their eclectic programming offered a new take on the seemingly staid uptown-downtown binary. Their concerts were fun, feisty, and well-attended. The performers they hired were refreshingly virtuosic, the composers themselves were developing compelling musical voices, and their operation seemed simultaneously scrappy and professional.

The 1990s were harder. Federal arts funding, under attack from the right, steeply declined, and states, cities, and corporations followed suit. Institutional models that had emerged during the Cold War were no longer sustainable. Major record labels invested, but not for long. Big presenters like Lincoln Center provided resources and reach, but their support didn't guarantee long-term stability. Diversity remained Bang on a Can's strategy for subsistence: diversifying the genres they programmed, diversifying the constituencies they served, diversifying the streams of funding they sought. Their audience-oriented focus helped them demonstrate relevance to the many stakeholders that they needed to win over in a lean time. But the decade was also one of consolidation for Bang on a Can, the reimagining of a ramshackle festival into a more compact presence at Lincoln Center, within carefully crafted commercial albums, and on All-Stars tours. "When things are tough all around us we dream," they wrote. They were willing to—they wanted to—adapt to survive.

***

Julia Wolfe and Michael Gordon had just dropped their daughter off at kindergarten and were standing with their young son, a few blocks away from the World Trade Center, when the first plane struck. David Lang, too, had been standing in a schoolyard with his daughter and eldest son right before he saw the jet streak overhead through the clear Manhattan sky. For years, the three composers had lived in downtown New York—Gordon's home composition studio had a direct view of the Twin Towers. "People were crying and running toward the building, people running away from the building, it was just crazy, and it was like that for months," Wolfe later recalled. "Not the intensity, obviously, of when it first hit, but the experience of living there and feeling like you're going to die."[2] She wrote several works responding to September 11, including the gritty, foreboding *Big Beautiful Dark and Scary*, composed for the All-Stars. In Gordon's *The Sad Park*, the voices of young children speaking about the day's events—recordings made at the Lower Manhattan nursery school that Gordon and Wolfe's son attended—are transformed into doleful contrapuntal lines for string quartet. Lang composed a pensive cello solo, for former All-Star Maya Beiser, titled *world to come*. He also lent some inspiration to Steve Reich's *WTC 9/11*, in which the melodic contours of prerecorded voices serve as the basis for churning repetitions played by the Kronos Quartet. "The world to come," states Lang in piece's final minutes, as serene strings trail his speech. "I don't really know what that means."

A new seriousness infused the music that Gordon, Lang, and Wolfe composed in the new century (Figure E.1). The ironic grunge of *cheating, lying, stealing* and the funky riffs of *Lick* seemed to recede. They collaborated as a trio, composing music in which they each contributed individual movements, including the haunting oratorios *Lost Objects* and *Shelter*. In 2007, Lang composed a work for small chorus, *the little match girl passion*, that drew together Hans Christian Andersen's story and Bach's *St. Matthew Passion* into

Figure E.1 David Lang, Michael Gordon, and Julia Wolfe. Photograph by Peter Serling.

a spare and deeply expressive meditation on suffering. The piece won the Pulitzer Prize the following year. (One of the jurors was the critic and former Catalyst producer Tim Page.) Further institutional consecration followed, and Lang began writing large-scale theatrical works for commissioners like the Brooklyn Academy of Music, and even Oscar-nominated film music.[3]

Wolfe continued exploring her fascination with folk music while placing a new focus on the history of American labor, culminating in two extended works written for the All-Stars with vocalists: *Steel Hammer*, which draws together hundreds of versions of the John Henry ballad into a powerful discourse on the American worker, and *Anthracite Fields*, a grandly seething oratorio dramatizing the history of Pennsylvania coal mining, which won the Pulitzer in 2015. Gordon operates a bit more on the experimental side of classical music, with major projects from European commissioners such as *Decasia*, a monumental sonic onslaught for detuned orchestra and one of several collaborations with the filmmaker Bill Morrison. Tending toward the abstract, his music harkens back to its minimalist roots, as in *Timber*, in which six percussionists unleash waves of overtones by beating amplified wooden planks, and *Rushes*, in which cascades of rhythmic pulses played by seven bassoons accumulate into strange and forlorn textures.

In 2006, Bang on a Can's marathons found perhaps their most audience-friendly site yet: the palm-tree filled Winter Garden Atrium of the World

Financial Center, a shopping mall and office complex across from the World Trade Center. Sponsored by the River To River festival, itself part of a broader cultural initiative to revitalize Lower Manhattan after 9/11, the setting sacrificed ideal listening conditions for the ability to reach more than a thousand attendees at a time—a concept reminiscent of when, back in the mid-'80s, Bang on a Can briefly discussed hosting their marathon on the Staten Island Ferry.

If the 1990s evinced a narrowing of Bang on a Can's curatorship, as they honed their identity for the marketplace, the new century has broadened and broadened their eclectic supermix. A twenty-six-hour marathon concert in 2007, celebrating the organization's 20th anniversary, included Burmese and Uzbek music, modern jazz, indie rock, *Music for Airports*, and longtimers like Lois V Vierk and Steve Reich. Despite some qualms raised by leftist composers—the World Financial Center is owned by Brookfield Office Properties, which evicted Occupy Wall Street protesters from one of its other holdings, Zuccotti Park, in 2011—Bang on a Can held their marathons near the center of global finance for nearly a decade, their longest-lasting home ever.[4] For May 2020, Bang on a Can looked to the culture of multiday festivals such as Coachella and Big Ears for a full-scale reimagining of their festival: Long Play, a three-day affair with concerts held across multiple spaces in Brooklyn. But then came the coronavirus pandemic, and they instead returned to their perennial format, hosting a series of livestreamed online marathons with musicians performing from home.

The All-Stars still serve as a house band. A mixture of old and new personnel tours internationally with the music of the founders as well as a bevy of works written by outside composers, including many supported by the ongoing People's Commissioning Fund.[5] The indie label Cantaloupe Music releases albums from a wide stable of collaborators, from newer acquaintances such as the Wilco drummer Glenn Kotche and the composer John Luther Adams to old friends like Jeffrey Brooks. There are, unsurprisingly, many fresh undertakings, such as the Asphalt Orchestra, a contemporary music street band, and Found Sound Nation, a social engagement initiative. The organization's annual budget, which has increased in the past decade, hovers around $1.5 million.[6] It has an office in downtown Brooklyn and, along with the three artistic directors, four full-time staffers.

This book, then, has told only the first half of Bang on a Can's story, from their student days in the Ivy League to their DIY years as a downtown marathon to their storming of the classical music mainstream. It would be in the twenty-first century, as they earned prestigious prizes and university appointments—Lang became a professor at Yale in 2008, Wolfe at New York

University in 2009, and Gordon has been adjunct faculty at NYU since 2010—that they secured themselves positions in the establishment, or perhaps crafted a new establishment in their image.

In the wake of the Great Recession, however, much of the institutional infrastructure that supported Bang on a Can's earlier efforts eroded. In 2011, Meet the Composer merged with the American Music Center to become New Music USA, a grantmaking and media organization that perpetuates the vital work of Duffy but on a much smaller scale—in 2019 it awarded a little over $1 million in grant support, only a fifth of the annual funding that it provided composers back in 1990.[7] Many younger musicians instead now know the name "Meet the Composer" as a short-lived educational podcast about contemporary music. The National Endowment for the Arts and state arts councils have recovered somewhat since the 1990s, but still reflect only a fraction of their pre-Reagan budgets and influence. Beginning with the rise of Napster, continuing through the age of iTunes downloads, and now in the era of streaming services, the record industry is a shadow of its former self. And what the future of the arts in America might look like after the devastation of the coronavirus pandemic remains uncertain.

***

"If you're a talented, intellectually curious young musician and you want to learn from the revolutionary composers and performers of our time there is no place you can go," Bang on a Can wrote in a 2001 grant proposal.[8] In the same year that Cantaloupe Music launched, they were envisioning yet another new initiative: a summer institute for young composers and performers, at the Massachusetts Museum of Contemporary Art in the Berkshires. They imagined the festival would supply a home for the young renegades in new music, those a bit too outré for the nearby Tanglewood Music Center. Indeed, they playfully nicknamed the enterprise "Banglewood." For nearly two decades since, the summer program has brought together musicians to collaborate, rehearse, and premiere new works, with faculty including the Bang on a Can founders and All-Stars, guest composers such as Louis Andriessen and Steve Reich, daily concerts in the museum's galleries, workshops in Latinx music and African drumming, and a culminating summer marathon. Participants are instilled with Bang on a Can's stylistic omnivory as well as their institutional savvy, attending fundraising and business workshops.

The very first crop of Bang on a Can student fellows, back in 2002, represented a generation that grew up in the midst of the marketplace turn. Composition fellow Judd Greenstein, who had bought Bang on a Can's Sony albums as a teenager and interned for the organization in college, described the summer program as a "seminal event," one that introduced him to a community of likeminded collaborators and instilled the idea that "music can be a very open place."[9] Inspired by the festival, he co-founded his own group, NOW Ensemble, as well as a label, New Amsterdam Records. Another 2002 attendee was the composer Missy Mazzoli, who went on to start a "bandsemble" called Victoire to play her melancholic, indie rock-influenced music. Both composers also studied at Yale with Martin Bresnick and Lang after the summer program (Druckman died of lung cancer in 1996). Greenstein and Mazzoli participated in a new scene oriented around New Amsterdam and dubbed "indie classical," a name that reflected its musicians' do-it-yourself attitude and embrace of genre-crossing.[10] Hipster bandleaders had side careers as composers; composers had side careers as DJs. Debates about uptown and downtown had faded into irrelevance.[11] "There's a very broad mix of programming in every ZIP code," Wolfe said in 2014. "There's a real spirit of entrepreneurship."[12]

The trajectories of Gordon, Lang, and Wolfe are now the standard model: attend an elite school, move to a metropolitan area, launch a concert series or an ensemble, release a record, start touring, partner with a local concert hall. And, perhaps surprisingly, the classical music establishment supports these endeavors. It is no longer a choice, as it was at Yale in the 1980s, between a career as an orchestral conformist or a DIY maverick. Mazzoli toured with her band while composing for symphony orchestras and opera houses. Carnegie Hall opened Zankel Hall in 2003, a chic black-box theater designed to host new music, jazz, and world music, and Nonesuch had its own series at the venue. Until stepping down in 2020, Jane Moss oversaw programming for Lincoln Center, and its Mostly Mozart festival now includes nearly as much contemporary music as it does eighteenth-century fare. The *New York Times* dubbed the Los Angeles Philharmonic "America's most important orchestra" largely because of its devotion to new work.[13] In 2019, the New York Philharmonic gave premieres of Wolfe's *Fire in my mouth*, an oratorio reflecting on the women who worked in the garment industry in the early twentieth century, and Lang's *prisoner of the state*, a reimagining of Beethoven's *Fidelio*. "It's a much better time for composers than when I was in my 20s," John Adams told the *Chicago Tribune* in 2017. "There's much more support now for commissioning new work. And there are all kinds of ensembles such as ICE [International Contemporary Ensemble], and Eighth Blackbird and various groups in L.A. dedicated to keeping contemporary composers in front of the public."[14] A composer who made his career working with mainstream orchestras and opera companies sees the culture of self-starting ensembles as the future.

In many ways, then, Bang on a Can was ahead of their time, building a lasting institution through individual perseverance and go-getting. But Bang on a Can was also a product of their time. They amassed support from the government and foundations, from record labels and presenters, because their ambitions were attuned to a marketplace ethos pervasive in the late twentieth century. In this present-day era of arts austerity, however, the resources that they marshalled are not necessarily available to those who seek to imitate their entrepreneurial spirit.[15] In separate interviews in the winter of 2016, Wolfe and Gordon both made an analogy between the current new-music world and the restaurant industry—if there is more than one restaurant on a city block, they might compete with one another, but they also draw more people to that area generally, and thus everyone wins.[16] When the composers first started out, new music was still a fringe phenomenon. Now, it is a cottage industry with a bigger audience and a seemingly limitless expanse of opportunities, in which everyone can find their own niche. But it's also a crowded market, and every new ensemble and record label has to build its own brand and relentlessly fundraise and market itself.[17] Opportunities have proliferated; stability remains elusive.

***

In August of 2019, during one of the final interviews I conducted for this project, I asked Lang if the three founders had ever considered rotating Bang on a Can's curatorship, of giving the reins of the organization over to an outside perspective. He was not terribly interested in the idea. "My feeling is that this organization exists to reflect our curiosity about the world," he said. "And when we're not curious about the world anymore we should stop, and when other people are curious about other things they should go start them themselves."[18] He described his pride in the summer program, where we were speaking, because its graduates went on to start their own organizations. Bang on a Can has sought to cultivate an open-minded spirit, in which their students do not replicate their aesthetic worldview but instead carve out their own pathways. Those values have contributed to today's healthy and pluralistic world of contemporary music, one much friendlier than the divisive old days of uptown and downtown. But I have also wondered whether such growth has mirrored the contemporaneous fragmentation of our public sphere, the proliferation of news sources and social media feeds and filter bubbles that—amidst a landscape of corporate malfeasance and elite profiteering—have threatened our democracy and compromised efforts at transformative political change.

Our conversation kept circling back to the legacy of John Duffy, who had passed away in 2015, and whom Lang called "the unsung hero." Bang on a Can's work has extended Duffy's marketplace philosophy into the twenty-first century; they represent perhaps the most prominent inheritors of his legacy today. But one aspect of his vision has not yet been realized. In his 1981 essay "Creating a Marketplace for Today's Composers," Duffy dreamed of a future after his organization had attained its objectives:

> As Meet the Composer comes closer to its goal, there will be a need to create an organization to represent the composing profession. A nationwide Guild of composers. This Guild will help set a schedule of gainful fees for composers. Oversee Performance Rights Societies so that composers are justly paid for concert, radio, and T.V. performances. Publish a geographical newsletter to inform people when composers will be in their area for performances and audience encounters. The Guild would help minority, women and young beginners who are now at the bottom of our musical culture. The Guild would speak for all the arts and serve as a link between various disciplines and the general public.[19]

John Duffy's long-dormant idea might be revived. A guild, or union, of composers might band musicians together to resist omnipresent neoliberal ideology that prizes individual entrepreneurship at the expense of societal change. It might define composition broadly, encompassing symphonic composers and film scorers and singer-songwriters and hip-hop beatmakers. It might fight against white supremacy and economic inequality and the destruction of our planet. It might advocate for a renewal of public arts agencies and the restoration of grants for individual artists. It might align its members in solidarity with locked-out orchestral musicians, and striking teachers and fast-food workers, and the newly unionizing tech and media industries. It might argue for orchestras and opera companies to program the music of underrepresented composers. It might push universities that rely on precarious adjunct labor to ensure more stable positions for their creative faculty. It might uphold Duffy's belief that composers are workers deserving of resources and support from the American public. And it would make decisions as a democratic, participatory body. Upstart musical institutions would still flourish, but they would participate in a larger coalition that governed contemporary music as a genre and profession, one that aligned its laborers with those of other genres and professions.

This work, of building solidarity and political power through democratic means, would likely be slow, and all-consuming, and possibly fruitless. It would be easier for composers to instead continue to start their own festivals, their own ensembles, and their own record labels, to build their own audiences. Perhaps, though, it is time to dream bigger.

Acknowledgments

Writing about the living is an enormous privilege and responsibility: I hope that this book honors those it portrays, and that they recognize themselves among its pages. None of it would have been possible without the extraordinary generosity of Michael Gordon, David Lang, and Julia Wolfe, who granted me access to themselves and their organization while understanding my need for editorial independence. The sixty-four people that I interviewed for this project, who charitably gave me their time and insights, provided invaluable context and stories. I have wondered how much better this book might have been had I been able to speak with those who inhabit its pages but no longer inhabit this earth. Jacob Druckman, Bette Snapp, and K. Robert Schwarz died many years ago; James Jordan and John Duffy passed more recently, but before I got the chance to interview them; I was deeply fortunate to spend time with Charles Wuorinen before he passed. I hope that the preceding pages have done justice to their memories.

Research is an inherently collaborative process, a dialogue with people and texts. The image of the solitary scholar is a powerful fiction, but a fiction nonetheless. The existence of this book rests on the foundational work of many archivists, librarians, and administrators over many years, and I am deeply indebted to all of them. First and foremost is the singular Oral History of American Music project at Yale, a legacy of the great Vivian Perlis and now under the direction of Libby Van Cleve; Libby and Anne Rhodes provided me with voluminous and crucial oral history recordings and transcripts. The work that OHAM has done for the past half-century remains vital and necessary to our understanding of American musical history. Tim Thomas and Kenny Savelson shepherded my access to Bang on a Can's archives and generously gave me free rein to explore. New Music USA allowed me to examine Meet the Composer's archives, and I am grateful to Ed Harsh for his support. I am thankful for the work of the staff at the Music Division of the New York Public Library for the Performing Arts, the New York State Archives, NYU's Fales Library and Special Collections, and Northwestern University's John Cage collection; Andy Lanset at WNYC's archives; the New York Philharmonic Archives and their intrepid, now-retired leader Barbara Haws as well as Sarah Palermo; and Bonnie Marie Sauer of the Lincoln Center Archives. I am grateful to the photographers Peter Serling, Robert Lewis, Bial Bert, RJ Capak, Elliot Caplan, Stephanie Berger, and Jack Vartoogian for the powerful images that you see in this manuscript.

Supportive conversations, over many years and in many settings, made this project much, much stronger than it could have been. Since my graduate school days, my colleagues D. Edward Davis, Ryan Ebright, Christa Bentley, David VanderHamm, Christopher Campo-Bowen, Gina Bombola, Kerry O'Brien, Patrick Nickleson, Emily Richmond Pollock, and Paula Harper have been encouraging friends and stalwart allies. Fellow new-music scholars John Pippen, Andrea Moore, and Marianna Ritchey have been the affable interlocutors that my work needs. I am grateful to Bernard Gendron, Steve Smith, Nicholas Tochka, Michael Uy, Douglas Shadle, Micaela Baranello, Martin Bresnick, Evan Ziporyn, Tim Page, and Dale Chapman for reading portions of the book and providing invaluable feedback. My dissertation committee at Chapel Hill—Andrea Bohlman, Mark Evan Bonds, Tim Carter, and Benjamin Piekut—made me a more thoughtful and mature scholar, as did my studies with Philip Vandermeer and Annegret Fauser. Anne Shreffler has long been a kind mentor and inspiration; my superb editor at the *New York Times*, Zachary Woolfe, has made me a sharper writer. Much of how I think about music, scholarship, and the world has been shaped by two longtime mentors. Alex Ross was and is my idol, the genius whose voice I've tried to imitate since college. I am honored, and still surprised, to call him my friend, and his feedback means the world to me. Mark Katz is the advisor every grad student wants to have, replete with work and life advice that simultaneously reassures you and pushes you to be a better scholar and person. All my musicological efforts aspire to be as good as his.

I have had the enormous privilege to research and write this book in the supportive environment of the University of Maryland's School of Music. My mentor Patrick Warfield has helped make my academic career remarkably pain free, and I am continually thankful to have such generous and brilliant colleagues as Siv Lie, Fernando Rios, Larry Witzleben, Olga Haldey, Richard King, and Barbara Haggh-Huglo. My students have been equally inspiring, and I am deeply, deeply grateful to the graduate student workers who taught alongside me and whose labor made my life infinitely easier: Joshua Bermudez, Sarah England, Rachel Ruisard, Alexander Devereux, Kevin O'Brien, Evangeline Athanasiou, Simon Polson, Elizabeth Massey, and Meghan Creek. I am also thankful for funding from Maryland towards this project, including an ARHU Faculty Fund seed grant and subvention, and a Summer Graduate School Research and Scholarship Award. My other teaching gig at Bang on a Can's media workshop certainly gave me additional insight into my subject matter, and has been a very happy way to spend a week each summer. I can't believe I get to work alongside the great John Schaefer, and I'm grateful to Philippa Thompson for making it all happen.

The inimitable Suzanne Ryan guided me through the publication process; her keen eye, steady hand, and editorial wisdom made everything easier, and this book better. Norm Hirshcy, Mary Horn, Jeremy Toynbee, Tim Rutherford-Johnson, and the team at Oxford University Press brought this book into existence, and for that I am ever grateful. I received helpful feedback from students and faculty at Rutgers University, Bowling Green State University, Peabody Conservatory, University of Chicago, Wesleyan University, Oberlin College Conservatory, and the Catholic University of America.

Writing a book is a crazy thing to do, but it's a lot less crazy if you have people who care about you. My late grandfather's slogan was "The joy of family," and I am extraordinarily lucky to feel that joy every day. The aunts, uncles, cousins, and grandmother I get to see each Thanksgiving and Passover make everything easier, and better. My parents Amy and Fred and my brother Michael have supported me for my entire life. Much what you read was written in my head on walks with Georgia, the best pooch in the world.

This book is dedicated to my wife Emily, the most amazing person I have ever met. Every day I wake up grateful for knowing you, and feeling your love, support, kindness, intelligence, and smile. My son Ira came into this world right after I finished writing this. The next one's for him.

Chronology

1979 Undergraduate collective Sheep's Clothing hosts second marathon concert at Yale
New Music, New York mounted at The Kitchen (subsequent annual festivals called New Music America)

1980 Michael Gordon enters master's program in composition at Yale (age 24)

1981 Ronald Reagan inaugurated; unsuccessfully attempts to cut budget of National Endowment for the Arts by 50 percent
After serving as faculty in Yale's undergraduate Department of Music, Martin Bresnick joins School of Music graduate faculty
David Lang enters master's program in composition at Yale (age 24)
Brooklyn Academy of Music's Next Wave Festival presents sold-out run of Philip Glass's *Satyagraha*

1982 Founding of the Michael Gordon Philharmonic
Meet the Composer announces the Orchestra Residencies Program, a partnership with Exxon, the Rockefeller Foundation, and the National Endowment for the Arts
Gordon graduates from Yale
Founding of *The New Criterion* by Hilton Kramer and Samuel Lipman
Philip Glass signs exclusive contract with CBS Masterworks, releases *Glassworks*

1983 The New York Philharmonic hosts first Horizons festival, subtitled "Since 1968, A New Romanticism?" and curated by Jacob Druckman
Lang graduates from master's program at Yale

1984 Julia Wolfe enters master's program in composition at Yale (age 25)
ECM creates New Series imprint
Robert Hurwitz becomes director of Nonesuch

1985 Lang works with Druckman as Revson Fellow to prepare the New York Philharmonic's Horizons '86 festival

1986 Wolfe graduates from Yale

1987 Bang on a Can produces first festival, a marathon concert at the gallery Exit Art
Lincoln Center launches its Serious Fun! avant-garde summer festival

1988 Bang on a Can stages second marathon festival, at the RAPP Arts Center
Charles Wuorinen complains to the *New York Times* about changes in New York State Council on the Arts' funding and effects on the Group for Contemporary Music

1989 Meet the Composer publishes handbook *Composers in the Marketplace*
Lang earns doctorate from Yale
Bang on a Can produces four-event festival at RAPP Arts Center
Political controversies over art by Andres Serrano and Robert Mapplethorpe lead to passing of NEA obscenity guidelines
New Music America's tenth anniversary festival held at the Brooklyn Academy of Music

234 Chronology

1990   NYSCA implements handbook guidelines advocating for programming for diverse audiences and supporting underserved populations
Bang on a Can presents weeklong festival at RAPP Arts Center
Joseph Dalton becomes managing director of Composers Recordings, Inc.
New Music Distribution Service closes
New Music America's final festival mounted in Montreal

1991   Bang on a Can presents fifth annual festival at multiple venues, after RAPP Arts is unexpectedly closed
NYSCA's budget slashed by 44 percent in response to the economic recession
John Duffy tells *EAR Magazine* that the "healthiest thing for the arts is for them to be profit-making"
Directors of several new-music ensembles tell the *New York Times* about their worries that funders, including NYSCA, are considering audience size when awarding grants
Group for Contemporary Music ends its live concert series and dedicates itself to recording

1992   Meet the Composer's Orchestra Residencies Program concludes
Debut of the Bang on a Can All-Stars
Jane Moss appointed director of programming at Lincoln Center
Nonesuch releases its recording of Henryk Górecki's Symphony No. 3
CRI launches Emergency Music imprint, releases *Bang on a Can Live Volume 1* (first of three live albums)
Philips founds imprint Point Music, overseen by Philip Glass, Kurt Munkacsi, and Michael Riesman
Bang on a Can produces festival at the Society for Ethical Culture

1993   Bang on a Can presents festival at The Kitchen, with a focus on activist art
BMG launches imprint Catalyst, overseen by Tim Page

1994   Bang on a Can receives three-year expansion grant from Chamber Music America and hires full-time staff
Bang on a Can has first season at Lincoln Center
All-Stars perform at Tanglewood
Milton Babbitt criticizes the NEA and other funders in *The Musical Times*
Republicans sweep midterm elections with Newt Gingrich's Contract with America

1995   Congress slashes NEA funding by 40 percent and eliminates nearly all fellowships awarded to individual artists
Sony Classical releases Bang on a Can's *Industry*
Bang on a Can has second season at Lincoln Center

1996   Bang on a Can's two-year NEA advancement grant is cut off because of funding changes
Sound engineer Andrew Cotton joins the All-Stars
Sony Classical releases *Cheating, Lying, Stealing*
Bang on a Can has third season at Lincoln Center, conducts survey of audience

1997   Bang on a Can mounts tenth-anniversary season, including All-Stars tour and final Lincoln Center residency
Bang on a Can launches People's Commissioning Fund
Bang on a Can receives major grant from NEA's new Planning and Stabilization category
Kenny Savelson hired to manage All-Stars as production associate; later becomes executive director of Bang on a Can

1998	Point Music releases Bang on a Can's *Music for Airports* *Music for Airports* premiere at Lincoln Center, followed by US and European tours Bang on a Can hosts gala benefit in honor of John Duffy First year in which Bang on a Can does not mount a festival
1999	Bang on a Can produces festival at Henry Street Settlement
2000	The Brooklyn Academy of Music hosts Bang on a Can's "Millennium Marathon" as part of the Next Wave Festival
2001	Cantaloupe Music label launches, releases Bang on a Can's *Renegade Heaven*
2002	Bang on a Can starts Summer Music Institute at the Massachusetts Museum of Contemporary Art

Notes

Introduction

1. Michael Gordon, "What Kind of Music Is This Anyway?" *New York Times Opinionator*, 5 March 2007, https://opinionator.blogs.nytimes.com/2007/03/05/what-kind-of-music-is-this-anyway/.
2. Lauren Iossa and Ruth Dreier, *Composers in the Marketplace: How to Earn a Living Writing Music* (Meet the Composer: New York, 1989).
3. John Duffy, "Creating a Marketplace for Today's Composers," April 1981, Meet the Composer archive, New Music USA, Box 30. It is not clear if this text was published, or given as a lecture.
4. Aaron Copland, "I Am the Bearer of Brutal Tidings," 10 May 1966, https://www.pulitzer.org/article/aaron-coplands-turn-crystal-ball.
5. See, for example, Copland, "Is the University Too Much with Us?" *New York Times*, 26 April 1970; reprinted in Richard Kostelanetz, ed., *Aaron Copland: A Reader Selected Writings 1923–1972* (New York: Routledge, 2004).
6. See Jennifer DeLapp, "Copland in the Fifties: Music and Ideology in the McCarthy Era" (PhD diss., University of Michigan, 2006).
7. See William J. Baumol and William G. Bowen, *Performing Arts: The Economic Dilemma* (New York: Twentieth Century Fund, 1966), 36–39; see also David Pankratz, *Multiculturalism and Public Arts Policy* (Westport, CT: Bergin & Garvey, 1993), 53–54.
8. Milton Babbitt, "Who Cares if You Listen," *High Fidelity* 8, no. 2 (February 1958): 38–40. Reprinted with the essay's original title as Babbitt, "The Composer as Specialist," *The Collected Essays of Milton Babbitt*, ed. Stephen Peles (Princeton, NJ: Princeton University Press, 2003), 48–54.
9. Babbitt, "The Composer as Specialist," 53.
10. See Anne Shreffler, "Ideologies of Serialism: Stravinsky's *Threni* and the Congress for Cultural Freedom," in *Music and the Aesthetics of Modernity*, ed. Karol Berger and Anthony Newcomb (Cambridge, MA: Harvard University Press, 2005), 217–45.
11. Quoted in Allen Edwards, *Flawed Words and Stubborn Sounds: A Conversation with Elliott Carter* (New York: W.W. Norton, 1971), 35.
12. Richard Taruskin, *The Oxford History of Western Music*, vol. 5, *Music in the Late Twentieth Century* (Oxford: Oxford University Press, 2009), 293–95.
13. For example, see Taruskin, "Afterword: *Nicht blutbefleckt?*" *Journal of Musicology* 26, no. 2 (Spring 2009): 274–84; Michael Uy, "The Big Bang of Music Patronage in the United States: The National Endowment for the Arts, the Rockefeller Foundation, and the Ford Foundation" (PhD diss., Harvard University, 2017); and Rachel Vandagriff, "The History and Impact of the Fromm Music Foundation" (PhD diss., University of California, Berkeley, 2014).

14. Taruskin, *Music in the Late Twentieth Century*, 478; and Uy, *Ask the Experts: How Ford, Rockefeller, and the NEA Changed American Music* (Oxford: Oxford University Press, 2020). These dollar figures are contemporary; $175,000 in 1958, when the grant was awarded, is equivalent to approximately $1.6 million in August 2020.
15. Susan Deaver, "The Group for Contemporary Music 1962–1992" (DMA diss., Manhattan School of Music, 1993), and William Robin, "Balance Problems: New-Music Ensembles, the University, and Neoliberalism," *Journal of the American Musicological Society* 71, no. 3 (Fall 2018): 749–94.
16. Vandagriff, "An Old Story in a New World: Paul Fromm, the Fromm Music Foundation, and Elliott Carter," *Journal of Musicology* 3, no. 4 (Fall 2018): 535–66; and Vandagriff, "Perspectives and the Patron: Paul Fromm, Benjamin Boretz and Perspectives of New Music," *Journal of the Royal Music Association* 142, no. 2 (2017): 327–65.
17. Charles Wuorinen, *Simple Composition* (New York: Longman, 1979), 3.
18. Joseph Straus has attempted to debunk this idea as a myth, drawing on statistical analysis to show that serial composers did not command the totalizing influence that is often attributed to them. But he differentiates serialism from atonality, a distinction that, as Anne Shreffler points out, might make sense to music theorists but was not audible to contemporary audiences. Joseph N. Straus, "The Myth of Serial 'Tyranny' in the 1950s and 1960s," *Musical Quarterly* 83, no. 3 (Autumn 1999): 301–43. Shreffler, "The Myth of Empirical Historiography: A Response to Joseph N. Straus," *Musical Quarterly* 84, no. 1 (Spring 2000): 30–39.
19. Benjamin Piekut has drawn on actor-network theory to rethink experimentalism as a "grouping, not a group," one that has stabilized through the work of a heterogeneous array of actors. Benjamin Piekut, *Experimentalism Otherwise* (Berkeley and Los Angeles: University of California Press, 2011), 6. I follow Piekut in my approach to experimental music as well as the other subgenres of new music addressed in this study, scrutinizing them less as sets of predetermined, coherent aesthetic practices than as discursive communities of musicians, listeners, and institutions. In deploying terms like "uptown" and "downtown," I draw specifically on a pervasive discourse that existed during my period of study, when the Bang on a Can founders and others regularly deployed these terms to describe their musical worlds. See Samuel Gilmore, "Schools of Activity and Innovation," *The Sociological Quarterly* 29, no. 2 (Summer 1988): 203–19.
20. Amy Beal, *New Music, New Allies: American Experimental Music in West Germany from the Zero Hour to Reunification* (Berkeley and Los Angeles: University of California Press, 2006).
21. John Cage, "The Future of Music," in Cage, *Empty Words: Writings '73–'78* (Middletown, CT: Wesleyan University Press, 1979), 183.
22. For Oliveros, see Kerry O'Brien, "Experimentalisms of the Self: Experiments in Art and Technology (E.A.T.), 1966–1971" (PhD Diss., Indiana University, 2018); for Young, see Jeremy Grimshaw, *Draw a Straight Line and Follow It: The Music and Mysticism of La Monte Young* (Oxford: Oxford University Press, 2012); for Subotnick, see Theodore Barker Gordon, "Bay Area Experimentalism: Music and Technology in the Long 1960s" (PhD diss., University of Chicago, 2018); for the AACM, see George E. Lewis, *A Power Stronger Than Itself: The AACM and American Experimental Music* (Chicago: University of Chicago Press, 2008).

23. Pauline Oliveros, "Sonic Meditations," in *Source: Music of the Avant-Garde, 1966–1973*, ed. Larry Austin and Douglas Kahn (Berkeley and Los Angeles: University of California Press, 2011), 342.
24. Tony Conrad, "MINor premise," *Early Minimalism Volume One* liner notes (Table of the Elements, 1997), 44; see also Branden Joseph, *Beyond the Dream Syndicate: Tony Conrad and the Arts After Cage* (New York: Zone Books, 2011).
25. Quoted in Lewis, "Experimental Music in Black and White: The AACM in New York," *Current Musicology* 71–73 (Spring 2001–Spring 2002): 100.
26. Beal, "'Music Is a Universal Human Right': Musica Elettronica Viva," in *Sound Commitments: Avant-Garde Music and the Sixties*, ed. Robert Adlington (Oxford: Oxford University Press, 2009), 99–120.
27. See Ryan Dohoney, "John Cage, Julius Eastman, and the Homosexual Ego," in *Tomorrow Is the Question: New Directions in Experimental Music Studies*, ed. Benjamin Piekut (Ann Arbor: University of Michigan Press, 2014), 39–62; and Piekut, *Experimentalism Otherwise*, 140–76.
28. An exception were populists like Musica Elettronica Viva who sought, in the spirit of the British leftist composer Cornelius Cardew and the Scratch Orchestra, to bring experimental music directly to the masses.
29. Babbitt, "The Composer as Specialist," 48 and 53.
30. Cage, "Diary: Audience 1966," in Cage, *A Year from Monday: New Lectures and Writings* (Middletown, CT: Wesleyan University Press, 1969), 51.
31. See Henry Pleasants, *The Agony of Modern Music* (New York: Simon & Schuster, 1955), 3.
32. See Piekut, *Experimentalism Otherwise*, 20–64; and Winthrop Sergeant, "First Causes," *New Yorker*, 15 February 1964, 125.
33. Quoted in John Rockwell, *All American Music: Composition in the Late Twentieth Century* (New York: Da Capo Press, 1997), 83.
34. See Judy Lochhead and Joseph Auner, eds., *Postmodern Music/Postmodern Thought* (New York and London: Routledge, 2002); and Kenneth Gloag, *Postmodernism in Music* (Cambridge: Cambridge University Press, 2012). David Brackett argues that close attention to aspects of "contemporary musical production and consumption" such as marketing, funding, discourse, and institutional ties reveals that the categories of "high" and "low" purportedly dissolved by postmodernism have remained largely intact; he points specifically to Bang on a Can, and how its "relationship to official institutions could not be more a part of institutionalized art." David Brackett, "'Where's It At?': Postmodern Theory and the Contemporary Music Field," in *Postmodern Music/Postmodern Thought*, 207 and 213.
35. K. Robert Schwarz, "John Adams: Music of Contradictions," *New York Times*, 11 January 1987.
36. Taruskin, "Afterword."
37. Rockwell, "New-Music Symposium Raises Some Hackles," *New York Times*, 27 January 1981.
38. Quoted in Nicholas Kenyon, "Musical Events: Incantations," *New Yorker*, 2 March 1981, 112.
39. Gregory Sandow, "Classical Music Counterculture," New York Philharmonic, *Horizons '84: The New Romanticism—A Broader View*, 1984, 14.

40. See, in particular, Georgia Born, *Rationalizing Culture: IRCAM, Boulez, and the Institutionalization of the Musical Avant-Garde* (Berkeley and Los Angeles: University of California Press, 1995); as well as Seth Brodsky, *From 1989, or European Music and the Modernist Unconscious* (Berkeley and Los Angeles: University of California Press, 2017); Tim Rutherford-Johnson, *Music after the Fall: Modern Composition and Culture since 1989* (Berkeley and Los Angeles: University of California Press, 2017); and Alastair Williams, *Music in Germany Since 1968* (Cambridge: Cambridge University Press, 2013).

41. Gordon, program note to *Industry*, 1992, https://michaelgordonmusic.com/music/industry.

42. Schwarz, "Bang on a Can Issues a Manifesto," *New York Times*, 21 May 1995.

43. Michael Gordon, David Lang, and Julia Wolfe, liner notes to Bang on a Can All-Stars, *Industry*, Sony Classical 66483, 1995.

44. Robert Fink, "(Post-)minimalisms 1970–2000: The Search for a New Mainstream," *The Cambridge History of Twentieth-Century Music*, ed. Nicholas Cook (Cambridge: Cambridge University Press, 2004), 546.

45. I take after David Harvey's definition of neoliberalism as "a theory of political economic practices that proposes that human well-being can best be advanced by liberating individual entrepreneurial freedoms and skills within an institutional framework characterized by strong private property rights, free markets, and free trade." David Harvey, *A Brief History of Neoliberalism* (New York: Oxford University Press, 2005), 2. See also Timothy Taylor, *Music and Capitalism: A History of the Present* (Chicago: University of Chicago Press, 2015); and Marianna Ritchey, *Composing Capital: Classical Music in the Neoliberal Era* (Chicago: University of Chicago Press, 2019).

46. See, for example, Wendy Brown, *Undoing the Demos: Neoliberalism's Stealth Revolution* (Cambridge, MA: MIT Press, 2015).

47. In his review of the *Industry* album, K. Robert Schwarz writes of the music's aesthetic that "For a time it went by the awkward term Totalism, but if this disk is any indication, it might be called Bang-on-a-Can-ism"; in a 2013 essay on minimalism, Robert Fink similarly analogizes totalism and "Bang-On-A-Can-ism." Schwarz, "Bang on a Can Issues a Manifesto"; Fink, "Going with the Flow: Minimalism as Cultural Practice in the USA Since 1945," in *The Ashgate Research Companion to Minimalist and Postminimalist Music*, ed. Keith Potter, Kyle Gann, and Pwyll ap Siôn (London: Routledge, 2013), 216.

48. Jeremy Grimshaw has persuasively examined this issue in the artistic trajectory of Philip Glass; see Grimshaw, "High, 'Low,' and Plastic Arts: Philip Glass and the Symphony in the Age of Postproduction," *Musical Quarterly* 86, no. 3 (Fall 2002): 472–507.

49. Quoted in Frank J. Oteri, "The Who and Why of Bang on a Can," *NewMusicBox*, 1 May 1999, https://nmbx.newmusicusa.org/bang-on-a-can/.

50. Throughout this manuscript, unless otherwise mentioned, contemporary dollar amounts will be used, rather than adjusting for inflation; for reference, the cumulative rate of inflation from 1987 to August 2020 is 128.1 percent, which is to say that an item that cost $1 in 1987 would cost approximately $2.28 in 2020. This rate declined through the 1990s, such that by 1997, that same $1 item would cost $1.61 in August 2020. Bang on a Can's 1987 budget of $11,000 translates to approximately $25,089 in August 2020; its 1996–97 budget of $429,000 is equivalent to approximately $708,441 in August 2020.

51. Alex Ross, *The Rest Is Noise* (New York: Farrar, Straus & Giroux, 2007).

52. My dissertation ultimately focused on the post-2000 scene of "indie classical" composers and performers, many of whom were strongly influenced by Bang on a Can, and who developed their own attendant scene of institutions such as New Amsterdam Records and the ensemble yMusic. Robin, "A Scene without a Name: Indie Classical and American New Music in the Twenty-First Century" (PhD diss., University of North Carolina at Chapel Hill, 2016).
53. Julia Wolfe, interview with author, 28 February 2016.

Chapter 1

1. Michael Gordon, interview with author and Julia Wolfe, 28 July 2018. My description of this work is based on an archival recording of the original performance provided by Gordon.
2. For the "Shut Up!" anecdote, see Julia Wolfe, "Embracing the Clash" (PhD diss., Princeton University, 2012), 31.
3. Jeffrey Brooks, interview with author, 8 June 2017.
4. "The Composer of Modern Life: David Lang, Paycheck to Paycheck," *Politico*, 19 October 2010, https://www.politico.com/states/new-york/albany/story/2010/10/the-composer-of-modern-life-david-lang-paycheck-to-paycheck-000000.
5. Elliott Carter, quoted in Michael Newman, "The Heart Is Back in the Game," *Time* 120, no. 12 (20 September 1982): 182.
6. Quoted in John Rockwell, *All American Music: Composition in the Late Twentieth Century* (New York: Da Capo Press, 1997), 111.
7. Gordon, interview with author and Julia Wolfe, 28 July 2018.
8. Martin Bresnick, interview with author, 18 December 2015.
9. Milton Babbitt, "The Composer as Specialist," *The Collected Essays of Milton Babbitt*, ed. Stephen Peles (Princeton, NJ: Princeton University Press, 2003), 53. See also Martin Brody, "'Music for the Masses': Milton Babbitt's Cold War Music Theory," *Musical Quarterly* 77, no. 2 (Summer 1993): 161–92; and Brian Harker, "Milton Babbitt Encounters Academia (And Vice Versa)," *American Music* 26, no. 3 (Fall 2008): 336–77.
10. Richard Taruskin has described this proliferation of post-Princeton programs as "the countless other degree programs that Princeton's made not just possible but necessary." Richard Taruskin, "Afterword: *Nicht blutbefleckt?*" *Journal of Musicology* 26, no. 2 (Spring 2009): 275.
11. Morton Feldman, "Boola Boola," in *Give My Regards to Eighth Street: Collected Writings of Morton Feldman* (Cambridge, MA: Exact Change, 2000), 47. Prominent scholars have echoed Feldman's concerns; Susan McClary famously attacked academic composition in 1989 as an "ivory tower" that has "sought to secure prestige precisely by claiming to renounce all possible social functions and value." Susan McClary, "Terminal Prestige: The Case of Avant-Garde Music Composition," *Cultural Critique* no. 12 (Spring 1989): 61 and 62. Jann Pasler offers a more nuanced view, cogently analyzing how universities have served as "power brokers" in the world of composition that "rival the old cultural capitals as centers of musical production and consumption." Jann Pasler, *Writing through Music: Essays on Music, Culture, and Politics* (Oxford and New York: Oxford University Press, 2007), 321.

12. Joseph N. Straus, "The Myth of Serial 'Tyranny' in the 1950s and 1960s," *The Musical Quarterly* 83, no. 3 (Autumn 1999): 301–43. In a retort to Straus's argument, *New York Times* critic Anthony Tommasini actually pointed to Yale: "As a music student at Yale in the early 1970s, I remember countless instances in which the prejudice against tonal music was voiced unabashedly." Anthony Tommasini, "Midcentury Serialists," *New York Times*, 9 July 2000.
13. Further, Yale in this period was also home to several students who would have major careers, including Aaron Jay Kernis, Michael Daugherty, and Michael Torke. In an exploration of the legacies of minimalism since 1970, Robert Fink echoes art critic Hal Foster's analysis of postmodernism to identify the Bang on a Can composers as participants in a "post-minimalism of resistance"—one that drew together radical politics and modernist dissonance—as opposed to a "post-minimalism of reaction"—as emblematized in the neo-Romantic orchestral music of Torke. It is significant, then, that both sides of this purported binary studied together at Yale, absorbing shared understandings about style and the marketplace even while their careers ultimately took different shapes, and forging a musical politics less overtly radical than the model Composer As Specialist offered by Sheep's Clothing. Robert Fink, "(Post-)minimalisms 1970–2000: The Search for a New Mainstream," *The Cambridge History of Twentieth-Century Music*, ed. Nicholas Cook (Cambridge: Cambridge University Press, 2004), 546 and 550.
14. David Lang, interview with Libby Van Cleve, 29 April 1997, Yale Oral History of American Music: Major Figures in American Music, 185 j–m.
15. Gordon, interview with Libby Van Cleve, 29 August 1997, Yale Oral History of American Music: Major Figures in American Music, 254 a–f.
16. Gordon, interview with Libby Van Cleve.
17. Gordon, interview with Libby Van Cleve.
18. Gordon, interview with Libby Van Cleve.
19. Gordon, interview with Libby Van Cleve.
20. Gordon, interview with Libby Van Cleve.
21. Lang, quoted in Ann McCutchan, *The Muse that Sings: Composers Speak about the Creative Process* (Oxford: Oxford University Press, 1999), 220. It is not clear what video Lang actually saw at age nine, or if the Bernstein anecdote he describes actually exists; Bernstein's Young People's Concert birthday tribute to Shostakovich, which focuses on the Ninth Symphony, does not mention the First Symphony or Shostakovich's overnight fame. See https://leonardbernstein.com/lectures/television-scripts/young-peoples-concerts/birthday-tribute-to-shostakovich.
22. Lang, interview with Ev Grimes, 14 December 1986, Yale Oral History of American Music: Major Figures in American Music, 185 a–g.
23. Lang, interview with Ev Grimes.
24. Lang, interview with Ev Grimes.
25. See Michael Uy, *Ask the Experts: How Ford, Rockefeller, and the NEA Changed American Music* (Oxford: Oxford University Press, 2020).
26. Lang, group interview with Bang on a Can media workshop fellows, 27 July 2018.
27. The Master's of Musical Arts program he entered was designed to lead directly into the School's DMA doctoral degree. Lang was the only one of the three composers to pursue his doctorate at Yale; Gordon only completed a master's degree, and Wolfe subsequently attended Princeton from 1989–92 and earned her doctorate in 2012. In 1958, Yale's School of Music became dedicated exclusively to graduate studies: where the School would

function as a professional training program for performers and composers, in the manner of a conservatory, Yale's Department of Music would supervise undergraduates pursuing a more liberal arts-oriented music major, a division that continues to this day. But it was the Department, rather than the School, that hosted graduate programs in music history and theory, establishing a setup quite different from programs like Princeton that envisaged a close dialogue between theory and composition. Thus, rather than a PhD for composition, the School began offering a Doctor of Musical Arts (DMA) degree in 1968.

28. Bresnick, interview with author, 18 December 2015.
29. It was established in 1967. See Gene Robinson, "Residential College," *Michigan Daily*, 7 September 1972; and Mitch Cantor, "RC, Pilot programs: More than a Classroom," *Michigan Daily*, 7 September 1978.
30. Wolfe, "Embracing the Clash," 31.
31. Wolfe, interview with Libby Van Cleve, 14 August 1997, Yale Oral History of American Music: Major Figures in American Music, 255 a–e. In the early 1960s, Ann Arbor had been home to the ONCE Festival, a hub for avant-gardism founded by Michigan graduates including Robert Ashley and Gordon Mumma, but it petered out around 1965 after it lost funding, so Wolfe would not have had contact with it. Ralf Dietrich, "ONCE and the Sixties," in *Sound Commitments: Avant-Garde Music and the Sixties*, ed. Robert Adlington (Oxford: Oxford University Press, 2009), 169–86.
32. Wolfe, "Embracing the Clash," 35.
33. See Uy, *Ask the Experts*.
34. Wolfe, "Embracing the Clash," 34.
35. Wolfe, interview with author, 28 February 2016.
36. Wolfe, interview with Libby Van Cleve.
37. Wolfe, interview with author, 28 February 2016.
38. Wolfe, interview with author, 28 February 2016.
39. Gordon, interview with Libby Van Cleve.
40. Martin Brody, interview with author, 20 June 2017.
41. Jacob Druckman, interview with Gene Cook, 11 July 1981, Yale Oral History of American Music: Major Figures in American Music, 106 p.
42. Scott Lindroth, interview with author, 27 August 2014.
43. Feldman, "Boola Boola," 47.
44. Bresnick, interview with Libby Van Cleve, 21 March 1998, Yale Oral History of American Music: Major Figures in American Music, 107 e–k.
45. Gordon, interview with Libby Van Cleve.
46. Druckman, quoted in Cole Gagne and Tracy Caras, *Soundpieces: Interviews with American Composers* (Metuchen, NJ: Scarecrow Press, 1982), 156.
47. Druckman, quoted in Charles Moritz, ed., *Current Biography Yearbook 1981* (New York: H.W. Wilson Company, 1981), 130; see also Nicholas Papador, "Jacob Druckman: A Bio-Bibliography and Guide to Research" (DMA diss., Northwestern University, 2003), 64–71.
48. Walter Wager, "Jacob Druckman, ASCAP '63, Pulitzer '72," *ASCAP Today* 6, no. 2 (1974): 17.
49. Gordon, interview with Libby Van Cleve.
50. Because of its compression of minimalist processes, combative edge, and unpredictable repetition, critic Kyle Gann has considered *Thou Shalt* emblematic of postminimalism

and totalism. Gann, *Music Downtown: Writings from the Village Voice* (Berkeley and Los Angeles: University of California Press, 2006), 13, 129, and 247.
51. Bresnick, interview with author, 18 December 2015.
52. Wolfe, interview with author, 28 February 2016.
53. Wolfe, interview with Libby Van Cleve.
54. Bresnick, interview with Libby Van Cleve. For Bresnick's broader exploration of how his pedagogy fits in with his critique of modernism and the avant-garde, see Bresnick, "We, Rhinoceros," *New Observations* 86 (November/December 1991): 3–5; and Bresnick, "Thoughts About Teaching Composition, or Self-Portrait as Hamlet and Polonius and Whitman Is Also There," *Contemporary Music Review* 31, no. 4 (2012): 269–76.
55. Wolfe, interview with Libby Van Cleve; and Wolfe, *On Seven-Star Shoes*, program note, https://juliawolfemusic.com/music/on-seven-star-shoes.
56. Wolfe, interview with Libby Van Cleve.
57. Wolfe, interview with Libby Van Cleve.
58. Lang has used all-lowercase titles for his titles since the early 1990s, and applied the casing retroactively to his earlier work.
59. Rachel Resnick, "'Rounds' Rewards Lang: Vietnam Score Garners Top Award," *Yale Daily News* 7, 17 September 1982.
60. Lang, interview with Ev Grimes.
61. Bresnick, interview with Libby Van Cleve.
62. Brooks, interview with Jack Vees, 1 August 2014, Yale Oral History of American Music: Major Figures in American Music, 470 a–c.
63. Brooks, interview with author, 8 June 2017.
64. Lindroth, interview with author, 27 August 2014.
65. Lang, interview with author, 19 January 2016.
66. Lang, interview with author, 19 January 2016.
67. Wolfe, quoted in Kyle Gann, "After Ugly Music," *Village Voice*, 1 June 1993. See also Lang's lengthy description of Bang on a Can's origins in a 1994 Lincoln Center program booklet, in which he links his work in the Sheep to the origins of Bang on a Can; Lang, quoted in "Bang on a Can Conversations . . . " with Deborah Artman, "Bang on a Can Marathon," *Lincoln Center Stagebill*, program booklet, 8 May 1994, Bang on a Can online archives.
68. Frederic Rzewski, *Les Moutons de Panurge*, score.
69. Bresnick, quoted in Julie Flanders, "'Sheep's Clothing's' Midnight Music," *Yale Daily News* 103, 30 March 1979.
70. Jenny Rycenga, quoted in Flanders, "'Sheep's Clothing's' Midnight Music."
71. Bresnick, interview with Libby Van Cleve.
72. Jonathan Rauch, "When Familiarity Breeds Content—Two Intimate Composers' Concerts," *Yale Daily News* 91, 22 February 1980.
73. David Cole, "Sheep's Clothing to Play New Music All Night Long," *Yale Daily News* 121, 23 April 1981.
74. Rauch, "When Familiarity Breeds Content."
75. Evan Ziporyn, "Contemporary Group Performs New and Old," *Yale Daily News* 59, 7 December 1978.
76. Ziporyn, "Cummings Copes with Public Apathy," *Yale Daily News* 45, 14 November 1978.
77. Ziporyn, interview with Libby Van Cleve, 9 December 1997, Yale Oral History of American Music: Major Figures in American Music, 270 a–g.

78. Lang, interview with Ev Grimes.
79. Martin Brown, "Sheep's Clothing Baffles Listeners; Unusual Singing Group Tours Area," *Yale Daily News* 31, 22 October 1982.
80. Bresnick, interview with Libby Van Cleve.
81. Lindroth, interview with author, 27 August 2014.
82. Lindroth, interview with author, 27 August 2014.
83. Cornelius Cardew, "Stockhausen Serves Imperialism," in *Stockhausen Serves Imperialism* (UbuClassics, 2004), 54.
84. Ivan Tcherepnin, quoted in Tom Johnson, "New Music New York New Institution," *Village Voice*, 2 July 1979, reprinted in Johnson, *The Voice of New Music*, digital edition, http://www.editions75.com/Books/TheVoiceOfNewMusic.PDF.
85. Flanders, "Sheep's Clothing's' Midnight Music." In that article, Plonsey said of the organization's outlook that "It's about as close to a democracy as I can imagine."
86. Flanders, "Sheep's Clothing's' Midnight Music."
87. Daniel Plonsey, interview with author, 28 May 2017.
88. Plonsey, interview with author, 28 May 2017.
89. Ziporyn, "Who Listens if You Care," *New Observations* 86 (November/December 1991): 25.
90. Lang, interview with author, 1 August 2019.
91. Lang, interview with author, 1 August 2019.
92. Bresnick, interview with Libby Van Cleve.
93. Plonsey, interview with author, 28 May 2017.
94. Lang, interview with Ev Grimes. This oral history is a crucial document for understanding the prehistory of Bang on a Can, as it is the only longform interview with one of the Bang on a Can founders prior to the first marathon.
95. Lang, interview with Ev Grimes.
96. Lang, interview with Ev Grimes.
97. Quoted in Aaron Girard, "Music Theory in the American Academy" (PhD diss., Harvard University, 2007), 410.
98. Feldman, "Boola Boola," 47.
99. Lang, interview with Ev Grimes.
100. Brody, interview with author, 20 June 2017.
101. Feldman, "Boola Boola," 47.
102. Bresnick, interview with author, 18 December 2015.
103. Lang, interview with Ev Grimes; Brooks, interview with author, 8 June 2017; Michael Daugherty, interview with author, 25 November 2015.
104. Lang, interview with author, 19 January 2016.
105. Daugherty, interview with author, 25 November 2015.
106. Daugherty, interview with author, 25 November 2015.
107. Michael Torke, interview with Ev Grimes, 13 November 1986, Yale Oral History of American Music: Major Figures in American Music, 188 a–b.
108. Torke, interview with author, 13 June 2017.
109. "Jacob Druckman: Chronological Biography," likely dated 1988. Jacob Druckman Papers, Music Division, New York Public Library for the Performing Arts, Folder 436. Jann Pasler notes that, between 1969 and 1985, 20 percent of all NEA composer grants were awarded to graduates of Yale. Pasler, *Writing through Music*, 352.

110. Daugherty, interview with author, 25 November 2015; Lindroth, interview with author, 27 August 2014.
111. Gordon, "Fierceness Devoted to Truth: Remembering Glenn Branca (1948–2018)," *NewMusicBox*, 25 July 2018, https://nmbx.newmusicusa.org/fierceness-devoted-to-truth-remembering-glenn-branca-1948-2018/.
112. Gordon, interview with Libby Van Cleve.
113. Gordon, interview with Libby Van Cleve.
114. Ian Minniberg, "Composition Prizewinners," *Music at Yale and Alumni News* 18 (May 1989): 6.
115. Wolfe's entry also incorrectly lists "Junior Fellow of Society of Fellows Harvard University, Guggenheim Fellow, commissions and awards from American Academy of Arts and Letters." She did not in fact receive those accolades in this period.
116. Wolfe, interview with author, 28 February 2016. Presumably, this would have been an October 1987 performance reviewed in the *New York Times*; see Bernard Holland, "Music: Chamber Group," *New York Times*, 27 October 1987.
117. Wolfe, "Embracing the Clash," 68.
118. Minniberg, "Composition Prizewinners," 6.
119. Lang, interview with Ev Grimes.

Chapter 2

1. Lang was born on 8 January 1957, so he would have been twenty-eight at the time of the photograph. David Lang, Twitter post, 30 August 2017, https://twitter.com/davidlangmusic/status/902897823703818240. The composer was responding to an article that I had written about the Horizons festivals for *NewMusicBox*, which included the photograph. See William Robin, "New Horizons, Old Barriers," *NewMusicBox*, 30 August 2017, https://nmbx.newmusicusa.org/new-horizons-old-barriers/.
2. Lang to John Duffy, 11 March 1986, Meet the Composer archives, New Music USA, Box 74.
3. Julia Wolfe, "Embracing the Clash" (PhD diss., Princeton University, 2012).
4. Bang on a Can, New York State Council on the Arts grant application materials, 1990–91, New York State Archives, Grant Application Files, Series 14064–95–B06.
5. Robert Commanday, "Cultivating an Audience for American Music," *San Francisco Chronicle*, 5 February 1989, 14.
6. Benjamin Patterson to Jacob Druckman, 27 February 1970, Jacob Druckman Papers, Music Division, New York Public Library for the Performing Arts, Folder 1008.
7. Carol Tuynman, "John Duffy: Meet the Composer," *EAR Magazine* 10, no. 5 (June/July 1986): 22.
8. Frances Richard, interview with author, 27 June 2017.
9. Meet the Composer application guidelines, June 1984, Composers' Forum Inc. Records, Music Division, New York Public Library for the Performing Arts, Box 9, Folder 1.
10. Charles Wuorinen, interview with author, 11 June 2017.
11. John Duffy, "Creating a Marketplace for Today's Composers," April 1981, Meet the Composer archive, New Music USA, Box 30.
12. Duffy, "Creating a Marketplace for Today's Composers."
13. Richard, interview with author, 27 June 2017. Richard strongly emphasized this component of Meet the Composer's mission: "We didn't even trust the organizations that would

write us an application and say, 'We would like to present John Doe next Tuesday night at Town Hall.' We made check to John Doe, not to the organization." Some organizations would apparently ask the composer to sign their check over to them, which Meet the Composer fought against. Richard, interview with author, 27 June 2017. Indeed, contracts made explicit that "Meet the Composer checks are made payable to the Composer and may not be used for other program costs." Meet the Composer, "Sponsor Final Report Form," September 1986, Composers' Forum Inc. Records, Music Division, New York Public Library for the Performing Arts, Box 9, Folder 1.

14. "Profile: Meet the Composer," *New Music: An Activity of The Composers' Forum, Inc.* (October 1979), Meet the Composer archive, New Music USA, Box 30.
15. Libby Larsen, interview with author, 8 June 2017.
16. Lauren Iossa, John Duffy, and Frances Richard, *Commissioning Music* (New York: Meet the Composer, 1984); and Lauren Iossa and Ruth Dreier, *Composers in the Marketplace: How to Earn a Living Writing Music* (New York: Meet the Composer, 1989).
17. New York State Council on the Arts, *Program Guidelines, 1987/88–1988/89*, 94–95.
18. Iossa and Dreier, *Composers in the Marketplace*, 28.
19. Iossa and Dreier, *Composers in the Marketplace*, 29.
20. Duffy, quoted in "Meet the Composer: A Dialogue," *American Music Center Newsletter* 27, no. 4 (1985): 12. Richard similarly said in a 1980 interview that "One of the reasons that we think we can build a network through the Meet the Composer program is because we are not stressing the difference between composers and their various aesthetic opinions, which they have their right to, but rather to take the common goals of composers." Richard, quoted in Peter Wetzler, "Meet the Composer Interview," *EAR Magazine East* 6, no. 1 (November/December 1980).
21. Iossa, Duffy, and Richard, *Commissioning Music*, 5
22. Tower, quoted in Kyle Gann, "Uptown Dropout," *Village Voice*, 22 September 1998.
23. Jann Pasler has documented how women composers were consistently "at a disadvantage" in the activities of the National Endowment for the Arts music program from the late 1960s to mid-1980s, in terms of both serving on panels and being awarded grants. Jann Pasler, *Writing through Music: Essays on Music, Culture, and Politics* (Oxford and New York: Oxford University Press, 2007), 355.
24. Meet the Composer Application Guidelines, June 1984, Composers' Forum Inc. Records, Music Division, New York Public Library for the Performing Arts, Box 9, Folder 1.
25. Michael Uy, for example, has noted the "underrepresentation of women and racial minorities" among consultants and panelists for music at the Ford Foundation, Rockefeller Foundation, and National Endowment for the Arts in the 1950s and 1960s. Uy, "The Big Bang of Music Patronage in the United States" (PhD diss., Harvard University, 2017), 118. According to the 1984 *Commissioning Music* handbook, the 1984 Meet the Composer advisory board comprised: Muhal Richard Abrams, John Adams, T.J. Anderson, Larry Austin, Milton Babbitt, Jack Beeson, Earle Brown, Joseph Celli, Ornette Coleman, Michael Colgrass, Charles Dodge, Douglas Ewart, Morton Feldman, Lukas Foss, Philip Glass, Leroy Jenkins, Karl Korte, Libby Larsen, Tania León, Edwin London, Otto Luening, Marian McPartland, Kermit Moore, Kirk Nurock, Pauline Oliveros, Bernard Rands, Gregory Reeve, Roger Reynolds, Robert Xavier Rodríguez, Ned Rorem, Eric Salzman, Gunther Schuller, Elie Siegmeister, Robert Starer, Carl Stone, Cecil Taylor, Joan Tower, Nancy Van de Vate, Hugo Weisgall, Olly Wilson, Charles Wuorinen, and La Monte Young.

Abrams, Anderson, Coleman, Ewart, Jenkins, León, Moore, Taylor, and Wilson were Black; Larsen, León, McPartland, Oliveros, Tower, and Van de Vate were women. In 1990, an advisory board of forty-seven composers included ten Black composers and eight women. Jane S. Moss, "Meet the Composer/Reader's Digest Commissioning Program in Partnership with the National Endowment for the Arts Proposal," Appendix D, Meet the Composer archive, New Music USA, Box 24.

26. Tania León, interview with author, 2 June 2017.
27. T.J. Anderson to "To Whom It May Concern," 18 July 1986, Meet the Composer archive, New Music USA, Box 84. That support encountered setbacks when Meet the Composer worked with major symphony orchestras for the Orchestra Residencies Program; despite Meet the Composer's petitioning, for example, the 1983 Horizons festivals included no works by Black composers and only one piece by a female composer. See William Robin, "Horizons '83, Meet the Composer, and New Romanticism's New Marketplace," *Musical Quarterly* 102, nos. 2–3 (Summer–Fall 2019): 158–99.
28. This incident was described to me by Frances Richard and Tania León; Richard, interview with author, 27 June 2017; León, interview with author, 2 June 2017.
29. León to Duffy, 27 July 1986; Ned Rorem to Duffy, 21 July 1986; and Milton Babbitt to Duffy, 2 September 1986. All quoted letters from Meet the Composer archive, New Music USA, Box 84.
30. John Rockwell, "'Horizons' Gives a Hearing to Living Composers," *New York Times*, 27 May 1984.
31. Uy, "The Big Bang," 223–24.
32. Mark Carrington, "Bringing 'Em Back Alive," *American Arts* 12, no. 6 (November 1981): 1.
33. Duffy, quoted in K. Robert Schwarz, "Is There a Composer in the House? Not Always," *New York Times*, 1 September 1996.
34. Duffy to Leonard Fleischer, Howard Klein, and Ezra Laderman, 9 August 1981, Meet the Composer archive, New Music USA, Box 84.
35. Duffy to Fleischer, Klein, and Laderman.
36. See Donna M. Binkiewicz, *Federalizing the Muse* (Chapel Hill: University of North Carolina Press, 2005); and Chin-Tao Wu, *Privatizing Culture* (London: Verso, 2003).
37. Duffy, quoted in "Meet the Composer: A Dialogue," *American Music Center Newsletter* 27, no. 4 (1985): 12; "John Duffy Honors the Residencies' Funders," *Meet the Composer Orchestra Residencies Newsletter* (Fall 1991), 1, Meet the Composer archive, New Music USA, Box 84.
38. "Financial Summary 1982–1987 Orchestra Residencies Program," Meet the Composer archive, New Music USA, Box 55.
39. Duffy to Fleischer, Klein, and Laderman.
40. Duffy, quoted in Carol Tuynman, "John Duffy: Meet the Composer," *EAR Magazine* 10, no. 5 (June/July 1986): 23.
41. Duffy, quoted in Tuynman.
42. The 1984 Pulitzer Prize was awarded to Bernard Rands for his *Canti del Sole*, premiered by the New York Philharmonic during the 1983 Horizons festival, and the 1991 Pulitzer was given to Shulamit Ran for her 1991 Symphony, commissioned as part of Rands's Philadelphia Orchestra residency; further, the 1990 Grawemeyer Award was granted to Joan Tower for her *Silver Ladders*, a St. Louis Symphony residency commission, and the 1991 Grawemeyer was awarded to John Corigliano for his Symphony No. 1, a Chicago

Symphony residency commission. A 1992 newsletter also noted a "long run in high positions" of the *Billboard* classical charts for Adams's *Harmonielehre*, as well as "Over one year in top 25" and "Highest position: No. 3" for the Chicago Symphony recording of Corigliano's Symphony No. 1. "Meet the Composer: Orchestra Residencies Program, 1982–92," Meet the Composer archive, New Music USA, Box 84.

43. Edward Rothstein, "Classical View; Supply-Side Composers Join the Band," *New York Times*, 30 October 1994.
44. Joan Tower, "Statement of Reasons for the Importance of the Residency Program," undated letter (likely 1986), Meet the Composer archive, New Music USA, Box 84.
45. John Adams, "The Making of a Professional Composer," in *Composer in Residence: Meet the Composer's Orchestra Residencies Program, 1982–1992*, ed. Theodore Wiprud and Joyce Lawler (New York: Meet the Composer, 1995), 21.
46. Adams, "The Making of a Professional Composer," 22.
47. As Ricky O'Bannon calculated in a survey of the 2016–17 seasons of 85 US orchestras, Adams was the most-performed living composer, with a total of 102 performances of his works; this is significantly more than the second most-performed living composer, John Williams, with a total of thirty-four performances of his works. See Ricky O'Bannon, "The Data Behind the 2016–2017 Orchestra Season," *Baltimore Symphony Orchestra Stories*, 31 October 2016, https://www.bsomusic.org/stories/the-data-behind-the-2016-2017-orchestra-season/. The importance of the Orchestra Residencies Program for Adams's career is strikingly unmentioned in scholarship on the composer, which typically focuses on his position as New Music Advisor rather than the subsequent Meet the Composer residency; in his own memoir, Adams does not mention Duffy or Meet the Composer by name and describes the residency as "sponsored by Exxon and the Ford Foundation," incorrectly citing the Ford Foundation rather than the Rockefeller Foundation. Adams, *Hallelujah Junction* (New York: Farrar, Straus & Giroux, 2008), 128.
48. Samuel Lipman, "The Philharmonic's New Horizons," *New Criterion*, September 1983.
49. Druckman, interview with Erwin Nigg, 14 June 1994, quoted in Erwin K. Nigg, "An Analysis of Jacob Druckman's Works for Wind Ensemble: *Engram* (1982), *Paean* (1986), *In Memoriam Vincent Persichetti* (1987), *With Bells On* (1993)" (DMA diss., University of Cincinnati, 1995), 221.
50. Jacob Druckman, "Music Since 1968: A New Romanticism?" New York Philharmonic, *Horizons '83: Since 1968, A New Romanticism?*, 1983, 6–7.
51. Druckman, "Music Since 1968: A New Romanticism?"
52. Minutes for a 1982 planning meeting for the festival, for example, state that "Mr. Druckman believes that the Berio is one of the major works in the 'new romantic' style." New York Philharmonic, "Minutes of the Music Policy Committee Meeting," 3 November 1982, Jacob Druckman Papers, Music Division, New York Public Library for the Performing Arts, Folder 685.
53. Nigg, "An Analysis," 221.
54. Kathy Erlandson, "Minutes Contemporary Festival Meeting, November 17, 1982," 1 December 1982, New York Philharmonic Archives, Box 076-01-19.
55. Erlandson, "Meeting—January 20," 20 January 1983, New York Philharmonic Archives, Box 076-01-19.
56. "Draft: Contemporary Music Festival," undated, New York Philharmonic Archives, Box 076-01-17.

57. Erlandson, "Minutes Contemporary Festival Meeting, November 17, 1982."
58. "Horizons '83 Spring Concerts Promotional Campaign Budget Revised," New York Philharmonic Archives, Box 076-01-26.
59. Erlandson, "Meeting—January 20."
60. Promotional flyer, New York Philharmonic Archives, Box 076-01-17.
61. Prices for typical single tickets in subscription concerts in 1983–84 outside of Horizons ranged from $6 for the third tier of the hall to $22–25 for first tier. "Press Releases, Jan 19, 1983–Dec 27, 1983," New York Philharmonic Leon Levy Digital Archives ID 765-28-02, 23.
62. Nigg, "An Analysis," 221.
63. Rockwell, "All-Ligeti Bill to Open Horizons '86 Festival," *New York Times*, 21 May 1984. A Philharmonic document outlining plans for the 1984 festival described the 1983 Horizons as a "dramatic success, receiving critical acclaim and popular support. Avery Fisher Hall was filled to an average capacity of over 70%, and the publicity was exceptional." "New York Philharmonic: Horizons '84: 'A New Romanticism?—A Broader Review,'" undated, New York Philharmonic Archives, Box 076-01-12.
64. Richard S. Ginell, "On the Horizons, a Coastal Tug-of-War," *Los Angeles Daily News*, 19 June 1983.
65. Lipman, "The Philharmonic's New Horizons."
66. Rockwell, "Critic's Notebook; Is 'New Romanticism' Music of the Future?" *New York Times*, 16 June 1983.
67. Edward Rothstein, "The Musical Avant-Garde: An Idea Whose Time May Have Gone," *New York Times*, 26 June 1983.
68. Rothstein, "The Musical Avant-Garde."
69. Milton Babbitt, "The More Than The Sounds of Music," New York Philharmonic, *Horizons '84: The New Romanticism—A Broader View*, 1984, 10. Reprinted in Stephen Peles, ed., *The Collected Essays of Milton Babbitt* (Princeton, NJ: Princeton University Press), 383–87.
70. Tim Page, "The New Romance with Tonality," *New York Times*, 29 May 1983.
71. Ginell, "On the Horizons."
72. Alan Rich, "Invaders From the New West," *Newsweek*, 20 June 1983, 81.
73. Lipman, "The Philharmonic's New Horizons."
74. Gregory Sandow, "Man of Our Time," *Village Voice*, 21 June 1983.
75. Charles Ruggles, "Looking Glass Catcalls," *Village Voice*, 5 July 1983.
76. Evan Ziporyn, email to author, 9 October 2018.
77. Poster for 25 April 1981 Sheep's Clothing concert, obtained from Ziporyn. The quote is from the Dutch composer Peter-Jan Wagemans; see Roland Beer, "Peter-Jan Wagemans: We Should Turn Towards the People without Falling into the Neo-Romantic Trap," *Key Notes* 10, no. 2 (1979): 4. (The Sheep poster comprises text printed directly on the title page of this interview.)
78. See Rockwell, "All-Ligeti Bill"; and Joan La Barbara, "The Orchestra Residency Program," *Musical America* 33, no. 11 (November 1983): 14.
79. "Horizons Comments," undated, New York Philharmonic Archives, Box 076-01-12.
80. Howard Klein to Jacob Druckman, 18 July 1983, Jacob Druckman Papers, Music Division, New York Public Library for the Performing Arts, Folder 687.
81. "Horizons Comments."
82. See National Endowment for the Arts, "National Endowment for the Arts Five-Year Planning Document, 1986–1990" (1984), 271.

83. Lang, "Jacob Druckman's Horizons," 1 January 2000, https://davidlangmusic.com/about/writings/jacob-druckmans-horizons.
84. See Leta E. Miller, *Aaron Jay Kernis* (Urbana: University of Illinois Press, 2014), 27–42.
85. Aaron Jay Kernis, interview with Ev Grimes, 13 November 1986, Yale Oral History of American Music: Major Figures in American Music, 181 a–f.
86. Unlike Leonard Bernstein and Pierre Boulez, the two previous Philharmonic music directors, Mehta was not a composer, and did not command a strong reputation as a new-music advocate. For a discussion of Bernstein's and Boulez's contemporary music programming, see Benjamin Piekut, *Experimentalism Otherwise* (Berkeley and Los Angeles: University of California Press, 2011) and Joshua Plocher, "Presenting the New: Battles around New Music in New York in the Seventies" (PhD diss., University of Minnesota, 2012).
87. Kernis, interview with Ev Grimes; Miller, *Aaron Jay Kernis*, 27.
88. Lang, "Jacob Druckman's Horizons."
89. "Horizons Comments," undated, New York Philharmonic Archives, Box 076-01-12.
90. Scott Lindroth, interview with author, 27 August 2014.
91. Barbara C. Phillips-Farley, "A History of the Center for New Music at the University of Iowa, 1966–1991" (DMA diss., University of Iowa, 1991), 4.
92. Leighton Kerner, "Music: Nu, Romanticism?" *Village Voice*, 26 June 1984, 92–93.
93. Rockwell, "All-Ligeti Bill."
94. Rockwell, "All-Ligeti Bill."
95. "Meet the Composer Receives Grant from the Revson Foundation for Composer Fellowships at New York Philharmonic," press release, 9 May 1984, Jacob Druckman Papers, Music Division, New York Public Library for the Performing Arts, Folder 658.
96. Lindroth to Eli N. Evans, 3 May 1985, Meet the Composer archives, New Music USA, Box 74.
97. Lindroth to Duffy, 2 May 1985, Meet the Composer archives, New Music USA, Box 74.
98. Lang to Duffy, 13 June 1984, Meet the Composer archives, New Music USA, Box 74.
99. "February 1985 Opportunity Update," Meet the Composer archives, New Music USA, Box 74.
100. Meeting notes from Meet the Composer/Orchestra Residencies Program Conference, Exxon Corporation, 28 May 1985, Meet the Composer archives, New Music USA, Box 51.
101. Lang to Duffy, 11 March 1986, Meet the Composer archives, New Music USA, Box 74.
102. Lang to Duffy, 11 March 1986.
103. Lang to Duffy, 11 March 1986.
104. Erlandson, "Meeting—January 20," 20 January 1983, New York Philharmonic Archives, Box 076-01-19.
105. Klein to Jacob Druckman, 18 July 1983, Jacob Druckman Papers, Music Division, New York Public Library for the Performing Arts, Folder 687.
106. Lang describes convincing Druckman in his 1997 oral history; see Lang, interview with Libby Van Cleve, 29 April 1997, Yale Oral History of American Music: Major Figures in American Music, 185 j–m.
107. Page, "Steve Reich, A Former Young Turk, Approaches 50," *New York Times*, 1 June 1986.
108. Rockwell, "Concert: Dresher and Reich Works," *New York Times*, 4 June 1986.
109. Michael Gordon to Jacob Druckman, 12 April 1986, Jacob Druckman Papers, Music Division, New York Public Library for the Performing Arts, Folder 592.

252 Notes to pages 70–76

110. According to a letter from Meet the Composer's development director to the administrator of the Revson Foundation, between December 1990 and January 1991, Wolfe was interviewed by Mehta for a subsequent Revson Fellowship. But the position was briefly suspended and ultimately went to Tania León in 1993. Joyce Lawler to Pamela Poland, 25 January 1991, Meet the Composer archives, New Music USA, Box 74. Wolfe, however, recalled meeting Mehta quickly in a hallway but that he did not show up to the formal interview. Wolfe, interview with author and Michael Gordon, 28 July 2018.
111. Wolfe, interview with author and Michael Gordon, 28 July 2018.
112. Donal Henahan, "Music View; Pondering the New-Music Dilemma," *New York Times*, 15 June 1986.
113. Financial issues are described in Albert K. Webster, interview with K. Robert Schwarz, 9 May 1992, K. Robert Schwarz Papers, Queens College Department of Special Collections and Archives, CD 2654 v. 39.
114. Druckman to Duffy, 11 October 1986, Meet the Composer archives, New Music USA, Box 84.
115. "Financial Summary, 1982–1987, Orchestra Residencies Program, Meet the Composer," Meet the Composer archives, New Music USA, Box 55.
116. Wiprud and Lawler, *Composer in Residence*, vii.
117. Wiprud and Lawler, *Composer in Residence*, 57.
118. Wiprud and Lawler, *Composer in Residence*, 19.
119. Wiprud and Lawler, *Composer in Residence*, 3.
120. Duffy to Druckman, 28 October 1991, Jacob Druckman Papers, Music Division, New York Public Library for the Performing Arts, Folder 661.
121. Tower, interview with Jenny Raymond, 4 January 1998, Yale Oral History of American Music: Major Figures in American Music, 55 g–h.
122. Schwarz, "Is There A Composer in the House?"
123. Lang, interview with Ev Grimes, 14 December 1986, Yale Oral History of American Music: Major Figures in American Music, 185 a–g.
124. Lang, interview with Ev Grimes.
125. Lang, interview with Libby Van Cleve.
126. Lang, interview with author, 19 January 2016.
127. Lang, interview with author, 19 January 2016.
128. Lang, interview with author, 19 January 2016.

Chapter 3

1. Gordon, spoken introduction at Bang on a Can Festival, 11 May 1987. These descriptions and all subsequent transcriptions of composers' introductions come from the archival audio captured by WNYC at the first Bang on a Can marathon.
2. Robert Black, interview with author, 6 December 2015.
3. In 1988, McMillin was renovated, and has since been known as Miller Theatre.
4. Wolfe, interview with author, 28 February 2016.
5. Drawing on the work of Pierre Bourdieu, Eric Drott argues that "the avant-garde may be conceived not so much as a succession of discrete movements in the various arts, but as a particular structural location within the social space of the artistic field." It is not only a particular philosophical or aesthetic stance, then, that characterizes the avant-garde, but also

how that stance is expressed: "Rhetoric and self-presentation contribute as much to the articulation of a particular artistic position as do aesthetic, ideological and/or stylistic factors." Eric Drott, "Spectralism, Politics, and the Post-Industrial Imagination," in *The Modernist Legacy: Essays on New Music*, ed. Björn Heile (Aldershot, UK: Ashgate, 2009), 43 and 44.
6. Ken Smith, "The Big Bang," *Time Out New York*, 29 May–5 June 1996.
7. Jeffrey Brooks, interview with author, 8 June 2017.
8. John Rockwell, "Avant Garde Music, the Bouquet of May," *New York Times*, 4 May 1990. In her dissertation, Wolfe recalls the line as: "Some composers sit around and bang on a can." Wolfe, "Embracing the Clash" (PhD diss., Princeton University, 2012), 8.
9. This anecdote was told to me by Brooks; Gordon did not recall proposing the ferry concert, but was not surprised that the idea was floated. Brooks, interview with author, 8 June 2017.
10. Lang, quoted in Tim Page, "New Music with a Bang, but No Cans," *New York Newsday*, 12 May 1987.
11. "Bang on a Can Festival [1987.08]: Project Description and Budget," Exit Art Archive, MSS 343, Box 11, Folder 13, Fales Library and Special Collections, New York University Libraries.
12. Wolfe attended performances of atonal music at Michigan, including a festival of Carter's music, but after arriving in New York, she did not attend concerts in the uptown scene.
13. Nicholas Kenyon, "Musical Events: Politics," *New Yorker*, 4 February 1980, 116; quoted in Joshua Plocher, "Presenting the New: Battles around New Music in New York in the Seventies" (PhD diss., University of Minnesota, 2012), 317.
14. Samuel Gilmore, "Collaboration and Convention: A Comparison of Repertory, Academic, and Avant Garde Concert Worlds" (PhD diss., Northwestern University, 1984), 92.
15. Gilmore, "Schools of Activity and Innovation," *Sociological Quarterly* 29, no. 2 (Summer 1988): 208.
16. Wolfe, quoted in "Bang on a Can Conversations," *Lincoln Center Stagebill*, program booklet, 15 March 1994, Bang on a Can online archives.
17. Lang, quoted in Kyle Gann, "After Ugly Music," *Village Voice*, 1 June 1993.
18. Lang, interview with author, 19 January 2016.
19. Associated Press, "Upscale Music Festival Considers Its Future," *The Intelligencer / The Record*, 20 March 1994, K. Robert Schwarz Papers, Queens College Department of Special Collections and Archives, Box 13.
20. John Rockwell, "What Happened to Our Vanguard," *New York Times*, 22 December 1985. Bernard Gendron similarly describes a "waning" of the downtown scene in this period. Bernard Gendron, "The Downtown Music Scene," in *The Downtown Book: The New York Art Scene, 1974–1984*, ed. Marvin J. Taylor (Princeton, NJ: Princeton University Press, 2006), 63.
21. Lang, interview with Libby Van Cleve, 29 April 1997, Yale Oral History of American Music: Major Figures in American Music, 185 j–m.
22. "Samuels ltr draft," 1994, Bang on a Can digital archives.
23. "Bang on a Can Final Report: 1995–1996 season," 1996, "jonathan," Bang on a Can digital archives.
24. Josef Woodward, "Ready for Takeoff," *Los Angeles Times*, 18 October 1998.
25. Audience numbers from "Program Schedule," Speculum Musicae, New York State Council on the Arts grant application materials, 1985–86, New York State Archives, Grant Application Files, Series 14064-90-B47. Concerts held 12 December 1984, 30 January 1985, and 12 March 1985. For Speculum Musicae and Group for Contemporary Music's

254 Notes to pages 81–83

audience numbers, I chose to focus only on their concerts at their primary venue of performance in New York City, as these were their core subscription performances and thus representative of typical audience draw.

26. Steven Swartz, "Speculum Musicae at the McMillin Theater, 3/12/85," in Speculum Musicae, New York State Council on the Arts grant application materials, 1985–86, New York State Archives, Grant Application Files, Series 14064-90-B47.
27. See "Program Schedule," Speculum Musicae, New York State Council on the Arts grant application materials, 1986–87, New York State Archives, Grant Application Files, Series 14064-91-B43. The ensemble reported that a 27 October 1985 concert had 180 attendees; a 19 February 1986 concert had 105 attendees; and a 24 February 1986 concert had 245 attendees.
28. Rockwell, "Music: Carter's 'Syringa,' by Speculum Musicae," *New York Times*, 18 May 1986.
29. Alice Tully Hall's capacity is identified in Speculum's grant materials, but they do not record attendance numbers for that concert. See "Program Schedule," Speculum Musicae, New York State Council on the Arts grant application materials, 1986–87, New York State Archives, Grant Application Files, Series 14064-91-B43.
30. See "Program Schedule," Group for Contemporary Music, New York State Council on the Arts grant application materials, 1985–86, New York State Archives, Grant Application Files, Series 14064-91-B21. In 1986, a 5 January concert attracted 200, a 29 January concert attracted 200, a 23 February concert attracted 175, and a 16 April concert attracted 250.
31. The writer, composer Peter Zummo, attended three concerts in December 1980 on behalf of the New York State Council on the Arts. Peter Zummo, "Experimental Intermedia Foundation/New Music Series," in Experimental Intermedia, New York State Council on the Arts grant application materials, 1981–82, New York State Archives, Grant Application Files, Series 14064-85-B072.
32. Swartz, "Bonnie Barnett at Experimental Intermedia Foundation, 10/18/86," in Experimental Intermedia, New York State Council on the Arts grant application materials, 1986–87, New York State Archives, Grant Application Files, Series 14064-91-B18.
33. "Project Request Sheet," Experimental Intermedia, New York State Council on the Arts grant application materials, 1981–82, New York State Archives, Grant Application Files, Series 14064-85-B072.
34. Experimental Intermedia, New York State Council on the Arts grant application materials, 1980–81, New York State Archives, Grant Application Files, Series 14064-85-B072.
35. Group for Contemporary Music, New York State Council on the Arts grant application materials, 1985–86, New York State Archives, Grant Application Files, Series 14064-91-B21.
36. Sasha Metcalf, "Funding 'Opera for the 80s and Beyond': The Role of Impresarios in Creating a New American Repertoire," *American Music* 35, no. 1 (Spring 2017): 17.
37. Metcalf, "Funding 'Opera for the 80s and Beyond,'" 16.
38. Wolfe, quoted in Smith, "The Big Bang."
39. Wolfe, quoted in K. Robert Schwarz, "Upstarts from Downtown," Lincoln Center *Stagebill*, April 1994.
40. "Where It All Came From," March 1995, Bang on a Can digital archives.
41. Lang, interview with author, 1 August 2019.
42. Lynn Garon, "Bang on a Can festival [1987.08]: Press Release," Exit Art Archive, MSS 343, Box 11, Folder 12, Fales Library and Special Collections, New York University Libraries.

43. Garon, "Bang on a Can festival [1987.08]: Press Release."
44. Scott Lindroth, interview with author, 27 August 2014.
45. Garon, "Bang on a Can festival [1987.08]: Press Release."
46. Lang, quoted in Page, "New Music with a Bang, but No Cans."
47. "Bang on a Can Festival [1987.08]: Project Description and Budget."
48. Bernard Holland, "Music: The Bang on a Can Festival," 14 May 1987. Holland's review did not actually name the gallery itself, and Ingberman sent him a scathing letter in response in which she informed him that "Exit Art is more than just 'an eighth floor loft fitted out with folding chairs.'" Jeanette Ingberman to Bernard Holland, 18 May 1987, "Bang on a Can Festival [1987.08]: Press Clippings and Listings," Exit Art Archive, MSS 343, Box 11, Folder 18, Fales Library and Special Collections, New York University Libraries.
49. Page, "New Music with a Bang, but No Cans."
50. Page, "New Music with a Bang, but No Cans."
51. Holland, "Music: The Bang on a Can Festival."
52. Garon, "Bang on a Can festival [1987.08]: Press Release."
53. Described in Lang, interview with author, 19 January 2016.
54. Wolfe, "Embracing the Clash," 51.
55. Lang, quoted in Gann, "After Ugly Music."
56. Lang, interview with Libby Van Cleve.
57. Sumanth Gopinath, "'Departing to Other Spheres': Psychedelic Science Fiction, Perspectival Embodiment, and the Hermeneutics of Steve Reich's *Four Organs*," in *Rethinking Reich*, ed. Sumanth Gopinath and Pwyll ap Siôn (Oxford: Oxford University Press, 2019), 19–52.
58. Lang, interview with Libby Van Cleve.
59. Lang, interview with Libby Van Cleve.
60. Lang, interview with Libby Van Cleve.
61. Wolfe, "Embracing the Clash," 51.
62. Lang, interview with author, 19 January 2016.
63. Lang sang in a performance of *Ktaadn* organized by Bresnick while at Stanford.
64. See Michael Palmese, "A Portrait of John Adams as a Young Man: The 1970s Juvenalia," *American Music* 37, no. 2 (Summer 2019): 229–56.
65. Gordon, Wolfe, and Lang to John Cage, 18 September 1986, John Cage Correspondence 72.9.5, Northwestern University Music Library, Evanston IL.
66. Lang, interview with Libby Van Cleve.
67. See Wolfe, "Embracing the Clash," 37. Though Wolfe does not mention Crawford Seeger, Bang on a Can did program *String Quartet 1931* on their 1989 marathon.
68. Gordon, quoted in Gann, "After Ugly Music."
69. Gordon, interview with author, 21 January 2016.
70. Bang on a Can, New York State Council on the Arts grant application materials, 1988–89, New York State Archives, Grant Application Files, Series 14064-93-B06.
71. In his 1997 oral history, Lang recalls it slightly differently: that Reich had been at the marathon for many of the earlier performances, but "went out in the hallway during Milton Babbitt's piece so he wouldn't have to hear it." Lang, interview with Libby Van Cleve.
72. Wolfe, interview with Libby Van Cleve, 14 August 1997, Yale Oral History of American Music: Major Figures in American Music, 255 a–e.

73. Gordon, quoted in Frank J. Oteri, "The Who and Why of Bang on a Can," *NewMusicBox*, 1 May 1999, https://nmbx.newmusicusa.org/bang-on-a-can/5/.
74. Wolfe, interview with Libby Van Cleve.
75. Steve Reich, spoken remarks at Bang on a Can Summer Festival, 30 July 2018. Private recording by Lasse D. Hansen, obtained and transcribed by author.
76. Brooks, interview with author, 8 June 2017.
77. Milton Babbitt, spoken introduction at Bang on a Can Festival, 11 May 1987.
78. Lang to Pauline Oliveros, undated, Pauline Oliveros Papers, Music Division, New York Public Library for the Performing Arts, Box 16, Folder 17.
79. Gordon, interview with author, 21 January 2016.
80. Babbitt to David Lang, 10 August 1987, Bang on a Can online archives.
81. "Marching to Their Own Drummers," *New York Magazine*, 9 June 2003, 137.
82. Bang on a Can, New York State Council on the Arts grant application materials, 1987–88, New York State Archives, Grant Application Files, Series 14064-92-B05.
83. Lang, quoted in Page, "New Music with a Bang, but No Cans."
84. Wolfe to Pauline Oliveros, 13 August 1987, Pauline Oliveros Papers, Music Division, New York Public Library for the Performing Arts, Box 29, Folder 26.
85. John Cage, 13 June 1988, Bang on a Can, New York State Council on the Arts grant application materials, 1988–89, New York State Archives, Grant Application Files, Series 14064-93-B06.
86. Martin Hoyle, "Can Can Do It," *Time Out London*, 17–24 January 1996, 119.
87. Rita Putnam, program review, 12 January 1988, Bang on a Can, New York State Council on the Arts grant application materials, 1987–88, New York State Archives, Grant Application Files, Series 14064-92-B05.
88. Lindroth, interview with author, 27 August 2014.
89. Gann, "The Missing Center," *Village Voice*, 31 May 1988.
90. Lang, interview with author, 19 January 2016.
91. "Final Report 1990," Bang on a Can digital archives.
92. Dean Drummond, quoted in "Earwitness," *EAR Magazine* 16, no. 2 (May 1991): 17.
93. Budget based on "Bang on a Can Financial Statement 1991," "1991 Budget Final-2," Bang on a Can digital archives; audience figures from "Final report 1991," Bang on a Can digital archives.
94. Freda Eisenberg, "New Music on WNYC-FM," *EAR Magazine* 8, no. 5 (March 1984): 24.
95. John Schaefer, "Facing the Risks," *EAR Magazine* 10, no. 5 (June/July 1986): 26.
96. Quoted in Michael Cooper, "WNYC Is Dropping 'New Sounds' After 37 Years. Musicians Are Mourning," *New York Times*, 11 October 2019. In October 2019, WNYC announced that it was dropping New Sounds after thirty-seven years on the air; following sustained protest from musicians and fans, the decision was reversed.
97. Gann, "Out of the Din," *Village Voice*, 23 May 1989.
98. Press Release for New Music, New York, The Kitchen Archives. Quoted in Plocher, "Presenting the New," 318–19.
99. Beth Anderson, "Reviews for the Critics: June 8 at The Kitchen," *Report from the Front*, June 1979. Obtained from the author, and available online at https://reportfromthefront.wordpress.com/. Also quoted and discussed in Plocher, "Presenting the New," 324.
100. As Joshua Plocher writes, "Entering the world of corporate and government politics meant trading creative anarchy for the business of consecration—the change that would

eventually lead Dmitri Devyatkin to call SoHo 'a syndrome of artists pitching projects to foundation executives over expensive lunches.'" Plocher, "Presenting the New," 347.
101. Detailed in Carol E. Tuynman, "New Music America 1985," *Ear Magazine* 10, no. 2 (November/December 1985): 3.
102. Gene Santoro, "New Music America," in *Tower Records Pulse!: The New Music America Supplement* (1989): 32.
103. Rockwell, quoted in Santoro, "New Music America," 35.
104. Lang, interview with author, 19 January 2016.
105. Described in Wolfe to Sara Burstein, 26 November 1990, "Jerome 1991 Pro Follow Up," Bang on a Can digital archives.
106. Rockwell, "His Forte Is Massive Sonic Grandeur," *New York Times*, 2 May 1982. Quoted in Bernard Gendron, *Between Montmatre and the Mudd Club: Popular Music and the Avant-Garde* (Chicago: University of Chicago Press, 2002), 296.
107. Tim Lawrence, "Pluralism, Minor Deviations, and Radical Change: The Challenge to Experimental Music in Downtown New York," in *Tomorrow Is the Question: New Directions in Experimental Music Studies*, ed. Benjamin Piekut (Ann Arbor: University of Michigan Press, 2014), 65. Despite the breadth of this approach, the festival's claims to multiculturalism, George Lewis notes, were not necessarily substantiated in the predominant whiteness of its programming. George E. Lewis, "Experimental Music in Black and White: The AACM in New York, 1970–1985," *Current Musicology* 71–73 (2002): 137.
108. Carl Stone, quoted in Tuynman, "New Music America 1985," 3.
109. Rockwell, quoted in Santoro, "New Music America," 35.
110. Wolfe, quoted in Rockwell, "Avant-Garde Music, the Bouquet of May," *New York Times*, 4 May 1990.
111. Lang, interview with Libby Van Cleve.
112. Gordon, quoted in Gann, "After Ugly Music." George Lewis has labelled that '80s improvisation scene "Downtown II," to distinguish it from the post-Cagean experimental and minimalist composers of the '60s. Lewis, "Experimental Music in Black and White," 116.
113. Lois V Vierk, *Go Guitars* (New York: L.V. Vierk, 1981).
114. Vierk, interview with author, 10 December 2015.
115. Gann, "Spring of Dissonance," *Village Voice*, 5 June 1990.
116. Gann, "The Missing Center," and Gann, "Out of the Din," *Village Voice*, 23 May 1989.
117. Gann, "Spring of Dissonance" and Gann, "After Ugly Music." For Gann's first in-depth column on totalism see Gann, "Totally Ismic," *Village Voice*, 20 July 1993, 69; reprinted in Gann, *Music Downtown* (Berkeley and Los Angeles: University of California Press, 2006), 127–29. For Gann's history of the term, see Gann, "A Technically Definable Stream of Postminimalism, Its Characteristics and Its Meaning," in *The Ashgate Research Companion to Minimalist and Postminimalist Music*, ed. Keith Potter, Kyle Gann, and Pwyll ap Siôn (New York: Routledge, 2016), 39–60.
118. Edward Rothstein, "Classical View; Minimalism Pumped Up to the Max," *New York Times*, 18 July 1993. The term was soon deployed by publicists, according to Timothy Taylor; see Timothy Taylor, "Music and Musical Practices in Postmodernity," in *Postmodern Music/ Postmodern Thought*, ed. Judy Lochhead and Joseph Auner (New York: Routledge, 2002), 107 and 111.
119. Mark Swed, "Bang on a Can Festival," *American Record Guide*, September/October 1992.

258 Notes to pages 100–106

120. David LL Laskin, "Bang on a Can Festival May 4–13 RAPP Arts Center, NYC," *EAR Magazine* 15, no. 2 (July–August 1990), 55.
121. Laskin, "Bang on a Can Festival."
122. Laskin, "Bang on a Can Festival."
123. "Preview, Bang on a Can Festival, New York City, May 9," *EAR Magazine* 16, no. 1 (April 1991), 43.
124. Stone, interview with author, 18 March 2019.
125. Lang, quoted in Gann, "After Ugly Music."

Chapter 4

1. Mervyn Rothstein, "Archdiocese Orders Play to Vacate Church," *New York Times*, 20 September 1990.
2. Peter Goodman, "Music Festival Loses Its Home," *Newsday*, date unknown; see Bang on a Can Festival: Clippings, New York Public Library for the Performing Arts.
3. Figure mentioned in Kyle Gann, "Alive at Zero," *Village Voice*, 4 June 1991, 62. In a 1991 final report to the New York State Council on the Arts, Bang on a Can noted that "$20,740 deficit due to closing of RAPP Arts Center three (3) weeks before festival. Other, more expensive venues were substituted at the last minute." Bang on a Can, New York State Council on the Arts grant application materials, 1990–91, New York State Archives, Grant Application Files, Series 14064-95-B06.
4. Quoted in Gann, "Alive at Zero."
5. Andrew Hartman, *A War for the Soul of America: A History of the Culture Wars* (Chicago: University of Chicago Press, 2015), 7. *Village Voice* critic Richard Goldstein, for example, placed the RAPP incident alongside court cases concerning the work of Mapplethorpe and hip-hop group 2 Live Crew that were considered landmark controversies in the Culture Wars; see Richard Goldstein, "Doowutchyalike: In the Brave New World, Sex Sells," *Village Voice*, 6 November 1990, quoted in *Culture Wars: Documents from the Recent Controversies in the Arts*, ed. Richard Bolton (New York: New Press, 1992), 288.
6. David Lang, "The New Politeness," *Symphony*, January–February 1990, 9. This citation is a reprint of the article that ran in the October 1989 issue of *Premiere*, the American Composers Orchestra's newsletter, which I was not able to obtain. In a column in *EAR Magazine*, Mary Charlotte Domandi raised similar points, describing the Robert Mapplethorpe and PMRC controversies and writing that "Experimental musicians have not (yet) been dealt the same sort of attacks. Perhaps this is because their work, if it does not contain text, tends to be more abstract or less overtly symbolic than other forms. Also, since experimental music is generally distributed through non-mainstream channels, it reaches a much smaller audience. So while there's little direct censorship, there is instead marginalization through lack of funding." Mary Charlotte Domandi, "Funding and Censorship: Put Your Money Where Your Mouth Is," *EAR Magazine* 15, no. 1 (March 1990): 15.
7. Lang, "The New Politeness," 9.
8. Lang, "The New Politeness," 10.
9. Donna Binkiewicz, *Federalizing the Muse: United States Arts Policy and the National Endowment for the Arts, 1965–1980* (Chapel Hill: University of North Carolina Press, 2004), 4.

10. National Foundation on the Arts and the Humanities Act of 1965 (P.L. 89-209), https://www.neh.gov/about/history/national-foundation-arts-and-humanities-act-1965-pl-89-209.
11. Quoted in Fanny Taylor and Anthony L. Barresi, *The Arts at a New Frontier: The National Endowment for the Arts* (New York: Springer, 2013), 229.
12. For a discussion of the role of "expertise" in early NEA music granting, see Michael Uy, *Ask the Experts: How Ford, Rockefeller, and the NEA Changed American Music* (Oxford: Oxford University Press, 2020).
13. James Allen Smith, "Foundations as Cultural Actors," in *American Foundations: Roles and Contributions*, ed. Helmut K. Anheier and David C. Hammock (Washington, DC: Brookings Institution Press, 2010), 277.
14. See National Endowment for the Arts, "National Endowment for the Arts Five-Year Planning Document, 1986–1990" (1984), 261. When accounting for inflation, this represents an approximately fifty-seven-fold increase.
15. Jann Pasler, *Writing through Music: Essays on Music, Culture, and Politics* (Oxford and New York: Oxford University Press, 2007), 353.
16. Pasler, *Writing through Music*, 358.
17. See Elizabeth A.C. Weil, "Introduction," in Diane J. Gingold, *Business and the Arts: How They Meet the Challenge* (Washington, DC: National Endowment for the Arts, 1984), xi.
18. Gingold, *Business and the Arts*, 12.
19. Lang, interview with author, 1 August 2019.
20. Quoted in Fraser Baron, "A Mission Renewed: The Survival of the National Endowment for the Arts, 1981–1983," *Journal of Cultural Economics* 11, no. 1 (June 1987): 23.
21. In terms of money allocated, the NEA budget was at its highest under George H.W. Bush, but in real purchasing power, its funding actually peaked in 1979 and declined by approximately 40 percent over the next decade. Paul DiMaggio, "Decentralization of Arts Funding from the Federal Government to the States," in *Public Money and the Muse: Essays on Government Funding on the Arts*, ed. Stephen Benedict (New York: W.W. Norton, 1991), 222.
22. Chin-Tao Wu, *Privatizing Culture* (London: Verso, 2003), 51.
23. "Washington News," *American Music Center Newsletter* 23, no. 2 (Spring 1981): 3.
24. Donald Erb, "A Note From the President of AMC," *American Music Center Newsletter* 24, no. 2 (Spring 1982): 1.
25. Ezra Laderman, "This Fragile Network," *American Music Center Newsletter* 24, no. 3 (Summer 1982): 5. Laderman's speech was originally given to the Music Publisher's Association in June 1982.
26. Julia Wolfe, interview with author, 28 February 2016.
27. "Cary Trust Final Report 1990," "Final Report Special 1990," Bang on a Can digital archives.
28. My comparison is based on examining the New York State Council on the Arts grant applications for these organizations.
29. Bang on a Can, New York State Council on the Arts grant application materials, 1990–91, New York State Archives, Grant Application Files, Series 14064-95-B06.
30. $216,685 in 1991 is equivalent to approximately $412,212 in August 2020.
31. Bang on a Can, New York State Council on the Arts grant application materials, 1990–91.
32. Red Poppy is an independent entity from Bang on a Can.
33. Bang on a Can, "Bang on a Can Announces Expansion," Bang on a Can Festival: Clippings, New York Public Library for the Performing Arts.

34. Bang on a Can, "Bang on a Can Announces Expansion."
35. "Samuels ltr draft," 22 December 1994, Bang on a Can digital archives.
36. "Samuels ltr draft."
37. Karen Sander, interview with author, 5 July 2019.
38. Sander, interview with author, 5 July 2019.
39. Alphonse D'Amato, statement in the Senate, 18 May 1989, quoted in *Culture Wars*, 28.
40. Pat Robertson, Christian Coalition direct mail, 25 October 1989, quoted in *Culture Wars*, 123.
41. Hartman, *A War for the Soul of America*.
42. Patrick Buchanan, 1992 Republican National Convention Speech, 17 August 1992, https://buchanan.org/blog/1992-republican-national-convention-speech-148.
43. Proposed Senate Amendment No. 420, 26 July 1989, quoted in *Culture Wars*, 73–74.
44. Public Law 101–121, 23 October 1989, quoted in *Culture Wars*, 121.
45. Pauline Oliveros and Ione, "Dear Ear," *EAR Magazine* 15, no. 15 (March 1991): 8.
46. Oliveros and Ione, "Dear Ear."
47. Duffy to John Frohnmayer, 7 June 1990, Meet the Composer archive, New Music USA, Box 24.
48. Quoted in David LL Laskin, "Composer to Composer," *EAR Magazine* 15, no. 6 (October 1990): 43.
49. Karen de Witt, "New Fiscal Year Ends Anti-Obscenity Pledge," *New York* Times, 31 October 1990.
50. American Family Association, press release, 25 July 1989, quoted in *Culture Wars*, 71.
51. Jesse Helms, Debate in Senate over Helms amendment, 26 July 1989, quoted in *Culture Wars*, 76.
52. Robert Anbian, "Bigots, Not NEA, Promote Social Decay," 22 June 1990, quoted in *Culture Wars*, 243.
53. Laskin, "Composer to Composer," 43.
54. John Duffy, quoted in "Discussion Two," *EAR Magazine* 16, no. 1 (April 1991): 30.
55. "Discussion Two," 30.
56. "Discussion Two," 32.
57. "Discussion Two," 32.
58. "Discussion Two," 38.
59. See Eleanor Blau, "Some U.S. Arts Grants Turned Down in Protest," *New York Times*, 9 July 1990.
60. Rebecca Sayles, "Arts Forward Fund Phase I Planning Grant," 10 June 1992, "Arts Forward," Bang on a Can digital archives.
61. Robert Hughes, "A Loony Parody of Cultural Democracy," *Time*, 14 August 1989; quoted in *Culture Wars*, 90.
62. In 1987, for example, he described Copland's music as "the golden age of American musical composition, the period when modernism and a musical audience seemed to come together." Samuel Lipman, "Doing New Music, Doing American New Music," *New Criterion*, 1987, quoted in Lipman, *Arguing for Music, Arguing for Culture* (Boston: D.R. Goldine, 1990), 54. As director of the Waterloo Music Festival, Lipman championed the so-called "lost generation" of American symphonists like Samuel Barber, William Schuman, and David Diamond. (Diamond, who was a Communist in his youth, saw the irony that a sound steeped in '30s leftism was being revived by a neocon; he told the *Times*

that "The whole leftist mentality has disappeared . . . Now it's the conservatives who are interested in my music.") John Rockwell, "Returning to the Music of a Lost Generation," *New York Times*, 21 July 1989. For Lipman quotes about new music, see "Doing New Music," 55; "The Road to Now," *New Criterion*, 1985, quoted in *Arguing for Music, Arguing for Culture*, 31; "From Avant-Garde to Pop," *Commentary*, 1979, quoted in *The House of Music: Art in an Era of Institutions* (Boston: D.R. Godine, 1984), 31; "From Avant-Garde to Pop," 47.

63. Michael S. Joyce, "The National Endowments for the Humanities and the Arts," in *Mandate for Leadership*, ed. Charles L. Heatherly (Washington, DC: Heritage Foundation, 1981), 1040 and 1052. The essay itself states that Lipman was among several figures who contributed to it, but several outside sources attribute its primary authorship to Lipman; see, for example, Baron, "A Mission Renewed," 25.
64. Joyce, "The National Endowments," 1052.
65. Joyce, "The National Endowments," 1055.
66. Joyce, "The National Endowments," 1055.
67. See Richard J. Margolis, "Moving America Right," *Foundation News* 24, no. 7–8 (1983): 47.
68. Hilton Kramer, "A Note on the New Criterion," *New Criterion*, September 1982, in *The New Criterion Reader: The First Five Years*, ed. Hilton Kramer (New York: Simon & Schuster, 1988), 3.
69. Margolis, "Moving America Right," 48.
70. Lipman, "Say No to Trash," *New York Times*, 23 June 1989, quoted in *Culture Wars*, 42.
71. Kramer and Lipman, "There Is Only One Magazine That Tells You What Is Right," direct mail for *New Criterion*, August 1990, quoted in *Culture Wars*, 260. The mailer was referring to the pamphlet *An American Dialogue*, a set of recommendations for performing arts presentation published in 1989 by a task force convened by the NEA, Rockefeller Foundation, and Pew Charitable Trusts; it advocated for cultural equity across racial and ethnic groups, and opened with a capsule history of the performing arts in the United States that was rooted in the immigrant experience and described "European-derived" art as having its "roots in the same kind of local 'ethnic activities' that we see today among newer immigrants." National Task Force on Presenting and Touring the Performing Arts, *An American Dialogue* (Washington, DC: Association of Performing Arts Presenters, 1989). Lipman had critiqued the pamphlet in an essay for *Commentary* in 1990; see Lipman, "Backward & Downward with the Arts," *Commentary*, May 1990, reprinted in Lipman, *Music and More: Essays 1975–1991* (Evanston, IL: Northwestern University Press, 1992), 300–9.
72. There is an immense body of scholarly literature theorizing and historicizing multiculturalism; Stuart Hall has pointed out that "The term 'multiculturalism' is now universally deployed. However, this proliferation has neither stabilized nor clarified its meaning . . . multiculturalism is now so discursively entangled that it can only be used 'under erasure.'" Stuart Hall, "Conclusion: The Multi-cultural Question," in *Un/settled Multiculturalisms: Diasporas, Entanglements, Transruptions*, ed. Barnor Hesse (London: Zed Books, 2000), 209.
73. "Special attention will be given to innovative and imaginative programming. Organizations are encouraged to present the works of living composers, including premieres of new works and repeat performances of recently composed works." See "Music Program," New York

State Council on the Arts, *Program Guidelines, 1985/86–1986/87*, 59. For a discussion of the touring New York State New Music Network, see Scott Cantrell, "The Hills Are Alive with the Sound of New Music," *New York Times*, 18 September 1988.
74. James Jordan, quoted in "Discussion Two," 36.
75. Thomas Morgan, "Arts Groups Seek Ethnically Broader Audience," *New York Times*, 1 January 1987.
76. See New York State Black and Puerto Rican Legislative Caucus's Cultural Arts Task Force, "Towards Cultural Democracy," January 1989.
77. "Towards Cultural Democracy," 40.
78. Samuel Gilmore, "Minorities and Distributional Equity at the National Endowment for the Arts," *Journal of Arts Management, Law, and Society* 23, no. 2 (Summer 1993): 137.
79. Gilmore, "Minorities and Distributional Equity."
80. Joan Peyser, "Music; Wuorinen's Bleak View of the Future," *New York Times*, 5 June 1988.
81. Peyser, "Wuorinen's Bleak View of the Future."
82. Peyser, "Wuorinen's Bleak View of the Future."
83. Jonathan Goldberg, program review, 15 September 1986, in Group for Contemporary Music, New York State Council on the Arts grant application materials, 1986–87, New York State Archives, Grant Application Files, Series 14064-91-B21.
84. The Group's programs are listed in Susan Deaver's dissertation; see Deaver, "The Group for Contemporary Music, 1962–1992" (DMA diss., Manhattan School of Music, 1993), 183–210.
85. Michael Leavitt to James Jordan, 1 November 1986, in Group for Contemporary Music, New York State Council on the Arts grant application materials, 1986–87.
86. Group for Contemporary Music, New York State Council on the Arts grant application materials, 1986–87.
87. Speculum Musicae, New York State Council on the Arts grant application materials, 1986–87, New York State Archives, Grant Application Files, Series 14064-91-B43.
88. Experimental Intermedia, New York State Council on the Arts grant application materials, 1985–86, New York State Archives, Grant Application Files, Series 14064-90-B18.
89. New York State Council on the Arts, *Program Guidelines, 1990/91–1991/92–1992/93*, 6.
90. Jordan, quoted in Neil Strauss, "New York," *EAR Magazine* 15, no.1 (March 1991): 19. As David Pankratz points out, this approach committed conceptually to a model of distributive justice, while also allowing for contingencies shaped by individual organization's approaches. David Pankratz, *Multiculturalism and Public Arts Policy* (Westport, CT: Bergin & Garvey, 1993), 93.
91. Quoted in Deaver, "The Group for Contemporary Music," 164.
92. Group for Contemporary Music, New York State Council on the Arts grant application materials, 1990–91, New York State Archives, Grant Application Files, Series 14064-95-B18.
93. Charles Wuorinen, interview with Richard Douglas Burbank; in Richard Douglas Burbank, *Charles Wuorinen: A Bio-Bibliography* (Westport, CT: Greenwood Press, 1994), 18. Burbank's interview transcript is a compilation of several interviews he conducted between 1987 and 1992.
94. Group for Contemporary Music, New York State Council on the Arts grant application materials, 1990–91.
95. New York State Council on the Arts, *Program Guidelines, 1990/91–1991/92–1992/93*, 87.

96. Bang on a Can, New York State Council on the Arts grant application materials, 1990–91, New York State Archives, Grant Application Files, Series 14064-95-B06.
97. Allan Kozinn, "For Contemporary Music, Times Are Hard," *New York Times*, 8 January 1991.
98. Kozinn, "For Contemporary Music, Times Are Hard."
99. Kozinn, "For Contemporary Music, Times Are Hard."
100. Kozinn, "Festival Shows There Is a New-Music Audience," *New York Times*, 3 June 1991.
101. Lang, "Body Count," *New York Times*, 26 June 1988.
102. Lang, "Body Count."
103. Bang on a Can, New York State Council on the Arts grant application materials, 1990–91, New York State Archives, Grant Application Files, Series 14064-95-B06.
104. Bang on a Can Festival, "Meet the Composer/Reader's Digest Commissioning Program" application, 1990, Meet the Composer archive, Box 69, New Music USA. In terms of gender, an average of 22 percent of works presented on the Bang on a Can marathons between 1987 and 1993 were by women composers.
105. Michael Gordon to Sara Burstein, 15 October 1991, "Sara Burstein_oct 91~1," Bang on a Can digital archives.
106. Gordon to Sara Burstein, 15 October 1991.
107. Jonathan Goldberg, program review, 24 June 1991, in Bang on a Can, New York State Council on the Arts grant application materials, 1991–92, New York State Archives, Grant Application Files, Series 14064-98-B01.
108. Grace Glueck, "Arts Officials Voice Shock at Cuomo Cuts," *New York Times*, 2 February 1991.
109. Jordan, quoted in "Discussion Two," 30.
110. See New York State Council on the Arts, Funding Report 1989–1990; New York State Council on the Arts, Funding Report 1991–1992; and New York State Council on the Arts, Funding Report 1992–1993. The 1992–93 report includes a graph documenting the Council's budget.
111. See DiMaggio, "Decentralization," 222. NYSCA funding gradually rebounded over subsequent years, but never fully recovered.
112. Lang, interview with author, 1 August 2019.
113. Experimental Intermedia, New York State Council on the Arts grant application materials, 1995–96, New York State Archives, Grant Application Files, Series 14064-99-B76.
114. Milton Babbitt, "Brave New Worlds," *Musical Times* 135, no. 1816 (June 1994): 330.
115. Babbitt, "Brave New Worlds," 330.
116. Babbitt, "Brave New Worlds," 330.
117. Babbitt, "Brave New Worlds," 331.
118. Toward the end of the *Musical Times* piece, he quotes a similarly grim prognostication by Samuel Lipman; Babbitt and Lipman were friends, and he read the critic's writing. Babbitt, "Brave New Worlds," 333.
119. See Martin Brody, "'Music for the Masses': Milton Babbitt's Cold War Music Theory," *Musical Quarterly* 77 (1993): 161–92.
120. Babbitt, "Brave New Worlds," 330.
121. The New Music Performance category was dissolved in 1985.
122. Sylvia Glickman and Tina Davidson to Fran Richard, 1 December 1987, Meet the Composer archive, New Music USA, Box 24. Pasler notes that "Between 1979 and 1985,

only 10 percent of NEA composers' grants went to women." Pasler, *Writing through Music*, 349.
123. Paul Dresher to Jan Stunkard, 18 January 1994, Meet the Composer archive, New Music USA, Box 84.
124. George Lewis discusses similar issues emerging around submissions to NEA fellowships by "jazz-identified experimentalists," which Muhal Richard Abrams fought to change while serving on panel juries. George E. Lewis, *A Power Stronger Than Itself: The AACM and American Experimental Music* (Chicago: University of Chicago Press, 2008), 400–3.
125. Edward Rothstein, "Bang on a Can Festival Seeks Political Relevance," *New York Times*, 27 May 1993.
126. Gann, "Politics in a Can," *Village Voice*, 22 June 1993, 82.
127. Newt Gingrich, Richard K. Armey, Ed Gillespie, and Bob Schellhas, *Contract with America: The Bold Plan by Rep. Newt Gingrich, Rep. Dick Armey and the House Republicans to Change the Nation* (New York: Times Books, 1994), 7.
128. See Diane Haitman, "Year in Review 1995: The Arts: Reports of NEA's Death Are Greatly Exaggerated (Yes—Listen Up, Newt)," *Los Angeles Times*, 31 December 1995.
129. Carl Stone and Randall Davidson to Jane Alexander, 13 March 1995, Meet the Composer archive, New Music USA, Box 84.
130. Quoted in Thomas Peter Kimbus, "Surviving the Storm: How the National Endowment for the Arts Restructured Itself to Serve a New Constituency," *Journal of Arts Management, Law, and Society* 27, no. 2 (Summer 1997): 15 and 18.
131. Phill Niblock, interview with author, 27 May 2017.
132. Experimental Intermedia, New York State Council on the Arts grant application materials, 1985–86; Experimental Intermedia, New York State Council on the Arts grant application materials, 1986–87, New York State Archives, Grant Application Files, Series 14064-90-B18; and Experimental Intermedia, New York State Council on the Arts grant application materials, 1995–96.
133. Dresher, interview with author, 21 October 2016.
134. Scott Johnson, interview with Jack Vees, 8 March 2006, Yale Oral History of American Music: Major Figures in American Music, 338 a–b.
135. National Endowment for the Arts, Annual Report 1995.
136. Bette Snapp, "PLAN," 5 October 1995, Bang on a Can digital archives.
137. Snapp, "Chamber Music America Presenter Expansion Program Interim Report," 27 August 1996, "june interim 96," Bang on a Can digital archives.
138. Snapp, "Chamber Music America Presenter Expansion Program Interim Report."
139. David Lang, Michael Gordon, and Julia Wolfe, "Merge letter 1996," 22 February 1996, Bang on a Can digital archives.
140. "Bang on a Can Summer Fundraising," 10 July 1996, "1996 summer funders," Bang on a Can digital archives.
141. For budget and total foundation/corporate funding, see Snapp, "Bang on a Can: Ten Years of Growth 1987–1997," 14 January 1998, "growth facts supp. info," Bang on a Can digital archives. For Rockefeller funding, see "10th Anniversary Bang on a Can Festival Budget," 30 September 1997, "fest. Budget," Bang on a Can digital archives. For general description of 1996–97 fundraising, including Bang on a Can's claims that it received first major corporate support that year, see Snapp, "Final Report 1996–97 Season," 26 August 1997, "96-97 final report Jerome," Bang on a Can digital archives. For Philip Morris, see Rachel

Cohen to Marilynn Donini, 12 January 1997, "ack. To Marilynn Donini 1," Bang on a Can digital archives. For AT&T, see Snapp, "Interstate Bang on a Can Final Budget," 1 October 1997, "97 Final Budget," Bang on a Can digital archives.
142. Snapp, "Bang on a Can: Ten Years of Growth 1987–1997."
143. National Endowment for the Arts, Annual Report 1997.
144. Christine Williams to Leah Krauss, 12 November 1998, "NEA Match NYCT," Bang on a Can digital archives.
145. Years listed on the X axis correspond to fiscal years as calculated by the organizations discussed (e.g. 1988 is equivalent to 1987–1988). With the exception of FY1996, all figures for Bang on a Can here were drawn from final reports to NYSCA attached to successful grant applications, obtained from the New York State Archives. FY1996, missing from the NYSCA files I obtained, is from "budgets for last 2 years," 15 February 1997, Bang on a Can digital archives. Discrepancies between the totals listed here and those described above in-text—for example, for the anniversary season budget and FY1997—are due to differences between how the organization calculated their budget for a concert season and how they did so for the financial year, as well as inconsistencies in how Bang on a Can described their budgets at various stages of the financial year. Total NEA and NYSCA music program granting numbers are drawn from the annual reports for both organizations; the NEA figures end in 1996 because the agency's granting was reorganized to eliminate discipline-specific categories. Note that for both government agencies, music program granting does not encompass all granting to musical organizations; the NEA's Music division, for example, was distinct from its Opera/Musical Theater program.
146. Amy Roberts Frawley, quoted in Kozinn, "For Contemporary Music, Times Are Hard."
147. John J. Condon, review of Bang on a Can, 7 June 1999, Bang on a Can, New York State Council on the Arts grant application materials, 1999–2000, New York State Archives, Grant Application Files, Series 14064-04-B37.
148. "To the Robert Sterling Clark Foundation," 5 February 1998, "97–98 proposal."
149. Inaugural People's Commissioning Fund postcard, 1997, Bang on a Can online archives.
150. *The People's Commissioner* 1, no. 1 (Spring 1997); obtained from Lois V Vierk.
151. Described in Michael Gordon, Karen Sander, and Christine Williams, "97 proposal," 8 December 1997, Bang on a Can digital archives.
152. Christine Williams, "Challenge 97 report," 29 May 1998, Bang on a Can digital archives; "1999 Season Final Report," Final Report 98–99, 18 April 2000, Bang on a Can digital archives.
153. "1999 Season Final Report."
154. "1999 Season Final Report."
155. Performances listed in Christine Williams to Joyce Carol Oates, 16 July 1998, "7-16 joyce carol oates," Bang on a Can digital archives. Oates had collaborated with Duffy on an opera adaptation of her novel *Black Water*, and was invited to speak at the gala; it is not clear whether she attended.
156. Figure from Bang on a Can, New York State Council on the Arts grant application materials, 1999–2000, New York State Archives, Grant Application Files, Series 14064-04-B37.
157. Duffy, "Passion for Music," 22 November 1998, "Catalogue duffy," Bang on a Can digital archives.

158. "Bang on a Can: The People's Commissions," flyer, May 1998, Bang on a Can online archives.
159. "Bang on a Can: The People's Commissions."
160. Pamela Z, interview with author, 31 July 2019.
161. Lang, Gordon, and Wolfe, fundraising letter, 11 December 1997, "fall 97 renew merge," Bang on Can digital archives.
162. Gordon to Rackstraw Downes, 13 September 1999, "rackstraw letter," Bang on a Can digital archives.
163. "The People's Commissioning Fund," 26 January 2000, "pcf 98-99," Bang on a Can digital archives.
164. "Newsletter 2.7," 12 March 1997, Bang on a Can digital archives.
165. Lang, interview with Libby Van Cleve, 7 April 2011, Yale Oral History of American Music: Major Figures in American Music, 185 t–u.
166. See Jane Alexander, *Command Performance: An Actress in the Theater of Politics* (New York: Da Capo Press, 2000), 239.
167. Binkiewicz, *Federalizing the Muse*, 221. Stefan Toepler writes that "With the NEA's restructuring in the mid-1990s, all disciplinary grant-making programs and most fellowships were eliminated; the NEA lost its ability to define the parameters of the policy field; and private donors lost their ability to delineate their own roles within the framework set by the NEA." Stefan Toepler, "Roles of Foundations and Their Impact in the Arts," in *American Foundations*, 302.

Chapter 5

1. See Julia Wolfe, "*Lick*: Excerpt," Bang on a Can online archives.
2. Wolfe, "Lick," in "Bang on a Can All-Stars," 4 August 1994, *Tanglewood Music Center Yearbook*, 1994, https://archive.org/stream/tanglewoodmusicc1994bost#page/n443/mode/2up, 444.
3. Wolfe, "Lick," *Tanglewood Music Center Yearbook*.
4. Mark Stewart, interview with author, 25 July 2018.
5. As Rachel Vandagriff has detailed, Schuller had clashed with Paul Fromm, the principal patron of the festival, over whether it should program the music of Steve Reich and John Adams, and Fromm subsequently withdrew his support from Tanglewood because he felt Schuller's purview was too narrow. Rachel Vandagriff, "The History and Impact of the Fromm Music Foundation, 1952–1983" (PhD diss., University of California, Berkeley, 2014), 237–40.
6. Alex Ross, "Tanglewood Series Gets a Change of Air in Its New Home," *New York Times*, 8 August 1994.
7. "Bang on a Can All-Stars," *Tanglewood Music Center Yearbook*, 447.
8. Kyle Gann, "The Missing Center," *Village Voice*, 31 May 1988.
9. Gann, "Out of the Din," *Village Voice*, 23 May 1989.
10. John Rockwell, "Review/Music; The Experimental Bang on a Can Festival," *New York Times*, 12 May 1989.
11. Michael Gordon, interview with Libby Van Cleve, 29 August 1997, Yale Oral History of American Music: Major Figures in American Music, 254 a–f.

12. Patrick Nickleson, "Transcription, Recording, and Authority in 'Classic' Minimalism," *Twentieth-Century Music* 14, no. 3 (2018): 361.
13. Gordon, *Thou Shalt!/Thou Shalt Not!* (New York: Red Poppy, 1983).
14. Gordon, spoken introduction at Bang on a Can Festival, 11 May 1987.
15. Gordon, interview with Libby Van Cleve.
16. Wolfe, quoted in Frank J. Oteri, "The Who and Why of Bang on a Can," *NewMusicBox*, 1 May 1999, https://nmbx.newmusicusa.org/bang-on-a-can/.
17. David Lang and Wolfe to Gayle Morgan, 1 December 1991, "Cary Commission 1991," Bang on a Can digital archives.
18. "Bang on a Can Festival, May 12–17, 1992," Bang on a Can online archives. This configuration of the All-Stars performed their own evening of works by Conlon Nancarrow, Pelle Gudmundsen-Holmgreen, Bunita Marcus, and Frederic Rzewski on May 14, and also played Steve Martland's *Remix* and Allison Cameron's *Blank Sheet of Metal* on the marathon on May 17.
19. Lang to Susan Lipman, 5 February 1992, "Lipman," Bang on a Can digital archives.
20. Lisa Moore, interview with K. Robert Schwarz, 23 March 1995, K. Robert Schwarz Papers, Queens College Department of Special Collections and Archives, CD 2654 v. 138b.
21. Gordon, interview with K. Robert Schwarz, 22 March 1995, K. Robert Schwarz Papers, Queens College Department of Special Collections and Archives, CD 2654 v. 138a.
22. Lang, interview with author, 19 January 2016.
23. Gordon to Margaret C. Ayers, 22 January 1993, "marketing proposal 5_93~1," Bang on a Can digital archives.
24. Gordon to Ayers, 22 January 1993.
25. These budgets are drawn from 1992 grant applications to the Aaron Copland Fund for Music; see Jacob Druckman Papers, Music Division, New York Public Library for the Performing Arts, Folder 1518.
26. Rachel Cohen to Gayle Morgan, 3 October 1995, "Admin," Bang on a Can digital archives; work after meeting with Cowperthwaite detailed in "Booking," 19 July 1997, Bang on a Can digital archives; Christine Williams to Leah Krauss, 12 November 1998, "NEA Match NYCT," Bang on a Can digital archives.
27. The Nirvana cover is described in Gann, "View from the Gap," *Village Voice*, 21 March 1995.
28. "Walker Arts Center and the Minnesota Composers Forum Present Bang on a Can All-Stars," 21 November 1992, Bang on a Can online archives.
29. "Bang on a Can All-Stars," *Tanglewood Music Center Yearbook*, 447.
30. "Bang on a Can Final Report: 1995–1996 season," 10 October 1996 "jonathan," Bang on a Can digital archives.
31. Snapp, "Chamber Music America Presenter Expansion Program Interim Report," 27 August 1996, "june interim 96," Bang on a Can digital archives.
32. "budgets for last 2 years," Bang on a Can digital archives.
33. Snapp, "Chamber Music America Presenter Expansion Program Interim Report."
34. See Tim Lawrence, "Pluralism, Minor Deviations, and Radical Change: The Challenge to Experimental Music in Downtown New York," in *Tomorrow Is the Question: New Directions in Experimental Music Studies*, ed. Benjamin Piekut (Ann Arbor: University of Michigan Press, 2014), 63–85.
35. Lang, interview with Ev Grimes, 14 December 1986, Yale Oral History of American Music: Major Figures in American Music, 185 a–g.

36. K. Robert Schwarz, "Pop Goes The Music—Classical, Too," *New York Times*, 20 January 1991.
37. Ned Rorem, "Pop Classical; Speaking in Tongues," *New York Times*, 3 February 1991.
38. Lang, interview with Libby Van Cleve, 29 April 1997, Yale Oral History of American Music: Major Figures in American Music, 185 j–m.
39. Wolfe, interview with Libby Van Cleve, 27 July 2014, Yale Oral History of American Music: Major Figures in American Music, 255 h–m.
40. Lang, quoted in Page, "New Music with a Bang, but no Cans," *New York Newsday*, 12 May 1987.
41. Lynn Garon, "Bang on a Can festival [1987.08]: Press Release," Exit Art Archive, MSS 343, Box 11, Folder 12, Fales Library and Special Collections, New York University Libraries.
42. Gordon, quoted in "Bang on a Can All-Stars," *Lincoln Center Stagebill*, program booklet, 11 April 1994, Bang on a Can online archives.
43. Gordon, quoted in "Bang on a Can All-Stars."
44. Allan Kozinn, "Into the Middle, Where There's Gravity," *New York Times*, 16 March 1995.
45. Schwarz, "Bang on a Can Issues a Manifesto," *New York Times*, 21 May 1995.
46. The quote is featured, for example, at the top of a poster for the group's 1996 tour to England. CMN Tours, "Bang on a Can," "1996 England Tour Poster," Bang on a Can online archives.
47. Gann, "Vision in a Can," *Village Voice*, 2 June 1992.
48. Gordon, interview with Libby Van Cleve.
49. Lang, interview with Libby Van Cleve.
50. Lang, interview with Libby Van Cleve.
51. "Bang on a Can All-Stars," *Lincoln Center Stagebill*, program booklet, 14 March 1994, Bang on a Can online archives.
52. Lang, Gordon, and Wolfe, liner notes to Bang on a Can, *Industry*, Sony Classical 66483, 1995.
53. Lang, quoted in Michael Blackwood, *New York Composers: Searching for a New Music* (Michael Blackwood Productions, 1997).
54. Maya Beiser, interview with author, 9 July 2018.
55. Robert Black, interview with K. Robert Schwarz, 23 March 1995, K. Robert Schwarz Papers, Queens College Department of Special Collections and Archives, CD 2654 v. 138b.
56. Evan Ziporyn, email to author, 24 December 2019.
57. Tim Page, "No Tinny Music by These Can-Bangers," *Newsday*, 13 April 1994.
58. Ziporyn, email to author, 24 December 2019.
59. Wolfe, "Embracing the Clash," 81.
60. Gordon, interview with K. Robert Schwarz, 22 March 1995.
61. Gordon, interview with K. Robert Schwarz, 22 March 1995.
62. Lang, interview with Ev Grimes.
63. See John Rockwell, "All for the Cause of New Music," *New York Times*, 8 March 1981.
64. Wolfe, *Arsenal of Democracy*, undated program note, https://juliawolfemusic.com/music/arsenal-of-democracy.
65. See Robert Adlington, "Organizing Labor: Composers, Performers, and 'the Renewal of Musical Practice' in the Netherlands, 1962–72," *Musical Quarterly* 90, no. 3–4 (Fall–Winter 2007): 539–577.
66. Quoted in Adlington, "Organizing Labor," 567.

67. Quoted in Wolfe, "Embracing the Clash," 126.
68. Lang, interview with author, 16 January 2016.
69. Amy Beal, *New Music, New Allies: American Experimental Music in West Germany from the Zero Hour to Reunification* (Berkeley and Los Angeles: University of California Press, 2006), 200.
70. Kerry O'Brien, "'Machine Fantasies into Human Events': Reich and Technology in the 1970s," in *Rethinking Reich*, ed. Sumanth Gopinath and Pwyll ap Siôn (Oxford: Oxford University Press, 2019), 329.
71. O'Brien, "Machine Fantasies," 338.
72. Moore, interview with K. Robert Schwarz, 23 March 1995.
73. Stewart, interview with author, 25 July 2018.
74. Moore, interview with K. Robert Schwarz, 23 March 1995.
75. Black, interview with author, 6 December 2015. Ziporyn, interview with author, 5 January 2016.
76. "Telsta Adelaide Festival '96," program booklet, 1–17 March 1996, Bang on a Can online archives.
77. "Bang on a Can Final Report: 1995–1996 Season," 10 October 1996, "jonathan," Bang on a Can digital archives.
78. Andrew Cotton, interview with author, 26 July 2018.
79. Ziporyn, interview with author, 5 January 2016.
80. Mark Stewart, interview with author, 25 July 2018.
81. Beiser, interview with author, 9 July 2018.
82. Kenny Savelson to Judith Hurtig, 22 November 1998, "Hancher note," Bang on a Can digital archives.
83. The memo's shorthand refers Lang's *cheating, lying, stealing*; Wolfe's *Believing* and *Lick*; Ziporyn's *Tsimindao Ghmerto*; and Gordon's *I Buried Paul*.
84. "All-Stars Mtg; June 28, 1999," 25 June 1999, "6/28 All Stars Mtg Agenda," Bang on a Can digital archives.
85. Savelson to Gordon, Lang, and Wolfe, 18 June 1998, "Immediate," Bang on a Can digital archives.
86. Gordon to Ayers, 22 January 1993.
87. Lang, interview with author, 1 August 2019.

Chapter 6

1. Allan Kozinn, "Bang on a Can and Lincoln Center Survive First Concert Unmarked," *New York Times*, 16 March 1994.
2. Kozinn, "Bang on a Can."
3. James Allen Smith, "Foundations as Cultural Actors," in *American Foundations: Roles and Contributions*, ed. Helmut K. Anheier and David C. Hammock (Washington, DC: Brookings Institution Press, 2010), 273.
4. See Stephen Stamas and Sharon Zane, *Lincoln Center: A Promise Realized, 1979–2006* (Hoboken, NJ: John Wiley & Sons, 2007), 52.
5. Nan Robertson, "Lincoln Center Goes Outdoors for a Spree," *New York Times*, 14 August 1981.

6. Charles Wuorinen, interview with Richard Douglas Burbank; in Richard Douglas Burbank, *Charles Wuorinen: A Bio-Bibliography* (Westport, CT: Greenwood Press, 1994), 18.
7. Rachel Vandagriff, "The History and Impact of the Fromm Music Foundation, 1952–1983" (PhD diss., University of California, Berkeley, 2014), 315–17.
8. Quoted in Stamas and Zane, *Lincoln Center*, 67.
9. Described in Bruce Weber, "A Transition in Definition for Serious Fun," *New York Times*, 13 July 1994. Seating capacities differ in different descriptions of Alice Tully: here, the *Times* identifies it as 1,100, whereas the Speculum Musicae grant report described in Chapter 3 describes it as 1,200, and Bang on a Can's own grant reporting describes it as 1,001.
10. Weber, "A Transition in Definition."
11. Heidi Waleson, "At Lincoln Center, A Time for Experimenting," *New York Times*, 5 July 1987.
12. Rockwell, "An Avant-Garde Series Is Set at Lincoln Center," *New York Times*, 20 May 1987.
13. Rockwell, "An Avant-Garde Series."
14. Stephen Holden, "A Second Festival of Serious Iconoclasm," *New York Times*, 4 May 1988.
15. Holden, "Serious Fun Events to Open with Opera on Vision via Music," *New York Times*, 14 July 1988.
16. Kozinn, "The Multiple Epiphanies of a New-Age Composer," *New York Times*, 28 July 1988.
17. Kozinn, "The Multiple Epiphanies."
18. Kozinn, "Chamber Society Seeks Lost Listeners," *New York Times*, 24 June 1992.
19. Jane Moss, interview with author, 23 September 2019.
20. Moss, interview with author, 23 September 2019.
21. Kozinn, "Lincoln Center Nominates Programming Director," *New York Times*, 16 September 1992.
22. Edward Rothstein, "Lincoln Center Programming: Rough Terrain," *New York Times*, 3 December 1992.
23. Leventhal quoted in Kozinn, "Lincoln Center Nominates Programming Director"; Moss quoted in Rothstein, "Lincoln Center Programming."
24. Samuel Lipman, "The Culture of Classical Music Today," *New Criterion*, September 1991; reprinted in Lipman, *Music and More: Essays, 1975–1991* (Evanston, IL: Northwestern University Press, 1992), 21.
25. Kozinn, "New Office at Lincoln Center to Oversee Programs," *New York Times*, 26 May 1993. See also Tim Page, "Coming to Lincoln Center," *Newsday*, 26 May 1993.
26. Moss, interview with author, 23 September 2019.
27. See Stamas and Zane, *Lincoln Center*, 55.
28. See Page, "Coming to Lincoln Center."
29. Lincoln Center Productions, Great Performers Press Release, October 1993, K. Robert Schwarz Papers, Queens College Department of Special Collections and Archives, Box 42.
30. Weber, "A Transition in Definition for Serious Fun."
31. See Stamas and Zane, *Lincoln Center*, 74.
32. Jane Moss, quoted in Susan Elliott, "Great Performers at Lincoln Center," *New York Magazine*, 18 October 1993.
33. Elliott, "Great Performers at Lincoln Center."
34. K. Robert Schwarz, "Upstarts from Downtown," *Stagebill*, April 1994, K. Robert Schwarz Papers, Queens College Department of Special Collections and Archives, Box 13.
35. Karen Sander, interview with author, 5 July 2019.

36. Julia Wolfe, "Embracing the Clash" (PhD diss., Princeton University, 2012), 62.
37. "Wolfe, "Embracing the Clash," 62.
38. Wolfe, interview with Libby Van Cleve, 27 July 2014, Yale Oral History of American Music: Major Figures in American Music, 255 h–m. In 2019, she clarified that it was actually "all of the work." Wolfe, email to author, 15 November 2019.
39. David Lang, interview with Libby Van Cleve, 29 April 1997, Yale Oral History of American Music: Major Figures in American Music, 185 j–m.
40. "93 Project Background," 22 April 1993, Bang on a Can digital archives.
41. Trudi Miller Rosenblum, "Bang on a Can Festival Goes Uptown," *Billboard Magazine*, 19 March 1994.
42. Lang, interview with Libby Van Cleve.
43. Lang, interview with Libby Van Cleve.
44. Associated Press, "Upscale Music Festival Considers Its Future," *The Intelligencer/The Record*, 20 March 1994, K. Robert Schwarz Papers, Queens College Department of Special Collections and Archives, Box 13.
45. Lang, interview with Libby Van Cleve.
46. K. Robert Schwarz, "Upstarts from Downtown," *Stagebill*, April 1994, K. Robert Schwarz Papers, Queens College Department of Special Collections and Archives, Box 13.
47. Wolfe, interview with Libby Van Cleve.
48. Wolfe, interview with Libby Van Cleve.
49. Bette Snapp, "Plan," 5 October 1995, Bang on a Can digital archives.
50. Michael Gordon to Matthew Glass, 17 March 1994, "Glass ltr," Bang on a Can digital archives; Karen Sander to Matthew Glass, 15 April 1994, "Marketing Fax," Bang on a Can digital archives.
51. Snapp, quoted in "Downtown Repercussions," *International Arts Manager*, October 1995, Bang on a Can online archives.
52. "Bang on a Can All-Stars to Perform Walter Reade Theater Concerts on March 13 and May 1," press release draft, Lincoln Center for the Performing Arts Archives, Marketing or Communication Workpaper—Bang on a Can—Pitches, Record Group 20, Location 06–01, Box ID 200157.
53. "Bang on a Can All-Stars to Perform."
54. Sander to John Kelly, 21 April 1995, Lincoln Center for the Performing Arts Archives, Marketing or Communication Workpaper—Bang on a Can—Pitches, Record Group 20, Location 06–01, Box ID 200157.
55. Sander to Michele Balm, 5 May 1994, "Umbrella Tables Fax," Bang on a Can digital archives.
56. Snapp, "NEA final report 95," 16 November 1995, Bang on a Can digital archives.
57. Schwarz, "BOAC Notes," K. Robert Schwarz Papers, Queens College Department of Special Collections and Archives, Box 13.
58. Wolfe, "Embracing the Clash," 101.
59. Kenny Savelson, interview with author, 31 July 2019.
60. Wolfe, interview with author, 28 February 2016.
61. Sander to Victoria Roth, CMA, 11 November 1995, "1995 clarif," Bang on a Can digital archives.
62. Michael Gordon to Jane Moss, 11 March 1994, "Moss Ltr Clarification," Bang on a Can digital archives.
63. Sander to Roth, 11 November 1995.

64. Rothstein, "Hunting for the Musical Thread," *New York Times*, 2 June 1993.
65. Kyle Gann, "Politics in a Can," *Village Voice*, 22 June 1993.
66. Snapp to Peter Goodman at Newsday, 22 February 1994, Lincoln Center for the Performing Arts Archives, Record Group 20, Location 27-25, Box ID 200399.
67. Michael Redman, "Lincoln Center Festival Looks, Longingly, into the Future," *The Star-Ledger*, 13 March 1994.
68. Kozinn, "Bang on a Can."
69. Gann, "Ain't Misbehavin'," *Village Voice*, 26 April 1994.
70. Kozinn, "Quirky Harmony: Maracas and Synthesizer," *New York Times*, 11 May 1994.
71. Gann, "When In Rome..." *Village Voice*, 24 May 1994.
72. Gann, "When In Rome."
73. Kozinn, "A New-Music Magazine's Struggle to Stay Alive," *New York Times*, 20 April 1992.
74. Lang, interview with Libby Van Cleve.
75. Lang, interview with Libby Van Cleve.
76. Wolfe, interview with Libby Van Cleve.
77. Ken Smith, "Return of the Big Bang," *Stagebill*, March 1995.
78. Justin Davidson, "In a Rut by Rote at Bang on a Can," *Newsday*, 23 May 1995.
79. Gann, "Ballad of Lincoln Center," *Village Voice*, 20 June 1995.
80. Gann, "Ballad of Lincoln Center."
81. Arlene Sierra, interview with author, 12 May 1997.
82. Smith, "The Big Bang," *Time Out New York*, 29 May–5 June 1996, 17.
83. James R. Oestreich, "Staying Hot on the Trail of Whatever Is New," *New York Times*, 2 June 1996.
84. Oestreich, "Staying Hot on the Trail."
85. Wolfe, interview with author, 28 February 2016.
86. Smith, "The Big Bang."
87. Lang, interview with Libby Van Cleve.
88. Wolfe, interview with K. Robert Schwarz, 6 January 1994. Quotation from transcript in K. Robert Schwarz Papers, Queens College Department of Special Collections and Archives, Box 13; this quotation was not included in the final article, Schwarz's "Upstarts from Downtown."
89. Schwarz, "Upstarts from Downtown."
90. Lang, interview with K. Robert Schwarz, 6 January 1994. Quotation from transcript in K. Robert Schwarz Papers, Queens College Department of Special Collections and Archives, Box 13; this quotation was not included in the final article, Schwarz's "Upstarts from Downtown."
91. Harvey Lichtenstein, "Voices from New York," *Daedalus* 115, no. 4 (Fall 1986): 149.
92. Lichtenstein, "Voices from New York."
93. Kozinn, "Festival Shows There Is a New-Music Audience," *New York Times*, 3 June 1991.
94. See Kozinn, "Festival Shows There Is a New-Music Audience"; and Final Report to the National Endowment for the Arts, 10 November 1991, "Final Report 1991-NEA," Bang on a Can digital archives.
95. Final Report to the National Endowment for the Arts, 8 November 1993, "Final Report 1992-NEA," Bang on a Can digital archives. The Kitchen also attracted over 2,500 attendees; see Final Report 1993, 14 December 1993, "final report 1993," Bang on a Can digital archives; this figure is also cited in Rosenblum, "Bang on a Can Festival Goes Uptown."

96. Philip Glass, quoted in Michael Blackwood, *New York Composers: Searching for a New Music* (Michael Blackwood Productions, 1997).
97. "attendance figures 1994," 23 May 1994, Bang on a Can digital archives. This document records Alice Tully's capacity as 1,001.
98. "attendance figures 1994."
99. The previously cited document places attendance at 838. "attendance figures 1994."
100. Final Report to the National Endowment for the Arts, 16 November 1995, "NEA Final Report 95," Bang on a Can digital archives; and Bang on a Can Final Report, 9 October 1996, "final report 95–96," Bang on a Can digital archives.
101. See Amy Virshup, "BAM Goes Boom," *New York Magazine*, 12 October 1987, 45.
102. "Notes from mtg," 16 March 1996, Bang on a Can digital archives.
103. Incomplete documentation of the survey is spread across four documents in one folder, "audience survey," in Bang on a Can's digital archives. No document records the total number of survey respondents, but the survey does record the number of responses to each question; I am approximating the total responses based on this information. These charts draw together information in all four documents to provide the clearest picture of both the questions and responses. See "raffle 2nd draft," 31 May 1996; "results stats," 19 June 1996; "stats for pm," 24 October 1996; and "stats in sum," 22 August 1996, in Bang on a Can digital archives.
104. "stats for pm," 24 October 1996, Bang on a Can digital archives.
105. Kozinn, "Bang on a Can Uptown Cultivates Crossover," 23 May 1995.
106. Smith, "Return of the Big Bang."
107. "What, When, and How? The Programming Shakeout," *Musical America*, 1995, http://www.musicalamerica.com/features/?fid=244&fyear=1995.
108. WCBS Evening News, 13 March 1995. Obtained from Lincoln Center Archives.
109. Snapp, quoted in "Downtown Repercussions."
110. See "raffle 2nd draft," Bang on a Can digital archives.
111. "1997 10th Anniversary Poster," Bang on a Can online archives.
112. "1995 Spit Orchestra Postcard," Bang on a Can online archives.
113. Davidson, "The Revolutionaries Won. Now What?" *Fanfare Magazine*, 4 May 1997, Bang on a Can online archives.
114. Quoted in Stamas and Zane, *Lincoln Center*, 55.
115. Moss, interview with author, 23 September 2019.
116. "Staff Meeting Notes 8/21/97," 22 November 1998, "Staff Mtg 8_21_97~1," Bang on a Can digital archives.
117. See folder "Festival 1998" in Bang on a Can digital archives.
118. "10-27 staff retreat notes," 2 November 1999, Bang on a Can digital archives.
119. "narratives," 16 June 2000, Bang on a Can digital archives.
120. Kenny Savelson to Thurston, Kim, Lee, and Steve, 21 January 2000, "1-21-00 to SY," Bang on a Can digital archives; Savelson to "John and the Tortoise Band," 21 January 2000, "1-21-00 to Tortoise," Bang on a Can digital archives.
121. Nadine Goellner to Joan Shigekawa, Lynn Szwaja, and Peter Helm at the Rockefeller Foundation, 30 March 2001, "Final Report Final," Bang on a Can digital archives. Gann remained skeptical, writing that "The thrill of continuous discovery is gone . . . Where BOAC used to define the newest currents around, it's beginning to look like the Museum of Great 1990s Music." Gann, "Dog Food for Justice," *Village Voice*, 2 January 2001.

122. Brooklyn Academy of Music, "2000 Next Wave Festival," *Stagebill*, December 2000, Bang on a Can online archives.

Chapter 7

1. Peter G. Davis, "Money Changes Everything," *New York Magazine*, 28 March 1994, 117.
2. Davis, "Money Changes Everything," 119.
3. Joseph Dalton, interview with author, 15 January 2018.
4. Adrian Gnam, quoted in Stephen Sinclair, "Recording American Composers," *American Music Center Newsletter* 25, no. 2 (Spring 1983): 54.
5. Michael Hicks, "Mass Marketing the American Avant-Garde, 1967–1971," *American Music* 35, no. 3 (Fall 2017): 281–302.
6. Quoted in Hicks, "Mass Marketing the American Avant-Garde," 288.
7. Hicks, "Mass Marketing the American Avant-Garde," 286.
8. John Rockwell, *All American Music: Composition in the Late Twentieth Century* (New York: Da Capo Press, 1997), 137.
9. Rockwell, *All American Music*, 138.
10. In practice, according to one former director, many recordings fell briefly out of print in the 1980s because the label did not have sufficient resources. Howard Stokar, interview with author, 11 June 2017. For the origins of New World, see Michael Uy, "The Recorded Anthology of American Music and the Rockefeller Foundation: Expertise, Deliberation, and Commemoration in the Bicentennial Celebrations," *American Music* 35, no. 1 (Spring 2017): 75–93.
11. Bob Davis, "The Lovely Music Series: New Music, New Label," *Synapse* 3, no. 1 (January/February 1979): 42.
12. Foster Reed, quoted in Tim Page, "New Albion: New Label for New Music," *New York Times*, 8 February 1987.
13. See Amy Beal, *Carla Bley* (Urbana: University of Illinois Press, 2011), 51–56.
14. Advertisement for New Music Distribution Service Catalog, "New Music America '81 Festival," San Francisco, 1981. Program digitized by Michael Galbreth and available at https://www.michaelgalbreth.com/new-music-america.
15. Page, "They Sell the Small Record Labels," *New York Times*, 14 March 1982.
16. Kozinn, "New-Music Distributor Is Closing," *New York Times*, 12 June 1990.
17. This institutional approach was also consistent with, as David Grubbs has documented, an ideological skepticism toward the recorded medium among experimental musicians; see David Grubbs, *Records Ruin the Landscape* (Durham, NC: Duke University Press, 2014).
18. Allan Kozinn, "Composers Recordings, Inc.—Surprising Survivor," *High Fidelity*, September 1979, 83.
19. Keith Potter, *Four Musical Minimalists: La Monte Young, Terry Riley, Steve Reich, Philip Glass* (Cambridge: Cambridge University Press, 2000), 209.
20. Robert Fink, *Repeating Ourselves: American Minimal Music as Cultural Practice* (Berkeley and Los Angeles: University of California Press, 2005), 26.
21. Robert Hurwitz, essay in liner notes to Steve Reich, *Works 1965–1995*, Nonesuch 79451-2, 1997. Also quoted in Potter, *Four Musical Minimalists*, 210.
22. Tim Rutherford-Johnson, *Music after the Fall: Modern Composition and Culture since 1989* (Berkeley and Los Angeles: University of California Press, 2017), 31.

23. I am grateful to Dale Chapman for sharing with me an unpublished paper discussing how Warner's structural shifts affected Sterne's ouster. Dale Chapman, "Private Equity Blues: Warner Music Group, Nonesuch, and Jazz in the Era of Financialization," 2019.
24. Quoted in Anthony Tommasini, "Teresa Sterne, Musical Prodigy, Sacrificed Her Own Art So Others Might Be Heard," *New York Times*, 31 July 2000.
25. Charles Wuorinen, interview with author, 11 June 2017; Morton Subotnick, interview with author, 28 June 2017; Michael Hill, "The Nonesuch Story," http://www.nonesuch.com/about.
26. Jon Pareles, "Recordings; Nonesuch Seeks to Break Down Musical Barriers," *New York Times*, 9 November 1986.
27. Carol Silverman, "Move Over Madonna: Gender, Representation, and the 'Mystery' of Bulgarian Voices," in *Over the Wall/After the Fall*, ed. Sibelan Forrester, Magdalena J. Zaborowska, and Elena Gapova (Bloomington: Indiana University Press, 2004).
28. Difficulties with CBS are recounted in Allan Kozinn, "Glass's *Satyagraha* (1986)," in *Writings on Glass: Essays, Interviews, Criticism*, ed. Richard Kostelanetz (Berkeley and Los Angeles: University of California Press, 1997), 181.
29. "Masterworks Launches Glass LP Promo," *Billboard*, 6 March 1982; and Alan Penchansky, "Glass Gets 'Walkman Mix,'" *Billboard*, 27 March 1982, 83.
30. Kozinn, "Nonesuch Makes a Deal With Glass That Looks Ahead and Into the Past," *New York Times*, 14 September 1993.
31. Gene Santoro, "New Music America," in *Tower Records Pulse!: The New Music America Supplement* (1989): 32.
32. Quoted in Santoro, "New Music America," 32.
33. Santoro, "New Music America," 32.
34. Dalton, interview with author, 15 January 2018.
35. Kozinn, "New-Music Label Loses a Champion; After 10 Years at Composers' Haven, The Director Decides to Resign," *New York Times*, 29 May 2000.
36. David Lang, interview with author, 19 January 2016.
37. "CRI Communiqué," 1 April 1992, Composers Recordings, Inc. Records, Music Division, New York Public Library for the Performing Arts, Box 12, Folder 12.
38. Kozinn, "New-Music Label Loses a Champion."
39. "Bang on a Can, Live Volume 1," press materials, K. Robert Schwarz Papers, Queens College Department of Special Collections and Archives, Box 13.
40. Kyle Gann, "Notes," printed in *Bang on a Can Live Volume 1*, Composers Recordings, Inc., 1992, NWCR628.
41. K. Robert Schwarz, "Uptown, Downtown: Who Can Tell?" *New York Times*, 10 May 1992.
42. Davis, "Money Changes Everything," 119.
43. Trudi Miller Rosenblum, "Bang on a Can Festival Goes Uptown," *Billboard Magazine*, 19 March 1994.
44. Dalton, interview with author, 15 January 2018.
45. Kozinn, "New-Music Label Loses a Champion."
46. Robert Hurwitz, interview with author, 25 May 2017.
47. Luke B. Howard, "Motherhood, *Billboard*, and the Holocaust: Perceptions and Receptions of Górecki's Symphony No. 3," *Musical Quarterly* 82, no. 1 (March 1998): 144.
48. Hurwitz, interview with author, 25 May 2017.

49. Steve Dollar, "Moods for Moderns," *The Atlanta Journal-Constitution*, 6 March 1994.
50. Rutherford-Johnson, *Music after the Fall*, 33. See also David Dies, "Defining 'Spiritual Minimalism,'" in *The Ashgate Research Companion to Minimalist and Postminimalist Music*, ed. Keith Potter, Kyle Gann, and Pwyll ap Siôn (London: Routledge, 2013), 315–336. Górecki's holy minimalism also fit neatly into Nonesuch's previous hits like *Le Mystère des Voix Bulgaires*, which, as Carol Silverman has described, the label marketed in such a way that downplayed the Bulgarian folk music's ethnic, peasant roots and instead "deliberately exoticized the music as ethereal and ancient" to appeal to a New Age demographic. Silverman, "Move Over Madonna," 217.
51. Norman Lebrecht, "Miracle Man of Music," *Daily Telegraph*, 12 February 1993, 15.
52. Keith Negus, *Music Genres and Corporate Cultures* (New York: Routledge, 2013), 49–50.
53. Chapman, *The Jazz Bubble: Neoclassical Jazz in Neoliberal Culture* (Berkeley and Los Angeles: University of California Press, 2018), 109.
54. Sedgwick Clark, "Boom or Bust," *Opera News*, August 1992.
55. Steven Swartz, interview with author, 29 August 2019. By summer 1990, when the distributor folded, it had amassed a deficit of nearly $160,000, also due to failure to pay New York State taxes. Kozinn, "New-Music Distributor Is Closing."
56. See Lebrecht, *The Life and Death of Classical Music* (New York: Anchor Books, 2007).
57. Clark, "Boom or Bust."
58. Is Horowitz, "Classical: Keeping Score," *Billboard*, 23 August 1986.
59. Timothy Taylor, *Music and Capitalism* (Chicago: University of Chicago Press, 2015), 59.
60. Horowitz, "Success of Górecki Symphony Leaves Labels Reevaluating Repertoire," *Billboard*, 25 December 1993.
61. Bambarger, "New Albion's New Age Spirit Fits Well At Harmonia Mundi," *Billboard*, 23 September 1995, 13.
62. Page, "A Crossroad for the Classics," *Newsday*, 10 January 1988.
63. Page wrote of the Górecki that he was "convinced that this incredibly moving work, a plaintive and affecting mix of Wagner, Messiaen, minimalism and folk song, has the makings of a warhorse and that intelligent marketing would put it across to a large audience." Page to Guenter Henssler, 2 January 1992, "BMG—First Letter to Guenter," obtained from Tim Page.
64. Page to Guenter Henssler, 2 January 1992.
65. Page, interview with author, 11 June 2017.
66. Page, interview with author, 11 June 2017.
67. Page, quoted in Scott Duncan, "Serious Sounds, in Fishnet: It Looks Like Pop, It Acts Like Pop but It's Classical Music," *Chicago Tribune*, 21 August 1994.
68. Tim Page, "BMG Catalyst in Retrospect," obtained from Tim Page. For the printed article, see Page, "Catalyst Means Change," *Classical Pulse!* (April 1996): 10–11.
69. Duncan, "Serious Sounds, in Fishnet."
70. Page, "BMG Catalyst in Retrospect."
71. Tommasini, "'Outing' Some 'In' Composers," *New York Times*, 6 August 1995.
72. Page, "BMG Catalyst in Retrospect." Unlike the previous quotes from the draft, which do not appear in the published article, this passage is also printed as the concluding words to the *Classical Pulse!* article.
73. Harry, interview with author, 8 June 2017.
74. Lang, interview with author, 19 January 2016.

75. Harry, interview with author, 8 June 2017.
76. "8. Recording FY95," Bang on a Can digital archives.
77. Lebrecht, *The Life and Death of Classical Music*.
78. Harry, interview with author, 8 June 2017.
79. Irv Lichtman, "Gelb Heads New Global Team at Sony Classical," *Billboard*, 18 March 1995.
80. Peter Gelb, interview with author, 24 May 2017.
81. Heidi Waleson, "Classical Continues Chorus of Success," *Billboard*, 9 September 1995.
82. Harry, interview with author, 8 June 2017.
83. Dalton, interview with author, 15 January 2018.
84. Louis Andriessen, liner notes to Bang on a Can, *Industry*, Sony Classical 66483, 1995.
85. Lang, Michael Gordon, and Julia Wolfe, liner notes to Bang on a Can, *Industry*, Sony Classical 66483, 1995. Quoted in Wolfe, "Embracing the Clash" (PhD diss., Princeton University, 2012), 163 and 164.
86. Davis, "Educating Violetta," *New York Magazine*, 3 April 1995, 71.
87. Heidi Waleson, "Classical: Keeping Score," *Billboard*, 20 May 1995.
88. Schwarz, "Bang on a Can Issues a Manifesto," *New York Times*, 21 May 1995.
89. Gordon, interview with K. Robert Schwarz, 22 March 1995, K. Robert Schwarz Papers, Queens College Department of Special Collections and Archives, CD 2654 v. 138a.
90. Evan Ziporyn, interview with author, 5 January 2016.
91. Grace Row, interview with author, 20 August 2019.
92. Heidi Waleson, "Classical Continues Chorus of Success," *Billboard*, 9 September 1995.
93. The recording's total expense was $100,530, a hefty budget for a new-music album—along with the NEA support, $22,000 of funding came from foundations, and Sony supplied the rest. Bang on a Can, "Final Descriptive Report," 28 January 1997, "final report recording 96," Bang on a Can digital archives.
94. Bang on a Can, "Final Descriptive Report."
95. Gelb, interview with author, 24 May 2017.
96. Lang, interview with author, 1 August 2019.
97. Harry, interview with author, 8 June 2017.
98. Gelb, "New Classical Music Can Expand Audience," *Billboard*, 21 September 1996.
99. Gelb, interview with author, 24 May 2017.
100. Bambarger, "Really Classic Rock," *Billboard*, 4 September 1999, 43.
101. See Negus, *Music Genres and Corporate Cultures*, 42 and 43.
102. Bambarger, "PolyGram Restructures Its Philips, Verve Groups," *Billboard*, 5 April 1997, 84.
103. Bambarger, "Really Classic Rock," 43.
104. Cecilia Sun offers a potent critique of Bang's transformation of Eno from ambient experimentalism into virtuoso live showcase; see Cecilia Sun, "Resisting the Airport: Bang on a Can Performs Brian Eno," *Musicology Australia* 29, no. 1 (2007): 135–59.
105. Josef Woodward, "Ready for Takeoff," *Los Angeles Times*, 18 October 1998.
106. "Bang on a Can: Music for Airports," one-sheet promotional materials, February 1998, Bang on a Can online archives.
107. Point Music, promotional video, February 1998, Bang on a Can online archives.
108. Brian Eno to "All Of You," 13 February 1998, fax, Bang on a Can online archives.
109. Nigel Williamson, "Global Music Impulse: U.K.," *Billboard*, 16 May 1998, 51.
110. "point mtg 5.15," 14 May 1998, Bang on a Can digital archives.

111. Woodward, "Ready for Takeoff."
112. Kyle Gann, "Framing Wallpaper," *Village Voice*, 24 March 1998, 126–27.
113. Jon Pareles, "Music Review; Calm and Exoticism in the Hovering Clouds," *New York Times*, 9 March 1998.
114. For sales figures, see Woodward, "A Logical Step in an Offbeat Journey," *Los Angeles Times*, 4 March 2001, and Frederick Kaimann, "Backbeat," *Chamber Music* 18, no. 2 (April 2001).
115. "Point Projects," 22 November 1998, Bang on a Can digital archives.
116. "record evidence," 27 October 1998, Bang on a Can digital archives. The author of these documents was likely Kenny Savelson, who was handling most of the back-and-forth with Point.
117. Unsigned letter to Rory Johnson, 4 November 1998, "Y2K," Bang on a Can digital archives.
118. Steve Smith, "Classical: Keeping Score," *Billboard*, 17 March 2001.
119. Kozinn, "The Year in Classical Music: The Critics' Choices; A Bridge to Rock; Fresh Beethoven," *New York Times*, 23 December 2001.
120. Cantaloupe Music is an independent LLC; it maintains an agreement with Bang on a Can for some shared administrative services.
121. Kenny Savelson, interview with author, 8 December 2015.
122. Bambarger, "P'Gram Divides Classical Duties," *Billboard*, 11 July 1998, 83.
123. Bambarger, "Classical: Keeping Score," *Billboard*, 11 July 1998, 37; Robert Baird, "Aural Robert," *Stereophile* 21 (September 1998), 161.
124. Dominic Pride, "Universal Classics and Jazz Integrating Philips, Decca," *Billboard*, 10 July 1999, 91.
125. "10-27 staff retreat notes," 2 November 1999, Bang on a Can digital archives.
126. See Gann, "Can't Help But CRI," *Village Voice*, 22–28 January 2003, 102.
127. Kaimann, "Backbeat."
128. Gordon, quoted in Smith, "Classical: Keeping Score."
129. Smith, "Classical: Keeping Score."
130. Gordon, interview with Libby Van Cleve, 29 August 1997, Yale Oral History of American Music: Major Figures in American Music, 254 a–f.
131. Gelb, interview with author, 24 May 2017.

Epilogue

1. Aaron Copland, quoted in *Aaron Copland: A Reader Selected Writings 1923–1972*, ed. Richard Kostelanetz (New York: Routledge, 2004), xvi.
2. Julia Wolfe, interview with Libby Van Cleve, 27 July 2014, Yale Oral History of American Music: Major Figures in American Music, 255 h–m.
3. Lang's "Simple Song #3," part of his score for the Paolo Sorrentino film *Youth*, was nominated for Best Original Song in 2016.
4. See John Halle, "Occupying New Music: Guest Blog," *PostClassic* blog, 13 February 2012, https://www.artsjournal.com/postclassic/2012/02/occupying-new-music-guest-blog.html. In 2014, the World Financial Center was renamed Brookfield Place.
5. Of the original members, Maya Beiser, Evan Ziporyn, Steven Schick, and Lisa Moore have left the group; as of August 2020, the line-up is Mark Stewart (guitars), Robert

Black (bass), Vicky Chow (piano), David Cossin (percussion), Arlen Hlusko (cello), Ken Thomson (clarinets), and Andrew Cotton (sound).

6. Bang on a Can's total revenue is actually higher—in 2017, for example, it was $2.13 million—but this includes funding for Found Sound Nation/OneBeat, a social-engagement initiative that has a budget of several hundred thousand dollars but is otherwise curatorially distinct from the main activities of the organization overseen by Gordon, Lang, and Wolfe.
7. Thanks to Vanessa Reed of New Music USA for providing this information. Meet the Composer's annual giving was about $2.5 million in 1990; when adjusted for inflation, it is the equivalent of $4.9 million in 2019.
8. "Proposal to the Robert Sterling Clark Foundation From Bang on a Can," 6 November 2001, "Clark Banglewood Proposal," Bang on a Can digital archives.
9. Judd Greenstein, "Banging," 29 July 2008, http://www.juddgreenstein.com/banging/; and Greenstein, interview with author, 26 April 2015.
10. See William Robin, "A Scene without a Name: Indie Classical and American New Music in the Twenty-First Century" (PhD diss., University of North Carolina, Chapel Hill, 2016); and Robin, "The Rise and Fall of 'Indie Classical': Tracing a Controversial Term in Twenty-First Century New Music," *Journal of the Society for American Music* 12 (2018): 55–88.
11. See, for example, Greenstein, "There Have Never Been Walls," *MUSO Magazine*, February 2008. Quoted in Robin, "A Scene without a Name," 15.
12. Wolfe, interview with Libby Van Cleve.
13. Zachary Woolfe, "Los Angeles Has America's Most Important Orchestra. Period," *New York Times*, 18 April 2017.
14. Quoted in John von Rhein, "John Adams Reflects What It Means to Compose Music in 'a Small Cultural Arena,'" *Chicago Tribune*, 18 July 2017.
15. For a critique of this entrepreneurship rhetoric, see Andrea Moore, "Neoliberalism and the Musical Entrepreneur," *Journal of the Society for American Music* 10, no. 1 (February 2016): 33–53.
16. Wolfe, interview with author, 28 February 2016; and Michael Gordon, interview with author, 21 July 2016.
17. For a discussion of branding in twenty-first century new music, see Robin, "Balance Problems: Neoliberalism and New Music in the American University and Ensemble," *Journal of the American Musicological Society* 71, no. 3 (Fall 2018): 749–94.
18. David Lang, interview with author, 1 August 2019.
19. John Duffy, "Creating a Marketplace for Today's Composers," April 1981, Meet the Composer archive, New Music USA, Box 30.

References

Interviews

Artman, Deborah. 14 June 2019.
Beiser, Maya. 9 July 2018.
Black, Robert. 6 December 2015.
Bresnick, Martin. 18 December 2015.
Brody, Martin. 20 June 2017.
Brooks, Jeffrey. 8 June 2017.
Cotton, Andrew. 26 July 2018.
Dalton, Joseph. 15 January 2017.
Daugherty, Michael. 25 November 2015.
Deak, Jon. 2 June 2017.
Dresher, Paul. 21 October 2016.
Froom, David. 4 April 2017.
Gelb, Peter. 24 May 2017.
Gordon, Michael. 21 January 2016.
Gordon, Michael and Julia Wolfe (joint interview). 28 July 2018.
Gosfield, Annie. 22 October 2019.
Greenstein, Judd. 26 April 2015.
Harry, Martyn. 8 June 2017.
Hurwitz, Robert. 25 May 2017.
King, John. 2 December 2015.
Kotik, Petr. 31 May 2017.
Kozinn, Allan. 11 November 2014.
Kuhn, Ted. 24 January 2016.
Lang, David. 19 January 2016.
Lang, David. 1 August 2019.
Larsen, Libby. 8 June 2017.
Leach, Mary Jane. 24 June 2017.
León, Tania. 2 June 2017.
Lindroth, Scott. 27 August 2014.
Lubman, Brad. 31 July 2019.
Mazzoli, Missy. 10 November 2015.
Mellits, Marc. 23 June 2017.
Moore, Lisa. 18 December 2015.
Morgan, Gayle. 22 December 2015.
Moss, Jane. 23 September 2019.
Niblock, Phill. 27 May 2017.
Page, Tim. 11 June 2017.
Peet, Shannon. 13 June 2018.
Plonsey, Dan. 28 May 2017.
Reynolds, Todd. 25 January 2017.

Richard, Frances. 27 June 2017.
Rockwell, John. 5 March 2015.
Roe, Grace. 20 August 2019.
Ross, Alex. 16 December 2015.
Ryan, Norman. 2 November 2015.
Sander, Karen. 5 June 2019.
Savelson, Kenny. 8 December 2015.
Savelson, Kenny. 31 July 2019.
Schaefer, John. 2 December 2015.
Schick, Steven. 21 December 2015.
Sierra, Arlene. 12 May 2017.
Stewart, Mark. 25 July 2018.
Stokar, Howard. 11 June 2017.
Stone, Carl. 18 March 2019.
Subotnick, Morton. 28 June 2017.
Swartz, Steven. 29 August 2019.
Swed, Mark. 29 October 2015.
Tenzer, Michael. 8 June 2017.
Thomas, Tim. 8 December 2015.
Thomson, Ken. 4 August 2019.
Torke, Michael. 13 June 2017.
Tower, Joan. 11 October 2018.
Vierk, Lois V. 10 December 2015.
Wolfe, Julia. 28 February 2016.
Wuorinen, Charles. 11 June 2017.
Z, Pamela. 31 July 2019.
Ziporyn, Evan. 5 January 2016.

Archival Collections

Bang on a Can digital archives, private institutional collection. All quotations printed with permission from Bang on a Can.
Bang on a Can Festival: Clippings, New York Public Library for the Performing Arts.
Bang on a Can online archives, accessible publicly at Canland.org.
Composers' Forum Inc. Records, Music Division, New York Public Library for the Performing Arts.
Composers Recordings, Inc. Records, Music Division, New York Public Library for the Performing Arts.
EAR Magazine Records, Music Division, New York Public Library for the Performing Arts.
Exit Art Archive, Fales Library and Special Collections, New York University Libraries.
Jacob Druckman Papers, Music Division, New York Public Library for the Performing Arts.
John Cage Collection, Northwestern University.
K. Robert Schwarz Papers, Queens College Department of Special Collections and Archives.
Lincoln Center Archives.
Major Figures in American Music series, Yale Oral History of American Music.
Meet the Composer archives, New Music USA, private institutional collection.
New York Philharmonic Archives and New York Philharmonic Leon Levy Digital Archives.
New York State Council on the Arts archives, Grant Application Files, New York State Archives.
Pauline Oliveros Papers, Music Division, New York Public Library for the Performing Arts.
SEM Ensemble archives, private institutional collection.
WNYC archives.

Books and Articles

Adams, John. *Hallelujah Junction*. New York: Farrar, Straus & Giroux, 2008.
Adlington, Robert, ed. *Red Strains: Music and Communism Outside the Communist Bloc*. Oxford: Oxford University Press, 2013.
Adlington, Robert, ed. *Sound Commitments: Avant-Garde Music and the Sixties*. Oxford: Oxford University Press, 2009.
Adlington, Robert. *Composing Dissent: Avant-Garde Music in 1960s Amsterdam*. Oxford: Oxford University Press, 2013.
Adlington, Robert. "Organizing Labor: Composers, Performers, and 'the Renewal of Musical Practice' in the Netherlands, 1962–72." *Musical Quarterly* 90, nos. 3–4 (Fall–Winter 2007): 539–77.
Alexander, Jane. *Command Performance: An Actress in the Theater of Politics*. New York: Da Capo Press, 2000.
Alonso-Minutti, Ana R., Eduardo Herrera, and Alejandro L. Madrid, eds. *Experimentalisms in Practice: Music Perspectives from Latin America*. Oxford: Oxford University Press, 2018.
Anheier, Helmut K., and David C. Hammock, eds. *American Foundations: Roles and Contributions*. Washington, DC: Brookings Institution Press, 2010.
Austin, Larry and Douglas Kahn, eds. *Source: Music of the Avant-Garde, 1966–1973*. Berkeley and Los Angeles: University of California Press, 2011.
Baron, Fraser. "A Mission Renewed: The Survival of the National Endowment for the Arts, 1981–1983." *Journal of Cultural Economics* 11, no. 1 (June 1987): 22–75.
Baumol, William J. and William G. Bowen. *Performing Arts: The Economic Dilemma*. New York: Twentieth Century Fund, 1966.
Beal, Amy. *Carla Bley*. Urbana: University of Illinois Press, 2011.
Beal, Amy. *New Music, New Allies: American Experimental Music in West Germany from the Zero Hour to Reunification*. Berkeley and Los Angeles: University of California Press, 2006.
Becker, Howard. *Art Worlds*. Berkeley and Los Angeles: University of California Press, 2008.
Bernstein, David W., ed. *The San Francisco Tape Music Center: 1960s Counterculture and the Avant-Garde*. Berkeley and Los Angeles: University of California Press, 2008.
Binkiewicz, Donna M. *Federalizing the Muse*. Chapel Hill: University of North Carolina Press, 2005.
Blake, David. "Musicological Omnivory in the Neoliberal University." *Journal of Musicology* 34, no. 3 (Summer 2017): 319–53.
Bolton, Richard, ed. *Culture Wars: Documents from the Recent Controversies in the Arts*. New York: New Press, 1992.
Born, Georgina. *Rationalizing Culture: IRCAM, Boulez, and the Institutionalization of the Musical Avant-Garde*. Berkeley and Los Angeles: University of California Press, 1995.
Born, Georgina. "The Social and the Aesthetic: For a Post-Bourdieuian Theory of Cultural Production." *Cultural Sociology* 42, no. 2 (2010): 1–38.
Bourdieu, Pierre. *The Field of Cultural Production: Essays on Art and Literature*. New York: Columbia University Press, 1993.
Bresnick, Martin. "Thoughts About Teaching Composition, or Self-Portrait as Hamlet and Polonius and Whitman Is Also There." *Contemporary Music Review* 31, no. 4 (2012): 269–76.
Bresnick, Martin. "We, Rhinoceros." *New Observations* 86 (November/December 1991): 3–5.
Brodsky, Seth. *From 1989, or European Music and the Modernist Unconscious*. Berkeley and Los Angeles: University of California Press, 2017.
Brody, Martin. "'Music for the Masses': Milton Babbitt's Cold War Music Theory." *Musical Quarterly* 77, no. 2 (Summer 1993): 161–92.
Brown, Wendy. *Undoing the Demos: Neoliberalism's Stealth Revolution*. Cambridge, MA: MIT University Press, 2015.

Broyles, Michael. *Mavericks and Other Traditions in American Music*. New Haven, CT: Yale University Press, 2004.
Burbank, Richard Douglas. *Charles Wuorinen: A Bio-Bibliography*. Westport, CT: Greenwood Press, 1994.
Cage, John. *A Year from Monday: New Lectures and Writings*. Middletown, CT: Wesleyan University Press, 1969.
Cage, John. *Empty Words: Writings '73–'78*. Middletown, CT: Wesleyan University Press, 1979.
Cardew, Cornelius. *Stockhausen Serves Imperialism*. UbuClassics, 2004.
Chapman, Dale. *The Jazz Bubble: Neoclassical Jazz in Neoliberal Culture*. Berkeley and Los Angeles: University of California Press, 2018.
Crist, Elizabeth B. *Music for the Common Man: Aaron Copland during the Depression and War*. Oxford: Oxford University Press, 2005.
Deaver, Susan. "The Group for Contemporary Music, 1962–1992." DMA diss., Manhattan School of Music, 1993.
DeLapp, Jennifer. "Copland in the Fifties: Music and Ideology in the McCarthy Era." PhD diss., University of Michigan, 2006.
DeNora, Tia. "After Adorno." In *The Routledge Reader on the Sociology of Music*, edited by John Shepherd and Kyle Devine, 341–48. New York: Routledge, 2015.
DiMaggio, Paul. "Decentralization of Arts Funding from the Federal Government to the States." In *Public Money and the Muse: Essays on Government Funding for the Arts*, edited by Stephen Benedict, 216–52. New York: W.W. Norton, 1991.
Drott, Eric. "Spectralism, Politics, and the Post-Industrial Imagination." In *The Modernist Legacy: Essays on New Music*, edited by Björn Heile, 36–60. Aldershot, UK: Ashgate, 2009.
Drott, Eric. "The End(s) of Genre." *Journal of Music Theory* 57, no. 1 (2013): 1–45.
Edwards, Allen. *Flawed Words and Stubborn Sounds: A Conversation with Elliott Carter*. New York: W.W. Norton, 1971.
Feldman, Morton. *Give My Regards to Eighth Street: Collected Writings of Morton Feldman*. Cambridge, MA: Exact Change, 2000.
Fink, Robert. "(Post-)minimalisms 1970–2000: The Search for a New Mainstream." In *The Cambridge History of Twentieth-Century Music*, edited by Nicholas Cook, 539–56. Cambridge: Cambridge University Press, 2004.
Fink, Robert. *Repeating Ourselves: American Minimal Music as Cultural Practice*. Berkeley and Los Angeles: University of California Press, 2005.
Gagne, Cole, and Tracy Caras, *Soundpieces: Interviews with American Composers*. Metuchen, NJ: Scarecrow Press, 1982.
Gann, Kyle. *Music Downtown: Writings from the Village Voice*. Berkeley and Los Angeles: University of California Press, 2006.
Gendron, Bernard. "The Downtown Music Scene." In *The Downtown Book: The New York Art Scene, 1974–1984*, edited by Marvin J. Taylor, 41–63. Princeton, NJ: Princeton University Press, 2006.
Gendron, Bernard. *Between Montmatre and the Mudd Club: Popular Music and the Avant-Garde*. Chicago: University of Chicago Press, 2002.
Gilmore, Samuel. "Collaboration and Convention: A Comparison of Repertory, Academic, and Avant Garde Concert Worlds." PhD diss., Northwestern University, 1984.
Gilmore, Samuel. "Minorities and Distributional Equity at the National Endowment for the Arts." *Journal of Arts Management, Law, and Society* 23, no. 2 (Summer 1993): 137–73.
Gilmore, Samuel. "Schools of Activity and Innovation." *The Sociological Quarterly* 29, no. 2 (Summer 1988): 203–19.
Gingold, Diane J. *Business and the Arts: How They Meet the Challenge*. Washington, DC: National Endowment for the Arts, 1984.

Gingrich, Newt, Richard K. Armey, Ed Gillespie, and Bob Schellhas. *Contract with America: The Bold Plan by Rep. Newt Gingrich, Rep. Dick Armey and the House Republicans to Change the Nation.* New York: Times Books, 1994.
Girard, Aaron. "Music Theory in the American Academy." PhD diss., Harvard University, 2007.
Gloag, Kenneth. *Postmodernism in Music.* Cambridge: Cambridge University Press, 2012.
Gopinath, Sumanth, and Pwyll ap Siôn, eds. *Rethinking Reich.* Oxford: Oxford University Press, 2019.
Gordon, Theodore Barker. "Bay Area Experimentalism: Music and Technology in the Long 1960s." PhD diss., University of Chicago, 2018.
Grimshaw, Jeremy. *Draw a Straight Line and Follow It: The Music and Mysticism of La Monte Young.* Oxford: Oxford University Press, 2012.
Grimshaw, Jeremy. "High, 'Low,' and Plastic Arts: Philip Glass and the Symphony in the Age of Postproduction." *Musical Quarterly* 86, no. 3 (Fall 2002): 472–507.
Grubbs, David. *Records Ruin the Landscape.* Durham, NC: Duke University Press, 2014.
Hall, Stuart. "Conclusion: The Multi-cultural Question." In *Un/settled Multiculturalisms: Diasporas, Entanglements, Transruptions,* edited by Barnor Hesse, 209–41. London: Zed Books, 2000.
Harker, Brian. "Milton Babbitt Encounters Academia (And Vice Versa)." *American Music* 26, no. 3 (Fall 2008): 336–77.
Hartman, Andrew. *A War for the Soul of America: A History of the Culture Wars.* Chicago: University of Chicago Press, 2015.
Harvey, David. *A Brief History of Neoliberalism.* New York: Oxford University Press, 2005.
Herrera, Eduardo. "The Rockefeller Foundation and Latin American Music in the 1960s: The Creation of Indiana University's LAMC and Di Tella Institute's CLAEM." *American Music* 35, no. 1 (Spring 2017): 51–74.
Hicks, Michael. "Mass Marketing the American Avant-Garde, 1967–1971." *American Music* 35, no. 3 (Fall 2017): 281–302.
Howard, Luke B. "Motherhood, *Billboard,* and the Holocaust: Perceptions and Receptions of Górecki's Symphony No. 3." *Musical Quarterly* 82, no. 1 (March 1998): 131–59.
Iossa, Lauren, John Duffy, and Frances Richard. *Commissioning Music.* New York: Meet the Composer, 1984.
Iossa, Lauren and Ruth Dreier. *Composers in the Marketplace: How to Earn a Living Writing Music.* New York: Meet the Composer, 1989.
Jakelski, Lisa. *Making New Music in Cold War Poland: The Warsaw Autumn Festival, 1956–1968.* Berkeley and Los Angeles: University of California Press, 2017.
Joseph, Branden. *Beyond the Dream Syndicate: Tony Conrad and the Arts After Cage.* New York: Zone Books, 2011.
Joyce, Michael S. "The National Endowments for the Humanities and the Arts." In *Mandate for Leadership,* edited by Charles L. Heatherly, 1039–56. Washington, DC: Heritage Foundation, 1981.
Kimbus, Thomas Peter. "Surviving the Storm: How the National Endowment for the Arts Restructured Itself to Serve a New Constituency." *Journal of Arts Management, Law, and Society* 27, no. 2 (Summer 1997): 139–58.
Kostelanetz, Richard, ed. *Aaron Copland: A Reader Selected Writings 1923–1972.* New York: Routledge, 2004.
Kramer, Hilton, ed. *The New Criterion Reader: The First Five Years.* New York: Simon & Schuster, 1988.
Latour, Bruno. *The Pasteurization of France.* Trans. Alan Sheridan and John Law. Cambridge, MA: Harvard University Press, 1988.
Latour, Bruno. *Reassembling the Social: An Introduction to Actor-Network-Theory.* Oxford and New York: Oxford University Press, 2005.

Law, John and John Hassard, eds. *Actor Network Theory and After*. Oxford: Wiley Blackwell, 1999.
Lebrecht, Norman. *The Life and Death of Classical Music*. New York: Anchor Books, 2007.
Lewis, George E. *A Power Stronger Than Itself: The AACM and American Experimental Music*. Chicago: University of Chicago Press, 2008.
Lewis, George E. "Experimental Music in Black and White: The AACM in New York, 1970–1985." *Current Musicology* 71–73 (2002): 100–57.
Lipman, Samuel. *Arguing for Music, Arguing for Culture*. Boston: D.R. Goldine, 1990.
Lipman, Samuel. *Music and More: Essays, 1975–1991*. Evanston, IL: Northwestern University Press, 1992.
Lipman, Samuel. *The House of Music: Art in an Era of Institutions*. Boston: D.R. Godine, 1984.
Lochhead, Judy and Joseph Auner, eds. *Postmodern Music/Postmodern Thought*. New York: Routledge, 2002.
Margolis, Richard J. "Moving America Right." *Foundation News* 24, no. 7–8 (1983): 44–48.
McClary, Susan. "Terminal Prestige: The Case of Avant-Garde Music Composition." *Cultural Critique* no. 12 (Spring 1989): 57–81.
McCutchan, Ann. *The Muse that Sings: Composers Speak about the Creative Process*. Oxford: Oxford University Press, 1999.
Metcalf, Sasha. "Funding 'Opera for the 80s and Beyond': The Role of Impresarios in Creating a New American Repertoire." *American Music* 35, no. 1 (Spring 2017): 7–28.
Metzer, David Joel. *Musical Modernism at the Turn of the Twenty-First Century*. Cambridge and New York: Cambridge University Press, 2009.
Miller, Leta E. *Aaron Jay Kernis*. Urbana: University of Illinois Press, 2014.
Mol, Annemarie. "Actor-Network Theory: Sensitive Terms and Enduring Tensions." *Kölner Zeitschrift für Soziologie und Sozialpsychologie* 50, no. 1 (2010): 253–269.
Mol, Annemarie. *The Body Multiple*. Durham, NC: Duke University Press, 2002.
Moore, Andrea. "Neoliberalism and the Musical Entrepreneur." *Journal of the Society for American Music* 10, no. 1 (February 2016): 33–53.
Moritz, Charles, ed. *Current Biography Yearbook 1981*. New York: H.W. Wilson Company, 1981.
Negus, Keith. *Music Genres and Corporate Cultures*. New York: Routledge, 2013.
Nickleson, Patrick. "The Names of Minimalism: Authorship and the Historiography of Dispute in New York Minimalism, 1960–1982." PhD diss., University of Toronto, 2017.
Nickleson, Patrick. "Transcription, Recording, and Authority in 'Classic' Minimalism." *Twentieth-Century Music* 14, no. 3 (2018): 361–389.
Nigg, Erwin K. "An Analysis of Jacob Druckman's Works for Wind Ensemble: *Engram* (1982), *Paean* (1986), *In Memoriam Vincent Persichetti* (1987), *With Bells On* (1993)." DMA diss., University of Cincinnati, 1995.
O'Brien, Kerry. "Experimentalisms of the Self: Experiments in Art and Technology (E.A.T.), 1966–1971." PhD diss., Indiana University, 2018.
Palmese, Michael. "A Portrait of John Adams as a Young Man: The 1970s Juvenalia." *American Music* 37, no. 2 (Summer 2019): 229–56.
Pankratz, David. *Multiculturalism and Public Arts Policy*. Westport, CT: Bergin & Garvey, 1993.
Papador, Nicholas. "Jacob Druckman: A Bio-Bibliography and Guide to Research." DMA diss., Northwestern University, 2003.
Pasler, Jann. *Writing through Music: Essays on Music, Culture, and Politics*. Oxford and New York: Oxford University Press, 2007.
Peles, Stephen, ed. *The Collected Essays of Milton Babbitt*. Princeton, NJ: Princeton University Press, 2003.
Phillips-Farley, Barbara C. "A History of the Center for New Music at the University of Iowa, 1966–1991." DMA diss., University of Iowa, 1991.

Piekut, Benjamin. "Actor-Networks in Music History: Clarifications and Critiques." *Twentieth-Century Music* 11, no. 2 (September 2014): 191–215.

Piekut, Benjamin. *Experimentalism Otherwise: The New York Avant-Garde and Its Limits*. Berkeley and Los Angeles: University of California Press, 2011.

Piekut, Benjamin. *Tomorrow Is the Question: New Directions in Experimental Music Studies*. Ann Arbor: University of Michigan Press, 2014.

Pleasants, Henry. *The Agony of Modern Music*. New York: Simon & Schuster, 1955.

Plocher, Joshua. "Presenting the New: Battles around New Music in New York in the Seventies." PhD diss., University of Minnesota, 2012.

Potter, Keith, Kyle Gann, and Pwyll ap Siôn. *The Ashgate Research Companion to Minimalist and Postminimalist Music*. Routledge: New York, 2016.

Potter, Keith. *Four Musical Minimalists: La Monte Young, Terry Riley, Steve Reich, Philip Glass*. Cambridge: Cambridge University Press, 2000.

Quillen, William. "Winning and Losing in Russian New Music Today." *Journal of the American Musicological Society* 67, no. 2 (2014): 487–542.

Ritchey, Marianna. *Composing Capital: Classical Music in the Neoliberal Era*. Chicago: University of Chicago Press, 2019.

Robin, William. "A Scene without a Name: Indie Classical and American New Music in the Twenty-First Century." PhD diss., University of North Carolina at Chapel Hill, 2016.

Robin, William. "Balance Problems: Neoliberalism and New Music in the American University and Ensemble." *Journal of the American Musicological Society* 71, no. 3 (Fall 2018): 749–94.

Robin, William. "Horizons '83, Meet the Composer, and New Romanticism's New Marketplace." *Musical Quarterly* 102, no. 2–3 (Summer–Fall 2019): 158–99.

Robin, William. "The Rise and Fall of 'Indie Classical': Tracing a Controversial Term in Twenty-First Century New Music." *Journal of the Society for American Music* 12, no. 1 (Spring 2018): 55–88.

Rockwell, John. *All American Music: Composition in the Late Twentieth Century*. New York: Da Capo Press, 1997.

Ross, Alex. *The Rest Is Noise*. New York: Farrar, Straus & Giroux, 2007.

Rutherford-Johnson, Tim. *Music after the Fall: Modern Composition and Culture since 1989*. Berkeley and Los Angeles: University of California Press, 2017.

Shreffler, Anne. "Ideologies of Serialism: Stravinsky's *Threni* and the Congress for Cultural Freedom." In *Music and the Aesthetics of Modernity*, edited by Karol Berger and Anthony Newcomb, 217–45. Cambridge, MA: Harvard University Press, 2005.

Shreffler, Anne. "The Myth of Empirical Historiography: A Response to Joseph N. Straus." *Musical Quarterly* 84, no. 1 (Spring 2000): 30–39.

Silverman, Carol. "Move Over Madonna: Gender, Representation, and the 'Mystery' of Bulgarian Voices." In *Over the Wall/After the Fall*, edited by Sibelan Forrester, Magdalena J. Zaborowska, and Elena Gapova, 212–37. Bloomington: Indiana University Press, 2004.

Stamas, Stephen and Sharon Zane. *Lincoln Center: A Promise Realized, 1979–2006*. Hoboken, NJ: John Wiley & Sons, 2007.

Straus, Joseph. "The Myth of Serial 'Tyranny' in the 1950s and 1960s." *Musical Quarterly* 83, no. 3 (Autumn 1999): 301–43.

Sun, Cecilia. "Resisting the Airport: Bang on a Can Performs Brian Eno." *Musicology Australia* 29, no. 1 (2007): 135–59.

Taruskin, Richard. "Afterword: *Nicht blutbefleckt?*" *Journal of Musicology* 26, no. 2 (Spring 2009): 274–84.

Taruskin, Richard. *The Oxford History of Western Music*, vol. 5, *Music in the Late Twentieth Century*. Oxford and New York: Oxford University Press, 2010.

Taylor, Fanny and Anthony L. Barresi. *The Arts at a New Frontier: The National Endowment for the Arts*. New York: Springer, 2013.

Taylor, Timothy. *Music and Capitalism*. Chicago: University of Chicago Press, 2015.
Uy, Michael. *Ask the Experts: How Ford, Rockefeller, and the NEA Changed American Music*. Oxford: Oxford University Press, 2020.
Uy, Michael. "The Big Bang of Music Patronage in the United States: The National Endowment for the Arts, the Rockefeller Foundation, and the Ford Foundation." PhD diss., Harvard University, 2017.
Uy, Michael. "The Recorded Anthology of American Music and the Rockefeller Foundation: Expertise, Deliberation, and Commemoration in the Bicentennial Celebrations." *American Music* 35, no. 1 (Spring 2017): 75–93.
Vandagriff, Rachel. "An Old Story in a New World: Paul Fromm, the Fromm Music Foundation, and Elliott Carter." *Journal of Musicology* 3, no. 4 (Fall 2018): 535–66.
Vandagriff, Rachel. "The History and Impact of the Fromm Music Foundation, 1952–1983." PhD diss., University of California, Berkeley, 2014.
Vandagriff, Rachel. "Perspectives and the Patron: Paul Fromm, Benjamin Boretz and Perspectives of New Music," *Journal of the Royal Music Association* 142, no. 2 (2017): 327–365.
Williams, Alistair. *Music in Germany Since 1968*. Cambridge: Cambridge University Press, 2013.
Wiprud, Theodore and Joyce Lawler, ed., *Composer In Residence: Meet the Composer's Orchestra Residencies Program, 1982–1992*. New York: Meet the Composer, 1995.
Wolfe, Julia. "Embracing the Clash." PhD diss., Princeton University, 2012.
Wu, Chin-Tao. *Privatizing Culture*. London: Verso, 2003.
Wuorinen, Charles. *Simple Composition*. New York: Longman, 1979.
Ziporyn, Evan. "Who Listens if You Care." *New Observations* 86 (November/December 1991): 28.

Index

For the benefit of digital users, indexed terms that span two pages (e.g., 52–53) may, on occasion, appear on only one of those pages.

9/11, 222–24

Abbado, Claudio, 206
Abrams, Muhal Richard, 6–7, 52–53, 124–25, 128n.124, 135–36
academic composition
　see uptown
Adams, John, 8–9, 54–59, 68–71, 89, 128, 167–68, 194–95, 212, 215, 226–27
　Grand Pianola Music, 63
　Harmonielehre 57, 195
　Harmonium, 58
　Ktaadn, 88
　Nixon in China, 9
Adams, John Luther, 224
Adelaide Festival, 156
affirmative action, 118, 120, 122, 127
AIDS, 112–13, 129, 176, 204–5
Ailey, Alvin, 168
Albert, Stephen, 57
Alexander, Jane, 130, 137
Alice M. Ditson Fund, 93–94
Alice Tully Hall, 80–81, 165–68, 173–77, 180–82, 186–88, 210, 214, 218
All-Stars
　see Bang on a Can All-Stars
Alternative Contemporary Music Line, 203, 206–12
ambient music, 152, 157–60
American Academy and Institute of Arts and Letters, 43
American Academy in Rome, 24
American Composers Orchestra, 67
American Music Center, 43, 50, 68, 109, 130, 225
amplification, 10, 14–15, 18, 29–30, 87, 89, 93, 99, 135–36, 138–39, 141, 145, 148–49, 156–57, 163, 169, 223
Anderson, Beth, 97

Anderson, Laurie, 26–27, 82, 97–98, 113–15, 165, 169, 196–97, 221
　"O Superman," 8–9, 196
Anderson, T.J., 53
Andriessen, Louis, 19, 72, 77, 83, 88–89, 94–96, 139, 149–51, 154, 178, 208–10, 225
　De Staat, 27, 69, 70, 75, 141
　De Tijd, 94–96, 140
　Hoketus, 208
　Hout, 138–39, 206–8
　Workers Union, 15–16
Argo, 203
Artman, Deborah, 146–47, 149–50, 172, 209–10
arts boom, 107
　see also cultural boom
Arts Forward Fund, 115–16, 144
ASCAP, 32, 42–44, 93–94
Ashley, Robert, 78, 193
Aspen Music Festival 22, 26–27, 43, 117–18
Asphalt Orchestra, 224
Association for the Advancement of Creative Musicians (AACM) 6–7, 124–25
audiences, 1–10, 12–17, 19–20, 34–36, 43, 48–52, 54–55, 57, 59–70, 75–76, 79–85, 100–1, 105, 109–10, 116–27, 131–33, 139–40, 147, 152–53, 156–59, 162–69, 180, 181–86, 188–89, 190–91, 194–95, 202–3, 207, 210, 212, 215–19, 221–24, 227–29
avant-garde, 1–10, 12, 18–19, 24, 34, 38–39, 41–42, 48–49, 62–64, 69, 75–77, 83, 96–98, 104–5, 117–18, 135–36, 139, 144, 161, 165, 168–69, 181, 193, 196, 208, 210–11, 215, 218–21

Index

Babbitt, Milton, 3, 5, 8–9, 24, 27–28, 41, 52–53, 60, 63–64, 98–99, 122, 166
   at Bang on a Can 13–14, 77, 88–91, 102, 118, 150–51, 176, 198–200
   and multiculturalism, 117, 126–28
   Philomel, 87
   Vision and Prayer, 86, 89, 150–51
   "Who Cares if You Listen?" ("The Composer as Specialist"), 4–5, 7–8, 19–20, 44, 51, 105
Bachmann, Maria, 204–6
Bang on a Can
   1987 festival (Exit Art), 1, 11, 13, 47–48, 75–92, 96, 102, 105, 141–43, 147–51, 153, 198, 209–10
   1988 festival (RAPP Arts Center), 91–93, 100, 140, 143, 198–200
   1989 festival (RAPP Arts Center), 94–97, 100, 143, 150–51
   1990 festival (RAPP Arts Center), 94–96, 100–1
   1991 festival (multiple venues), 89, 94–96, 99–100, 101, 104–5, 180–82
   1992 festival (Society for Ethical Culture), 100, 142–43, 150–51, 161, 178–82, 197–98
   1993 festival (The Kitchen), 129, 175–77, 180–82
   1994 series (Lincoln Center), 15, 146, 161–63, 168–77, 182, 185
   1995 series (Lincoln Center), 172–74, 177–78, 185–86
   1996 series (Lincoln Center), 178–85
   1997 series (Lincoln Center), 186–87
   1999 festival (Henry Street Settlement), 188
   2000 marathon (Brooklyn Academy of Music), 188–89
   audiences at, 1–2, 12, 15–16, 36, 82–85, 105, 116, 123–24, 131–32, 139–40, 147, 152, 156–59, 181–86, 188–91, 207, 210, 215–16, 218–19, 221–24
   funding of, 85, 93, 105–6, 109–12, 115–16, 124–25, 131–37, 144–45, 174, 184–85, 224
   governance of, 12, 40, 102–3, 154–55, 159–60, 179–80, 227–28
   influence on younger composers of, 225–27
   and Horizons festivals, 13, 47–49, 68–74, 105
   and Lincoln Center, 10–11, 15–16, 132–33, 146–47, 149–51, 153, 156, 158f, 160–63, 168–89, 190–91, 202, 209–10, 214–15, 218–19, 221–22
   Lost Objects, 76
   marketing of, 1, 11, 83, 85, 124–25, 134–35, 145–47, 150–52, 172–74, 185–86, 208–9, 211
   and Meet the Composer, 74, 83–85, 90–91, 93–94, 102, 109–10, 124, 151
   and multiculturalism, 14, 123–25, 129
   musical style of, 86–91, 99–101, 105–6, 147–52, 210, 213, 215–17, 222–23
   program notes for, 83–85, 146–47, 149–50, 172, 209–10
   recordings of, 10–11, 13–15, 96, 116, 132–33, 144–45, 150–52, 157, 163, 188–89, 190–91, 197–200, 206–20
   and Sheep's Clothing, 33–34, 36–37, 39–40, 75–77, 116, 154–55
   Shelter, 222–23
   summer institute of, 187, 225–28
   and touring, 1, 11, 14–15, 111–12, 116, 131–32, 142–45, 147, 156–61, 163, 186–88, 206–7, 213–15, 221–24
   and uptown/downtown, 13–14, 75–76, 78–80, 86–91, 99–102, 123–24, 149–52, 177–78, 221
Bang on a Can All-Stars
   amplification of, 138–39, 156–57
   funding of, 116, 131–33, 144–45
   governance of, 152–60
   marketing of, 145–47, 152
   and *Music for Airports,* 157–60
   musical style of, 147–52
   origins of, 142–47
   at Tanglewood, 138–39
   touring of, 147
Bang on a Can Live Volume 1, 197–98, 199f
Banglewood, 187, 225–28
Beatles, The, 25, 152, 216
   Introducing the Beatles, 215–16
Beck, John, 96
Beethoven, Ludwig van, 3, 22–23, 50–51, 64–65, 83, 118–19, 152, 164, 211, 226–27

Behrman, David, 191–92
Beiser, Maya, 10–11, 138, 142–43, 146, 152–53, 157–59, 222
Berio, Luciano, 69, 192
  Sinfonia, 60–61
Bermuda Triangle, 129
Bernstein, Leonard, 3–4, 7–8, 22, 192
Binkiewicz, Donna, 106, 137
Birtwistle, Harrison
  Secret Theatre, 176–77
Bittová, Iva, 188–89
Black composers, 6–7, 53, 119, 121, 124–25
Black, Robert, 75, 138, 142–43, 146, 152–53, 156, 198–200
Blackwood, Michael
  New York Composers: Searching for a New Music, 152, 178–79, 181–82
Bley, Carla, 193
BMG, 15, 193, 203–6
BMI, 24–25, 32, 42–43
Bolcom, William, 26–27, 98–99
Boosey & Hawkes, 42–43
Boston Symphony Orchestra, 54, 170
Boulez, Pierre, 8, 60, 62–63, 140
Bouwhuis, Gerard, 75, 94f
Brahms, Johannes, 24–26
Branca, Glenn 43–44, 89, 94–96, 98–100, 104, 135–36, 141, 147–48, 170–71, 186, 193
  Movement Within, 216–17
branding, 15, 85, 116, 227
Breest, Günther, 206–8
Bresnick, Martin, 13, 19, 24–25, 27–39, 42–44, 75, 79–80, 89, 173, 225–26
Brody, Martin, 27–28, 32–33, 41–42
Brookfield Office Properties, 224
Brooklyn Academy of Music, 80, 82, 97–98, 107–8, 131, 162–63, 165–66, 170, 187, 196–97, 221–23
  see also Next Wave Festival
Brooklyn Philharmonic, 42–43
Brooks, Jeffrey, 18, 29, 32–33, 75, 77, 90, 142, 198–200, 224
Brown, James, 148
Brubaker, Bruce, 205
Brubeck, Dave, 25–26
Bryars, Gavin
  Jesus' Blood Never Failed Me Yet, 213
Buchanan, Pat, 112–14, 116–17

Budd, Harold, 203
Bush, George H.W., 109, 112–14, 130

Cacioppo, George, 26–27
Cage, John, 6–9, 34–39, 58, 78, 79, 98–99, 168, 191–92
  Atlas Eclipticalis, 7–8
  and Bang on a Can 83, 88, 91, 92, 92f, 94–96, 99–100, 101, 104, 110, 129, 149, 175–76
  Ryoanji, 75
  Six Melodies, 101
California E.A.R. Unit, 93, 140
Cameron, Allison
  Two Bits, 198–200
Cantaloupe Music, 189, 191, 217–18, 224–25
capitalism, 11–12, 38, 51–52, 101–2, 115–16, 120–21, 169–70
Cardew, Cornelius, 38–40
  Stockhausen Serves Imperialism, 37–38
Carlos, Wendy
  Switched-On Bach, 192
Carnegie Hall, 16, 82, 87, 170, 181, 226–27
Carnegie Recital Hall, 21, 32, 78, 80–81
Carter, Elliott, 4–5, 18–21, 60, 78, 98–99, 150–51, 166–68, 194, 198–200
  Duo, 176–77
  Piano Concerto, 117–18
  String Quartet No. 3, 195
Catalyst, 190, 203–6, 208–10, 222–23
Catholic Church, 104–6
CBS Masterworks, 190–91, 195–96, 206, 208
  see also Columbia Records, Sony Classical
CDs, 16, 157, 160, 182–84, 190, 197–200, 202–6, 211–13, 215, 217
censorship, 105, 113–14, 126
Chamber Music America, 110–11, 131, 145, 147, 172–73
Chamber Music Society of Lincoln Center, 163–64, 166
Chant, 201, 211, 216–17
Chapman, Dale, 202
Chatham Square, 193
Chatham, Rhys, 77, 97, 147–48, 165–66, 177
Chicago Symphony Orchestra, 8, 57
Christian Coalition, 112–13
Christianity, 114, 116–17
Circle in the Square, 104

Clark, Sedgwick, 202
Classic FM, 200–1
Clayton, Laura, 26, 75
Clinton, Bill, 129–30
Cohen, Jeffrey, 104
Cold War, 3–4, 5, 6, 19–20, 24, 106, 112–13, 120–21, 127, 221–22
Coleman, Ornette, 52–53, 119
    The Shape of Jazz to Come, 215–16
collective, 6–7, 12–13, 20, 33–34, 37–40, 152–53, 154–55
Colo, Papo, 83
Columbia Records, 191–92, 195
    see also CBS Masterworks, Sony Classical
Columbia University, 4–6, 41–42, 75–76, 78, 93–94, 96, 150–51
Columbia-Princeton Electronic Music Center, 5, 24–26, 29
Composer in Performance
    see Meet the Composer
composer-performers 13–14, 67, 78, 98–100, 135–36, 169, 177
Composer's Cafeteria, 39–40
Composers Recordings, Inc. (CRI), 15, 190–94, 196–200, 210, 216, 217–18
Congress, 2–3, 14, 104–8, 112–14, 129–31, 191, 211
Conrad, Tony, 6–7
Consoli, Marc-Antonio, 62
Contract With America, 129–31
Cooper-Hewitt Museum, 77
Copland, Aaron, 3–4, 8, 117–18, 195–96, 221
    Appalachian Spring, 3
Corcoran Gallery, 112
Corigliano, John, 69, 134–35, 167–68, 212
    Symphony No. 1, 57
coronavirus pandemic, 224–25
corporate funding, 48–49, 51–52, 55–56, 106–9, 114–15, 125–26, 131–33, 147, 163–64, 182, 184–85, 221–22
Cotton, Andrew, 157, 161
Cowperthwaite, Janet, 145
Crawford Seeger, Ruth
    String Quartet 1931, 88–89
crossover, 152, 157–59, 191–92, 194–96, 202–3, 208, 213, 216–17, 219
Crumb, George, 8, 26, 83, 194
    Black Angels, 21, 75
cultural boom, 3–4, 163–64

Culture Wars, 11, 14, 104–6, 112–19, 127, 129–33, 136–37, 167, 180, 198
Cummings, Conrad, 197–98
Cunningham, Merce, 168
Cuomo, Mario, 125
Curran, Alvin, 204–5

D'Amato, Alphonse, 112
Da Capo Chamber Players, 66, 126f, 143, 154
Dallas Symphony, 55, 68–69
Dalton, Joseph, 190–91, 196–200, 208–9, 217
Dance Theater Workshop, 83, 186
Darmstadt, 6, 62–63
Daugherty, Michael, 20n.13, 22, 29, 32–33, 42–43, 203
Davidovsky, Mario, 4–5, 21, 150–51, 176–77
    Synchronisms No. 6, 93, 150–51
    Synchronisms No. 10, 150–51
Davidson, Justin, 177, 187–88
Davidson, Randall, 130
Davidson, Tina, 128
Davies, Peter Maxwell, 62
Davis, Peter G., 190, 200, 210
Decca, 202–3, 206, 217
Del Tredici, David, 8, 60–62, 70–71, 89, 98–99
    All in the Golden Afternoon, 63–64
    Final Alice, 8
democracy, 12, 101–2, 108–9, 137, 154–55, 228
Dempster, Stuart, 67
Depression, 3–4, 221
Deutsche Grammophon, 194, 203, 206, 217
Di Pietro, Rocco
    Three Black American Folk Songs, 178–79
Didkovsky, Nick, 153, 173, 211
Disney, Abigail, 92
diversity, 28–29, 53, 60, 116–28, 171–72, 178, 208, 221–22
DIY (do-it-yourself), 37, 170, 172, 221, 224–27
DJ Spooky, 134–35
Donaueschingen, 6
Douglas Dunn and Dancers, 165
downtown, 1–4, 6–9, 13–15, 19–22, 27, 43–44, 52, 67, 69–70, 72, 75–85, 87, 89–91, 93, 96, 97, 99–102, 115, 123–24, 131,

139–40, 147–52, 154, 161–62, 165–66, 168–71, 175–78, 185, 187–88, 197–200, 216, 221–28
see also experimentalism
Downtown Ensemble, 123, 180–81
Dresher, Paul, 128, 131, 137
Slow Fire, 70
Dreyblatt, Arnold, 78, 104, 216
Escalator, 216–17
Druckman, Jacob, 72, 75, 83, 225–26
and Horizons festivals, 13, 47, 51–52, 58–62, 64–71, 88–89
and New Romanticism, 13, 18, 29, 60–61, 63
Windows, 29
at Yale, 13, 27–30, 32–33, 37, 40–46, 68–69, 79–80
Duffy, John, 1–2, 13, 49–57, 59–60, 65–76, 83–85, 86–87, 90–91, 96, 113–16, 119–20, 124–25, 134–35, 151, 166–67, 187–88, 191, 198, 218–20, 225, 228

EAR Magazine, 48–49, 100–1, 113–15, 122, 125, 176, 196–98
Eastman School of Music, 42–43, 58
Eastman, Julius, 6–7
ECM, 8, 15, 194–95, 201, 206
New Series, 194, 203
economic recession, 101, 125–26, 225
Eicher, Manfred, 194–95
electric guitar, 9, 29–30, 39–40, 75, 89, 98–100, 138, 140–44, 148–49, 165–66
Elektra, 194–96, 203
see also Nonesuch
Emergency Music, 190–91, 197–200, 208–9
Eno, Brian, 97, 213, 216
Music for Airports, 15, 152, 157–60, 161, 187–88, 191, 213–15, 217, 218–19, 224
entrepreneurship, 13–14, 39–40, 66–67, 76, 102, 132, 186, 225–28
Euphorbia Productions, 213
evangelical right, 112–13
Exit Art gallery, 75, 77–78, 80, 82–83, 85, 88, 147–48

Experimental Intermedia, 13–14, 75–76, 78, 81–82, 97–100, 109–10, 116, 121–22, 125–26, 131
experimental music, 1–2, 6–10, 12–14, 19–20, 24, 27, 34–39, 52–53, 58, 64, 67, 79, 81–82, 97, 99, 107, 119, 122–25, 153, 165, 168–69, 191–94, 213, 215, 221, 223
see also downtown
Exxon, 13, 54–56, 59, 68–69, 71, 107–8

Feldman, Morton, 6, 19–20, 28–29, 41–42, 143, 176
Coptic Light, 69
The King of Denmark, 93
Fennelly, Brian, 21–22, 41–42
financialization, 202
First Amendment, 105
Fleischer, Leonard, 54, 56–57
Fleisher, Leon, 138–39
Fluxus, 6, 36, 49–50
Ford Foundation, 106–7, 163–64
Forte, Allen, 21–22
Found Sound Nation, 224
Foundation for Contemporary Performance Arts, 110
foundations, 2–3, 5, 11–12, 19–20, 48–49, 51–52, 55–56, 71, 106–12, 119, 124–27, 131–35, 163–64, 224, 227
Franklin, Aretha
"Think," 149
Fred Frith Guitar Quartet, 188
free market, 2–3, 8, 104–5, 108, 115, 117–18, 137, 191, 198, 219–20
Frohnmayer, John, 113–14, 120, 129
Fromm Foundation, 5, 164–65
Fromm, Paul, 5, 139n.5, 164–65
Fulbright grant, 44, 149
Fullman, Ellen, 78
Fulmer, Mimmi, 86
funk, 31–32, 138, 148–49

gagaku, 99–100, 147–48
Galás, Diamanda, 67, 169
gamelan, 147–48, 156
Gamelan Galak Tika, 186, 188–89
Gann, Kyle, 33–34, 79, 88–89, 93–94, 97–102, 129, 140, 150–51, 175–78, 180, 185, 188, 198, 214–15
Garon, Lynn, 83, 86

Gay American Composers, 200
Gelb, Peter, 207–8, 211–12, 219–20
genre, 6, 86, 96, 99, 139–40, 149–50, 183–84, 194, 201, 204, 215–16, 221–22, 225–26, 228
gentrification, 166
Gilmore, Samuel, 79, 120
Gingrich, Newt, 129–30
Glass, Philip, 8–10, 18–20, 21, 27, 52–53, 64, 69–70, 85, 87–88, 97–98, 99, 101–2, 115, 128, 134–35, 140, 154, 165, 173, 175–76, 181–82, 193, 195–97, 203–4, 207–8, 210, 213, 215, 218–19, 221
  Einstein on the Beach, 8
  Glassworks, 195–96
  Koyaanisqatsi, 195–96
  "Low" Symphony, 213
  Mishima, 195
  Music in Similar Motion, 88, 93
  Music in Twelve Parts, 8
  Satyagraha, 82
  Songs from Liquid Days, 195–96
  Symphony No. 5, 188–89
Glennie, Evelyn, 204–6
Glickman, Sylvia, 128
Globokar, Vinko
  Corporal, 185–86
God's Love We Deliver, 129
Godfrey, John, 154–55
Goode, Daniel, 35
Gordon, Michael
  academic training of, 21–22, 29–30, 33, 39, 43–44
  Decasia, 223
  Earthwork, 21–22
  Four Kings Fight Five, 149
  I Buried Paul, 152, 159, 216
  Industry, 5–6, 138–39, 143, 153, 208
  musical style of, 18, 21–22, 88–89, 140–41, 149, 223
  Rushes, 223
  The Sad Park, 222
  Strange Quiet, 70, 88–89, 198–200
  Thou Shalt!/Thou Shalt Not!, 29–30, 33, 70, 89, 91, 140–42
  Timber, 223
  Trance, 203
  The Tree Watcher, 18–20, 27, 30, 42, 72, 89
  Van Gogh Video Opera, 93, 96
  Weather, 213

  Yo Shakespeare, 149, 154–55
  youth of, 20–21
Gordon, Peter, 193
Górecki, Henryk, 214–15, 217–18
  Symphony No. 3, 15, 167–68, 190–91, 200–1, 203–8, 210, 212, 219
Gould, Glenn, 204
government funding, 11–12, 14, 52, 104–7, 109, 114–16, 117, 119, 125–28, 131–32, 136–37, 144–45, 147, 185, 193, 198, 211, 219–20
  see also National Endowment for the Arts, New York State Council on the Arts
graphic scores, 6, 37–38, 140–41
Great Performers (Lincoln Center series), 161, 164, 167–69, 187
Great Recession, 225
Great Society, 106, 108
Greenstein, Judd, 225–26
Group for Contemporary Music, 5, 14, 67, 78, 80–82, 120–23, 126–27, 154

Haas, Michael, 206
Hakmoun, Hassan, 188–89
Hanks, Nancy, 106–7
Harbison, John, 55, 57
Harmonia Mundi, 203, 218
Harrington, David, 145, 154
Harrison, Lou, 24, 148
Harry, Martyn, 15, 203, 206–8, 211–12, 217–18, 219
Hartman, Andrew, 104–5
Heirich, Jane, 25–26
Held, Barbara, 75
Helms, Jesse, 113–19, 126–27, 129, 137
Hendrix, Jimi, 8–9, 93, 148
  "Purple Haze," 145–46
Henze, Hans Werner, 72
Heritage Foundation, 108, 117–18, 129–30
Hibbard, William, 24
Hindemith, Paul, 21
Hirsch, Shelley, 75, 198–200
HMV, 214
Hodsoll, Frank, 109
Holland Festival, 169–70
Holland, Bernard, 85–86
holy minimalism, 201, 204–7, 210, 212, 214–17, 219
  see also spiritual minimalism

Hopkins, Karen, 182
Horizons festivals, 29, 43, 47–48, 96, 109,
    162–65, 170
  1983 festival, 48–49, 59–67, 82, 89,
    105, 117–18
  1984 festival, 9–10, 67
  1986 festival, 13, 47, 67–68, 69–71,
    88–89, 170
  effects on young composers of, 65–74
Houston Symphony, 57
Hovda, Eleanor, 161
Huddersfield Contemporary Music
    Festival, 207
Hurwitz, Robert, 194–97, 200–1, 203–5

Icebreaker, 140, 154–55, 176, 203, 207–8
improvisation, 6, 75–76, 78, 79, 98–99, 100,
    128, 140–41, 153, 198–200
indeterminacy, 6, 37–38, 98–99, 140–41
Indianapolis Symphony, 57
indie classical, 108
Industry (Sony album), 10–11, 16, 150–51,
    208–11, 214–15
Ingberman, Jeannette, 77–78, 83, 85n.48
Internet, 182–84, 218–20
Ione, 113–14
IRCAM, 32–33
iTunes, 225
Ives, Charles, 3–4, 26, 64, 77, 192
Ivy League, 2–3, 11, 18–20, 224–25

Jackson, John Shenoy, 6–7
Jagger, Mick, 200–1
Jarrett, Keith, 165–66
jazz, 9–10, 20–21, 23–24, 32–33, 35–36,
    49–50, 64, 96, 99, 119–20, 127, 145, 153,
    157, 165, 166–67, 171, 173, 193–94, 202,
    215–16, 224, 226–27
Jazz at Lincoln Center, 165, 168
Jeffries, Nancy, 196
Jenkins, Leroy, 52–53, 97, 124–25
Jerome Foundation, 124–25, 134–35
Johnson, Lyndon, 106
Johnson, Mimi, 193
Johnson, Scott, 131
Johnson, Tom, 35, 161
  *Failing: A Very Difficult Piece for String
    Bass*, 143, 157–59, 198–200
Jones, Bill T., 187

Joplin, Janis, 25
Joplin, Scott, 194
Jordan, James, 119, 121, 122–23, 124–25
Joyce, Michael S., 117–18
Judaism, 20–21, 23–24, 30
Juilliard, 20–21, 164–65

Kagel, Mauricio
  Pas de Cinq, 69
Kancheli, Giya, 206
Kazue Sawai Koto Ensemble, 94–96, 148
Kerner, Leighton, 67
Kernis, Aaron Jay, 20, 29, 42–44, 70, 72, 75,
    79–80, 197–98, 203
  dream of the morning sky, 65–67
King, John
  move, 75
Kitchen, The, 38, 78, 80–81, 97, 119, 129,
    165–66, 170–71, 175–77, 180–82, 186
Klein, Howard, 54, 56–57, 65
Kline, Phil, 188–89, 216
Knitting Factory, 97–99, 136*f*, 177, 186–88,
    198–200
Korf, Anthony, 123
Kotche, Glenn, 15–16
Koussevitsky Foundation, 43, 137
Kozinn, Allan, 123, 126–27, 132–33,
    150, 161–63, 175, 177, 181–82, 185,
    188, 216–17
Kraft, William, 55, 59*f*
Kramer, Hilton, 116–18, 120–21
Kronos Quartet, 8–9, 131, 138–46, 154,
    167–68, 195, 210, 218–19, 222

La Barbara, Joan, 101–2
La Mama, 104, 123–24, 170–71, 181–82
labor, 139–40, 174, 223, 228
Laderman, Ezra, 54–57, 109
Lam, Bun-Ching, 129
Lang, David
  academic training of, 22, 23–25, 32–33,
    36–37, 39–41, 44–46
  the anvil chorus, 138–39, 153
  are you experienced?, 148
  cheating, lying, stealing, 16, 148, 159,
    211, 222–23
  eating living monkeys, 68, 72, 88–89, 170
  flaming youth, 68
  frag, 88–89

Lang, David (*cont.*)
   and the Horizons festivals, 47–48, 65–66, 68–70, 71–74
   illumination rounds, 32–33, 39
   the little match girl passion, 15–16, 222–23
   musical style of, 24, 32, 39, 72, 88–89, 148
   press release, 148
   prisoner of the state, 226–27
   while nailing at random, 32, 72
   world to come, 222
   youth of, 22–24
Larsen, Libby, 51–53, 55, 59f, 71–72
Lasker-Schuller, Elsa, 30
Laskin, David LL, 100–1, 114–16, 119
Lazarof, Henri, 22–23
Le Mystère des Voix Bulgares, 195, 201
Le Nouvel Ensemble Moderne, 94–96, 176
Lebrecht, Norman, 201
Led Zeppelin, 152, 213, 215–17
Leeuw, Reinbert de, 139
LeGassick, Damien, 216–17
León, Tania, 53, 70n.110
Leventhal, Nathan, 165–68
Levin, Todd, 203, 211
Lewis, George, 97, 100–1
Lichtenstein, Harvey, 82, 165, 181
Lieberson, Goddard, 192, 206
Ligeti, György, 26, 60–61, 69, 88–89
Lincoln Center, 3–4, 47, 49–50, 59–60, 65–66, 73–74, 80–82, 114, 163–64, 166–68
   and Bang on a Can, 11, 15, 16, 132–33, 146–47, 149–51, 153, 156, 158f, 160–63, 168–89, 190–91, 202, 209–10, 214–15, 218, 221–22
   and new music, 2, 10, 164–66, 191, 226–27
   Lincoln Center Productions, 167–68
   New Works Fund, 167–68
   Discovery series, 167–68, 171
Lindroth, Scott, 22, 28–29, 32–33, 37, 43, 66–69, 83, 93
   Relations to Rigor, 75
Lipman, Samuel, 9–10, 62–63, 116–21, 124–25, 127, 167
London Records, 203, 217
London Sinfonietta, 157, 200
Long Play, 224
Los Angeles Philharmonic, 55, 167–68, 226–27
Louisville Orchestra, 57
Lounge Lizards, 165

Lovely Music, 193
loyalty oath, 113
LP, 192–93, 197–98, 202
Lucier, Alvin, 97
Lucinda Childs Dance Company, 188–89
Lutosławski, Witold, 26–27

Ma, Yo-Yo, 171, 212
MacArthur grant, 16
Madonna, 201, 205–6
Maguire, Michael, 173
Maher, Chris, 35–36, 38–39
Man, Wu, 186
Mandate for Leadership, 117–18
Manhattan School of Music, 21, 121
Mapplethorpe, Robert, 112–13, 118–19, 127
Marcus, Bunita, 142–43
   Adam and Eve, 198–200
marketplace, 1–3, 10, 12–16, 19–20, 41, 43–44, 48–49, 50, 58, 65–67, 72, 74, 76, 96, 105–6, 109, 114–16, 119, 128, 137, 139–40, 160, 162–63, 185–86, 191, 194–95, 198, 201, 204, 216, 218–21, 224–28,
Marsalis, Wynton, 167–68
Marshall, Ingram, 193, 196
Martino, Donald, 60–61
Martland, Steve, 142–43, 147–48, 157, 188–89, 205–6, 216
   Drill, 93
   Horses of Instruction, 138–39
Mary Flagler Cary Trust, 93–94, 109–10
Massachusetts Museum of Contemporary Art, 225
Mazzoli, Missy, 225–27
McMillin Theatre (Miller Theatre), 75–76, 78–81
Meet the Composer, 1–2, 10, 13, 16, 21–22, 48–49, 52–55, 59, 61–62, 65, 69–72, 74, 83–85, 90–91, 93–94, 96, 102, 108–10, 121, 124, 162–68, 221, 228
   Commissioning Music, 22
   Composers in the Marketplace, 1–2
   Composers Performance Fund, 50
   and diversity, 52–54, 124–25, 128, 151
   funding of, 11–12, 51–52, 54, 71, 113–15, 225
   and the marketplace, 50–52, 60, 115, 162–63, 191

origins of (as Composer in Performance), 49–52, 119
see also Orchestra Residencies Program
Mehta, Zubin, 66–70, 73
Mellits, Marc, 141
Memento Bittersweet, 204–6
Mendel, Arthur, 41
Merkin Concert Hall, 4–5, 78, 80–81
Messiaen, Olivier, 35, 122
Metropolitan Opera, 8, 28, 58, 69, 110–11, 161, 163–64, 219–20
Michael Gordon Philharmonic, 29–30, 44, 70, 77, 88–89, 142–43, 170–71, 193
Mikhashoff, Yvar, 93
Mills College, 34
minimalism, 2, 8, 12–14, 18–22, 26–30, 37–38, 43–44, 52–53, 63–64, 69–70, 79–80, 85, 87–89, 93, 96, 99–100, 117–18, 120–21, 123–24, 127–28, 139, 140–41, 152, 185–86, 192–93, 195, 206, 216, 221, 223
Minnesota Orchestra, 55
Mitchell, Joni, 25
Monk, Meredith, 97, 175–76, 194
Moore, Lisa, 138, 143, 150–51, 155–57
Moorefield, Virgil, 135–36
Moorman, Charlotte, 6–7
Morgan, Gayle, 109
Morris, Butch, 97–98
Morris, Robert, 27–28, 41–42
Morrison, Bill, 223
Moses, Robert, 163–64
Moss, Jane, 15, 162, 166–71, 173–74, 181–82, 185–87, 226–27
Mostly Mozart, 164–65, 167–68, 185–86, 226–27
Motown, 138, 149
Movement for the Renewal of Musical Practice, 154
Mozart, Wolfgang Amadeus, 64–65
multiculturalism, 14, 16, 105–6, 117–25, 127–28, 167, 180
Munkacsi, Kurt, 213, 218
Music Critics Association, 59, 62, 97
Music of Our Time, 191–92, 194–95, 203
Musica Elettronica Viva, 6–8, 97–98

Nancarrow, Conlon, 64, 142–43
Napster, 217, 225
National Council on the Arts, 118

National Endowment for the Arts (NEA), 43, 119, 137, 180, 225
Composer Fellowships, 44–45, 127–28
and the Culture Wars, 11–12, 104–5, 112–14, 116–17, 126–27, 129–30
funding cuts of, 9–10, 55, 108–9, 130–31
and new music, 13, 54, 55–56, 65, 80, 93–94, 107, 109, 113–14, 122, 128, 130–217, 219–20
origins of, 106–8
National Endowment for the Humanities, 106, 129–30
National Medal of Arts, 108–9
NEA Four, 113
Negus, Keith, 201
Neill, Ben, 129
neo-Romanticism, 8, 12, 52–53, 60–61, 63, 64, 70, 74, 123, 221
neoconservatives, 105–6, 116–17, 120–21, 164
neoliberalism, 11–12, 39–40, 202, 228
Netherlands Wind Ensemble, 176
Neutral Records, 193
New Age, 214–15
New Albion Records, 190–91, 193, 196, 203, 218
New Amsterdam Records, 225–26
New Criterion, The, 62, 118–20
New Music Across America, 142–43
New Music America, 13–14, 16, 97–103, 135–36, 142–43, 147–48, 176–77, 180, 193, 196, 221
New Music Distribution Service (NMDS), 193–94, 202
New Music New Haven, 42
New Music USA, 225
New Music, New York, 38, 97, 101–2, 119
see also New Music America
New Romanticism 15, 19, 29, 48–49, 59–65, 67, 105, 117–18, 185–86
New Sounds, 96
New World Records, 192–93
New York Foundation for the Arts, 77
New York Philharmonic, 2, 6–10, 13, 28, 29, 43, 45–50, 54–55, 58, 59–71, 72–73, 75–76, 92, 109, 119–20, 148, 161–64, 167–68, 170, 226–27
see also Horizons festivals

New York State Black and Puerto Rican
    Legislative Caucus, 119–20
New York State Council on the Arts
    (NYSCA), 14, 43–44, 47–48
    and audience outreach, 122–24, 218
    funding cuts of, 125–26, 176, 225
    and multiculturalism, 16, 105–6, 117, 119–
        24, 126–27, 155
    and new music, 49–50, 52, 80–81,
        91–92, 94–96, 109–10, 119, 124–25,
        132–35, 211
New York Youth Symphony, 44, 68, 92
new-music ensembles, 2–3, 5–6, 8–9, 15,
    19–20, 24, 26, 39–40, 66–67, 78, 82, 89,
    107, 120–21, 123, 140, 154–55, 157, 166,
    175–76, 226–27, 229
Niblock, Phill, 75, 81, 86, 97–98, 131
    Held Tones, 75
    see also Experimental Intermedia
Nirvana
    "Lithium," 145–46
No Wave, 141
non-profit, 15, 65, 76, 115–16, 118, 191,
    192–93, 196–97, 221
Nonesuch, 15, 145–46, 167–68, 190–91,
    194–96, 200–1, 203–6, 210, 212–13, 215,
    217, 226–27
NOW Ensemble, 225–26
Nyman, Michael, 165–66, 211

Oestreich, James R., 178–79
Ohga, Norio, 206
Olin Foundation, 117–18
Oliveros, Paulin, 35, 83, 91, 107, 113–14, 193
    Sonic Meditations, 6–7, 75, 93
Orange Mountain Music, 218
Orchestra of St. Luke's, 164–65
Orchestra Residencies Program, 13, 48–49,
    54–59, 64–66, 74, 98–99, 107–9,
    113–14
Orkest de Volharding, 94–96, 140, 154–55
Oscars, 222–23
Out Classics, 205–6
Out of Doors festival, 164, 167–68

Page, Tim, 15, 70, 83–85, 91–92, 96, 149,
    153, 203–6, 209–10, 211–12, 217–19,
    222–23
paleoconservatives, 108, 116–17, 126–27
Palmer, Juliet, 173

Pareles, Jon, 214–15
Parnassus ensemble, 123, 125, 126*f*
Pärt, Arvo, 167–68, 201, 204–5, 210,
    212, 214–15
    Fratres, 194, 204–5
    Tabula Rasa, 70, 194
Partch, Harry, 24, 94–96, 148, 176, 192, 200
    The Wayward, 104
Pascoal, Hermeto, 173, 211
Patterson, Benjamin, 49–50
Paulus, Stephen, 55
Penderecki, Krzysztof, 27–28, 60–61
People's Commissioning Fund, 14, 132–37,
    159–60, 186, 187–88, 189, 224
Performing Artservices, 193
Perspectives of New Music, 5, 21–22, 45–46
Peter and the Girlfriends, 21, 142
Pew Charitable Trust, 110
Peyser, Joan, 120–21, 123–24
Philadelphia Orchestra, 204
Philip Morris, 93–94, 97–98, 107–8, 131–32,
    182, 184–85
Philips, 15, 157, 190, 203, 206, 213, 217
Piano Circus, 149
Picker, Tobias, 57
Pierrot ensemble, 66–67, 144
Pink Floyd, 213, 216, 219
Pittsburgh Symphony, 55, 57
Pleasants, Henry
    The Agony of Modern Music, 7–8
Plonsey, Daniel, 35–40, 64, 135–36
Point Music, 15, 157, 190, 203, 213–17, 219
Poke, James, 154–55
PolyGram, 213–14, 217
Polyrock, 8–9
pop, 8–9, 14–15, 99, 117–18, 128, 138,
    139, 142, 145–50, 157–59, 164, 190,
    192, 194–95, 198, 200–3, 207–8,
    213, 214–15
postminimalism, 1, 9, 12, 27, 29–30, 43–44,
    70, 74–75, 88, 99, 128, 144, 178,
    198–200
Powell, Mel, 21–22
President's Committee on Arts and
    Humanities, 108–9
Presidential Task Force on the Arts and
    Humanities, 108
Previte, Bobby, 177
Princeton University, 4–5, 8, 19–20, 24–25,
    27–28, 41

producer, 2–3, 15, 101, 104, 106–7, 113, 190–91, 193–94, 206, 216–17, 218, 222–23
Pulitzer Prize, 3, 5, 15–16, 29, 43, 57, 66, 150–51, 194, 222–23
punk rock, 148, 170

Quintet of the Americas, 44

RAPP Arts Center, 93–94, 104, 161, 170–72
Ran, Shulamit
    Symphony, 57
Rands, Bernard, 52–53
    Canti del Sole, 57
RCA Mark II Synthesizer, 5
Reader's Digest, 71–72, 124, 166–67
Reagan, Ronald, 9–12, 55, 107–9, 114, 117–18, 125–26, 130, 137, 221, 225
recording new music, 15, 96, 165–66, 196–200, 206–20, 221–22, 225, 227, 229
    as a non-profit enterprise, 192–94
    sales potential of, 8, 57, 69–70, 97–98, 167–68, 185–86, 190–92, 194–96, 200–6, 218–20
Red Poppy Music, 110–11
Reed, Foster, 193, 196, 201, 203
Reich, Steve, 8–10, 18–19, 21, 24, 26–27, 52, 64, 69–70, 83, 85, 87, 99, 102, 105, 107, 115, 128, 134, 154–55, 194, 195–97, 203–4, 213, 215, 218–19, 221
    at Bang on a Can, 13–14, 86–91, 149, 151, 176, 224–25
    The Desert Music, 195
    Drumming, 87, 97, 155
    Eight Lines, 212–13
    Four Organs, 21, 86, 102
    Music for Eighteen Musicians, 8, 26, 70–71, 87, 140–41, 155, 194
    New York Counterpoint, 212–13
    Piano Phase, 37
    Tehillim, 31–32, 87
    WTC 9/11, 222
Relâche Ensemble, 140
religious right, 2–3, 104–6, 112–13, 129, 137
Renegade Heaven, 216–17
Republicans, 2–3, 104–5, 112–13, 129–30, 191, 211
Revson Fellowship, 43–45, 47, 66–70
Reynolds, Roger, 52–53, 67
Richard, Frances, 49–52, 166–67

Riesman, Michael, 93, 213
Rieu, André, 217
Rifkin, Joshua, 194
Riley, Terry, 25–26, 93–96, 191–92
    In C, 34–35, 187–88, 192
River To River Festival, 223–24
Robert Sterling Clark Foundation, 144–45
Rochberg, George, 9–10, 60–61
rock, 8–10, 12, 14–15, 20–21, 29–30, 43–46, 79–80, 82–83, 89, 99, 138–42, 147–53, 157, 159–61, 163–65, 169–71, 173–74, 181, 183–84, 191–92, 195–96, 201, 204–6, 214–17, 224–26
Rockefeller Foundation, 5, 13, 20, 26, 54–55, 65, 66, 69–70, 106–8, 119, 131–32, 163–64, 192–93
Rockwell, John, 8–9, 62–63, 70, 78, 80–81, 97–99, 140, 168, 192
Rodríguez, Robert Xavier, 55, 59f, 68–69
Roland SRE-555 tape delay machine, 18
Rome Prize, 43–44
Rorem, Ned, 3–4, 52–53, 63, 148
Ross, Alex
    The Rest Is Noise, 16
Rothstein, Edward, 62–63, 129, 167, 175
Roulette, 78–79, 81, 186
Rouse, Christopher, 57
Row, Grace, 211–12
Rozen, Jay, 36f
Ruggles, Carl, 64
Rutherford-Johnson, Tim, 194, 201
Rycenga, Jenny, 34–35, 39–40
Rzewski, Frederic, 28–29, 67–68, 94–96, 161, 211
    Coming Together, 93
    Les Moutons de Panurge, 34–35
    Piano Piece No. 4, 157–59

S.E.M. Ensemble, 75, 86, 140, 154
San Francisco Symphony, 8–9, 54–55, 58, 121
San Francisco Tape Music Center, 34
Sander, Karen, 110–12, 147, 169, 172–74
Sandow, Gregory, 9–10, 64, 67, 78
Satoh, Somei
    Toward the Night, 203
Savelson, Kenny, 157–59, 174, 217
Sayles, Rebecca, 110–11, 115–16
Schaefer, John, 96

Schick, Steven, 93, 138, 142–43, 153, 156–57, 185–86
Schindler's List, 211
Schoenberg, Arnold, 3–4, 60, 62–63, 90, 192
  Pierrot Lunaire, 66–67
Schuller, Gunther, 139
Schwantner, Joseph, 55, 58–61, 68–69
Schwarz, K. Robert, 71–72, 142–44, 148, 150, 152–53, 168–69, 171–74, 181, 200, 210, 218–19
Scorca, Marc, 131
Scratch Orchestra, 37–39
Seattle Symphony, 57
Seiji Ozawa Hall, 138
Sellars, Peter, 167–68, 187
Senate, 3–4, 112, 114
serialism, 3–6, 8–10, 13–14, 18–20, 21–22, 24, 26–27, 29, 32, 52–53, 60–64, 73, 79, 83, 87, 100, 120–21, 123–24, 149–50
  see also twelve-tone music, uptown
Serious Fun!, 161, 165–66, 167–69, 171, 181, 185–86
Serling, Peter, 26, 31*f*, 135*f*, 139*f*, 208–9, 223*f*
Serrano, Andres
  Piss Christ, 112
Shapey, Ralph, 175–76
Sheep's Clothing, 13, 20, 33–40, 42, 64, 65–66, 75–77, 99, 116, 135–36, 140–41, 143, 154–55, 180–81
Sherry, Fred, 166
Shifrin, David, 166
Shostakovich, Dmitri, 23–24, 148
  First Symphony, 22–23
Sierra, Arlene, 178
Silvestrov, Valentin, 206
Singh, Talvin, 188
Singleton, Alvin, 57, 134–35
Skempton, Howard, 206
Slatkin, Leonard, 57, 68–69
Smith, Geoff, 206
Smith, James Allen, 107, 163–64
Snapp, Bette, 110–11, 131, 147, 172–73, 175, 185–86
Society for Ethical Culture, 161, 170–71, 181–82
Sonic Arts Union, 6
Sonic Youth, 134–35, 188–89, 216–17

Sony Classical, 10–11, 15–16, 131, 150–51, 172–73, 190–91, 203, 206–13, 216–20, 225–26
  see also CBS Masterworks, Columbia Records
Speculum Musicae, 5, 13–14, 78–81, 83, 93–94, 109–10, 116, 121–22, 126*f*, 132–33, 154, 166, 195
spiritual minimalism, 167–68, 185–86, 201, 210, 214–15
  see also holy minimalism
SPIT Orchestra, 186, 212–13
St. John, Lara, 202–3
St. Louis Symphony, 55, 58, 68–69
Stanford, 23–24, 34, 36, 38–39
Sterne, Teresa, 194–95
Stewart, Mark, 138–39, 142–43, 156–59
Stockhausen, Karlheinz, 34–35, 37–38, 151, 175–76, 178, 191–92
  Der kleine Harlekin, 69
  Klavierstücke, 32
  Trans, 69
Stone, Carl, 98–99, 101–2, 130
Storer, Taylor, 193
Straus, Joseph, 19–20
Stravinsky, Igor, 3–4, 31–32, 60, 195–96
  Agon, 75, 86
  The Rite of Spring, 18
Subotnick, Morton, 6, 60–61
  Silver Apples of the Moon, 191, 194–95
SUNY Stony Brook, 143
Swed, Mark, 100

Takemitsu, Tōru, 27–28, 60–62
Talking Heads, 82–83
Tan Dun, 188–89
  Symphony 1997, 212
Tanglewood Music Center's Festival of Contemporary Music, 5, 42–44, 72, 138–39, 146, 150–51, 161, 170, 225
Tashi, 166
Tavener, John, 201, 210, 212
Tcherepnin, Ivan, 34–35, 38, 97
Tenney, James, 113–14
Tharp, Twyla, 165
The Red Violin, 212
Theatre of Eternal Music, 6–7
Threadgill, Henry, 52, 153
Three Tenors, 191, 211, 219
Titanic, 212, 219

Torke, Michael, 20n.13, 42–44, 203
totalism, 89, 100, 140, 175–76, 178, 210
"Towards Cultural Democracy," 120
Tower, Joan, 52–53, 57, 58, 71–72, 136–37
Tower Records, 182–84, 193, 196, 202, 205, 214, 217–18
Tudor, David, 6, 36
Tyranny, "Blue" Gene, 193
twelve-tone music, 18–20, 21–22, 60, 120–21, 149
see also serialism, uptown

UCLA, 22–23
union, 69, 172–74, 176–77, 228
Universal Music Group, 217
University of Illinois, 143
University of Iowa, 24–26, 32, 41–42, 45–46, 66, 143
University of Michigan, 21, 25–27, 73, 75
Upshaw, Dawn, 168, 200
uptown, 2–9, 13–14, 18–19, 20–22, 33–34, 41–42, 51, 66–67, 76, 78–82, 87, 89–91, 93, 99–100, 102, 120–21, 139–40, 144, 149–52, 154, 161, 165–66, 168–69, 175–78, 185, 195, 198–200, 210, 216, 221, 225–28

Varèse, Edgard, 77, 191–92
Vees, Jack
  John Henry, 93
Vega, Suzanne, 195–96
Victoire, 225–26
Vierk, Lois V, 147–48, 173, 178–79, 186, 189, 198–200, 211, 224
  Go Guitars, 99–100
  Red Shift, 206–7
Virgin, 196, 201, 203
virtuosos, 9, 11, 13–14, 32, 67, 99, 139, 142–44, 148–50, 157–60, 218–19, 221

Waits, Tom, 213
Walker Arts Center, 142–43, 145–46
Walter Reade Theater, 161, 162*f*, 167–68, 173, 176, 182, 186
Warner, 194–96, 200–1
Webern, Anton, 21–22, 29, 60, 192
Webster, Albert K., 61, 64–65, 69
Weinstein, David, 198–200
Wheeler, Jed, 165–66, 168

Wilco, 15–16, 224
Wild Swan, 26
Williams, John, 58, 211
Wilson, George Balch, 26–27
Wilson, Robert, 165, 168, 188–89
WNYC, 96, 189, 203–4
Wojnarowicz, David, 126
Wolfe, Julia
  academic training of, 25–27, 30, 44
  Anthracite Fields, 223
  Arsenal of Democracy, 154, 213
  Believing, 147, 159, 216
  Big Beautiful Dark and Scary, 222
  Fire in my mouth, 226–27
  Four Marys, 148–49
  Lick, 16, 138–55, 159, 208, 222–23
  musical style of, 22, 30, 88–89, 138, 148–49
  my lips from speaking, 149
  On Seven-Star Shoes, 26–27, 30–32, 44, 148–49
  Seamarks, 26–27
  Song at Daybreak, 30
  Steel Hammer, 223
  The Vermeer Room, 148–49, 198–200
  Williamsburg Bridge, 88–89
  youth of, 25
World Saxophone Quartet, 147–48, 165, 195
World Trade Center, 222–24
World War II, 2–6, 20–21, 221
Wright, Mary, 161
Wu Man, 186
Wu, Chin-Tao, 108–9
Wuorinen, Charles, 4–5, 32–33, 50, 52–53, 57, 67, 78, 98–99, 151, 154, 164, 167–68, 195
  and multiculturalism, 117, 120–24, 126–27, 128
  Simple Composition, 5–6
  Time's Encomium, 5, 194
Wyner, Yehudi, 27–28

Xenakis, Iannis, 83, 143, 178, 188

Y2K, 215–17
Yale, 13, 16, 18–23, 24–26, 57, 58, 65–67, 72–73, 75, 77, 79, 86, 89, 99, 143, 148–49, 178, 224–27
  pedagogy at, 27–33
  professional attitude at, 40–46, 68–69, 163
  and Sheep's Clothing, 33–40

Yale Contemporary Ensemble, 34–36
Yale Oral History of American Music, 40–41, 148, 188–89
Yates, Sidney, 108, 129–30
Young, La Monte, 6–7, 52–53
   Piano Piece for David Tudor #1, 36

Z, Pamela, 134–36
Zankel Hall, 226–27
Zeeland, Cees van, 75, 94*f*

Zero Hour, 3–4
Zinman, David, 167–68
Ziporyn, Evan, 29–30, 35–36, 38–39, 64, 66, 100, 138, 142–43, 145–48, 152–53, 155–57, 159, 161, 186, 211–13, 216–17
   Tsimindao Ghmerto, 159
   LUV Time, 198–200
   Waiting by the Phone, 75
Zorn, John, 78, 99